ANATOMY OF THE RED BRIGADES

ANATOMY OF THE RED BRIGADES

THE RELIGIOUS MIND-SET OF MODERN TERRORISTS

ALESSANDRO ORSINI

TRANSLATED FROM THE ITALIAN BY SARAH J. NODES

CORNELL UNIVERSITY PRESS
Ithaca and London

Originally published in Italian as Alessandro Orsini,
*Anatomia delle Brigate rosse: Le radici ideologiche del terrorismo
rivoluzionario,* by Rubbettino Editore S.r.l., Viale Rosario
Rubbettino n. 10, 88049 Soveria Mannelli (CZ), Italy.

English translation first published 2011 by Cornell
University Press

Printed in the United States of America

Library of Congress Cataloging-in-Publication Data

Orsini, Alessandro, 1975–
    [Anatomia delle Brigate rosse. English]
    Anatomy of the Red Brigades : the religious mind-set of
modern terrorists / Alessandro Orsini ; translated from the
Italian by Sarah J. Nodes.
       p. cm.
    Includes bibliographical references and index.
    ISBN 978-0-8014-4986-4 (cloth : alk. paper)
    1. Brigate rosse. 2. Ideology. 3. Terrorism. I. Title.
    HV6433.I82R436313   2011
    363.3250945—dc22   2010047281

Cloth printing   10 9 8 7 6 5 4 3 2 1

CONTENTS

Introduction 1

1. The Pedagogy of Intolerance 9

The Revolutionary Vocation 9
Violence as the Only Way 14
The "Binary Code" Mentality 17
Political Violence and Social
    Marginality 21
Eschatological Politics 26

2. The Sacralization of Politics 30

The "Fanaticism of a New Religion" 30
Radical Catastrophism 33
The Revolutionary Sect and the
    Obsession with Purity 36
The Hatred of Reformists 42

3. Toward the Bloodshed 48

Daily Life in a Revolutionary Sect 48
The Red Brigades' Organization Plan 54
The Blood Crime and Its "Story" 58
The Path to Bloodshed 66
Shedding Blood and the Role of the
    Revolutionary Sect 83
The Detachment from the Surrounding
    World 89

4. The Genesis of the Red Brigades 93

The Red Brigades' Social Roots 93
The "Cultural Lag" Theory 108
When Were the Red Brigades Born? 118

The Red Brigades: "Imbeciles" or
  Real Revolutionaries?   122
Antonio Gramsci and the "Hour
  of Redemption"   125
The Italian Communist Party's Role in
  the Genesis of the Red Brigades   131
An Oxymoron: The "Leninist-
  Reformist" Party   147

5. The Masters of the Red Brigades   155

Illustrious Predecessors: Thomas
  Müntzer   155
John of Leiden, King and
  Revolutionary   162
The English Revolution and the
  Puritan Movement   165
The French Revolution and the
  Jacobin Experiment   170
Babeuf: "The world has plunged
  into chaos"   184
Karl Marx's Pantoclastic Dream   187
The Revolutionary Tradition of
  Russian Populism   196

6. The Purifiers of the World in Power   208

Lenin and State Terrorism   208
The Bolshevik Revolution and the
  "Victims of the Victims"   213
The Gulag, or The Promise Kept   217
Mao and the Myth of the "New Man"   226
The Cambodian Revolution   237

Not a Conclusion: Portrait of a
  Red Brigadist   253

Appendix: Red Brigades and Black Brigades   263
A Note on Method   285
Bibliography   289
Index of Names   313

ANATOMY OF THE RED BRIGADES

Introduction

It is a frightening idea that envy, resentment, and hate can sometimes have a decisive effect on the course of history. A rational vision of politics, in which the actors' choices are always based on a cost-benefit calculation, is much more reassuring.[1]

In this book I tell the story of a pathos that became a political movement and kept an entire country under siege for almost twenty years, leading it to the brink of civil war.[2] We're talking not about an army but about a handful

---

1. J. Coleman, *Foundations of Social Theory.*

2. According to the comparative analysis of modern terrorism by G. Chaliand and A. Blin ("Dal 1968 all'islamismo radicale," 243), "Italy was by far the country most affected by terrorist activities between 1969 and 1985." The latest figures on terrorist violence in Italy in the 1969–2007 period are given by L. Manconi, *Terroristi italiani,* 22ff. A total of 333 people were killed in attacks and massacres in Italy between 1969 and 2007. Of these, 144 can be ascribed to left-wing terrorism, 54 to right-wing terrorism; 135 were killed in massacres. Victims of international terrorism are not included. No less impressive are the statistics concerning damage to things and violence against people. Between 1969 and 1980 12,690 political attacks were recorded. Of these, 4,035 were carried out between 1969 and 1974, and 8,655 from 1975 to 1980. Out of a total of 362 victims, 92 (25 percent) died during the first period, 270 (75 percent) in the second. Between 1969 and 1974, 63 people were victims of right-wing and 9 of left-wing terrorist attacks, and 10 were killed in shoot-outs with the police; for the remaining 10 the identity of the attackers is unknown. Between 1975 and 1980, 115 people were killed by right-wing terrorists, 110 by left-wing ones, 29 by the police, and 16 by unknowns. The least blood was shed in 1971 (6 deaths), the most in 1980 (135 deaths). The greatest number of people were wounded during the late seventies (551, including 200 in Bologna alone in 1980). At least 75 people had been "kneecapped" up to December 1978. See M. Galleni, ed.,

of men and women animated by a fierce ideological determination. The story of the Red Brigades and their homicidal fury is the story of a sociopsychological process that strips the victim of humanity.

I call this process the "pedagogy of intolerance."

The immediate object of pedagogical theories, as Émile Durkheim teaches us, is to guide behavior. Such theories do not identify with the action but prepare for it.[3] The pedagogy of intolerance finds its raison d'être in action; it is itself a tool of social change. Before being killed, the enemy is degraded to a subhuman species. For the Red Brigade terrorist who has finished his or her educational pathway, the enemy is a "pig"[4] who arouses "absolute loathing."[5] When the enemy becomes a "filthy pig,"[6] his life no longer has any value. Political homicide in the ultra-left terrorist groups is above all a narrative, a unilateral version of the facts without cross-examination; the world is a "marsh"[7] immersed "in the gloom of political slavery."[8] There are some men responsible for this state of affairs. Killing them is an "act of justice";[9]

Rapporto sul terrorismo; see also H. Hess, *La rivolta ambigua,* 125. For figures on "kneecapping," see G. Dossena, "Il polpaccio nel mirino," 30–41.

3. E. Durkheim, *L'educazione morale,* 466.

4. *Comunicato no. 1—D'Urso Campaign.* Red Brigades document issued on 13 December 1980. It states: "On Friday 12 December, an armed nucleus of the Red Brigades captured and placed in a people's prison the bastard, slave driver of thousands of workers, Giovanni D'Urso, judge, director-general of the Ministry of Justice. This pig is chiefly responsible for the treatment of all proletarian prisoners in both normal and special prisons. Everything that, in compliance with the directives imparted by the imperialistic head offices, concerns the prisoners' general and particular treatment, the differentiation between prisons, the transfers, the tortures, and the political-psychic-physical annihilation goes through his hands. Or rather went, because he is now in a people's prison and will be judged by that proletariat that the pig believed he could massacre with impunity" (see www.brigaterosse.org).

5. Document *claiming responsibility for the Labate kidnapping* issued on 12 February 1973. Bruno Labate was a manager at Cisnal. Now in *Dossier Brigate rosse,* 1:217.

6. Red Brigades document *claiming responsibility for the Taliercio kidnapping* issued on 11 June 1981. Giuseppe Taliercio was a director of the Montedison petrochemical company in Marghera. Kidnapped on 20 May 1981, his body was found riddled with sixteen bullets on 5 July 1981. Some extracts from this document are published in M. Clementi, *Storia delle Brigate rosse,* 299, from which I quote.

7. V. I. Lenin, *Che fare?* 39. Lenin writes: "We are marching in a compact group along a precipitous and difficult path, firmly holding each other by the hand. We are surrounded on all sides by enemies, and we have to advance almost constantly under their fire. We have combined, by a freely adopted decision, for the purpose of fighting the enemy, and not of retreating into the neighboring marsh....Oh, yes, gentlemen! You are free...to go yourselves wherever you will, even into the marsh. In fact, we think that the marsh is your proper place, and we are prepared to render you every assistance to get there. Only let go of our hands, don't clutch at us and don't besmirch the grand word "freedom," for we too are "free" to go where we please, free to fight not only against the marsh, but also against those who are turning toward the marsh!"

8. Ibid., 45.

9. The Red Brigadist Giulia Borelli speaking to L. Guicciardi, *Il tempo del furore,* 251. Borelli says, "What is most amazing, thinking back with a different mentality and maturity, is the naturalness with which we came to accept (and I personally accepted) the idea of political homicide as a positive

a loving gesture toward humanity awaiting an "apocalyptic palingenesis."[10] The enemy is a "monster."[11]

In brief, this is the thesis that I propose to illustrate and document through the history of the Red Brigades.

What do brigadists think as they are about to kneecap the enemy? What group dynamics and mental processes enable them to perform and justify shedding blood? Where do they find the strength and psychological support to live constantly at war with the world around them? To tackle these questions we have to attempt to see the world through the eyes of professional revolutionaries. We have to reconstruct the Red Brigades' mental universe, which "sees politics as indivisible from the use of force"[12] and is based on the "denial of reality."[13] Renato Curcio, Alberto Franceschini, Margherita Cagol, Mario Moretti, Mario Galesi, and Nadia Desdemona Lioce, to cite just some of the more famous names, are all part of a shared history: the history of revolutionary gnosticism and of the pedagogy of intolerance—the educational process that turns the rebel into a professional revolutionary.

A few notes on the phenomenon of revolutionary gnosticism are necessary to help the reader understand the interpretative key used in this book.

In a literal sense, "gnosis" (from the Greek verb meaning "to know") is a superior knowledge, to which only some have access (the elect). Understood as a sociological category, gnosis is an approach to the great issues of human existence.[14] The gnostic mentality has some recurring themes. I will focus on three: waiting for the end,[15] radical catastrophism, and obsession with purity. The gnostic design can be summarized as follows: the world is immersed in pain and sin; it is populated with "infected" presences that attack the purity of the elect; the last day is near, when evil people will be punished for their

---

form of battle, that is even an act of justice in a certain sense. It is also very difficult to explain how I could have arrived at this junction. I have to admit that things had become so contorted that, when we discussed serious actions, for me it was also a matter of choice in which I certainly did not question the matter in itself."

10. The interpretation of Marxism as a "religious" phenomenon is now accepted by the most famous Marxist historians. See E. J. Hobsbawm, *Il secolo breve,* 92: "Like the early Christians, the majority of Socialists before 1914 believed in a great apocalyptic palingenesis that would have canceled out all social evils and would have established a society without unhappiness, oppression, inequality, and injustice. Alongside the millenarianist hope, Marxism offered the guarantee of a doctrine that was proclaimed scientific and the idea of historic inevitability; the October revolution then offered the proof that the palingenesis had begun."

11. Lenin, *Che fare?* 59.

12. D. Novelli and N. Tranfaglia, *Vite sospese,* 197. I quote the brigadist Nitta.

13. Ibid., 240. I quote the brigadist Silvia Arancio.

14. See M. Introvigne, *Le sette cristiane,* 15–16.

15. See G. Filoramo, *L'attesa della fine,* 64: "There is a moment in the myth in which the different gnostic traditions appear not only to run in parallel but almost to flow into the same doctrinal bed in which any detailed distinctions are superfluous. This moment is 'the end time.'"

misdeeds. The gnostic revolution is a political practice that yearns for an "absolutely perfect world."[16] "I imagined a future in which every wrong would be righted, every inequality repaired, every injustice corrected.... This justified the means that we would have used," explains the brigadist Anna Laura Braghetti.[17]

Typical of the Red Brigades' mentality is their apocalyptic vision of history. Their "search for the absolute means that politics becomes a religious issue and the revolution the mundane form of the mystic."[18] In their documents, the revolution is "an immediate idea of radical change, of upturning the foundations,"[19] which will free men from every form of suffering and unhappiness after "a series of battles that mark *the beginning of the last war: the class war for a communist society*."[20] The revolution—we read in the document claiming responsibility for Marco Biagi's murder—"is a historic necessity."[21] The brigadist Gianluca Codrini said that the Red Brigades considered themselves "knights of a bloody apocalypse."[22] The brigadist Enrico Fenzi was convinced the revolution would be an apocalypse that would regenerate the world. He never wondered about the future. His millenarianist faith nailed him to the here and now. In his words: "I've never had any particular ability to imagine the new, I've never contributed to a novel and positive scenario! No, I'd say there was an *apocalyptic type of vision* rather than a vision projected toward the future."[23] In the words of the Red Brigades, the person who embraces the revolution is "the Christ who sacrifices himself to redeem humanity."[24] "In those years," the brigadist Mario Ferrandi recalls,

---

16. G. Filoramo, *Il risveglio della gnosi ovvero come si diventa Dio,* 13. Filoramo made the following distinction between ancient and modern gnosis: "Ancient gnosis, with its concept of an evil world supported by an ignorant or wicked demiurge, introduced an atheism in our cosmos based on the absolute transcendence of the unknown God, whereas the modern gnosis, whose most significant representative is Marxism, depreciates the present world in the name of an absolutely new future aeon. In other words, while the former tells you how to free the soul from the prison of the cosmos, the latter tells you how to construct an absolutely perfect world."

17. A. L. Braghetti, *Il prigioniero,* 17.

18. N. Matteucci, "La strategia del terrorista." For an in-depth study of the relationship between revolution and religion, see V. Mathieu, *La speranza nella rivoluzione,* 187ff.

19. Novelli and Tranfaglia, *Vite sospese,* 238. This is from the account of the brigadist Barbara Graglia, and merits citing in full: "The problems are at the source, as it was said in those years, and had to be solved at the source. For me the idea of fighting to change society is the idea of a radical change, of shaking the foundations."

20. "Document of Internal Reflection," published in the periodical *Brigate rosse,* no. 1, June 1975, in *Dossier Brigate rosse,* 1:372. Italics added.

21. Red Brigade document *claiming responsibility for the Marco Biagi murder* of 19 March 2002. The entire text is available at www.brigaterosse.org.

22. G. Codrini, *Io, un ex brigatista,* 18.

23. E. Fenzi, *Armi e bagagli,* 214. Italics added.

24. Brigadist Enzo Fontana to G. Bocca, *Noi terroristi,* 42.

"we never asked ourselves what base we had to build, the only thing we knew was that the present had to be destroyed."[25]

But not all the gnostic sects make use of revolutionary violence. To clarify this point, I distinguish between passive and active sects.

The former are characterized by their radical isolation. If the world is impure, one has to get as far away from it as possible. Waiting for the end involves mystical-religious practices, prompting a withdrawal from the profane world. The passive sects—as Max Weber has it—are in "flight from the world."[26] They don't want to destroy; they want to protect themselves against the imminent collapse caused by human corruption.

The latter, by contrast, are characterized by the presence of a premise that the former lack, and which I call *definition of evil*. In the active sects, the "obsession with purity" becomes the "obsession with purification" or the implacable fight against the forces of evil. It is no coincidence that the language of active sects is borrowed from parasitology: the enemies are "parasites"[27] that "infest" the world.[28] A Red Brigades militant who admires Pol Pot helps us understand the obsession with purification: "If I win, I don't want any positions or honors. I just want the job of getting rid of our enemies, all those who have to be got rid of. It'll be a difficult task because *there will be millions of people who have to be eliminated*. That's what I want to do after [the revolution]."[29] The typical attitude of the active sects is hate, even when they profess an ethics of peace and love.[30] As Lenin wrote: "The hate of the representative of the oppressed and exploited masses is the origin of every wisdom, the foundation of every Socialist and Communist movement and of its victories."[31]

A revolutionary sect is a sociopolitical organization formed by *separation* from a historically consolidated political-cultural tradition.[32] The experience

---

25. Interview with the brigadist Mario Ferrandi, "Una pistola per riconquistare il paradiso," 7 March 1984.

26. M. Weber, *Economia e società*, 2:233.

27. *The raid in the offices of "Iniziativa democratica."* Red Brigade document of 15 May 1975, in *Dossier Brigate rosse*, 1:369.

28. There are also religious sects that try to change the world with peaceful means, although obsessed with purity and rejecting this world, such as Quakers, called after their "quake" of religious fervor when, in their meetings, they have direct communion with the Divine Spirit. Radical pacifists and believers in nonviolent action, the Quakers believe it is possible to transform humankind through conversion. See A. Prosperi and P. Viola, *Storia moderna e contemporanea*, 2:39.

29. S. Zavoli, *La notte della Repubblica*, 221. Italics added.

30. See W. Stark, *The Sociology of Religion*, 2:101.

31. V. I. Lenin, "L'estremismo, malattia infantile del comunismo," 1432.

32. I found this definition in E. Pace, *Le sette*, 11ff. For an excellent introduction to the sociological concept of the sect, see M. L. Maniscalco, *Spirito di setta e società*.

of separation assumes an already existing system of values, united around a determinate institution. Therefore every revolutionary sect is a "church-party." The birth of a sect involves a minority group, willing to subject itself to a new interior and exterior discipline, setting itself against a constituted political authority. To justify this separation, the sects typically accuse the "church" of reaching a compromise with the powers of "this world."

Ernst Troeltsch, referring to Max Weber, has made a distinction between church and sect.[33] The church, like the state, is considered a "spiritual power" that addresses all humankind with a permanent body of officers. Its ecumenical vocation, underpinned by a bureaucratic apparatus, forces it to compromise with the systems of "this world." Instead the sect, at least in its initial stage, is a "product of the will." Its leaders are the founders of a new experience and not continuers of a tradition. One is born in the church; instead, the sect imposes a conversion that marks a "rebirth."[34] Through a ritual—of varying complexity—the initiate is required to change identity (*metanoia*), acquiring a new name. The church, because it wants to attract an increasing number of adherents, is prepared to compromise; the sect adopts the more drastic aspects of a determinate "message" to induce the radical rejection of the world. In short, the church tends to include and absolve; the sect excludes and condemns[35] in the name of purity.[36]

The history of the Red Brigades—created from "a real *schism*"[37] within the Italian Communist Party (PCI)—is the history of a political movement operating with the typical words, thoughts, and dogmas of a religious sect. It is an authentic part of the tradition of political messianism, which "postulates a scheme of orderly, harmonious and perfect things, toward which men are irresistibly led and which they are forced to achieve. They acknowledge only

---

33. See E. Troeltsch, *Le dottrine sociali delle chiese e dei gruppi cristiani,* 1:463ff. For a development of the Weber-Troeltsch church-sect typology, see J. M. Yinger, *The Scientific Study of Religion,* and B. Wilson, *Religious Sects.* What I call a "passive revolutionary sect" is similar to what Wilson calls an "introversionist sect."

34. Troeltsch, *Le dottrine sociali,* 1:481.

35. Troeltsch writes: "The sects thus gain an intense Christian life, but lose universalism, since they have to keep the Church for apostate and they do not believe it is possible to conquer the world with human forces, so that they are always forced to have eschatological expectations." Ibid., 1:478–79.

36. Sects can also be formed without the presence of a charismatic figure. It is not essential for a sect "to be able to boast a founder who has demonstrated himself to be a saint in life: *he asks his followers to become saints, to be pure and virtuous.* Thus the sect does not necessarily have to have a leader: mutual correction, the control that the community exercises over the individual, can sometimes be stronger than any established authority." E. Pace, *Le sette,* 24, italics added.

37. F. Alberoni, "Movimenti sociali e società italiana," in *Classi e movimenti in Italia 1970–1985,* 138.

one plan for living, the political one. They extend the scope of politics to embrace all of human existence."[38]

The Red Brigades' dream was to raze to the ground all aspects of current life, in order to build "the society of the just,"[39] a dream characterized by the "prevailing sensation of the inevitability of revolution."[40] The determination with which they operated came from the aspiration—present in all professional revolutionaries—for a "perfect society,"[41] which—the Red Brigades were convinced—would be born from the clash between the mighty forces of good and the dark forces of evil: "I felt cleaner, that is, I was the good and the others were the evil,"[42] recounts Roberto Minervino, a militant in Prima Linea, a revolutionary group second only to the Red Brigades in number of homicides.

The Red Brigades have always shouted to the entire world that they were animated by a "fatal" and "despotic" purity aimed at repressing the impure in the name of an unshakable faith.[43] In their documents they are "children of the light," arriving in this world to punish and redeem, to destroy and purify. The Red Brigades want to wash away the sins of capitalism with blood.

The Red Brigades documents all talk about waiting for the end, the idea of purity, and the radical rejection of the world. There is also a fourth aspect, with all too well-known effects: the purification of the world through the extermination of enemies. The *ruling logic* of the Red Brigades' mentality was not a "calculation of the effects" (albeit obviously present) but a political-religious concept of history whose main aim was to satisfy a spiritual need and achieve a political end: heaven on earth.[44] It was Friedrich Engels who highlighted the profound analogies between revolutionary and religious practices: "Both Christianity and the workers' socialism preach salvation from bondage and misery; Christianity places this salvation in a life beyond, after

---

38. J. Talmon, *The Origins of Totalitarian Democracy,* 1.

39. See L. Pellicani, *Revolutionary Apocalypse.*

40. Novelli and Tranfaglia, *Vite sospese,* 191. This is the full testimony of the brigadist Nitta: "My political culture was dominated by a sensation of the inevitability of revolution and the facts I witnessed further convinced me."

41. Ernesto Che Guevara, "Una nuova cultura del lavoro" (21 August 1962) in his *Leggere Che Guevara,* 174. Guevara writes: "Even if it involves a distant future, we must already think about communism, which is the perfect society, the fundamental aspiration of the first men who knew how to look beyond the present and foresee the prospects of humanity."

42. Brigadist Roberto Minervino talking to L. Guicciardi, *Il tempo del furore,* 304.

43. V. Morucci, *La peggio gioventù,* 114.

44. Sabino Acquaviva writes: "Individuals who shoot are people who, having lost traditional religious values, find a ritual in shooting and killing, the experience of the final and the absolute. And what is more final, more absolute than death? Than the almost ritual sacrifice of the 'guilty'?" S. Acquaviva, *Guerriglia e guerra rivoluzionaria in Italia,* 55.

death, in heaven; socialism places it in this world, in a transformation of society. Both are persecuted and baited, their adherents are despised and made the objects of exclusive laws, the former as enemies of the human race, the latter as enemies of the state, enemies of religion, the family, social order. And in spite of all persecution, nay, even spurred on by it, they forge victoriously, irresistibly ahead."[45]

What distinguishes the Red Brigades is their search for an all-absorbing ideology to guide militants' thoughts, sentiments, and actions, to a large extent independent of the political and institutional conditions in which they operate. The Red Brigades' logic is that of "all or nothing, of winning or dying. And nothing in between,"[46] because "the middle way has been wasted."[47]

We do not get a true picture of the Red Brigades' politics if we try to explain terrorism leaving out political-ideological variables. The violence they used can be correctly understood only within a specific ideological program.[48] As they have admitted: "The Red Brigades had another politics. Or rather the same politics but taken to the extreme. They were asking the other politics to be 'pure.' Just as Savonarola asked it of 'his' Church. *Purifiers of the world or exterminating angels.*"[49]

These were the Red Brigades.

---

45. F. Engels, *Sulle origini del cristianesimo*, 17.

46. They are Barbara Balzerani's words: "We were an underground group that couldn't just close an office, perhaps a newspaper office, return the keys to the landlord, and wait for better times at some other address. In that war, in which political bargaining was almost absent, we had introduced the logic of all or nothing, of winning or dying. And nothing in between." B. Balzerani, *Compagna luna*, 87–88.

47. *Il sequestro Amerio—Comunicato no. 1,* Communiqué dated 10 December 1973, in *Dossier Brigate rosse,* 1:226. Ettore Amerio was a Fiat personnel manager. He was kidnapped on 10 December 1973.

48. To decipher the Red Brigade universe, the words of the multiple killer Antonio Savasta are illuminating. Between the end of April and the beginning of May 1982, he testified for twenty-seven hours during eight sessions of the first "Moro trial." The presiding judge, Santiapichi, after inviting Savasta to testify to the kidnapping of Aldo Moro without expatiating in ideological speeches, was told that Aldo Moro's kidnapping and execution could be understood only in the terms of a specific ideology, according to which enemies deserved only to be exterminated. "Moro 1," Rome Court of Assizes, trial records, 28 April 1982, reel 2, p. 4. Savasta's testimony is also mentioned in R. Drake, *Il caso Aldo Moro,* 61–66.

49. Morucci, *La peggio gioventù,* 143. Italics added.

CHAPTER 1

The Pedagogy of Intolerance

> You will ask if these are the means to use?
> Believe me, there are no others.
>
> —Mara Cagol

The Revolutionary Vocation

The first lesson that the aspiring revolutionary receives is that *the world is in danger.*

The "children of the light" are engaged in a fight to the death against the "children of the shadows." The outcome of this battle—however steep and painful the road leading to the goal—is already written: society will be cleansed of the "pigs"[1] that infest it. After this, communism can finally be constructed and people will no longer suffer hunger and oppression.

"The politics on which our conduct was based," recounts the brigadist Valerio Morucci, "was revolutionary, and the revolution would have led to a society without conflict. A society without the need for mediation, compromise, or filthy bourgeois politics. *A pure politics.*"[2] Without these certainties you don't find the vocation to become a revolutionary. The Red Brigades conceived revolutionary action as a mission and not as a simple profession to be performed and paid for.

---

1. Red Brigades pamphlet no. 4. *Attack, strike, liquidate, and disperse the Christian Democrat Party, pillar of the restructuring of the State and of the imperialist counterrevolution.* This is a resolution of the Red Brigades' strategic management, November 1977. In *Dossier Brigate rosse,* 2:148.

2. V. Morucci, *La peggio gioventù,* 140.

The brigadist Patrizio Peci, arrested on 19 February 1980, accused of being directly or indirectly responsible for seven homicides, seventeen injuries, and dozens of other crimes, states: "It is obvious that you don't make this choice if you don't believe completely in communism, if you don't believe in the armed struggle as the only way to bring it about, if you don't believe in victory. I had these three certainties. . . . If I'd not been sure of winning, I wouldn't have continued."[3]

To achieve the grand design of a society in which conflicts are banned forever, the Red Brigades have to follow an ongoing training pathway. Their first task is to learn to think differently from the "common" person: the enemies of the proletariat are hidden everywhere. To recognize them, you have to embrace a new vision of the world, enabling you to grasp what others can't see. Evil has to be flushed out, fought, and destroyed because our enemies— this is written in a Red Brigades document of 26 November 1972—are "an army of bastards."[4] Only the dialectic method, that of Marx and Engels, gives access to the knowledge of reality. There is only one truth. True brigadists cannot and must not tolerate opinions other than theirs. Those who oppose the revolution are "pigs."[5] They must be killed or disabled for the rest of their lives.

To kill for the revolution is the noblest of gestures, a demonstration of love to humanity awaiting redemption. We read in a Red Brigades document of September 1977: "The revolution signifies continuity, solidarity, and love."[6] And it is in the name of love that the organization exercises the power of life or death over its enemies. Brigadists—according to the document claiming responsibility for the Labate kidnapping (12 February 1973)—must shake off their bourgeois morality and understand that the enemy has to be eliminated. Denying it would mean not being able "to distinguish between the violence of the oppressor and that of the slave."[7]

---

3. P. Peci, *Io, l'infame,* 41 and 103. It is the same determination we see in the testimony of the brigadist Raffaele Fiore: "I had an immense faith in the organization. I believed in its political programs and in the revolution. . . . I was sure that the way was sound, that it was just." See A. Grandi, *L'ultimo brigatista,* 64–65.

4. *Crush the fascists in Mirafiori and Rivalta! Throw them out of our factories and our districts,* leaflet issued in Turin on 26 November 1972, in *Dossier Brigate rosse,* 1:194.

5. Red Brigades—Fighting Communist Party's document *claiming responsibility for wounding the Labor Ministry adviser, Gino Giugni,* issued 3 May 1983 (full text available at www.brigaterosse.org).

6. *Diary of the Struggle: Special Tribunes of Bologna, Torino, Milano,* Red Brigades document of September 1977, in *Dossier Brigate rosse,* 2:128.

7. Red Brigades document *claiming responsibility for the Labate kidnapping* issued 12 February 1973, in ibid., 1:216. Bruno Labate was a Cisnal manager.

The Red Brigades are philanthropists, friends of the people. The brigadist Patrizio Peci is firmly convinced that political violence "is also a question of altruism and generosity: it means risking everything for a cause you believe is just, forgetting personal advantage."[8] The feeling that inspired the brigadist Sergio Segio "was basically, totally, a feeling of love."[9] "Love and strength," we read in a Red Brigades document of 26 May 1982, "will subdue and destroy the imperialist bourgeoisie; we shall build a society free from the slavery of salaried work."[10]

But the brigadist is not everyone's friend, because those who are against the revolution are enemies of humanity. They are accessories to and responsible for all unhappiness and suffering. This is what Renato Curcio writes to his mother in a letter from prison dated November 1974: "Yolanda dearest, mother mine, years have passed since the day on which I set out to encounter life. . . . Seeking my path, I found exploitation, injustice, and oppression. People who handed them out and people who submitted to them. I was one of the latter. And these latter were in the majority. I therefore understood that my history was their history, that my future was their future. . . . What more can I say? *My enemies are the enemies of humanity and of intelligence,* those who have built and still build their monstrous fortunes on the material and intellectual misery of the people. Theirs is the hand that has banged shut the door of my cell."[11]

The world is divided into two. On one side the oppressors of humanity, on the other the avengers. This is why "we have to kick the bosses' asses, after kicking those of some work colleagues; we have to kill the team leaders one by one; we have to kill the department heads, workshop heads, and all toadies." Brigadists have to "organize teams for lynching scabs and managers; the struggle continues without respite: strikes, thrashings, and beatings; violent struggles,"[12] until it is clear that "those who intervene to stop the workers' struggle and their interests are our enemies and as such must be struck down!"[13]

---

8. Peci, *Io, l'infame,* 42.

9. S. Zavoli, *La notte della Repubblica,* 387.

10. *In honor of Umberto Catabiani.* Red Brigades document issued 26 May 1982. Catabiani was a member of the Red Brigades–Fighting Communist Party strategic management. He was shot in the stomach and killed by the police not far from Pisa on 24 May 1982. The document is available at www.brigaterosse.org.

11. Letter from Renato Curcio to his mother, November 1974, in D. Settembrini, *Il labirinto rivoluzionario,* 2:295.

12. From interviews in *Potere Operaio* with workers in the Mirafiori factory in Turin, April 1969, quoted in P. Casamassima, *Il libro nero delle Brigate rosse,* 25.

13. *Fogli di lotta di Sinistra proletaria* (July–October 1970), in *Dossier Brigate rosse,* 1:77.

And yet violence is never a choice. The Red Brigades are forced to violence by circumstances. They kill because the "imperialist system of the multinationals,"[14] "society," the "means of production," the "capitalist state," "imperialist technological fascism"[15] leave them no alternative. In other cases the formulas are even more abstract. It is "the antagonistic contradiction with the general system of economic, political, and cultural exploitation"[16] that means the enemy has to die.

For the Red Brigades, society is always "ready to explode."[17] The conviction that the revolution is imminent gives an extraordinary emotive charge to gnostic activists. This certainty enables them to cope with even the most dramatic consequences of the armed struggle, such as the death of one's fighting comrades, prison, or separation from the family, dictated by the choice of going underground.

The brigadist is convinced that everything is possible. Happiness is around the corner. The world might live in abundance, but the "system," explains the brigadist Margherita Cagol, in a letter of 1969 to her mother, stops this. Society oppresses us; it "rapes" our lives continuously. We are never free, even when we think we are. Happiness is an illusion. It's the fruit of the manipulation of minds that "the system" uses to guarantee its own survival. The world has to be destroyed to be totally re-created. Those who don't fight to bring down society are guilty of a crime against humanity. It's the "rejection of everything"[18] that characterizes the militants of the ultra-left terrorist groups. The world is described as a "fierce monster," inhabited by "vampires."[19] The brigadists feel deprived of everything. Oppressed, humiliated, and degraded, they move in a "spectral" landscape from which every gleam of humanity has disappeared.

In the words of Cagol to her mother:

Milan is a great experience for me. At first sight this big city seemed full of light and attractions, but now it seems like a *fierce monster that*

---

14. *Resolution of the strategic management,* Red Brigade document of April 1975, in ibid., 1:356.

15. Written by Curcio from the Casale prison, published in the magazine *Abc* on 6 March 1975, in ibid., 1:341.

16. This expression comes from the "yellow book" (from the color of its cover), a twenty-eight-page document titled *Social Struggle and Organization in the Metropolis,* launched in Chiavari in the autumn of 1969 during a convention of the Metropolitan Political Collective. In ibid., 1:22.

17. This is the testimony of the Red Brigadist Enrico Fenzi to Sergio Zavoli, *La notte della Repubblica,* 225.

18. The testimony of a Prima Linea militant, Vincenza Fioroni, in L. Guicciardi, *Il tempo del furore,* 228.

19. Document of the Prima Linea terrorist group *claiming responsibility for the attack on the offices of the Association of Small Industries in Turin,* 4 January 1976, quoted in C. Stajano, *Il sovversivo,* 211.

devours everything that is natural, human, and essential in life. There is bar-barity in Milan, the true face of the society we live in. . . . *This society does violence to us all the time,* taking away anything that could eman-cipate us or make us really feel what we are (it makes it impossible to cultivate a family, to cultivate ourselves, our needs, it represses us on a psychological, physiological, and ethical level, it manipulates our needs, our information, etc., etc.). This society has to be changed by a profound revolutionary process. . . . When I think that all this could be easily remedied (remember I said to you last year that, by using mod-ern technology in the production process, it would be possible to pay 10 billion people the American average wage?) if we no longer had political systems like the European or American ones. But we now have the opportunity to change this society and *it would be criminal (toward humanity)* not to exploit it. We must do everything possible to change this system, because this is the profound meaning of our existence. These things are not impossible, you know, Mama. They are serious and difficult things that are really worth doing. . . . Life is too important to waste or fritter away in stupid chatter or squabbles. Every minute is vital.[20]

The Red Brigades document in which the catastrophic-radical concept of history is expressed most fully is *Gocce di sole nella città degli spettri* (Drops of Sun in the City of Ghosts), written by Renato Curcio and Alberto France-schini in 1982. The world, they write, has become a "total factory." Men are engulfed by the shadows and wander around like "ghosts," swallowed up by capital "that suffocates and kills everything."[21] Egoism triumphs. There are no longer any spaces for freedom. The most elementary needs are trampled on. Capital has taken over bodies and minds. No one, except the Red Bri-gades, is aware of this, because the "system" plays with its victims. Reality is just a show; happiness is self-deception. A happy person is a person who does not see. Only the Red Brigades know, see, and live. All the others are caught up in a "nonlife." A new social formation has been formed, called "comput-erized metropolises." It's a "huge prison," which one can escape from only with the extensive use of violence and by launching a "total social war." With high-flown and apocalyptic language, Curcio and Franceschini define "war as the mother/father of everything, a distinction that destroys everything

---

20. Letter from Mara Cagol to her mother (1969), quoted in Casamassima, *Il libro nero delle Brigate rosse,* 39. Italics added.

21. R. Curcio and A. Franceschini, *Gocce di sole nella città degli spettri,* 8.

to change it into something else. War as destruction/construction."[22] The recipe is always the same: to destroy and purify to construct a "new order" in which there is no trace of the present world. Revolutionary violence is "humanity's greatest conscious act."[23] Humanity will be saved after a revolutionary apocalypse that will devastate the world—completely—through a "catastrophic and revolutionary implosion/explosion." A minority of the "elect" have the task of destroying the "city of ghosts" to restore "light" to the kingdom of darkness.

The future of humanity is in the hands of the Red Brigades.

Violence as the Only Way

The Red Brigades are "forced" to violence because the system oppresses them and gives them no escape. For this reason they are never "executioners." Even when they shoot they are "victims." They are desperate people who have no real alternative to murder. Responsibility for their actions is always collective and never individual. According to the Red Brigadist Angela Vai, the Red Brigades "act for others, not for yourself; our comrades in the factory, the workers, were the ones who decided, and I was only their armed wing, the vanguard; *it is the system that imposes violence,* a necessary evil and not an aim in itself."[24]

This is how the brigadist Alessio Casimirri pleads for the release "without preliminary conditions" of all the Red Brigades members still in prison ten years after the death of Aldo Moro (1988): "I think that *all the responsibilities were collective and political and cannot be reduced to individual responsibilities,* when calculating single crimes, single indictments, or when calculating years or centuries of prison."[25]

This approach to the issue of violence—summed up in the formula "brigadist against my will"—is to be found in all the Red Brigades' documents.

"Revolutionary violence," we read in a document of the Metropolitan Political Collective (Collettivo politico metropolitano, or CPM), established on 8 September 1969 in Milan by the militants who would found the Red

---

22. Ibid., 266.

23. Ibid., 264.

24. G. Bianconi, *Mi dichiaro prigioniero politico,* 74. Italics added. The events described in Bianconi's book have been reconstructed on the basis of news reports, literature, legal and parliamentary proceedings, as well as the protagonists' testimonies.

25. Quoted from Grandi, *L'ultimo brigatista,* 162. Italics added.

Brigades the following year,[26] "is not a subjective fact or a moral need: it is imposed by a situation that is by now violent in its structure and superstructure. This is why its organization is now a parameter of discrimination...the violent struggle is an intrinsic need, systematic and continual, of the class struggle."[27]

In the words of the Red Brigadist Mario Moretti: "We chose the armed struggle because every other road was closed, we felt forced to it. Forced to do dreadful things.... Just as in war, where they do dreadful things because they're considered terrible and necessary."[28] Violence takes on such a central role that it becomes politics. *Violence is politics:* "For us," Moretti points out, "armed action is not just another way of being in politics. On the contrary, it is where politics is at."[29] No less significant is the testimony of another leader of the armed struggle: "I wasn't excited at taking up the armed struggle; in fact I said, 'Damn it, why can't someone else do it?' But I considered it a logical choice, the right choice.... I considered it a possible choice, the choice of someone who was aware of a whole series of things he had to do."[30]

Margherita Cagol, in a letter dated 18 September 1974, reassures her parents about her health. She tells them that her husband, Renato Curcio, was arrested because of a spy and that she has no intention of interrupting her fight for the good of humanity. The armed struggle is the only way to go and her battle is "just and sacrosanct." History, she asserts, will prove her right: "Dear parents, I write to tell you not to worry too much about me.... Renato was arrested thanks to a big international spy, Father Leone, a priest working for the CIA.... Now it is up to me and all the comrades who want to combat this rotten bourgeois power to continue the fight. Please don't think that I'm irresponsible.... What I'm doing is just and sacrosanct, history will prove me right as it did for the Resistance in '45. But you'll say, are these

---

26. On the Pecorile convention and the effect it had on the foundation of the BR (Brigate Rosse), see the testimony of A. Franceschini, *Mara, Renato e io,* 23. Franceschini: "A single act that founded the Red Brigades has never been documented but it is commonly thought they were created during a convention we held in Chiavari in the autumn of 1969. But this is not so. There we only discussed what the newly created Metropolitan Political Collective should do. We didn't talk about the armed struggle, and 'going underground,' as a means of political fighting, was rejected. To find an official occasion when what was to become the Red Brigades took their first steps we have to go to Pecorile, a town at the foot of the Apennines, 20 kilometers from Reggio Emilia." As we shall see later, the decision to take up armed struggle, contrary to what Franceschini wants us to believe, was made prior to September 1970.

27. Quoted from Casamassima, *Il libro nero delle Brigate rosse,* 40.

28. M. Moretti, *Brigate rosse,* 49.

29. Ibid., 47.

30. This is the testimony of an anonymous Red Brigades member interviewed by D. Della Porta, *Il terrorismo di sinistra,* 190.

the means to use? Believe me, there are no others. This police state relies on the strength of its weapons and those who want to fight it have to use the same means.... Therefore my revolutionary choices, despite Renato's arrest, remain the same ... no prospect shocks or frightens me."[31]

Society is a battlefield. Political ideas require a military organization. The streets of the cities of Rome, Milan, Turin, and Genoa are the "jungle" in which the warrior moves because—as we read in the *Communiqué on the death of Mara Cagol* of 5 June 1975—"it is the war that decides, in the final analysis, the question of power: the war of the revolutionary class."[32]

In the *Fogli di lotta di Sinistra proletaria,* published in the July–October 1970 period, the political clash is conceived in terms of an authentic "guerrilla warfare." No negotiation is possible. The enemy has to be eliminated: "The proletariat has experienced its first phase ... and is starting to understand that the class struggle is like a war. We have to learn to strike suddenly, concentrating our forces for the attack, rapidly dispersing when the enemy recovers."[33] The conclusion is always the same: "The organization of violence is a necessity of the class struggle."[34]

For the Red Brigades—old or new—violence is the only solution, the only road to take.

In the document claiming responsibility for the murder of Marco Biagi (19 March 2002), violence is the only tool to free the world from unhappiness: "Power cannot therefore be achieved without revolutionary violence."[35] The enemy, explains the BR assassin Enrico Galmozzi, can be tackled only "in terms of destruction."[36] Those who try to indicate an alternative way are supporters of reactionary forces. As such, they have to be struck down because they are openly on the side of the "continuous and systematic violence that the bosses have organized against the working class."[37]

---

31. *Letter from Mara Cagol to her parents* (18 September 1974) in *Dossier Brigate rosse,* 1:249–50.

32. *Communiqué on the death of Mara Cagol.* Red Brigade document of 5 June 1975, in *Dossier Brigate rosse,* 1:374.

33. *Fogli di lotta di Sinistra proletaria,* in ibid., 1:75. The magazine's editorial staff consisted of Renato Curcio, Sandro D'Alessandro, Gaio Di Silvestro, Marco Fronza, Alberto Pinotti, and Corrado Simioni. Contributors included Duccio Berio, Alberto Franceschini, and Vanni Mulinaris.

34. Ibid., 1:75–76.

35. Red Brigades document *claiming responsibility for the murder of Marco Biagi* of 19 March 2002. The entire text is available at www.brigaterosse.org.

36. Guicciardi, *Il tempo del furore,* 60. I quote from the testimony of the terrorist Enrico Galmozzi, assassin of Enrico Pedenovi, MSI (Italian Social Movement) provincial councillor killed in Milan on 29 April 1976.

37. Red Brigade *Communiqué on the Lonigo expropriation* issued on 14 July 1975, in *Dossier Brigate rossi,* 1:376. The document refers to an "expropriation" of 42 million lire by an armed group of the Red Brigades from the Banca Popolare di Lonigo (Vicenza, 14 July 1975).

The "Binary Code" Mentality

One of the aims of the pedagogy of intolerance is the dissemination and consolidation of "dichotomous thought."

The Red Brigades' mentality is elementary, instinctive, and brutal in its immediacy. This is why it is effective. It is a "binary code" mentality. By this I mean the mental process typical of the professional revolutionary that reduces even the most complex phenomena (the reasons for underdevelopment, for example) to two opposing concepts: good/evil, friend/enemy, exploited/exploiters, innocent/guilty. The "binary code mentality" is a mechanism that simplifies reality, that favors the use of political violence. The Red Brigades are well aware that "to fight you need an easily identifiable enemy, without fine distinctions and without having to follow circuitous paths to find it."[38]

The brigadist Adriana Faranda considers slaughter a demonstration of love of one's neighbor. Her political sentiments, she recounts, were of two kinds: love and hate. To her, humanity seemed divided into two sectors: those who deserve love and those who deserve hate: "I considered that the armed struggle, the choice of taking up arms, could only go together with an implacable passion for humanity. And the love-hate bipolarity *automatically* implied hate for those who prevented the achievement of harmony and the different quality of life of which we dreamed."[39] For Faranda, the difference is not only between those who deserve love and those who deserve hate, but also between those who hate and those who don't hate. Those who don't hate don't know how to love. In the Red Brigades' logic, the absence of hate is a sure index of moral baseness. Speaking of a friend who was not politically committed, Faranda expresses herself in these terms: "Well, I'm fond of her, but what separates us is that she doesn't hate."[40]

Hatred of the enemy dominates every moment of the Red Brigades' life. Their thoughts, their words, their gestures are filled with it. When this hatred slackens, they doubt, hesitate, and step back.

Enrico Fenzi tells of a punitive expedition against a local representative of the Christian Democrat Party in Genoa with a heavy sentence hanging over his head. He is a "diabolical" presence in the service of "evil" forces. In the Red Brigades' judgment he is "the minor agent of diabolic power strategies and evil plans."[41] The victim lives in Cornigliano, in a working-class area.

---

38. Morucci, *La peggio gioventù,* 130.

39. Testimony of the brigadist Adriana Faranda to Silvana Mazzocchi, *Nell'anno della tigre,* 76. Italics added.

40. Valerio Morucci recounted this episode to Silvana Mazzocchi in ibid., 75.

41. Zavoli, *La notte della Repubblica,* 217.

The Red Brigades spring into action. They intercept him and are about to shoot him. Suddenly they realize they're looking at a middle-aged man, owner of a small, beat-up car. He lives in a miserable public-housing apartment building. He's a Christian Democrat activist, but he's also working class. The hatred abates, the sentence is not carried out. "All this," concludes Red Brigades member Fenzi, "is interesting because it shows the schizophrenia between the reality and the consequences of an ideological, abstract way of reasoning."[42]

Without their resentment, their hatred, and their desire for revenge, the Red Brigades would be paralyzed.

In the words of a leader of the armed struggle: "I participate emotionally in what I do. And I want to have a reason that echoes within me if I'm going to attack someone or rob a bank. . . . My gun is something I hope will serve everyone. But meanwhile this is also my rebellion, my hatred, my revolution, just as it is my road that has led me to take up a gun."[43]

Valerio Morucci, in his autobiography covering the years prior to his entry into the armed struggle, blames his errors on "that same fucking rigidity—it has to be said—that later ruined my life. Always black or white, without gray areas, either friends or enemies, either love or hate, either moral or immoral."[44] Paolo Zambianchi, a Prima Linea ex-terrorist, recalls: "I split the world into two parts: on one side the exploited who worked and sweated, on the other the bosses. And I always felt a great moral indignation."[45]

A leader of the armed struggle has very effectively described the power of the pedagogy of intolerance and binary code mentality.

The revolutionary ideology—the witness explains—radically changes the way in which we perceive reality. The world appears divided into two sides: on one side there are your friends, and on the other your enemies. Your enemies are not human beings but just symbols to be attacked. This way of perceiving the political conflict strips the enemy of their humanity, so the brigadist can carry out political homicide with great naturalness. Assassination thus becomes a routine task, leaving its perpetrator entirely indifferent to the victim's feelings.

Also here, the words leave nothing to the imagination: "For me it was like carrying out a routine job. . . . This is the aberration, because you're on

---

42. Ibid.
43. *Memorie dalla clandestinità,* 71. This is an anonymous work in which a Red Brigadist tells his story.
44. V. Morucci, *Ritratto di un terrorista da giovane,* 31.
45. See D. Novelli and N. Tranfaglia, *Vite sospese,* 144.

a side with your friends, on the other instead are your enemies. And your enemies are a class, they are functions, symbols to strike, not human beings. Treating these people with the symbology of the enemy means that you have an entirely abstract relationship with death. So that if I'd worked in the land registry office instead of killing, nothing would have changed. I left home in the morning, went to check on people and prepare the operations. Obviously this was when I wasn't going directly to kill someone. Then I calmly returned home, continuing with my life, which was that of a normal housewife."[46]

As we shall see later on (chapter 3), murder assumes a change in the relationship with reality. The brigadist is formed through a sociopsychological process, the aim of which is to create a "new man" programmed to kill. This educational pathway enables militants to be "reborn." Their previous life belongs to a very remote past. They have performed an interior revolution so that they can now look at the world through the eyes of a redeemer. They are no longer like the "others." They are different, with a superior vision of reality. They are the keepers of a knowledge reserved for the chosen people—the revolutionary gnosis—that contains the message of salvation to be revealed to the entire world. They are "missionaries of the revolution." They redeem people and look for new converts.

The brigadist Nitta's testimony merits particular attention because it summarizes, with extreme clarity and incisiveness, the typical traits of the Red Brigades' mentality.

Nitta recounts that encountering the materialistic concept of history was the decisive moment of his life. After having embraced Marx's texts, "my tensions lead me to identify the duty of the revolution with my need-duty to fight against 'evil.' I will finally understand the children of Biafra with their swollen bellies and I'll have enemies to face. Imperialism, capitalism, a class-conscious society, and the exploitation of man by man for me symbolized the incarnation of evil, the enemy to destroy, everything that I couldn't nail down found a response in the fideist value of revolution."[47]

In Nitta's testimony there are all the elements of the gnostic scheme: (a) the *"binary code mentality"* that identifies reality as the battle between the forces of "good" and the forces of "evil"; (b) *"radical catastrophism,"* according to which the world is immersed in pain and suffering; (c) the *identification of an "enemy"* on whom to heap the blame for all human unhappiness; and

---

46. This is told by a leader of the armed struggle to D. Della Porta, *Il terrorismo di sinistra,* 183. The same extract appears in D. Biacchessi, *Una stella a cinque punte,* 41.

47. See Novelli and Tranfaglia, *Vite sospese,* 190.

(d) *the salvific conception of the revolution* that sweeps away the shadows, vanquishing "the dark forces of the counterrevolution"[48] and establishing "a perfect society."[49]

The Red Brigades never imagined they would be defeated. They were convinced that capitalism was on the way out. For them, armed militancy was a "sacrificial gesture." This spirit is, under some aspects, similar to that of the "apocalyptic fanatics" so masterfully described by Norman Cohn:[50] "We were the *saviors*," states the brigadist Roberto Rosso, "and we wanted to bring valid values to support our judgments."[51] Anna Laura Braghetti also lived in "a time of waiting, looking for a way to change the world and attempting to understand if the Red Brigades were an instrument for making the revolutionary dream come true."[52]

For the Red Brigades, society is always "ready to explode."[53] The conviction that the revolution is imminent gives an extraordinary emotive charge to the gnostic activists. This certainty means that even the most dramatic consequences of the armed struggle can be overcome, such as the death of your fighting comrades, prison, or separation from the family, imposed by the choice of going underground.

Sergio Segio, founder of Prima Linea—a political group second only to the Red Brigades for number of homicides—saw the revolution as a salvific event that would liberate people: "The revolution and communism were nothing else for me but the possibility of being happy and free, knowing that you can be free only if everyone is."[54] In other words, "a revolutionary project of that stature, of that ambition, cannot be carried out if any margin of doubt remains."[55]

Absolute faith in the revolution, understood as the final solution to all humanity's problems, is a typical trait of the Red Brigades' mentality.

---

48. *Sossi kidnapping—Communiqué no. 1*, document issued on 19 April 1974, *Dossier Brigate rosse*, 1:258.

49. The expression is Nitta's, interviewed by D. Novelli and N. Tranfaglia, *Vite sospese*, 186. "In the Catholic environment I'd never been totally influenced by a particular figure, I stood out with all my diversities; now, in contact with the communist ideology, which did not propose perfect models for living but a perfect model of reality, I was strongly influenced by the people living in that environment."

50. N. Cohn, *I fanatici dell'apocalisse*, 1976.

51. Testimony of the brigadist Roberto Rosso to S. Zavoli, *La notte della Repubblica*, 378. Italics added.

52. A. L. Braghetti, *Il prigioniero*, 15.

53. Brigatist Enrico Fenzi talking to S. Zavoli, *La notte della Repubblica*, 225.

54. S. Segio, *Una vita in prima linea*, 78.

55. Braghetti, *Il prigioniero*, 36.

Political Violence and Social Marginality

The brigadist is a "marginal" individual who perceives the condition in which he lives as profoundly unjust. But "marginality" is not "marginalization," which is a condition of objective privation. Marginality instead is a state of mind that can also involve those of high social status. It is seen when individuals consider that their role in society is inferior to their merits or abilities. Hence the conviction of being the "victim" of an injustice. Typical marginal individuals have a neurotic and frustrated personality that makes them project the reason for their unhappiness on an external enemy. They wait obsessively for their day of deliverance.

Whether we are talking about a promising assistant at the University of Trento, like Margherita Cagol,[56] a literature teacher in a high school, like Maria Rosaria Roppoli, or a worker at the fruit and vegetable market in Bari, like Raffaele Fiore, the Red Brigades reject the values of the society in which they live. Their aspiration for a better world clashes with a reality that appears impossible to change through reforms and good intentions. For them, violence is a compulsory route. As Vincenzo Guagliardo explains, "The brigadist doesn't choose violence, he accepts it."[57] In the words of Fiore: "We considered that the only way to achieve our aims, those of the revolutionary Left, was through armed struggle, and we rejected the parliamentary path since we didn't consider it capable of altering society in the way we wanted. *We wanted to change it completely.*"[58]

No less significant is the way in which Patrizio Peci describes his frustration and anger when employed in the factory: "The work was always the same, the most stupid and monotonous that exists. Every day I had to make a hole in 3,000 pieces of a very tough material that was softened with oil. The oil burned with the heat of the drill and gave off a terrible smell. Holes, holes, holes all day. 10,000 holes a day, 50,000 holes a week, 200,000 holes a month, 2,400,000 holes a year. Was this living? Was this the fate of the proletariat? And why? The boss acted paternalistic. . . . And if we'd drilled a hole in his legs? Would he and his kind have continued to hassle us for a hole done badly?"[59]

---

56. Margherita Cagol graduated with honors on 26 July 1969 from the Sociology Faculty at the University of Trento. Her thesis was on "The Qualification of the Labor Force during Capitalistic Development." She was offered a two-year assistant professorship in sociology at the Milan Umanitaria. See P. Agostini, *Mara Cagol,* 62–63.

57. V. Guagliardo, *Di sconfitta in sconfitta,* 53.

58. Grandi, *L'ultimo brigatista,* 65. Italics added.

59. P. Peci, *Io, l'infame,* 52.

Fiore was born in Bari. The oldest of six children, he started working at the age of ten, first as apprentice builder, then auto-body repairer, then factory worker, and finally in the wholesale food market as a goods handler. Fiore moves from Bari to Milan in October 1970, aged sixteen, to attend a course for turners. He recounts that his encounter with the city and its smog, leaden sky, and traffic, is awful. It is a chaotic, hostile, and depressing environment in which he feels an outsider. In Milan he earns the same money he would have earned in Bari. All in all, he would have been better off at home, but, he recounts, a desire to improve his social condition gets the better of him. He's convinced that Milan can give him more. He decides to stay. After finishing his training course, he finds employment in the Breda factory as a turner. He observes the other workers, their efforts, their sacrifices, and their alienating life. He's certain he can aspire to a better future. He refuses to think that he'll spend all his life in a factory. He starts to ask himself questions about politics and society, but he has little education (it's not clear from his autobiography whether he even completed junior high school). He needs to meet someone who knows more than he does, who is able to answer his questions about the world. In 1972, he meets a Red Brigades militant, Arialdo Lintrami, who will lead him to the armed struggle.

Fiore lives in the suburbs. He doesn't have a house, just a bed. He hates his life. He irons his own clothes, eats always in the same café with other workers. His days are monotonous and repetitive. He leaves home at half past six in the morning to reach the factory by eight. He finishes work at five o'clock and by seven he's home again. He just has time to wash, eat something, and go out for a stroll to meet his friends. At midnight he has to be back home, otherwise he's forced to spend the night in the street. This isn't the life he wanted. It's a life that forces him to live on the margins and he finds it unsupportable.

When he starts working in the factory, Fiore is faced with a depressing sight: "Men who've been working for over thirty years on the same machine, pathologically wedded to their job and their alienation; workers who empty flagons of wine to endure the casting fumes, like soldiers at the front who, aware they're cannon fodder, cloud their minds as they go into battle; workers hard of hearing, because they've hammers in their heads like football fans have the ball. I slowly started to feel a strong conviction: *I would never spend all my life doing that work.* At the time I wasn't able to see any solutions, but I knew I would have found them."[60]

---

60. Grandi, *L'ultimo brigatista,* 35. Italics added.

Fiore was to find his "solution" in the Red Brigades, where he became a leader of the Turin faction.

The aspiring brigadists have the same ambitions for money and success as any normal person. They want to improve their social status. They dream of a world in which they'll be respected and admired. But the reality they encounter causes them constant frustration. If the "boss system" relegates them to the margins of society, the only thing left to do is to demolish it. It has to be destroyed and rebuilt in the image and semblance of the Red Brigades' ambitions. To succeed in this undertaking, they have to possess power. They also feel a "lust for power" and the "will to power."

Nitta, recalling his youth, writes: "I wanted to draw on that will to power in which I could fully tap my thirst for justice. . . . What was voluntary service against the possibility of changing the material cause of injustice?"[61]

Although the Red Brigades feel a lust for power, their mission is not completed when they gain it. Taking over the coercive apparatus is the first step in the regeneration of humanity through violence. Do not forget that, in eschatological politics, power is a means and not an end.

In a document of July 1970, the Red Brigades explain their immediate objective: "*What do we want? We want power!* We said it at the outset: we want power. Because as long as the bosses have power, our condition cannot change. And we don't want just a part of it, we want it all. There's no possibility for cooperation. Our interests are conflicting."[62] This is because "all the contradictions in this society are resolved only on the basis of specific strength relationships."[63] "The workers' movement . . . must concentrate on the issue of power, on the dictatorship of the proletariat."[64] In the document claiming responsibility for the Biagi murder it is written that "power cannot therefore be gained without revolutionary violence; that is, without an armed struggle to destroy the state machine that creates class dictatorship and constitutes the armed instrument that protects and guarantees the interests of the ruling class. The communist revolutionary process is thus essentially a class war against the state and the ruling class."[65]

---

61. Novelli and Tranfaglia, *Vite sospese*, 188.

62. This is what can be read in "Fogli di lotta di Sinistra proletaria," published July–October 1970. See *Dossier Brigate rosse,* 1:76.

63. *Sossi kidnapping—Communiqué no. 8.* On 23 May 1974 the BR released Mario Sossi with the task of distributing communiqué no. 8. The text, published by the Roman daily *Il giornale d'Italia* on 24–25 May 1974, is in *Dossier Brigate rosse,* 1:297.

64. *Communiqué for the liberation of Curcio.* Red Brigade document of 19 February 1975, in ibid., 1:338.

65. Red Brigades document *claiming responsibility for the Biagi murder* of March 2002. The entire text is available at www.brigaterosse.org.

Hatred, envy, resentment, and the desire to avenge one's marginal status are among the sentiments that prompt people to enter the Red Brigades: "We hated with all our hearts,"[66] recalls Valerio Morucci, who added these important words: "I had learned that you couldn't be a communist without hating, that those who understand hate, and those who don't understand don't hate."[67]

I call the reader's attention to the next passage because it offers sociological considerations. Besides providing an excellent picture of the Red Brigades' mental universe, it also shows once again how important the ideological dimension is in their actions and, more precisely, when shedding blood.

This is what the brigadist Peci thought before shooting Antonio Munari, then shop foreman at Fiat, eight times in his legs (22 April 1977): "I didn't have any second thoughts. This man—he must have been around forty to forty-five, balding—was a boss, someone the factory comrades had indicated was harsh with the workers, a servant of the boss. I didn't know if he was a bully, I didn't work at Fiat, but as I waited I thought: 'This is a man who's doing well, he goes home for lunch while the workers eat in the canteen. He has a nice car given to him by Fiat, he lives in a pleasant place, in a residential suburb, possibly also given to him by Fiat, while the workers' houses...' What struck me most of all was the fact that he would go home to eat, while the workers probably ate disgusting food in the canteen, then he'd come back, happy and well fed, and make them work like dogs. I thought about my father, who is a builder, when he left for the site with his cold lunch. I geared myself up in this way..., thinking about what I would have said to the factory brigade: Munari didn't behave well; besides being a boss—which in itself has a specific meaning—he was inflexible, demanding. I was there, I told myself, for an act of justice. Strike one to educate one hundred.... An infernal din, with that gun echoing loudly in that garage and him yelling like a madman....I could have lost my nerve but I stayed cool and finished the magazine, eight shots. Too many, but I was so tense I couldn't stop myself. He was shouting like a madman. As I left, out of the corner of my eye I saw him drag himself toward the door, but he didn't make it, because I read in the papers that he was there for about twenty minutes."[68]

Brigadists are prompted by a feeling of deep frustration caused by their marginality. But before acting they have to define the reasons for their deprivation. The Marxist-Leninist doctrine is their beacon. It tells them that the

66. Morucci, *La peggio gioventù*, 103.
67. Morucci, *A guerra finita*, 17.
68. Peci, *Io, l'infame*, 14–16.

roots of their exploitation are to be found in "relations of production," in the relations established between capitalists and proletarians during the production process. These relations are based on the private ownership of means of production. Communism is the solution to all evils. Once established, there will no longer be any distinction between rich and poor, employers and workers, exploiters and exploited. But every attempt to demolish the present order of things comes up against the reaction of the ruling class. For this reason, politics is an ongoing war in which the army of the "good" fights against the army of the "bad." There is no room for dialogue or consultation. Revolutionaries have to be intolerant because their enemies live in error, far from the scientific and incontestable truth of Marxism-Leninism. However, the Marxist-Leninist formula is not in itself sufficient to save the world. The revolution needs a handful of trained and well-organized people to transform Marx's thinking into a tool of social change. The professional revolutionaries have the task of saving humanity from the tyranny of capitalism and from people's wickedness.

Conclusion: the conquest of power is the antechamber of happiness.

Paraphrasing Max Weber, we could say that "they work with the striving for power as an unavoidable means. Therefore, the 'power instinct,' as it is called, belongs indeed to their normal qualities."[69] The Red Brigades could see themselves in this description, where Weber is referring to the "professional politician," except for one thing: they do not have the same ambitions as the middle classes. The Red Brigades consider themselves anthropologically different from their enemies. They could never admit that they have the same impulses as those who infest the world with their corrupt presence, and their daily life must continually confirm this unshakable "diversity." The Red Brigades are absolutely certain that their war is in the interests of humanity and they think it entirely justified "to respond to the fascist atrocities with armed justice."[70] They practice terror and preach love. With one hand they kill, kneecap, and terrorize; with the other they outline the perfect society. It will be built with their heroism, their love for others, day after day, death after death, because—as we read in the first communiqué of the Sossi kidnapping

---

69. M. Weber, *La politica come professione,* 95–96.

70. Leaflet *claiming responsibility for the Padua assassination,* 18 June 1974, in *Dossier Brigate rosse,* 1:299. The document refers to the actions of 17 June 1974, when an armed Red Brigade group occupied the MSI (Italian Socialist Movement) provincial headquarters on via Zabardella, Padua. There were two MSI victims: Graziano Giralucci and Giuseppe Mazzola. According to the Red Brigades, Mazzola and Giralucci reacted violently and were "executed." According to forensic findings, they were handcuffed and shot in the back of the head.

(19 April 1974)—"there can be no compromise with the executioners of freedom."[71]

Political violence always needs to justify itself. It has to define an abstract principle as its foundation.

Eschatological Politics

At this point the reader may be tempted to conclude that the communist ideal, along with the utopia of the perfect society, the liberation of the oppressed, and heaven on earth, were the Red Brigades' "political formulas."[72] That is, they were the ornaments with which they tried to embellish the crude reality of politics, which is the battle for power. But this would be a hasty conclusion, because the *final aim* of the Red Brigades' action is not the conquest of power and the enjoyment of the pleasures it involves, but the radical transformation of the world. The Red Brigades' mission has a very real goal: to take over the establishment and purify the world from the moral corruption generated by private property. Taking power—it can never be repeated enough—is only a stage in the brigadist plan whose final goal is the extermination of their enemies through revolutionary terror and the construction of a perfect society. In other words, the political realism lecture can hinder our understanding of the brigadist mentality. Machiavelli and Pareto, Mosca and Michels—according to whom politics in the end comes down to the struggle for power—can illuminate only some minor aspects of the phenomenon we are analyzing.

In the words of Dolf Sternberger, the Red Brigades' type of politics is "eschatological."[73] Author of a fundamental work on the great metamorphoses of the concept of politics, Sternberger is worth studying in depth. He has pinpointed three "roots" of political thought in the West: the "politology" of Aristotle, the "demonology" of Machiavelli, and the "eschatology" of Augustine. For Aristotle—writes Sternberger—politics is the administration of the state for the "common good," whereas for Machiavelli it is the art of command. There is also a third tradition, Saint Augustine's eschatological

---

71. *Sossi kidnapping—communiqué no. 1*, Red Brigades document of 19 April 1974, in ibid., 1:259.

72. See G. Mosca, "Elementi di scienza politica," 2:633: "The political class does not exclusively justify its power with its de facto possession, but tries to give it a moral and also legal basis, making it a necessary consequence of doctrines and beliefs that are generally recognized and accepted in the society it governs."

73. D. Sternberger, *Le tre radici della politica*.

politics, described in his famous work *De civitate Dei,* written between 413 and 425 during the reign of the Christian emperor Honorius.

Eschatological politics aims to prepare people spiritually for the day of the apocalypse and universal judgment. In eschatological politics—explains Sternberger—the "great transformation" is awaited with profound faith. This "living in expectation" requires a strict ethical self-discipline, conceived as a daily "sacrifice." Eschatological politics is thus the politics of believing, since only an invincible faith can relieve the anguish of those waiting for the apocalypse. It is also a politics that leads to a fierce ethical radicalism. Since it is focused on the opposition between those who live in the light of Christ and those enveloped in the darkness of Lucifer, it is destined to condemn obsessively anything not included in the church orthodoxy. Lastly, it is a politics of conversion. Believers consider themselves the guardians of an absolute truth because it is of divine origin. There will be no tolerance for reprobates. Saint Augustine admonishes pagans who do not believe in the "true God" with the Hebrew commandment: "Those who offer a sacrifice to the gods, and not to the Lord alone, will be cursed."

The Red Brigades never worried about the governance of the state nor asked themselves how they would exercise power once they had gained it. There are no traces of Aristotle or Machiavelli in their thinking. As Nitta explains, recalling his political training: *"The communist ideology was offering me a perfect model for real life."*[74]

The Red Brigades' documents—hundred and hundreds of pages— obsessively reiterate the same concept: *this sickening and putrefying world is about to die.* A radical upheaval will change the course of history. A "new world" will come, in which every form of exploitation will be eliminated forever and people will live in universal harmony. A terrible anger will overthrow the "ungodly" bourgeoisie, who will pay for their atrocious crimes with their blood. In the "Red Brigades' city" there will be room only for the pure in spirit. Its doors will open only to those who, during the dark age of waiting, have lived in the "catacombs," renouncing the sinful temptations of this world.

The Red Brigades' actions are prompted by hatred of the enemy, an obsession with purity, pantoclastic fury, and the fideistic concept of the revolution. Their ideology is not a simple reflection of underlying material concerns; it is not a trite "anecdote" to embellish the fight for power—as a follower of Hans J. Morgenthau would say[75]—but the *primum movens* of the Red

---

74. Novelli and Tranfaglia, *Vite sospese,* 186. Italics added.
75. H. J. Morgenthau, *Politica tra le nazioni,* 1997.

Brigades' thoughts and actions. The brigadist ideology—to recall Karl Mann-heim's fundamental work—is itself an "instrument of collective action."[76] The Red Brigades are not simple "creatures of prey,"[77] as political realists would assert. They are not satisfied with gaining power. They are much more ambitious. They want a "new world" and a "new person."[78] The Marxist-Leninist ideology—in the hands of a group of people willing to use violence—is in itself a very powerful instrument of political and social change; it is a way of perceiving reality and of reconstructing it. For the Red Brigades it is the only link between people and reality. In other words, it is the most powerful of bullets.

The words of the Red Brigades' brigadist Anna Laura Braghetti are re-vealing here. They make us reflect, once again, on the importance the Red Brigades placed on ideology. Braghetti writes: "*Our only medium was ideol-ogy....Ideology was the crime that permitted me to enter the Red Brigades and to shoot other people. But it was also the crime against my very existence. Against all our lives.*"[79] For the brigadist Paolo Lapponi, "the revolution has a moral aspect that in some way justifies [political violence]."[80] The brigadist Alfredo Buo-navita states that "the issue of violence . . . is treated as something absolutely normal."[81] And for the brigadist "Piero," violence is "a method, an instru-ment of liberation."[82] In the Red Brigades—explains Morucci—"it had be-come a mark of distinction and of courage to have killed someone when you had no idea who he was."[83] The Red Brigades militant Alberto Franceschini describes the brigadist ideology as a "killer drug." These were his words: "We were only drug addicts, with a particular kind of drug, ideology. You just need a few cubic centimeters and you're stoned for life."[84]

---

76. K. Mannheim, *Ideologia e utopia,* 7.

77. R. Niebuhr, *Uomo morale e società immorale,* 18.

78. *Social Struggle and Organization in the Metropolis* (see n. 16 above), 57. The passage is worth quoting in full: "The fight for a 'new world' is also the fight for a 'new person.' The political revolu-tion finally becomes a real and profound process of social and cultural revolution. The revolution that has left utopia behind becomes relevant first of all in the revolutionary community. It passes 'inside' and 'outside' each of us at the same time, inside and outside every revolutionary community, inside and outside every labor collective. It requires a real contemporaneity between the transforma-tion of man and the transformation of his institutions, between the transformation of needs and the transformation of the production and consumption apparatus."

79. Anna Laura Braghetti talking to S. Mazzocchi, *Nell'anno della tigre,* 14.

80. R. Catanzaro and L. Manconi, eds., *Storie di lotta armata,* 197.

81. Ibid., 98.

82. Ibid., 255. The authors do not give the surname of the terrorist quoted.

83. Morucci, *Ritratto di un terrorista da giovane,* 219.

84. Franceschini, *Mara, Renato e io,* 204.

The Red Brigades would not have been content just to gain power. Everything leads us to believe that, if they had succeeded in doing so, they would have conscientiously and scrupulously carried out their promised "purification" of society through an extortionate use of political violence and terror, exactly as happened in all the societies in which the purifiers of the world succeeded in taking over the state machine. The Red Brigades wanted to free humanity from any form of unhappiness and oppression; they wanted to build a world based on solidarity and love. And they wanted it to last forever.

The Red Brigades cannot tolerate a world inhabited by individuals not inspired by the revolutionary ideal. The complete elimination of their enemies could require many years, because the world is infested with them. There could be millions of people to kill, but no matter. True revolutionaries are willing to devote their entire lives to this project of total annihilation. As we saw in the testimony of the brigadist who admired Pol Pot, many gnostic activists do not want to obtain privileges or honorary appointments. They want to exterminate their enemies; they want to punish the reprobates and inflict "fair punishment" on those who have refused to take the "path of light" that leads to salvation. They are intransigent. No party in this corrupt world could stop them. They will win or die.

CHAPTER 2

The Sacralization of Politics

> Politics is beyond people's lives.
> It's a "great plan" close to the divine.
>
> —Valerio Morucci

The "Fanaticism of a New Religion"

One of the typical traits of the Red Brigades' mentality is the sacralization of politics. The Red Brigades have the task of redeeming people, showing them the way to salvation: "We were the saviors," says the brigadist Roberto Rosso, "and we wanted to bring people convincing values to judge with."[1] Like all self-respecting saviors, the Red Brigades are the guardians of an absolute truth that contains the "formula" for eliminating every form of human suffering. This formula consists of the destruction of the present world through revolutionary violence. Which means that the future of humanity depends on politics. That politics is certainly not a "bourgeois politics" vulgarly aimed at the conquest of power. Rather, the Red Brigades practice a "new" politics that aspires to a metapolitical aim: the perfect society. Human conduct is meaningful only in the service of the revolution. Someone who does not espouse the Marxist ideal is not even a person.

The brigadist Nitta recalls that for him politics had a marginal importance. But everything changed after his encounter with Marxism. From then on, the meaning of his life depended solely on the revolution: "My cultural and existential baggage was not focused on politics, but I gradually started

---

1. S. Zavoli, *La notte della Repubblica,* 378.

to interpret reality through political criticism according to Marxist categories.... I encountered a mentality in which the value of an individual life was
relative and *man was such only if he was revolutionary.*"[2]

Nitta ends with these words: "The communist ideology did not propose
perfect models of man, but *a perfect model for real life.*"[3]

Thus the Red Brigades' politics has a soteriological nature and as such is
"sacred." As Morucci wrote about his militancy in the Red Brigades: "*Politics is beyond people's lives. It's a 'great plan' close to the divine.*"[4] Only those who
follow Marxism can see the world with "pure" eyes. This "privilege" makes
the Red Brigades "gnostic" activists, or people who have "a revolutionary
gnosis," a knowledge reserved for the select few, who have the "duty" to save
humanity, defeating—after "a series of battles that mark the beginning of the
last war"[5]—"the vast army of black soldiers."[6]

Everything has to be sacrificed on the altar of politics, including life—
your own and that of your enemies. The Red Brigades' mission—as Morucci
wrote—was the result of the "fanaticism of a new religion."[7]

The communist ideal enabled the Red Brigades to pour their mystic-
religious vocation into politics, which takes on a salvific character. Politics
becomes their obsession: "Politics was everything,"[8] asserts the brigadist Enrico Baglioni. Outside revolutionary politics, life has no significance whatsoever. Through it, it is possible to resolve all the contradictions that afflict
human coexistence. But it has to be a politics illuminated by the Marxist
"truth" and supported by the "faith" in the palingenetic power of the revolutionary procedure. The Red Brigades' need for the "absolute" is thus fulfilled. All their psychic energies can be addressed to an ideal of redemption,
giving an elevated meaning to their existence. The Red Brigades can shake
off their status as marginal individuals to become "heroes." They choose to
sacrifice themselves for the good of humanity, shouldering the task of leading the oppressed and the exploited to the kingdom of light.

You enter the Red Brigades "with the same absolutism as that involved
in a sacrifice." Entering the Red Brigades—these are the words of Valerio

---

2. D. Novelli and N. Tranfaglia, *Vite sospese,* 185. Italics added.

3. Ibid., 186. Italics added.

4. V. Morucci, *La peggio gioventù,* 104.

5. *Internal Reflection Document;* published by the periodical *Brigate rosse,* no. 1, June 1975, in
Dossier Brigate rosse, 1:372.

6. "Giornale 'Brigate rosse' no. 2. Br di Roma," from the periodical *Brigate rosse,* no. 2, May
1971, in ibid., 1:112.

7. Morucci, *La peggio gioventù,* 108.

8. R. Catanzaro and L. Manconi, eds., *Storie di lotta armata,* 99.

Morucci—is "like going to the stake."[9] As Sergei Nechaev, whose teaching the Red Brigades eagerly imbibed, wrote: "The revolutionary is a dedicated man; he must not be driven by his personal impulses but must be directed by the common interests of the revolution. For him, the only thing that is moral is that which contributes to the triumph of the revolution. All that obstructs this is immoral and criminal."[10] The Red Brigades practice an authentic "secular alternative" to religion. Therefore—and this is my core theory—they fall within the vast phenomenology of religious phenomena.[11] For the Red Brigades, the choice of the armed struggle is an authentic "sacrificial gesture."[12]

To understand the phenomenon of the Red Brigades we have to realize that they, by their explicit admission, were "invaded with political purity."[13] Their enemies' ideas were only an instrument to oppress the workers. The ideas of those who support the revolution are instead "just," "true," and "indisputable." Imposing them with force is nothing to be ashamed of, since violence is necessary when its aim is to purify the world of reprobates. We read in a Red Brigades document of April 1974: "Striking the fascists with every means and in every place is just and necessary."[14] "The claim that a fascist's life is worthless," clarifies the brigadist Alfredo Buonavita, "was a cultural legacy. . . . In the sense that the fascist as an enemy whose life is worthless is not the legacy of youthful extremism, it's the acceptance of a whole left-wing mentality that has filled the squares of Milan."[15]

The Red Brigades documents show the perspicacity of the social psychologist Milton Rokeach, who had been suggesting the existence of "left-wing authoritarians" since 1956. These would be those left-wing extremists who preached equality and liberty but oppressed and crushed those who expressed

---

9. Testimony of the brigadist Valerio Morucci to S. Mazzocchi, *Nell'anno della tigre,* 74.

10. Quoted in M. Nomand, *Apostles of Revolution,* 232.

11. As Pellicani says: "The modern, secularized, and positive society has not entirely succeeded in suppressing religious need. It satisfies this need through ethical-political utopias." L. Pellicani, *I rivoluzionari di professione,* 12–23.

12. The testimony of a brigadist to D. Della Porta, *Il terrorismo di sinistra,* 174. With his entry into the Red Brigades, the militant recalls that he underwent "a profound change and upheaval in my life, in the sense that I, devoting myself practically body and soul to this type of commitment spiritually linked to my comrades on the run, to this idea of our lives overturned, had a series of virtual pictures before my eyes: the need, the legitimacy, the justice and, if you want, also the beauty of that type of sacrificial gesture." Mark Juergensmeyer's comparative study of religious terrorism, *Terror in the Mind of God,* is a good resource for understanding the religious mindset of the Red Brigadists. See also Jessica Stern, *Terror in the Name of God.*

13. Morucci, *La peggio gioventù,* 141.

14. *Against neo-Gaullism to strike at the heart of the State.* Red Brigades document issued in April 1974, in *Dossier Brigate rosse,* 1:256.

15. Catanzaro and Manconi, *Storie di lotta armata,* 64.

different opinions. This narrow and intolerant mentality is similar to the fascist one.[16] The brigadist Patrizio Peci's testimony is very instructive. Both fascism and the Red Brigades, explains Peci, want to impose their vision of the world with force, but fascism supports "impure" principles and ideas not in line with the Marxist "truth." This is Peci on the difference between Red Brigades and fascists: "My benchmark was always fascism as the opposite of communism. Fascism is the arrogance of wanting to impose one's ideas with force and with violence. You could say, and someone has said it, that the Red Brigades also did this; they wanted to classify the Red Brigades with fascism because both use violence and want to impose, as an elitist group, their ideas on the majority. I think they exaggerate. Fascism is the exaltation of individualism, communism is the exaltation of collectivism. But above all, communism is in the interests of the majority class, of the proletariat, of the class that works, not of a select group."[17]

Radical Catastrophism

So those who live outside the Marxist doctrine must open their eyes. They are blind and must accept a vanguard that will conduct them to the kingdom of "truth." It is only under these conditions—we read in a Red Brigades document issued in Milan in 1971—"that the pigs won't crush the people."[18]

Imposing the "right" way of thinking is a duty. But the "boss system" is everywhere. There is no respite. It takes over minds and thoughts. As soon as they are born, people are inserted in a machine that humiliates, degrades, and exploits them twenty-four hours a day. The political, economic, cultural, and legislative systems have to be eliminated. Everything is "bourgeois" and thus impure. State, political parties, trade unions, legal institutes, the entire capitalistic productive-distributive apparatus, the dominant ideology in all its aspects, customs, "morals"—there is nothing in this world that deserves to be preserved. This is what we read in the first programmatic document of the Metropolitan Political Collective (CPM), *Social Struggle and Organization in the Metropolis,*

---

16. See M. Rokeach, "Political and Religious Dogmatism"; see also his *The Open and Closed Mind*. See also P. E. Tetlock, "Cognitive Style and Political Belief Systems in the British House of Commons," 1314–24. Tetlock questioned a random sample of the British House of Commons on their political convictions. It was found that Conservatives and extremist Socialists had the same tendencies toward absolutism and intolerance.

17. P. Peci, *Io, l'infame,* 45.

18. *Class against Class: Class War.* Red Brigade document issued in Milan during 1971, quoted in ibid., 118.

drafted in November–December 1969, and printed and issued in Milan in the form of a pamphlet in January 1970.[19]

Television, the press, cinema, schools, even kindergartens are tools of social oppression. In a leaflet of the Metropolitan Political Collective, *Emancipation of Women?* issued in Milan in March 1970, we read: "But emancipation from whom? From husbands who are exploited in the factory eight hours a day, who work in dangerous conditions, who are made to believe they have privileges by the boss system? Emancipation because women 'can' work? Emancipation because today women 'can' go to the pub or cinema alone, buy a few more clothes or necklaces, take the pill? *In our society based on exploitation twenty-four hours a day.... In the name of their emancipation, the bosses offer women the right to be exploited in the factory, which they call the right to work. So women are super exploited: once because they have to work in the factory to manage to pay the rent, to buy books for their children and send them to school....And again when they have to look after the home and children and maybe 'fight' to have a kindergarten built, with mimosa branches! All this serves to support the boss system;* in fact, in the terms of the system, the kindergarten serves to remove the so-called 'weight' of the education of your children so that you can work when and how it wants; to delegate the education of your children to it from birth for its own interest."[20]

The world is caught up in permanent disaster. No one can escape alienation. For the brigadist Codrini: "The rot is there, it's spreading, ruining everything: we're become increasingly aware of it every day. A quagmire in which we're inexorably sinking. The soul of modern society is in tatters, it's bleeding everywhere, there's no hope for it."[21] He observes "the behavior of children from the so-called well-off families and realize[s], with dismay, that the seeds of the drugs they will inject in a few years' time are already germinating inside them."[22]

Our thoughts, our desires, are not really "ours." They're the reflection of "forces" extraneous to us, occult powers that move like shadows in our minds. The "boss system" thinks and desires for us: "We're profoundly marked by an alienated social life," the Red Brigades write, "in which 'separation' seems to be the prevailing law: separation between public and private, separation between being and awareness, separation between your mind and your balls."[23] To escape this condition of unsupportable privation, a revolution

---

19. *Social Struggle and Organization in the Metropolis,* in *Dossier Brigate rosse,* 1:21–58.

20. *Emancipation of Women?* Red Brigades leaflet issued in Milan in March 1970, in *Dossier Brigate rosse,* 1:71–72.

21. G. Codrini, *Io, un ex brigatista,* 52.

22. Ibid., 61.

23. *Social Struggle and Organization in the Metropolis,* 56–57.

that changes only the nation's political-institutional system is not sufficient. Much more is needed. An anthropological revolution is needed, able to up-root the egoism that "the system" has sown in people's hearts. This is the Red Brigades' ambition: to change people. To purify their eyes and minds from the contamination of a corrupt and evil society: "The 'new man's' fixation on constructing," writes the brigadist Prospero Gallinari, "raises the criticism of middle-class morals, the theory of militant abnegation, to embarrassing levels."[24]

With the radicalization of their revolutionary ideology, the Red Brigades adopt a rigid dividing line. On one side the "pure," the "elect" who have the task of judging and carrying out sentences; one the other "the black fascist soldiers."[25] In Mario Moretti's words: "On one side the armed struggle, on the other all the rest."[26]

In the programmatic document of the Metropolitan Political Collective, *Social Struggle and Organization in the Metropolis* (1969) cited earlier, the range of enemies to attack is extended with effects that were to be devastating. No longer only those who "deliberately" defend the system, but also those who unconsciously support it.[27] It is the distinction—typical of totalitarian terror—between "objective enemy" and "potential enemy." The former de-liberately and resolutely oppose the revolutionary project; the latter instead, even if they haven't actually carried out any counterrevolutionary behavior, are persecuted for the sole fact of belonging to a social group considered "hostile."[28]

But who are the enemies? They are all those who are not friends; all those who are not deployed in the armed struggle. The "binary code" of the Red Brigades' mentality leaves no way out because—as their document of September 1971 states—the boundaries between "good" and "evil" are rigorously "scientific." As such they have nothing arbitrary or subjective about them. They are inspired by Marxism-Leninism, the Chinese Cultural

---

24. P. Gallinari, *Un contadino nella metropoli,* 80.

25. *"Giornale 'Brigate rosse' no. 2. Br di Roma,"* from the periodical *Brigate rosse* no. 2, May 1971, in *Dossier Brigate rosse,* 1:113.

26. Moretti's statement: "It was as ideological as you want, but it consisted of the armed struggle on one side, and on the other all the rest." M. Moretti, *Brigate rosse,* 44.

27. We read in the document of the Metropolitan Political Collective, *Social Struggle and Orga-nization in the Metropolis,* 51: "'To act with the masses like fish in water' for us means preventing the powers that be from forming a real idea of their strength, hounding them in their dens and unloading on them and their representatives (*or on those who consciously or unconsciously take their defense and become their accomplices*) all the violence that they continually use against the great majority of the people." Italics added.

28. See H. Arendt, *Le origini del totalitarismo,* 580; and also D. Fisichella, *Totalitarismo,* 40.

Revolution, and the experience of the metropolitan guerilla movements.[29] Following the Marxism-Leninism doctrine means upholding a principle of absolute truth that brooks no contradiction: "The working class and the working masses," we read in another Red Brigades document issued in Milan in April 1972, "cannot defeat the armed middle classes without the power of guns. This is a Marxist law, not an opinion."[30]

Revolutionary violence is an appealing ideal because it meets a fundamental need for self-fulfillment. A need that cannot be met through the exaltation of individual qualities (the "boss system" systematically represses any "real" attempt at social ascent) but through the violent and radical transformation of the world.

The Revolutionary Sect and the Obsession with Purity

The political group confers significance on human existence. It becomes the only link with reality. The relationship with your comrades, sharing a great project, the bonds of solidarity, take on an absolute value that transcends the meaning of individual existences.

With the language and mentality typical of the gnostic revolutionary, a brigadist describes the communist ideal as a choice that involves every moment of his existence. Politics has a "total" meaning with all the aspects of a mystic-religious experience: "Being part of a great organization justified me, at least that is what I felt, in front of the world and of history, and for years it was to become the only transcendence, the only immanence to which I could sacrifice myself. Not so much by unorganized reading but rather by daily experience, my conception of the world became strongly materialistic, dialectics was to rationalize even the irrational. I gradually became convinced that my ideals were fulfilled in my relationship with my comrades, in our unity of intentions and solidarity. Politics became my way of life, the way in which I related to reality.... My life is now completely immersed in political practice. I internalize the reasons for the revolt that drives thousands of young people... who during the demonstrations all become 'brothers' against the common enemy. The noise of thousands of people marching in

---

29. Self-interview. BR leaflet issued in Milan, September 1971, in *Dossier Brigate rosse*, 1:127: "*What ideology did you support?* Our benchmarks are Marxism-Leninism, the Chinese Cultural Revolution and the ongoing experience of the metropolitan guerilla movements; in brief, the scientific tradition of the international workers' revolutionary movement."

30. *Votes Don't Work, Guns Do!* Red Brigade document issued in Milan, April 1972, in ibid., 1:159.

the streets, yelling slogans at the top of their voices and the odor of the tear gas became synonyms of authenticity for me."[31]

In the light of all this, it becomes very difficult to agree with those who—like Luigi Bonanate—try to explain the phenomenon of terrorism in Italy leaving out ideological variables. According to Bonanate, when the political system is no longer able to answer the questions asked by civil society, it becomes "blocked." This political-institutional situation creates favorable conditions for subversive movements, since they come to believe that political violence is the only practical way to achieve their goals.

In Bonanate's words: "The appearance of a terrorist event becomes an indicator of a blocked situation . . . , one could say that the appearance of terrorism allows for a kind of 'early diagnosis'. . . of the fact that a determinate structured organization . . . is nearing, or has already entered, a blocked situation, that is, it is only able to perform its tasks repetitively, without adapting to new needs or new stimuli, without developing or regulating itself. In other words, the blocked situation is that of a system that has consolidated its base, its structural organization, to such an extent that no innovation of any kind is possible. . . . The terrorist thus knows he is in a blocked route: thus he needs a fighting technique that permits him to explode that block in his path."[32]

Less dogmatic is the position of Gianfranco Pasquino, who states that the "blocked system" does not in itself create the demand for terrorism. At most, it can be considered a facilitator: "The block of the system," writes Pasquino, "acts as a factor facilitating the approach of a consistent number of young people to the armed struggle; it is *not the cause* of terrorism in a technical sense."[33]

My theory is that the Red Brigades' action is the result of a gradual interaction in which the support of a particular political ideology plays a decisive role. This is in disagreement not only with Bonanate but also with Donatella Della Porta and Carlo Marletti. The former denies that ideology is one of the "causes for collective behavior."[34] The latter, using the economic approach to the study of political phenomena, claims that terrorism "*always* has a strategic

31. Ibid., 1:190.

32. L. Bonanate, *Dimensioni del terrorismo politico,* 176–78.

33. G. Pasquino, "Sistema politico bloccato e insorgenza del terrorismo," 218.

34. Della Porta, *Il terrorismo di sinistra,* 123–24. Della Porta's contributions also include *Terrorismi in Italia; Il terrorismo; Gli incentivi alla militanza nelle organizzazioni clandestine della sinistra; Social Movements and the States; Movimenti collettivi e sistema politico in Italia 1960–1995;* and with M. Rossi, *Cifre crudeli Bilancio dei terrorismi italiani.*

content; it is a type of selective action, calculated for the effects it can produce and that develops according to a specific logic of behavior."[35]

The Red Brigades documents—and the history of this revolutionary group—lead us to the opposite conclusion.

The Red Brigades are required to carry out the colossal mission of saving the world. They feel that the fate of humanity is their responsibility. Their life has a meaning only in the function of the revolution. The system can only be destroyed, since, we read in a Red Brigades document of 1971 published in Milan, "power is born from the gun barrel."[36] The Red Brigades' gnostic vision is a "mental barracks" that guides their behavior in a way mainly independent of the political system's capacity to reform. This explains how the Red Brigades reestablished themselves—not once but twice after their first defeat in the early eighties—in very different institutional political situations. The Red Brigades—we read in the document claiming responsibility for the Rossi attack (4 June 1977)—are fighting not to "unblock" the political system but, on the contrary, "to block and destroy the murdering and counterrevolutionary initiative the state is implementing to reorganize, on the back of the working class's sacrifices and deaths, the tottering power of multinational capital."[37] In *Comunicato no. 10,* Giovanni D'Urso kidnapping (14 January 1981), we read that "we of the Red Brigades have nothing either to ask or to barter. The guerrilla warfare achieves the goals of its program with its weapons in hand and it is not negotiable."[38]

The "blocked system" theory removes attention from the Red Brigades' particular characteristic, their political-religious vocation.[39] We can attempt to understand this phenomenon through what elsewhere I have called the "paradigm of Pareto."[40] According to this sociologist's typical approach, politics can be understood only in its innumerable relations with other social areas.

The Red Brigades have a particular vision of the world based on some deflagrating ingredients: (a) social marginalization, (b) denial of reality, (c) obsession

35. See C. Marletti, "Immagini pubbliche e ideologia del terrorismo," 191. Italics added.

36. "Classe contro classe," 117.

37. *Leaflet claiming responsibility for Rossi shooting* published on 4 June 1977, in *Dossier Brigate rosse 1976–1978,* 2:86. Emilio Rossi was director of RAI Channel 1 News.

38. *Comunicato no. 10—D'Urso kidnapping,* Red Brigade document issued on 14 January 1981 (www.brigaterosse.org).

39. The "blocked system" theory can be useful, at most, to investigate how the Red Brigades phenomenon gained its consensus, but not its genesis and persistence. We have to examine the professional revolutionaries' mental universe, the way in which they are formed and the social processes that encourage them on their path.

40. See A. Orsini, "Sociologia politica e scienza politica," 433–68.

with "purity," (d) hatred of capitalism, (e) fideistic expectation of the revolution, and (f) pantoclastic fury.

The choice to embrace the Red Brigades' cause is prompted mainly by sentiment and passion and only to a very limited extent by the capacity to adjust the means (the armed struggle) to the end (the communist revolution). The Red Brigades' vision of the world is mature when "principle of hope" prevails over the principle of reality.[41] Being educated for the revolution means espousing a new faith. The revolutionary sect is a very powerful agency for socialization with the task of forging the "ideological person." Its most important aspect is what Herman Schmalenbach has called "emotional sodality."

This concept needs to be examined.

Ferdinand Tönnies had distinguished between *community* and *society*.[42] The first, supported by the power of tradition, is founded on deep emotional links and on solidarity; the second is dominated by rationality and by egoistical interests. In the community, individuals are an "end"; in society they are a "means." Their value is commensurate with their "usefulness." Community bonds are given; social ones are acquired. This means that you are "born" into the community, whereas you "enter" society.

Alongside these two sociological categories, Schmalenbach introduces a third, called *Bund*.

You enter the *Bund* out of free choice, but the bonds of solidarity uniting its members are very tight. The *Bund* is a fusion model. Once inside, it is very difficult to leave because the emotional involvement is very intense. "Emotional sodality," explains Schmalenbach, "is typical of religious communities. You become a believer, but sharing the faith creates a 'fraternal' bond. The true disciple is prepared to die to defend his teachers and his 'fellow believers.'" "The sect," concludes Schmalenbach, "is a *Bund* in the pure state."[43] And so is the Red Brigades' community, whose militants are fused into a single body. The "sacrifice" in defending one's comrades—renouncing all the pleasures of *this world*—has a deeply religious connotation. The Red Brigades are ready to die with the same determination with which they are ready to kill. Their action is driven much more by "emotional sodality" than by instrumental logics. The revolutionary sect is a source of life. It has the power to confer a very high significance even on

41. E. Bloch, *Il principio speranza*, 2005.
42. See F. Tönnies, *Comunità e società*, 1963.
43. H. Schmalenbach, *La categoria sociologica del Bund*.

the most "insignificant" existences. Outside the sect, the brigadists are lost; in the *Bund,* they are heroes fighting for the salvation of humanity.

Morucci recounts that, before embracing the revolutionary cause, he was living a life he felt to be useless and aimless and of which he was ashamed. He felt a great need to battle against an "obscene" world. Man can redeem the world, he thought, because he is the "incarnation of the divine." His testimony is invaluable: "After being a kind of drifter, comfortable because I had some money that was no use for anything, I'd started to feel ashamed of myself. The world continued to be obscene. Violence after violence and abuse after abuse. And there I was thinking only of my problems. It wasn't right. There was something inside me, a sensation that brought me to tears, which wasn't even ideological. It came from before. From further away. I couldn't ignore it. An old itch. A cultural itch. Man 'has' to act to change the world. To 'improve it.' He has to be an active part of history. Whatever the cost. He bears everything, because he's the incarnation of the divine. The king of the universe. The breakup of the static and suffocating pyramid of God-Church-Man has given us magnificent things, but its stagnation and barely concealed arrogance has made everything in its way capitulate or be swept away: things, which is not so bad; nature, unavoidable but within certain limits; and people themselves. The fanaticism of a new religion."[44]

The Red Brigades have the same features Jean Guitton described for the "party of the pure." We can break them down into six categories.

Segregation: The Red Brigades have no contact with the social universe. Their existence is closed, invisible, and clandestine. Just as the church achieves its "incandescent state" when it takes shelter in the catacombs, so the Red Brigades become more themselves in segregation.

Permanent Indignation: The Red Brigades love to despise, which is why they tend to become so outraged. They need it because their inner purity is confirmed through indignation.

Desire to be Persecuted: The Red Brigades are gratified by being persecuted. The state's violence against the "pure" proves their extraneousness to *this world.* If everything that lives outside the "confraternity" is corrupt, every attack on its members confirms an implacably pure diversity. As the left-wing revolutionary Ulrike Meinhof writes: "If the enemy fights us, that is good, not bad.... If the enemy opposes us vigorously, paints us in the blackest

---

44. Morucci, *La peggio gioventù,* 107–8.

colors, and allows us no good points, that is even better; it shows that... we have drawn a clear dividing line between ourselves and the enemy."[45]

Purification of Means through the End: Another characteristic of the Red Brigades' mentality is the acceptance of a temporary evil in view of a greater good. Saying that evil is justified by good is the same as saying that the end purifies the means. Remember the words of Anna Laura Braghetti, one of Aldo Moro's executioners: "I imagined a future in which every wrong would be righted, every inequality repaired, every injustice corrected.... *This justified the means we would have used.*"[46] Vincenzo Guagliardo recounts that his decision to enter the Red Brigades was for an eminently "moral" reason. He felt like a "heretic" who would lead people back to the way of "purity." In his words: "When we decided to embark on the armed struggle for communism, in the very early sixties, I think we were all convinced we were heretics.... In the end, by deciding on the armed struggle, in our heresy we just wanted to be consistent compared to those we considered had abandoned the purity of the ideal by accepting middle-class values."[47]

The brigadist responsible for shedding blood is convinced that violence represents only a cruel interlude before communism is established. In this way, "the immaculate character of the end," explains Guitton, "gives the bloody means an aura of innocence. This is why the pure are violent and the violent feel pure. The stronger the force, the gentler it seems, since it saves the time of pain."[48] The Red Brigades' violence is "compassionate."

Principle of Secrecy: The "secret" is the fifth pillar of the Red Brigades' universe. Not only because the goal of destroying the world cannot be publicly declared but also because there is the utmost solidarity among comrades. The Red Brigades have a "very high" goal. The "traitor" jeopardizes the salvation of humanity and is guilty of a "very base" action that offends the sacred nature of the salvific mission. Treason is a "spiritual" crime.

Preventive Internal Terror: To prevent the spiritual collapse of the weaker members, the Red Brigades rely on preventive internal terror. What a "party of purists" fears most is betrayal. It is a duty to accuse those who could betray; it is a duty to eliminate anyone who has collaborated with the "guardians" of *this corrupt world*. The Red Brigades live in a state of permanent alert toward

---

45. This is an extract from the manifesto of the Rote Armee Fraktion, *The Urban Guerrilla Concept,* written by Ulrike Meinhof probably in 1971.

46. A. L. Braghetti, *Il prigioniero,* 17. Italics added.

47. V. Guagliardo, *Di sconfitta in sconfitta,* 23.

48. J. Guitton, *Il puro e l'impuro,* 31.

the surrounding world and toward themselves. The revolutionary fury moves in all directions.

The Hatred of Reformists

Hatred and disdain toward all reformists was a typical, and obsessive, trait of the Red Brigades' mentality.

What compromise would ever have been possible with that "filthy fascist scum"[49] who defend the "monstrous killing machine"[50] represented by the state? Those who claim they can reform the system are only "its puppets."[51] "The only feasible politics for the proletariat at this stage is the *revolutionary class war*."[52] The Red Brigades' task is to "wreak total havoc in the enemy front"[53] and in its "degenerate party"[54] because—we read in a Red Brigades leaflet issued in Milan on 5 February 1971—"asking us to fight by the bosses' laws is like asking us to cut off our balls!"[55] The Red Brigades' desire to destroy every aspect of the present world will never be changed by the political parties' strategic choices. As we read in the communiqué claiming responsibility for the Coco crime (8 June 1976), political elections do nothing else but establish "who gives the order to shoot on the working classes."[56]

---

49. Leaflet *claiming responsibility for the Brescia attacks* published by *Controinformazione* no. 7–8, June 1976, in *Dossier Brigate rosse 1976–1978*, 2:29.

50. Communiqué *claiming responsibility for the attack on the prison inspectorate* published by *Controinformazione* no. 7–8, June 1976, in ibid., 2:38.

51. *Milan Trial. BR Communiqué no. 1,* document issued by the BR on 15 June 1977, at the start of the Milan trial against Renato Curcio, Nadia Mantovani, Giuliano Isa, Vincenzo Guagliardo, and Angelo Basone, in ibid., 2:90.

52. *Lettera aperta al processo di Bologna,* "Open Letter" signed by the Red Brigades members on trial in Bologna, published by *Controinformazione* no. 9–10, November 1977, in ibid., 2:76.

53. Morucci. *La peggio gioventù,* 141.

54. *Raid in the offices of "Iniziativa democratica."* Red Brigades document of 15 May 1975, in *Dossier Brigate rosse,* 1:368.

55. *Red Brigades Pirelli. Communiqué no. 6,* leaflet distributed to Pirelli factory in Milan on 5 February 1971, in *Dossier Brigate rosse,* 1:99. The first Red Brigades' actions were signed in the singular: "Red Brigade."

56. Communiqué *claiming responsibility for the Coco crime* issued in Genoa on 8 June 1976, in ibid., 2:41. Francesco Coco was the Genoa state prosecutor. He was killed with his guards on 8 June 1976. The passage is worth citing in its entirety: "In this situation there are the elections of 20 June, that will have to establish the political framework, the political alliances that will manage the implementation of this project. On 20 June one can only choose who will give the order to shoot the proletariat. Anyone who considers that, with the elections, there could be a balance favorable to the proletariat or even an alternative power created is not only acting out a miserable falsification, but is also indicating an adventurist and suicidal line. The only alternative to power is the armed struggle for communism."

Those who assert that big changes require time and that the world cannot be altered through an act of will, those who attempt to broaden the range of problems, doubting the effectiveness of radical solutions, are just "guard dogs"[57] at the service of the exploiters. We read in a Red Brigades leaflet issued in Turin on 18 December 1972 that "we have to silence these enemies of working-class unity, we have to strike them hard, with method, in their persons and in their belongings."[58] As Patrizio Peci explains: "At the time I was naive enough to still think that, in the end, perhaps the trade unions were preferable to the Christian Democrats. Then I realized that the trade union was more harmful for the revolution because it did not directly attack the working classes but instead inveigled them to act in its interests. The Red Brigades claim that the same applies to the PCI (Italian Communist Party) because it restrains the proletariat's revolutionary tendencies."[59]

The Red Brigades' hatred of reformists is even greater than their hatred of capitalists. In the document claiming responsibility for the Traversi attack (13 February 1977), the reformists are "elements proposing laws and reforms that are basically ultrareactionary and counterrevolutionary."[60] In Renato Curcio's analysis, *L'ultrarevisionismo,* written from prison in 1976, we read that "the Social-Democratic, reformist parties are an organizational screen behind which the bosses construct their counterrevolutionary revenge. Their complicity consists of restraining the revolutionary drive, giving the bourgeois time to return to the attack."[61] Curcio had already started to launch his invective against the reformists in November 1969, in Chiavari, during the "congress" of the Metropolitan Political Collective: "The attack on reformism is today the only condition for the defense and development of proletarian autonomy."[62]

In the Red Brigades' *Strategic Management Resolution* in November 1977, Berlinguer's followers are the leading actors of a "shameful work" and "shabby maneuvers,"[63] whose aim is to make the working classes accept the interests

---

57. Communiqué *claiming responsibility for the Borello attack* published by *Controinformazione,* no. 7–8, June 1976, in ibid., 2:34. Giuseppe Borello was a Fiat manager shot twice in the legs on 13 April 1976.

58. *Mass Force,* leaflet issued in Turin on 18 December 1972, in ibid., 1:197.

59. Peci, *Io, l'infame,* 72

60. Document *claiming responsibility for the Traversi attack* issued by the Red Brigades on 13 February 1977, in *Dossier Brigate rosse,* 2:73. Valerio Traversi was a government minister in charge of prison reform. He was shot in the legs five times in Rome on 13 February 1977.

61. *L'ultrarevisionismo,* short study written in prison by Renato Curcio; published by *Controinformazione,* no. 7–8, 1976, in ibid., 2:47.

62. *Social Struggle and Organization in the Metropolis,* 37.

63. *Red Brigades pamphlet no. 4. Attack, strike and disperse the Christian Democrat Party, pillar of the State reorganization and of the imperialist counterrevolution.* This is the BR strategic management's resolution of November 1977. In ibid., 2:134–35.

of the bourgeoisie. The Red Brigades are an "elect class," the class of the "pure." They are children of the "light," and as such they have to guard against any possible contamination from the institutions and practices of bourgeois politics: "We could dirty our hands with blood," recounts the brigadist Morucci, "but never with the fetid fluid of compromise. That was the job of the 'bourgeois parties.'"[64]

In a Red Brigades communiqué of June 1977, we read: "For a communist worthy of the name, what you call 'democracy' is only and always a form of politics that conceals the dictatorship of big capital.... There is no continuity between our democracy and yours, as false as a lead coin, but an absolute historic antagonism that has its roots in the class structure of the capitalistic way of production, that is, in the unshakable antagonism that sets the exploited classes against the exploiting ones."[65] And in a previous *Joint Red Brigades-Armed Proletarian Nuclei Communiqué* of June 1976, Berlinguer's politics is nothing else but a "shameful compliance with the bosses."[66] Any self-respecting communist well knows that "behind its democratic appearance, the Imperialist State hides its true nature of harsh counterrevolutionary dictatorship of the bourgeoisie."[67] In the Red Brigades communiqué claiming responsibility for the Cacciafesta attack, issued on 21 June 1977, the "system" can neither be "unblocked" nor reformed: "The task of the vanguard is unquestionably that of organizing the proletariat for an armed struggle."[68]

A revolutionary education admits neither uncertainties nor doubts. Those who doubt, like those who hesitate, are potential enemies. And they are no less dangerous than the real enemies. They live in a healthy environment but are carriers of an infectious disease called critical thought. They question the orders of the "sect-party," seeking an alternative to violence and revolution. They are contemptible beings, "snitches," but they can be identified. They have a specific name: they are "reformers." The community is endangered by coming into contact with them. Revolutionaries must be constantly vigilant because the reformer attacks the purity of the group. They have to scrutinize the thoughts of those beside them along the path that leads to salvation. Weeding out the "impure" is a fundamental rule, "because it is better," as

64. Morucci, *La peggio gioventù*, 140.

65. *Milan Trial. BR communiqué no. 2* issued on 20 June 1977, in *Dossier Brigate rosse*, 2:92.

66. *BR-NAP Joint Communiqué,* published in *Controinformazione*, no. 7–8, June 1976, in ibid., 2:32. NAP stands for *Nuclei Armati Proletari,* an organization created at the beginning of 1974. Its founders include Pasquale Abatangelo, Domenico Delli Veneri, and Giorgio Panizzari.

67. *Turin Trial,* communiqué confiscated from the historic nucleus of the Red Brigades on trial in Turin, 3 May 1977, in ibid., 2:81.

68. Red Brigades communiqué *claiming responsibility for the Cacciafesta* attack issued on 21 June 1977, in ibid., 2:97.

written in a Red Brigades communiqué of March 1972, "to have your enemies in front of you instead of disguised as communists among the ranks of the combatants."[69]

The first Red Brigades' kidnapping (3 March 1972) happened immediately after the start of the trial for the anarchist Pinelli's death. The victim, to be released after a "political process," was Idalgo Macchiarini, a Sit-Siemens manager disliked by the workers for his dictatorial methods. In the tense climate of those months, fed by the clashes between police and demonstrators, Pino Masi wrote the song "Free Them All." There is no difference between reformers and bosses. Both deserve to be "done away with":

> Free them all
> It means going on fighting
> It means organizing ourselves
> Without losing one hour.
> Filthy bosses
> You're deceiving yourselves
> Prisons aren't enough
> To keep us in
> And all the reformers
> Who act as informers
> Together with the bosses
> We'll do away with them.

The normal democratic game, in which the political parties address in parliament the issues raised by the workers, is just a way of hiding the reality of a "stealthy civil war."[70] The reformist idea of fighting to improve the workers' conditions without violence is unacceptable. For the Red Brigades there is no alternative: "Either acceptance of exploitation or rejection of the capitalistic society."[71]

In the hierarchy of hatred, the *pentiti* take first place. Repenting is different from distancing oneself from terrorism. Those who have distanced themselves do not deny the past, and they refuse to collaborate with the police. They simply state that the historic conditions for continuing the armed struggle no longer exist. Instead the *pentito* strikes a harsh blow to the organization, revealing the places and personalities of the total war

---

69. *Taking Sides,* Red Brigades communiqué issued on 30 March 1972, in ibid., 1:155.

70. *Social Struggle and Organization in the Metropolis,* 1:43.

71. Ibid., 1:40.

against the world. It is not the contribution offered to the enemy that is unpardonable, but the ideological attack on the "community of absolute revolution." The *pentito* recants the revolutionary faith, and, since revolutionary politics are "sacred," recantation is the most atrocious of crimes. Penitence is an offense against the symbols and dogmas of the sect-party. Because the *pentiti* are guilty of a "symbolic" offense, they must be given a symbolically significant punishment: they have to die among garbage, their faces shot to disfigure them. Having lost the faith, they are no longer revolutionaries and thus are no longer people. As such they have no identity. Since they no longer identify with the group, they must be rendered unidentifiable to everyone.

Roberto Peci, Patrizio's younger brother, first and most important Red Brigades *pentito,* dies in this way.

Roberto enters the Red Brigades in the summer of 1976. In January 1977 he is arrested after the three pistols and a Sten machine gun he is keeping for the Red Brigades' Marche Committee were discovered. He spends a few days in prison. Once outside, he decides to leave the armed struggle. On 26 October 1979 he is again arrested for something that had occurred three years earlier. He is charged with breaking into the Ancona offices of Confapi (Association of Small Industries). He is arrested again and released after a few days. The next year, it is his brother Patrizio (19 February 1980) who is arrested and who starts to collaborate with the police. Patrizio was imprisoned for the first time in December 1979, and, according to the Red Brigades, in exchange for freedom he had accepted the role of "mole" in the Turin column up to his final arrest—a "fake" arrest therefore—organized with the police (this is the Red Brigades' theory of Patrizio Peci's double arrest).

On 10 June 1980, Roberto is taken from a house at via Boito 6 in San Benedetto del Tronto.[72] His jailers are Giovanni Senzani and Roberto Buzzati. The execution is filmed, with the notes of the "Internationale" in the background, so that all the Red Brigades can view the event. Roberto is killed on 3 August in front of a ruined wall in the Rome suburbs, surrounded by garbage. He is wearing the same clothes he had on fifty-four days before. His body is riddled with eleven bullets. His face is unrecognizable. They shoot him in the mouth, cheek, temple, and ear. His hands are tied with a chain. He has gauze and sticking plaster over his eyes, mouth, and ears. For his executioners: "There can be no hesitation, no uncertainty, no extension....Roberto

---

72. The story of the kidnapping of Roberto Peci has been reconstructed by G. Guidelli, *Operazione Peci.*

Peci is a traitor and must be treated as such."[73] "Death to traitors" is written on the wall. On the ground, next to the body, there is a Red Brigades document that reads as follows: "Annihilation is the only possible relationship between marginal proletariat and traitors."[74]

To cure the ideological wound inflicted by those who choose to leave the revolutionary faith, the Red Brigades deny the existence of the *pentiti*. The Red Brigades who turn state's evidence have been deceived or tortured by the police. They can no longer repent because those who have had access to the "kingdom of truth" cannot fall into error. This is the significance of the words that Roberto Peci writes under his jailers' vigilant gaze: "I realize that I have erred and because of this I submit to the judgment of the proletariat. I trust in the magnanimity that it has often shown, but I understand that everything I have done has been the result of a methodical plan prepared by Dalla Chiesa, Pignero, and Caselli, a plan that has been studied, calculated, and weighed up. Those people have played with the minds of some of the weaker comrades and they are the actual guilty ones. I've been controlled without fully realizing it. It's only recently that I've become aware of the political games behind all this. *There are no pentiti,* they are only the weaker comrades who don't want to shoulder their responsibilities and who've been manipulated like puppets, and I include myself among them."[75]

---

73. *Peci Kidnapping. Communiqué no. 5,* 10 July 1981. This document was then published by the magazine *Lotta Continua* of 30 July 1981, from which I quote.

74. See P. Casamassima, *Il libro nero delle Brigate rosse,* 247–49.

75. Roberto Peci's letter from the BR prison, in *Lotta Continua,* 30 July 1981.

Chapter 3

Toward the Bloodshed

> To kill someone, you rely on the most responsible person because you need a very great ideological and political conviction to do it.
>
> —Raffaele Fiore

Daily Life in a Revolutionary Sect

Discipline is very strict in the Red Brigades. Every moment of the militant's life is subjected to a serious of rigorous rules. The Red Brigades—explains Valerio Morucci—lead "a hidden life at all times."[1]

And this life is a "nightmare."

Going underground, testifies a brigadist, "isn't easy. You have to live a double life and keep the rules religiously and behave accordingly.... Going underground is a *nightmare* that follows you month after month and year after year, never changing."[2] The Red Brigades member Fiore recalls: "*If you wanted to carry out what they asked, you had to be very strict with yourself. This meant giving yourself rules; you needed an iron self-discipline, starting as soon as you got up.*"[3] "Life in the Red Brigades," Fiore continues, "was all-absorbing and highly demanding."[4]

There is no moment in the day that isn't taken up by the obsessive thought of the revolution. The life of professional revolutionaries is subject to a suffocating control even in their own homes.

---

1. V. Morucci, *A guerra finita*, 78.
2. A brigadist called "Claudio," in an interview by *Panorama*, 6 June 1978, 162. Italics added.
3. A. Grandi, *L'ultimo brigatista*, 82. Italics added.
4. Ibid., 57.

The internal document *Security and Work Rules,* presumably dating back to 1974, regulates all the Red Brigades' movements. Particularly significant is the fact that "the house belongs to the organization, which lends it to the militant. It has to be managed according to *specific and unbreakable rules, equal for all.*...When a comrade takes possession of an organization's house, the first task is to create, in the minutest detail, a well-defined *social character.*...The role that a comrade has assumed must be consistent with his or her everyday life. If, for example, a person has taken the role of craftsperson, he or she has to leave home before eight in the morning and not return until twelve thirty; he or she has to leave again at two o'clock and return at seven or later. This means that comrades have to organize a specific timetable for their work (appointments, investigations, etc.)."[5]

In the document, also described are the "bleak furnishings"[6] allowed ("a radio or television, a first-aid box, basic living necessities for at least two militants"), how to file bills, the type of keys to use, the noises to avoid so as not to arouse the neighbors' suspicions, how to do the shopping or buy newspapers, the rules for going to cafés and restaurants: everything is governed by rigid guidelines. There are also clear instructions on looking after a car—also belonging to the organization—and on keeping it clean inside. Even how to look in the rearview mirror. Dressing, combing your hair, tending your beard, nothing escapes the all-seeing eye of the revolutionary sect.

Valerio Morucci, in his *Ritratto di un terrorista da giovane* (Portrait of a Young Terrorist) has described the mental dimension of the professional revolutionary through his daily dialogues. It is a flood of obsessive, maniacal thoughts and gestures, repeated ad infinitum. Day after day, always the same:

> What instead was incredibly stressful was having to always check everything. Have you taken your gun? Is it loaded? And have you taken the spare magazine? Have you got your identity documents? Have you put on your sham spectacles? Have you locked the door properly? Have you looked out the window before going out? And don't look around you with that suspicious air because they only do this kind of bullshit in films; walk confidently along your way, you can check later. Have you got the car keys? Where have you parked it? Have you given all the instructions

---

5. *Security and Work Rules.* Red Brigades internal document, in *Dossier Brigate rosse,* 1:311–12. The first italics are added.

6. The expression is Anna Laura Braghetti's, who recounts that the Red Brigades lived in "anonymous apartments, with bleak furnishings; we ate hurriedly with plastic plates and glasses, without worrying about etiquette or material comforts." A. L. Braghetti, *Il prigioniero,* 26.

on what they have to do? Have you given them exact appointments? Why hasn't that guy arrived? Has he gone to the wrong place? Think of what you told him. Word by word. Did you forget anything? To take, do, see? Why do you always feel that you've forgotten something? Is there enough gas in the car? Have you locked it? And now have you unlocked it to get in after the action? And when you're inside don't keep your finger on the trigger, because if you knock it against something you could end up killing someone. Have you checked that there's no one else inside this crap place? That there isn't someone perhaps calling the cops? Have you unplugged the phones? Now don't burn rubber, drive fast but without speeding. This is also the kind of bullshit action that you only see in films. Who the hell are those three in that car? Is that a short police aerial? What do they look like? Now be careful where you park. Is there a nosy dickhead at the window? Have you put some magazines in the rear window? And the dog with the nodding head? Have you looked over your shoulder? Have you changed your bus? Did you take the second and not the first? And don't lift your arm to hang onto the strap because you can see the gun bulge. And who's that guy with a shoulder bag who's just gotten on? Is he a cop? See if he pays for a ticket. Did you get off two stops before? Have you done your shopping far away from the house or did you get lazy?[7]

The Red Brigades do not possess anything, not even their own thoughts, and are completely subject to the rules of the group. They are in permanent fighting trim. The place in which they live is like a barracks. The Red Brigades are forbidden to have children, nor are they allowed to create ties of friendship or love with people outside the professional revolutionaries' group.[8] Furthermore, the "regulars" (those who have gone underground) cannot have sentimental ties with "irregulars" (so-called fellow travelers). The brigadist Raffaele Fiore recalls that "the clandestine life was difficult because you're almost always alone and you needed a lot of self-control. You're hardly ever at home with someone else, even just to exchange a couple of words."[9]

---

7. V. Morucci, *Ritratto di un terrorista da giovane,* 157–58.

8. On the fact that the Red Brigades were not allowed to have children, see, among many, the testimonies of P. Peci, *Io, l'infame,* 103; R. Curcio, *A viso aperto,* 44–45; Braghetti, *Il prigioniero,* 31–32. This ban also dramatically involved Adriana Faranda, forced to have an abortion in July 1974. See S. Mazzocchi, *Nell'anno della tigre,* 55–56.

9. A. Grandi, *L'ultimo brigatista,* 81.

The brigadist Patrizio Peci also highlights the psychological consequences of going underground: "You cut off relations with your family, you don't talk with anyone else but the Red Brigades,"[10] and Guagliardo states: "Underground militants had to 'give up everything.'"[11]

A Red Brigades sympathizer who had come into contact with the revolutionary universe stated in 1974 that "the Red Brigades are people who've chosen a solitary and desperate life. They've given up everything: friendship, human relations, habits, and amusements; they spend their days with the nightmare of being discovered and recognized or running into an informer. They're forced to absolute obedience and rigid discipline."[12]

There is no chance at all of getting away, physically or mentally, from the "barracks," exactly like integralist sects in which any contact with the outside world is forbidden. It is impossible to escape the group: "All links with the outside world were dangerous," Fiore recalls, "so it meant that love affairs had to be created inside the organization."[13]

Besides the manifest function of protecting the group from the police, the social control over sex plays an important latent function, of the integrative and structuring type. It stresses the complete subordination to the group, which reserves the right/duty to legislate on the professional revolutionary's intimate relations. It is the triumph of that controlled personality the Red Brigades were fighting against. The reason becomes clear if we consider that the first function of the revolutionary sect is the fight against anomie. The Red Brigades have the task of reconstructing the psychological and social identity of new members, providing them with a redeeming mission and a new vision of "good" and "evil."

The success of such an undertaking depends on two basic conditions: the attack on the primary groups (mainly the family) and the attack on the ego. The Red Brigades have to distance themselves from their past life, removing all the emotional constraints that could affect them when preparing to shed blood. The bonds with their immediate family are the first obstacle to remove. Those with children have to abandon them. There is a categorical ban on making contact with family members. An absolute mission requires absolute self-denial. The group must be the revolutionary's only reality. The presence of "relational alternatives" is dangerous because it represents a possibility of flight, mental even before physical.

---

10. Peci, *Io, l'infame,* 91.

11. V. Guagliardo, *Di sconfitta in sconfitta,* 56.

12. *Panorama,* no. 424, 1974. M. Clementi cited this extract in his *Storia delle Brigate rosse,* 96.

13. Grandi, *L'ultimo brigatista,* 105.

Individuals also have to answer to the group for the most elementary impulses. Through the control of their sexual sphere, the militants are completely deprived of any areas of freedom. They become "transparent" to the group, which takes over their bodies as well as their minds.[14] The ego is merged into the group, and "we" becomes the only way to think and act.

The professional revolutionaries' "purity" is also measured by their ability to censor themselves. The revolutionary education invites people not to be tempted by reading works conflicting with the Marxist-Leninist "truth." Embracing the revolutionary ideal means becoming deaf to any other arguments. The freedom to criticize does not exist. Those who love the revolution hate any theoretical and contradictory arguments. In the Red Brigades' universe, freedom of speech is not a problem, since all those who distance themselves from Marxism-Leninism have either to be reeducated or exterminated. Hence any debate with gnostic activists is impossible because they consider it an offense against the revolutionary faith.

The Red Brigades make those they kidnap read the Marxist-Leninist classics. During their imprisonment, their victims have to prove they want to "reeducate" themselves. They are required to criticize what they are and to be ashamed of it. They are bourgeois, "filthy pigs," and they must realize this.

The following is the only dialogue possible with a brigadist. It took place in April 1974. The victim is a magistrate and replies under threat of death. As can be seen, the brigadist has no ability to carry on a debate. His binary code mentality means that his replies have no relation to his interlocutor's questions. The weakness of his argument is a consequence of the pedagogy of intolerance and what Eric Voegelin has called the "gnostic prohibition of questions."[15] In a revolutionary sect, no "mental escape" is possible. You can only believe and obey. The revolutionary training progressively weakens the adherent's intellectual faculties, who is reduced to reciting a "catechism":

> BR: You have to reflect, you have to carry out a sincere self-criticism and admit your errors.
> PRISONER: What errors?
> BR: Those that you've always committed, persecuting the working class.
> PRISONER: I don't persecute the workers, I suppress crimes.
> BR: The judiciary plays an instrumental role in the neo-Gaullist restructuring of the state and you have been a willing participant in this plan.

---

14. On the control of sexuality in fundamentalist religious sects, see E. Pozzi, *Il carisma malato*, 165–206.

15. E. Voegelin, *Il mito del mondo nuovo*, 85ff.

That's why we took you: to undo the bourgeoisie's plan to neutralize the initiative of the masses.

PRISONER: But the judiciary is independent, it doesn't take orders from the government.... We're in a democracy, there's the division of powers.

BR: Democracy doesn't exist. Democracy is an invention of the bourgeoisie to hide the counterrevolutionary nature of the imperialistic state. You've never understood anything about politics.

PRISONER: But these are slogans.

BR: Is communism a slogan? Communism is the liberation of the exploited and oppressed in all the world.

PRISONER: In the countries where the communists are in power, there's no liberation for the proletariat and the exploited, but only greater slavery.

BR: In the communist countries is the only form of justice possible, that which comes from the dictatorship of the proletariat. But that's enough talking. Read![16]

The Red Brigades' logic is elementary: freedom of thought is a "bourgeois" right. It belongs to a "putrid" world that deserves only to be destroyed. The very fact that society is organized to guarantee the exercise of such a right is the expression of its barbarism since the presence of conflicting opinions means that the "truth" has not yet triumphed. Freedom of speech is actually the freedom to live in error because there is only one "word." It flows directly from the works of Marx and Lenin and as such has to be accepted and not questioned. The brigadist Valerio Morucci explains that the Red Brigades were children of the Leninist culture, which "claimed that, since it brought Truth, it must force those who thought differently to embrace it."[17] The Red Brigades, he concludes, "were the beacon of the revolution. All the others were dead dogs."[18]

As the philosopher Vittorio Mathieu has observed, revolutionaries do not conceive of any form of effective dialogue.[19] Their only relation with "unbelievers" is the attempt to convert, deceive, or massacre. The revolutionary

---

16. Quoted from M. Sossi, *Nella prigione delle Br*, 69–70. No less significant are the dialogues between Hanns-Martin Schleyer, then president of the West German Confederation of Employers Associations, and his kidnappers, the terrorists of the Rote Armee Fraktion (RAF). See P.-J. Boock, *L'autunno tedesco*. See, in particular, 55, 56, 66, 87, 92, 93, 94.

17. V. Morucci, *La peggio gioventù*, 69.

18. Ibid., 87.

19. V. Mathieu, *La speranza nella rivoluzione.*

education—it goes without saying—has a very specific psychological effect: the progressive detachment from reality. We shall see later on that this detachment is one of the decisive conditions for passing to violence. It is no coincidence (see next paragraph) that the most brutal actions—requiring a greater ideological determination—are performed by the "regular" members, those militants who, living underground, are completely "separate" from the world.

The Red Brigades' Organization Plan

The Red Brigades had a strictly Leninist concept of the political struggle.

The proletariat is incapable of working out a coherent and effective plan for social change. To achieve their goals, the masses have to blindly entrust themselves to a select group of professional revolutionaries. Guiding the masses from outside is the task of a minority in possession of the "revolutionary gnosis," a knowledge reserved for the few elect. As Mario Moretti states: "A vanguard has never asked for a delegation. We were almost too Leninist in this....I never believed that the workers could initiate change."[20] For the brigadist Patrizio Peci, "the fact that a few dozen people, we Red Brigades, wanted to decide for all and guide these masses did not seem unreasonable, because history teaches that all revolutions were started by a handful of people....You need a vanguard, a small group that sees things first and pulls along the others."[21] "We thought," explains the brigadist Guagliardo, "that the masses had to be 'won over' to the cause, not 'involved.'"[22]

So the Red Brigades' organization plan is elitist. Only they, thanks to Marxist science, know the end of the story. As the brigadist Enrico Fenzi writes: "I and the Red Brigades knew everything, we understood everything. Our work was a simple extension of our capacity to understand the movement of things, their management."[23] The Red Brigades are aware of the proletariat's unconscious desires. This means that workers who do not agree with violence and the armed struggle have to be "reeducated," because their thoughts have been contaminated by a middle-class mentality. This means that what they think and say is entirely worthless, since their thoughts and words are not truly "theirs."

The Red Brigades also have the power of life and death over the same workers.

---

20. M. Moretti, *Brigate rosse,* 35 and 45.
21. Peci, *Io, l'infame,* 45.
22. Guagliardo, *Di sconfitta in sconfitta,* 41.
23. E. Fenzi, *Armi e bagagli,* 52.

In the leaflet claiming responsibility for the murder of Guido Rossa (24 January 1979)—the communist worker who had reported on a fellow worker distributing Red Brigades leaflets—we read that no one is immune to proletarian justice, not even the workers themselves. The worker who is against the revolutionary plan is a "lackey of Berlinguer" and as such deserves to be executed. The Red Brigades write that "those who join in this filthy action, the various Rossas and all the aspiring spies, should remember that you are not working class by birth but because of the interests you defend, and by this distinction we always know who belongs to the proletariat and who is a class enemy."[24] This means that the Red Brigades are not the party *of* the working class but the party *for* the working class. The leaflet claiming responsibility for the murder of Ezio Tarantelli of 27 March 1985 claims that "as a communist organization our duty is obviously to represent the general interests of the proletariat."[25]

Rather than a political group, the Red Brigades have the look of a military organization. This is not surprising if we consider their typical vision of human existence: evil is looming over us and our enemies are everywhere. Human existence is a battle and only a battle, and life has meaning only in relation to the conquest of power. No compromise is possible with those "filthy fascist pigs"[26] who are the enemy. The end of all things is the destruction of the world, which requires the conquest of the state and total dominance over civil society.

The Red Brigades were always very clear about the importance of the organization, viewing it in a strictly elitist key. The revolutionary goal requires an "immense" effort and can only be achieved by gathering up— that is, organizing—the forces of "good." The organization—we read in a document of March 1979—"enables the deficiencies and the weaknesses of individual comrades to be transformed into a collective capacity to fight any battle victoriously, to attack any objective."[27]

The Red Brigades' internal organization responds perfectly to its pantoclastic mission. It is based on the Leninist principle of "democratic centralism."

---

24. Red Brigades leaflet *claiming responsibility for the murder of the Italsider of Genoa communist worker—Guido Rossa* (24 January 1979). See www.brigaterosse.org.

25. Red Brigades document *claiming responsibility for the murder of the Political Economy lecturer— Ezio Tarantelli* issued on 27 March 1985. Available at www.brigaterosse.org.

26. Leaflet *claiming responsibility for the Brescia attacks* published by *Controinformazione,* nos. 7–8, June 1976, in *Dossier Brigate rosse,* 2:29. The leaflet refers to the destruction of the automobiles of Mario Chieco, militant of Movimento Sociale Italiano, and Mauro Pagliarini, Msi-Dn town councillor, and some shots at the garage of Giorgio Brunelli, head of traumatology at the hospital and clinic San Camillo di Brescia. These actions were carried out on 7, 8, 9 January 1976.

27. *The Spring Campaign.* Red Brigades document of March 1979. The whole text is available at www.brigaterosse.org.

This, in the words of the brigadist Peci, is an organizational principle conceived "to guarantee maximum representativeness with an elitist criterion."[28] The Red Brigades' internal structure is designed to prevent any distinction between those who think and those who act. For a chart of the organization, see figure 1.

The Red Brigades' life is run by the *logistic brigade,* on which all the practical organization depends. It deals with the falsification of identity documents and automobile license plates, health and legal assistance, finding accommodation, stealing cars, and, sometimes, collecting weapons. It consists of a maximum of five people, almost all "irregulars" or "active supporters," that is, members who haven't gone underground.

The *mass brigades,* instead, have different functions and are divided into three categories: (1) *triple brigades* dealing with *carabinieri,* police, judiciary, and prisons; (2) *political brigades,* whose job is to follow the political parties; and (3) *factory brigades,* involved with industry. The brigades inflict injuries and perform minor actions.

Political homicides are carried out only by the *columns.* They consist solely of "regulars" (why only the regulars carry out the most brutal crimes is something that will be explained later on).

Each column controls a certain geographical area (Turin, Genoa, Rome, Milan, Veneto, Sardinia) and has a management, consisting of the logistics manager, the mass brigades manager, and possibly other regulars.

Going up the hierarchical pyramid, we find the two national fronts: the *national logistic front* and the *national mass front.* The column leaders, who assess the actions and proposals from the various columns, belong to these.

The members of the executive, who do not participate in the life of the column, are also engaged (less often) in the actions.

The summit of the hierarchical pyramid is occupied by the executive committee. It consists of two militants from the *national logistic front* and two from the *national mass front,* the real leaders of the Red Brigades. They give final approval to the proposals from the fronts and columns and generally superintend the most serious situations. During the Moro kidnapping, for example, the executive was in a permanent meeting. The executive also manages relations with other terrorist organizations (ETA, IRA, RAF, Palestinians, etc.).

To guarantee democratic rule, there is a further body, the *strategic command,* that controls the executive and is the organization's highest political authority.

---

28. Peci, *Io, l'infame,* 58.

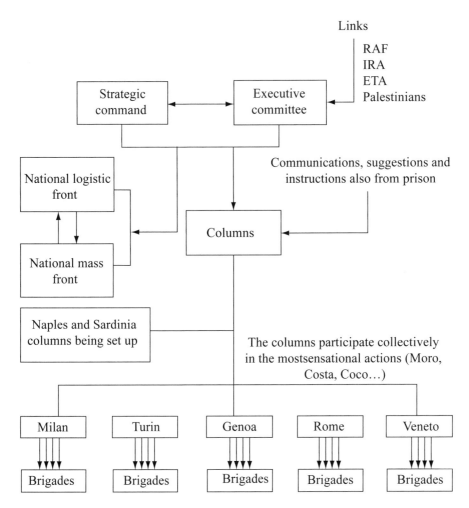

FIGURE 1. Red Brigades organizational chart. Information drawn from P. Peci, *Io, l'infame*, 56–59.

The strategic command meets once or at most twice a year. It consists of members of the executive, those of the fronts, and other regulars. Thus in the Red Brigades you can discuss what murders to commit, but once a decision has been made, no one can question it. "In the BR," recounts the brigadist Adriana Faranda, "the collective decisions are not questioned."[29] Even during the most dramatic moments, when the individual conscience would like to rebel against the group decisions, the members do not dare to oppose them. They have learned to obey blindly and to submit to the collective will.

---

29. Testimony of Adriana Faranda to S. Mazzocchi, *Nell'anno della tigre*, 12

The description of the Red Brigades' organization plan and the discipline it imposes is the best way to explain the stages that lead to political homicide. As Faranda explains, entry into a revolutionary sect marks the beginning of an anthropological mutation that strips gnostic activists of their individuality, turning them into a "means" at the service of the group.

Faranda's testimony about the dramatic moment when the Red Brigades decided to kill Aldo Moro merits being quoted in full: "I still can't accept the idea of killing a defenseless prisoner.... On 8 May the final decision is made. *There's no chance of any opposition. I feel desperate, but I have to bend to the decisions of the Organization. I've accepted this discipline,* how can I pull back at this point?"[30]

It is in the revolutionary sect that we have to seek the motives, support, and justification for shedding blood.

The Blood Crime and Its "Story"

Shedding blood is first of all a "story," a way of reporting the "facts" common to all professional revolutionaries: humanity is on the brink of ruin; the world is immersed in unhappiness and misery. You can get out of this deep hole of suffering, but you have to fight, because the bourgeoisie, the capitalists who guide "the dark forces of the counterrevolution,"[31] feed on the hunger and desperation of others. This is why it is just and necessary to eliminate them. Only in this way can evil be expelled from history.

For the Red Brigades members who have finished their educational pathway, the enemies are "parasites"[32] who arouse "absolute revulsion."[33] More specifically, the enemies are "shit,"[34] "filthy worms,"[35] "swine,"[36] "pigs,"[37]

---

30. This is again Adriana Faranda speaking to Silvana Mazzocchi (ibid., 132–33).

31. *Sossi Kidnapping—Communiqué no. 1.* Red Brigades document issued on 19 April 1974, in *Dossier Brigate rosse,* 1:258.

32. *Communiqué no. 4—D'Urso Campaign.* Red Brigades document of 23 December 1980 (www.brigaterosse.org).

33. Document *claiming responsibility for the Labate kidnapping* issued on 12 February 1973, in *Dossier Brigate rosse,* 1:217. Bruno Labate was a Cisnal manager.

34. Fenzi, *Armi e bagagli,* 52.

35. *Communiqué no. 2—D'Urso Campaign.* Red Brigades document of 15 December 1980. The whole text is available at www.brigaterosse.org.

36. *Class against Class: Class War,* in *Dossier Brigate rosse,* 1:118. This is a document attached to the leaflet "Red Brigades. Proletarian Revolutionary Communist Newspaper," issued in Milan during 1971.

37. Leaflet *claiming responsibility for automobile burning* issued in the Lorenteggio district in Milan on 15 January 1972, in *Dossier Brigate rosse,* 1:149.

"rabid dogs,"[38] "servants,"[39] "drudges,"[40] "wretches,"[41] "filthy bastards,"[42] "delinquents,"[43] and "neofascist bastards."[44] Therefore—we read in a Red Brigades document of April 1974—"striking the fascists with every means and everywhere is right and necessary,"[45] "because the fascists must not speak."[46] When the enemy becomes a "monster,"[47] a "State hangman,"[48] a "filthy mercenary,"[49] a "State hack,"[50] a "Zionist pig,"[51] their lives become valueless. The pedagogy of intolerance completes its "discourse" when the enemy is no longer seen as a human being, since, in the brigadist Valerio Morucci's words, "if you see him as a human being, you can no longer kill him."[52]

To eliminate the enemy, explains the brigadist Raffaele Fiore, multiple murderer, who never repented nor distanced himself from terrorism, you have to degrade the relationship between people to that between "animals."

---

38. Communiqué *claiming responsibility for Macchiarini kidnapping* issued in Milan on 3 March 1972. Idalgo Macchiarini was a Sit-Siemens manager. In ibid., 1:151.

39. *Class against Class: Class War.* Document attached to leaflet "Red Brigades: Proletarian Revolutionary Communist Newspaper," issued in Milan during 1971. Ibid., 1:118.

40. Grandi, *L'ultimo brigatista,* 95.

41. *Crush the Fascists in Mirafiori and Rivalta! Throw Them out of Our Factories and Our Districts.* Leaflet issued in Turin on 26 November 1972, in *Dossier Brigate rosse,* 1:194.

42. Leaflet *claiming responsibility for Brescia attacks* published by *Controinformazione,* nos. 7–8, June 1976, in ibid., 2:29.

43. *Raid in the Offices of "Iniziativa democratica."* Red Brigades document of 15 May 1975, in ibid., 1:369.

44. *A Terrible Fate.* Document issued in Milan, November 1971, in ibid., 1:135.

45. *Against Neo-Gaullism to Strike at the Heart of the State.* Red Brigades document issued in April 1974, in ibid., 1:256.

46. D. Novelli and N. Tranfaglia, *Vite sospese,* 198. I quote from the testimony of the brigadist Nitta.

47. *Fogli di lotta di Sinistra proletaria* (July–October 1970), in *Dossier Brigate rosse,* 1:77.

48. Document *claiming responsibility for Coco murder.* Francesco Coco, state prosecutor in Genoa, was killed on 8 June 1976. In ibid., 1:43.

49. Communiqué *claiming responsibility for Rome attacks* issued in Rome by the Red Brigades on 27 April 1978, in ibid., 2:327.

50. Communiqué *claiming responsibility for Casalegno homicide* issued by the Red Brigades on 16 November 1977, in ibid., 2:168. Casalegno was deputy editor of *La Stampa.* Partisan in the Partito d'Azione, he had undertaken a fierce battle against the Red Brigades, whom he repeatedly attacked from the columns of the Turin daily. He was murdered by Raffaele Fiore.

51. Document of Red Brigades–Communist Combatant Party (BR-PCC) *claiming responsibility for murder of former mayor of Florence—Lando Conti* issued on 10 February 1986. Lando Conti, member of the Republican Party, was killed on via Togliatti on 10 February 1986, close to his house. The epithet "filthy Zionist pig" refers to Giovanni Spadolini, with whom Landi was a close collaborator (See www.brigaterosse.org).

52. Quoted from G. Galli, *Piombo rosso,* 394. On this point, Morucci's testimony merits being quoted in full: "If they had asked me to kill Moro on via Fani, I would have been able to do it. But afterward he was no longer a target, he was a man. And I had started to prevent him being killed. If you recognize someone as a human being, you can no longer kill them. After seeing as human beings two policemen, aged nineteen, reading comics outside the delle Nuove prison in Turin, whom we were supposed to kill, I left the Red Brigades."

Before shooting: "*All the efforts humanity has made to recognize itself as such have to be eradicated: it was like returning to the very beginning of man's journey, when he didn't recognize the other person as a fellow creature, but as an animal from which to defend himself, to kill, to eat....At that junction we looked on the others not as people, but as an authority that had to be stripped of its power.*"[53]

"We had no type of direct relationship," continues Fiore, "with those we killed. Ours was a political bond. For us they were symbols, political targets, and *not people.*"[54]

Another testimony that sheds light on the effects of the revolutionary education comes from a brigadist called "Claudio" (June 1978). The recourse to political violence, explains "Claudio," requires "psychological training" to free yourself of sentiments against revolutionary violence. Compassion for the enemy stops the professional revolutionary from correctly performing his duties. In his words: "Believing in the armed struggle also means psychologically defending yourself against the trap of sentiment to achieve the necessary determination and lucidity for the best practical result."[55]

The revolutionary education transforms enemies into "parasites"[56] who "infect" the world surrounding them. Their existence is outrageous, their thoughts harmful.

Every Red Brigades member, we read in a leaflet issued in Milan on 15 July 1971, has the task of "sweeping away, with the aid of proletarian justice, the black bastards who are *infecting* the district."[57] Hate/love, infect/purify, oppress/liberate, the binary code mentality is an increasingly tight slipknot.

Fiore explains that shedding blood is the end of a "political pathway." Only those who are ideologically determined can pull the trigger. You don't become killers in a single day, he stresses. You have to follow an educational pathway—with massive doses of ideological ferocity—to know how to break all the socially constructed bonds: "*To kill someone, you rely on the most responsible person because you need a very great ideological and political conviction to do so.*"[58]

---

53. Grandi, *L'ultimo brigatista*, 89. Italics added.

54. Ibid., 104. Italics added.

55. *Panorama,* 8 June 1978, 224. In the interview, "Claudio," age twenty-six, tells Marco Ventura about the rules, the aims, the undertakings, and the programs of the organization he belonged to. It is not the Red Brigades but another subversive group of which "Claudio" is a national manager.

56. *Raid in the offices of "Iniziativa democratica,"* Red Brigades document of 15 May 1975, in *Dossier Brigate rosse,* 1:369.

57. Red Brigades leaflet *claiming responsibility for automobile burning* issued in the Milanese district of Quarto Oggiaro on 15 July 1971, in ibid., 1:115. Italics added.

58. Grandi, *L'ultimo brigatista*, 99. Italics added.

For the brigadist Silveria Russo, a Prima Linea militant, murder was "a normal operational task,"[59] rendered such by an ideology that enabled killing without feeling any emotional participation in the victim's torment: *"Everything was naturally mediated by ideology in the sense that, because of ideology, because of a choice of violence a priori, the action of killing is not different from any other action."*[60] Ideological ferocity, explains Russo, has the power to transform the terrorist's activity into "an ordinary activity. After which your personal life carries on as normal: it's the life of an ordinary person, exactly as it was before."[61] The conclusion is implicit in the premise: *"So everything was arbitrated by the ideology, and that meant seeing people as symbols. For me, that magistrate or any other person we had decided to eliminate was a symbol, he wasn't a person."*[62]

Ideology manages to lead militants to a condition of total "abstraction" from the human consequences of their actions. Reality is "abstract," the victims are "abstract," even death is "abstract." It is the brigadist Franco Bonisoli who explains that "it was the abstraction that was important, the abstraction of the idea of revolution. The revolution involved deaths on both sides, it involved brutal clashes, and if you accepted this type of choice, you were prepared for anything."[63]

It's a chorus of testimonies: you kill after you've finished an ideological pathway where the victim is stripped of his humanity. The ideology intervenes *before* striking the victim and not after. The dehumanization of the enemy comes before his physical elimination. The ideology is the *primum movens* that unleashes the homicidal fury and not a simple process of justification a posteriori. Shedding blood, to quote the brigadist Mario Ferrandi, is the result of "an absurd ideological inspiration."[64] Maurizio Costa prefers to express himself in these terms: *"We'd actually already eradicated people before killing them."*[65] The brigadist Enrico Baglioni considers it "a moral responsibility to permit the value of life to be ousted by ideology."[66] For Enrico Fenzi: "Human life didn't count for anything."[67] For Enrico Galmozzi, you begin killing after having reached "the highest level of ideological degeneration.... We didn't

59. Brigadist Silveria Russo talking to S. Zavoli, *La notte della Repubblica,* 374.
60. Ibid.
61. Ibid., 377.
62. Ibid., 385.
63. Testimony of brigadist Franco Bonisoli, in ibid., 289.
64. Testimony of brigadist Mario Ferrandi, in ibid., 373.
65. Testimony of brigadist Maurizio Costa, in ibid., 380.
66. Testimony of brigadist Enrico Baglioni, in ibid., 382.
67. Testimony of brigadist Enrico Fenzi, in ibid., 408.

even consider life."[68] For Vincenzo Guagliardo: "The victim was reduced to a symbol."[69]

Murder is nothing else but an "administrative" deed, a cold "practice" entrusted to a group of bureaucrats of death: "We saw death as an act of justice," explains Patrizio Peci, "and that was that."[70] Mario Moretti states: "I would never kill a person,"[71] which is why, the terrorist Silveria Russo points out, "we never raised the issue of the person living inside that symbol."[72] Anna Laura Braghetti, murderer of Vittorio Bachelet, recalling the gentle and caring nature of her comrade Prospero Gallinari, explains that ideology and political faith can transform even the mildest man into a killer: "I knew a lot of people like him in the Red Brigades, people who would never have hurt anyone, let alone shoot them, people who had never handled a gun and who, instead, shot, killed, and caused immense pain in the name of ideology, of political faith."[73]

Before settling on a victim, recounts another brigadist, you had to find a reasoning, an idea, a phrase to punish. Only after do you start hunting the person who is responsible for them. You come up against an "impure" thought and spend your days obsessed by this unsupportable presence. You search, read the papers, participate surreptitiously in political party meetings, until you discover the carrier of the "infected" message. You don't yet know your victim, but you'll manage to find him through his words. Once you're on his track you have to decide on the punishment. Kill him or kneecap him?

In the words of a witness:

> You make a person match a political need. That is, today I have the job of attacking the Christian Democrat Party in a district where a certain type of discourse is being made, but you don't go to take it out on the walls...so let's see who's making this speech and then you're off, that is, you start looking for him. It's as if you were raising your receptive aerials to understand where this message is coming from, then you read the papers, you participate undercover in the meetings of these people,

68. Testimony of brigadist Enrico Galmozzi to L. Guicciardi, *Il tempo del furore,* 60. In Galmozzi's words: "We didn't even consider life. This is the highest level of ideological degeneration in the opposition to the enemy. We didn't consider them as real people, as mothers, fathers, married men. They were fascists, republicans, and so on."

69. Guagliardo, *Di sconfitta in sconfitta,* 55.

70. Testimony of brigadist Patrizio Peci to S. Zavoli, *La notte della Repubblica,* 395.

71. Testimony of brigadist Mario Moretti, in ibid., 330.

72. Testimony of brigadist Silveria Russo, in ibid., 383.

73. Braghetti, *Il prigioniero,* 33.

you try to see and understand; then you've picked him out and so he's physically targeted, he's the one responsible, it's him at this time, there's already a logical process in which there's no relationship, in which you've already decided that he's the guilty one. Then you arrive and what makes the difference is the punishment, that is, what punishment should I give to this person guilty of these things? You go there and you have this fierce sense of justice,... for all the speeches that are there inside. So he isn't even that person any longer, *that person is emptied, and he's blamed for other crimes, other responsibilities....*He becomes another person, another thing... a small cog in the monstrous machine that is destroying us all.... When you reach that point, you can't help being totally involved, you can't feel any emotion, you're someone who's administering justice, who's affirming values and therefore has no place for hate.... In your heart of hearts you tell yourself, "I'm forced to do this thing."[74]

The pedagogy of intolerance molds the Red Brigades' thoughts, feelings, and actions. There is no gesture or breath that isn't dominated by the plot of their "story." This is a grueling educational pathway, explains Fiore, that disrupts the new adherent's inner life: "When you choose a path like the one we chose, there are inner ruptures that *tear you up* but which also enable you to overcome socially constructed limits. You don't become a killer immediately, but it is through a *political journey* that all your convictions are changed."[75]

Murder is thus the result of a sociopsychological process that degrades, debases, and stigmatizes the "enemy" until he or she is reduced to a reflection of the "system." The dialogue between Mario Sossi, at the time a public prosecutor in Genoa, and his kidnappers is very instructive (28 April 1974):

SOSSI: I had to come here to understand how distressing imprisonment is.
RB: Yes, we know. We communists have been going to prison for hundreds of years. Communists, vandals...
SOSSI: Communists, if we want to put it like that. But with the laws we have...
RB: It was you.
SOSSI: Not me, it was the law.
RB: All right. I'm talking about the system, not you.

74. Ibid.
75. Grandi, *L'ultimo brigatista*, 121. Italics added.

SOSSI: But why should I identify with the entire system when I disagree with so much of it?[76]

The revolutionary education completes its "dissertation" when the victim's pain, his cries, his anguish no longer arouse any emotion in his killer.

In October 1977 in Turin, Cocozzello, the Christian Democrat town councillor, was shot in the legs in front of onlookers. The emotional detachment with which brigadist Patrizio Peci performed the task assigned him proves how effective the revolutionary education is in freeing initiates from any individual responsibility. The "mature" brigadist can hand out death "very naturally." This time, Peci does not manage to find a particularly valid reason for attacking his victim, but the group's decisions are also his. His gun is only an extension of the proletariat's will. Attacking Cocozzello "was what the Organization wanted and I did it as best I could because I believed in it."[77] For Peci, kneecapping an enemy is only a matter of "technique."

Hatred drives someone to take up arms, but pressing the trigger is a *routine* job: "For me, shooting is like being a surgeon in an operating theater," a terrorist stated in 1978. "To treat the disease you have to use scalpels, that's all."[78]

This is the same mental condition with which Peci performed the task the "Organization" had entrusted to him:

He was called Cocozzello, a DC town councillor. . . . He was tall, with a paunch, not young, standing on the sidewalk. I calmly walked up to him, and when I was alongside him, almost face to face, *very naturally*— as if nothing was out of the ordinary—I shot him twice in his legs with the Nagant. Usually the target realizes you're about to shoot him a few seconds before and he tries to escape. Since he hadn't seen me, I was sure he would just fall to the ground, but he didn't. He heard the noise, he felt the pain, he looked down at his legs, he saw the blood, he looked at me, he looked at my gun, and—unbelievably—he ran away. Although he was fat, old, and wounded, he managed to take off like a runner, so I was taken by surprise and didn't even try to shoot him

76. *Interrogation of prisoner Mario Sossi arrested by a Red Brigades armed nucleus and taken to a people's prison.* Document published in part by the weekly *Panorama* of 10 July 1975, in *Dossier Brigate rosse,* 1:263–64.

77. Peci, *Io, l'infame,* 166.

78. *Panorama,* 8 June 1978, 224.

again. Finally he fell, after five or six meters, and I went up to him, standing beside him with the usual procedure. In the meantime he was shouting, shouting at the top of his voice, and despite the two bullets in his legs, he was trying to kick me. I thought, "Look at his courage: he's even kicking me while I shoot him!" In fact it wasn't a good move, because in this way there was the risk I would miss and shoot him somewhere else. Luckily I didn't miss and I just shot him four more times in the legs.[79]

The revolutionary education has achieved its final aim when political violence takes on an intrinsic meaning; when the homicidal rage against the enemy has a value in itself, independently of its effects.

Peci recounts the action in which Sergio Palmieri was kneecapped in April 1978. Also present is Angela Vai, who wants to redeem herself in the eyes of the group for an error committed during a previous shooting. Palmieri is hit by the brigadist Panciarelli and falls, the action is completed, "but not for Vai, who wants to show that she can shoot as well, after her poor showing the other time: she goes over to the poor man who is yelling on the ground with his legs shattered and shoots him again."[80]

No less significant is the way in which the Red Brigades eliminated Francesco Coco, state prosecutor in Genoa, and his guards, on 8 June 1976. Coco is shot a few paces from his house, together with the brigadier Giovanni Saponara. Both are hit in the head and back with dozens of bullets, with only one missing the target. Coco's driver, Antioco Dejana, is far away from the ambush and doesn't realize what is happening, also because silencers are used. Dejana is waiting calmly for his chief. He doesn't represent any danger for the Red Brigades. He is riddled with bullets and killed.[81]

On this point, the words of Valerio Morucci make us reflect, once again, on the effects and effectiveness of the pedagogy of intolerance: "The cop who was with Coco could've been disarmed and rendered harmless. There was enough time to do it on those deserted steps. And he wasn't a commando, he was just a police officer with a paunch. The other one, the one who was sitting waiting in the car, couldn't even see what was happening.

---

79. Peci, *Io, l'infame,* 156–57. Italics added.

80. Ibid., 87.

81. For a reconstruction of the Coco murder, see V. Tessandori, *Br. imputazione: Banda armata,* 11–13.

You just had to keep an eye on him. They were killed because they were soldiers of the enemy. And in war you kill the enemy soldiers."[82]

By ennobling bloodshed, the Red Brigades' ethical-political code allows the gnostic activist to hand out death without any emotional involvement.

Killing one's enemies is an "honor" and a "duty."

This is what we read in the document claiming responsibility for the murder of the "pig" Ray Leamon Hunt (15 February 1984): "Putting an end to the miserable existence of this filthy lackey of imperialism is an *honor* for our organization and at the same time a *duty* toward the international revolutionary movement."[83]

The Red Brigades leave nothing to chance. Before being killed, Marco Biagi was the subject of a very careful study. For months, all his habits were set down in a document of seventeen pages, divided into six chapters. This shadowing was needed to tackle a practical problem: how to kill Marco Biagi. The Red Brigades recorded, classified, and analyzed every movement of their victim, including the time needed to chain up his bicycle at the train station. There are twenty-one possibilities indicated for eliminating him, divided into three plans. In the document, he is not a person; he is "the subject." Biagi was killed before he died. This occurs when the pedagogy of intolerance has accomplished its task. It is not only for organizational reasons that the Red Brigades take so much time to eliminate their victims. They have to train themselves mentally; in order to pull the trigger they have first to dehumanize the enemy; they have to see him fall a thousand times and then another thousand; they have to get used to seeing him die before they kill him. The Red Brigades were factory workers, clerks, students, and teachers. They lived "normal" lives; they had never made use of violence. But now they had received a "call" that requires suitable spiritual preparation. To commit murder you have to follow an educational pathway—remember what the Red Brigades terrorist Fiore said—"that kills you instead."

The Path to Bloodshed

The Red Brigades arrive at bloodshed through a very complex process of interaction that is divided into several stages. I describe four stages, to which

---

82. Morucci, *La peggio gioventù*, 105.

83. Red Brigades document *claiming responsibility for the murder of U.S. General Ray Leamon Hunt* issued 15 February 1982. The victim was the director-general of the UN Multinational Force and Observers (MFO) in the Sinai. The document is available at www.brigaterosse.org. Italics added.

I give the acronym DRIA (Disintegration, Reconstruction, Integration, Alienation):[84]

1. Social marginality (*Disintegration of social identity stage*)
2. Acquisition of "binary code" mentality (*Reconstruction of social identity stage*)
3. Entry into a political-religious group or "community of absolute revolution"[85] (*Integration in the revolutionary sect stage*)
4. Detachment from reality (*Alienation from the surrounding world stage*)

The aim of this model is to reconstruct the "marginal" individual's route toward revolutionary behavior, of which the most intense expression is the willingness to give and receive death. It integrates micro- and macro-sociological variables in an explicative approach dealing with the psychological and social causes of subversive action. In the DRIA model, the first two stages concern the individual's personality with reference to his or her creative abilities.

---

84. The DRIA model has been developed from the testimony of numerous members of the Red Brigades. However, it presents some significant methodological problems. In contrast to Al Qaeda militants, who are still active and operating today, Red Brigades militants ended their killing many years ago. In addition, many of them have distanced themselves from what they once did, partly because the historical and social context that inspired their revolutionary action in the 1960s and 1970s has profoundly changed in the interim. The validity and reliability problems that always exist in inquiries that make use of the direct interview technique would have increased enormously under these circumstances. As Kenneth D. Bailey has noted in his *Methods of Social Research* (New York: The Free Press, 1982), a person being interviewed may answer in a manner that is socially acceptable but not accurate, sometimes because he could be ashamed to admit that he does not know the answer. Furthermore, it is probable that he will give accurate answers to questions that deal with recent developments but will commit many errors when answering questions about events that occurred long ago. After several failed attempts at using the direct interview method (due to, e.g., problems with entering maximum security prisons, tracing released ex-Red Brigades members, and convincing those members to speak about dramatic events in which they were involved), I decided to reconstruct the motives of Red Brigadists by using other sources that were contemporary to the events being discussed. This is exactly what scholars will be forced to do in a few years when the protagonists of that bloody period will have died. I have tried to analyze in this way a phenomenon that is historically recent but socially distant, with all the methodological problems that this choice presents, without claiming to be complete or exhaustive. In other words, I have attempted to historicize the Red Brigades phenomenon by combining the instruments of historical research with those of sociological theory. At any rate, the process that transforms an ordinary person into a militant of the Red Brigades is not always the same for everyone and cannot be expressed in a definitive scheme. In conclusion, the DRIA model is an instrument that can be used for the interpretation of reality. Max Weber would say that the sociologist's task is to verify, in each case being considered, the distance between reality and the conceptual framework that is being employed to interpret that reality (see M. Weber, *Economia e società*, 4 vol., *Edizioni di Comunità*, Milano, 1999, 1:17–18).

85. The expression "community of absolute revolution" belongs to the brigadist Roberto Rosso.

In the *disintegration* and *reconstruction* stages the individual plays an active role.

Individuals at the margin can either fall into despair or start searching for an *exit strategy*. As José Ortega y Gasset has written, man is an animal rich in imagination: it is the "liberating power possessed by man"[86] that enables him to place a utopian world of imaginary things against a present judged to be unbearable.[87] The brigadist Vincenzo Guagliardo states that the revolutionary choice is prompted by a "mental process" that starts by *negating reality* and ends up by *inventing* a "fantasy" world as a "psychological refuge." In Guagliardo's words: "It is important to remember that every crisis that triggers the victimization process begins by (*first stage*) rejecting reality; the future persecutor does not have a presumed enemy but simply tries to invent another reality to escape his own problems."[88]

The human being is a "fantasizing animal."[89] But the social actor's subjectivity means that not all reconstruction attempts have the same outcome. Some succeed while others fail. The *reconstruction of social identity* is above all a "psychological undertaking" that requires particular talents. The first of these is the "will to want," that is, the capacity to transform one's need for change into behavior (or "attempts to solve"). The *will to want* is effective through the fighting spirit, the desire for revenge, and the courage of the challenge, implying risk and danger.[90]

---

86. J. Ortega y Gasset, "La ribellione delle masse," in his *Scritti politici,* 922.

87. For this aspect of Ortega's thinking, see L. Pellicani, introduction to *L'uomo e la gente,* by J. Ortega y Gasset, 17.

88. Guagliardo, *Di sconfitta in sconfitta,* 60.

89. J. Ortega y Gasset, *Una interpretazione della storia universale,* 211.

90. It has been commonplace for scholars to agree that a predisposition to violence is a fundamental precondition to becoming a revolutionary. This conventional explanation, however, appears to have been negated by the Red Brigades' life history and by the recent study by Randall Collins, *Violence: A Micro-Sociological Theory* (Princeton-Oxford, 2008), who argued that violent confrontation goes against human physiological hardwiring. According to Collins, humans are not naturally good at violence in real-life situations. Violence comes neither easily nor automatically. Antagonists are by nature tense and fearful, and their confrontational anxieties put up a powerful emotional barrier against violence. That is why "any successful violence must overcome this tension and fear" (19). Many brigadists, albeit adverse to physical violence, turned into ferocious killers after entering the revolutionary sect. What seems decisive is not the predisposition to physical violence but the tendency to dehumanize the victims. In other words, it is the pedagogy of intolerance that is decisive and not a Red Brigadist's "genetic predisposition" to use force. As we have seen, the Red Brigades' political morality is typically justificationist ("terrorist despite myself") and can be summarized as follows: "My violence is always right because it aims at a noble objective, whereas the violence of others is always wrong because it defends shabby interests." All this makes us reflect, once again, on the revolutionary sect's enormous power over its members. If it is true, as the Red Brigades' testimonies seem to prove, that even those who never imagined being able to shoot were turned into killers, then revolutionary behavior is to a very large extent the outcome of an educational pathway

The *disintegration* and *reconstruction of the social identity* leads us back to what Kurt Lewin—in his studies on the "psychological field concept"—has called "life space," that is, a person's inner world made up of needs, motivations, anxieties, ideals, and so forth.[91] In the DRIA model, the life space is made up of the marginal individual and his or her psychological representation in the surrounding environment.

According to Lewin—father of modern social psychology—revolutionary behavior involves both the inner and outer worlds, besides the way in which the subversive action influences both of them. The Red Brigades' internal cognitive workings are closely linked with the outside environment in a relationship—mark well—that can only be that of hatred and annihilation. In these interrelationships and interdependencies, the revolutionary conduct cannot only be considered a function of the mental universe or social environment. This is because—as said earlier—the subversive action changes both the former and the latter. The brigadist attack, for example, does not only upset the external world but also affects the brigadist's psychological dimension, provoking new behavior in an uninterrupted chain of actions-reactions.

This approach helps us understand the very rare cases of defection from revolutionary sects. Brigadists might decide to leave the group because their perception of reality has changed and they no longer consider, for example, that revolutionary violence can be successful. They might repent and feel remorse for their victims. There is always the possibility of turning away from a revolutionary sect. But this is true more in theory than in practice because, as we shall see, you only leave a revolutionary sect feet first. The revolutionary sect is a group, but a group with very particular features. Lewin's theory, invaluable as it is, cannot shed light on its essential aspects.

In the field theory, the concept of the *relationship* between the subject and the external world is decisive. Lewin explains his point of view by noting the difference between Aristotelian and Galilean thought, with a preference for the latter.

In Aristotelian thinking, the focus is on the characteristics of the object, whereas with Galileo the study of situational factors becomes central (the

---

inexorably aimed at destruction. Thus revolutionary education can be seen as an education in hatred and in violence.

91. See K. Lewin, *Field Theory in Social Science.* An excellent summary of Lewin's thinking can be found in P. Amerio, *Teorie in psicologia sociale,* 157ff. Scholars who have analyzed Lewin's contribution include L. Ancona, *La psicologia sociale in America;* G. Petter, introduction to *Teoria dinamica della personalità,* by K. Lewin; A. Ossicini, *Kurt Lewin e la psicologia moderna;* G. Galli, ed., *Lewin;* and A. J. Marrow, *The Practical Theorist.*

inclined plane, for example). None of this means that the object loses its importance. It means that the environmental situation has the same importance as the object. Hence the laws of a field are not determined by the single features of its particular elements but by their configuration and movement in the entire field.[92]

The decisive point is that, for an individual who has withdrawn from the world, the "entire psychological field" Lewin talked about consists of the revolutionary sect. Those living in the "catacombs" no longer belong to *this world*.

In a revolutionary sect, the *life space* and the external environment are hypercompressed, in the sense that these two spheres—especially after the first homicides—tend to overlap and not to intersect.[93] The brigadists break into *this world* only to destroy. Their relationship with the surrounding environment is that of annihilation and not exchange. Here we have to be cautious when speaking about *feedback,* after having first specified the characteristics of what I call *subversive-revolutionary feedback.* This is what I propose to do in the last two stages of the DRIA model.

For the members of a revolutionary sect, the external environment tends to become that of the sect itself, in the sense that it is the professional revolutionary's *world,* an exclusive and all-absorbing world.

---

92. K. Lewin, "Conflict between Aristotelian and Galileian Modes of Thought in Contemporary Psychology," 141–77.

93. Serious scholars of radical religious sects agree in assigning a fundamental role to the isolation of their followers from the surrounding world in explaining phenomena of extreme deviance, like homicide and ritual suicide. An excellent summary, synthesis, and assessment of the socio-psychological consequences of alienation from the surrounding world in radical religious sects is L. L. Dawson, *Comprehending Cults.* The concept of subversive-revolutionary feedback presents significant points of contact with the concept of negative feedback elaborated by scholars who have attempted to explain the extreme forms of deviance found in fundamentalist religious sects. In my studies on revolutionary sects, I have used the conceptual categories of the sociology of religion that I then applied in the analysis of a political phenomenon. The subversive-revolutionary feedback theory is indebted to the following: T. Reiterman and J. Jacobs, *Raven;* J. R. Hall, *Gone from the Promised Land;* D. Chidester, *Salvation and Suicide;* M. M. Maaga, *Most Intimate Other;* M. Introvigne, "Ordeal by Fire," 267–83; J. G. Melton, "Violence and the Cults"; M. Galanter, *Cults;* E. Pozzi, *Il carisma malato;* W. S. Bainbridge, *Satan's Power;* R. Stark and W. S. Bainbridge, "Scientology," 128–36; R. Stark and W. S. Bainbridge, *The Future of Religion;* S. J. Palmer, "Purity and Danger in the Solar Temple," 303–18; J. Tabor and E. Gallagher, *Why Waco?;* D. G. Bromley and E. D. Silver, "Davidian Tradition"; S. J. Palmer and N. Finn, "Coping with Apocalypse in Canada," 397–415; R. W. Balch, "Waiting for the Ships," 137–66; E. W. Mills Jr., "Cult Extremism," 75–87; J. R. Hall and P. Schuyler, "Mystical Apocalypse of the Solar Temple," 285–311; M. Barkun, "Reflections after Waco," 41–49; N. T. Ammerman, *Bible Believers;* S. A. Wright, "Another View of the Mt. Carmel Standoff," xiii–xxvi; L. E. Sullivan, "'No Longer the Messiah,'" 213–34; T. Robbins and D. Anthony, "Sects and Violence," 236–59.

Georg Simmel had defined the freedom of modern people as the possibility of belonging to several social circles at the same time, that is, the freedom to be able to move between different social groups.[94] According to this theory, our level of freedom is proportional to the number of circles we can enter and exit without constrictions. Simmel was convinced that the individual's personality is enriched through *segmentation*. For this reason, the more social circles we belong to, the more we can develop our identity in many different ways. In Simmel's sociology, the concept of the *interaction of the parties* is crucial.[95] Each of us is constituted by our relations with others.

No less valuable is George Herbert Mead's theory, suggesting that our identity is the result of a continuous negotiation with the surrounding world.[96] Psychology, Mead explained, cannot study only the field of awareness. Although introspection is important as a method of analysis, we have to study the way in which the social group influences the conduct of the individual members. The "ego" is not something that exists before social life. Its genesis is the result of a dynamic process filtered through cognitive activity. As Herbert Blumer says: "Society consists in the interaction of individual human beings. The actions of its members are shaped largely by the actual and anticipated responses of others."[97]

Simmel, Mead, and Blumer help us understand subversive-revolutionary feedback.

Professional revolutionaries have declared that they reject society. Their lives are a relational microcosm in which each member of the group is identical to the other. This means that the Red Brigades never leave their mental universe, either because of their *obsession with purity,* which denies any real interaction with the corrupt and putrescent bourgeois world, or because their comrades are just a reflection of themselves. Those who live in a single social circle—and one founded on internal preventive terrorism—are taught to see any change in their convictions and behavior as the ultimate sin. Changing your view of the world means weakening your bond with the group.

Anyone who has lived in a revolutionary sect—whether a brigadist or a neo-Nazi skinhead like Ingo Hasselbach—defines his relationship with

---

94. See G. Simmel, *Sociologia,* 347ff. On Simmel's theory of social circles, see L. Coser, *I maestri del pensiero sociologico,* 274ff. An interesting analysis of Simmel's thinking can also be found in E. Rutigliano, *Teorie sociologiche classiche,* 139–66.

95. G. Simmel, *La differenziazione sociale,* 17.

96. G. H. Mead, *Mind, Self and Society.*

97. H. Blumer, *Interazionismo simbolico,* 39.

his companions as a "drug"[98] that changes his relationship with the outside world. He can no longer separate himself from them.

In short, in a revolutionary sect a person's inner and outer worlds tend to merge into an explosive whole: a brigadist is his group.

Adriana Faranda, one of those involved in the kidnapping of Aldo Moro, had second thoughts about her militancy in the Red Brigades. Any contact with the world outside the sect was forbidden. This meant she was not allowed to see her daughter, causing her immense pain. Her state of mind alarmed the others, who shut her up for two months in an apartment, isolating her from the rest of the group. In the end, Faranda resumed her salvific mission, convinced that it was for the good of her children because a revolution would enable them to live in a just world.[99]

In my analysis, the *subversive-revolutionary feedback* takes the place of the "frontier," which in Lewin's theory is the place in which the individual encounters the surrounding environment, that is, the zone in which the person's internal world interacts with the external world. The *subversive-revolutionary feedback* is a type of interaction aimed at strengthening revolutionary conduct. It is only in a revolutionary sect that the "frontier," where the subjective intersects with the objective, confirms the individual's mental universe instead of changing it. The "field" Lewin describes is a dynamic system, whereas the revolutionary sect is a "static" one. The life of the social groups Lewin analyzed is in continual change, whereas the life of a revolutionary sect is always the same. In a revolutionary sect, life is frenetic and at the same time petrified. An extremely strict system of rules and prohibitions dries up the source of change represented by contact with the outside world. It is the consequence of the *segregation* and *internal preventive terror* we talked about in chapter 2 with reference to Jean Guitton's studies on the party of the pure. This "interactive statics" of life in a revolutionary sect provides indispensable psychological support for gnostic activities. You need a very powerful motivation to initiate a total war against the surrounding world. You have to protect your inner world from any possible external disturbance. Don't forget that the sect—whether active or passive—is created to protect its members from external contagion. The world is corrupt and the end is imminent; you have to seek refuge in the catacombs. The Red Brigades— explains Laura Braghetti—must "remain as ghosts."[100]

---

98. I. Hasselbach, *Diario di un naziskin,* 122.
99. Brigadist Adriana Faranda talking to I. Pisano, *Io terrorista,* 186.
100. Braghetti, *Il prigioniero,* 34.

My *subversive-revolutionary feedback* theory is based on copious documents and life stories. Some of them we have already encountered, others we will come to later on. For now I want to cite the testimony of Patrizio Peci, a Red Brigades multiple murderer.

Peci explains that the Red Brigades have no relationship with the outside world. Their mental universe develops in total isolation from the surrounding environment. *Segregation*—which Peci calls going underground—produces people who live "out of the world": "When you live underground for a long time—as I did for over three years—even the strangest things start to seem normal to you, because *you end up meeting only other people in your same condition, you live out of the world.* Then one day [when you leave the revolutionary sect], you're faced with different experiences, and so you ask yourself, 'What am I doing, who am I, why?'"[101]

The importance of the *subversive-revolutionary feedback* becomes clearer in the last two stages of the DRIA model.

The *integration in a revolutionary sect* stage and that of *alienation from the surrounding world* have an impact on the group dimension and a markedly sociological import. In the search for an answer to his or her existential drama, the more enterprising marginal individual discovers that there is a universe of pain made up of similar individuals, who offer and ask for help. He or she approaches them and is conditioned by them.

The following dramatic words, written by the brigadist Gianluca Codrini in 1981, shed light on the sociopsychological motivations that prompt someone to enter a revolutionary sect: "Each of us comes from oceans of solitude and deserts of silence and meets other people with similar backgrounds; so solitude is added to solitude and silence joins silence."[102]

Even more than a political-military organization, a revolutionary sect is a psychological power, an emotional force field that binds the individual to it, stripping him or her of any relational alternative. It is an organization of atomized and isolated individuals who are asked for unconditional dedication and absolute loyalty. A revolutionary sect is a form of tyranny exercised on the human spirit through internal preventive terrorism, but it is also a psychological refuge. The success of extreme-left terrorist training is inversely proportional to the individual's level of integration in society. The fanaticism of revolutionaries is the product of their extraneousness to any social and political body. Only those who have cut every social bond with

---

101. Peci, *Io, l'infame,* 30. Italics added.
102. G. Codrini, *Io, un ex brigatista,* 65.

family members, friends, and acquaintances can guarantee total support and complete submission to the community of absolute revolution.

On entering a revolutionary sect, the marginal individual rediscovers the "lost society." Starting then, the group takes over the individual. Joining a revolutionary sect is a total and final choice; it's a road of no return. You leave the revolutionary community only when you die, either killed by the police or killed by your companions.

There is no need to investigate an accusation of betrayal. A suspicion is enough to receive a death sentence.

The brigadist Giorgio Soldati, nicknamed Tommy, suspected of being a *pentito* in Prima Linea, was strangled in the Cuneo prison on 10 December 1981 by numerous militants from different armed groups during the afternoon recreation hour. He was a twenty-six-year-old construction worker. A communiqué titled "Epitaph for a Despicable Crocodile," signed "Terrore Rosso," and sent to the Radio Popolare of Milan, claimed responsibility for the murder on 28 December. The brigadist Ennio Di Rocco, forced to give evidence under torture, was killed on 27 July 1982 in the Trani prison. He was a twenty-four-year-old plumber. Marino Pallotto, suspected of having collaborated with the magistrates, was hanged on 29 July 1980 in his cell in the Velletri prison. Bricklayer, age twenty-four. William Waccher, suspected of having betrayed the Red Brigades, was killed on 7 February 1980 in Milan, via Magliocco at Porta Ticinese. Surveyor, age twenty-six. Francesco Berardi, suspected of having collaborated with the magistrates, committed suicide in the Cuneo prison on 24 October 1979. Blue-collar worker, age fifty. Maria Giovanna Massa, distancing herself from the Red Brigades, managed to save herself from being killed in the Voghera prison, as did Maria Grazia Biancone in the Latina prison. Roberto Peci, as we know, was killed by multiple gunshots.[103]

In the sect, individuals give themselves up to the group as they would no longer have any chance of surviving without it. They have declared war on the world and the world is hunting them. It is a psychological war rather than a "military" one. They need to be supported to advance; leaving the group would mean giving themselves up to the enemy. For every revolutionary, we read in a Red Brigades document of 29 March 1980, "the choice was specific: fight and win with the possibility of dying, instead of submitting and dying slowly at the hands of the lackeys and by the tools used by a few

---

103. See *Progetto memoria*, 335, 340. See also Clementi, *Storia delle Brigate rosse,* 305–6.

jackals to become wealthy."[104] Once you enter a terrorist group, explains the Red Brigadist Guagliardo, there is no going back: "The military mechanisms impose very tight constraints because the means increasingly conditions the end, it is already the prerequisite of a fixed route. *The individual has compromised his life, and therefore the collectivity to which he belongs can no longer turn back or go forward along a new road.*"[105] Entering a revolutionary sect, explains the Red Brigadist Anna Laura Braghetti, means *uprooting your identity.*[106]

Milovan Djilas has methodically analyzed the educational strategies used by revolutionary sects to shape their adherents' identities.

Djilas, professional revolutionary as well as faithful supporter of Tito, was one of the principal artificers of the communist revolution in Yugoslavia. After a change of heart when he was still a key actor in the government, he denounced the failure of communism in his main work, *The New Class* (1956). He went to prison rather than abjure his ideas, convinced that "all the demons that communism thought it had banished from the present, as well as the future world, insinuated themselves in its soul, becoming part of its being."[107]

In Djilas's analysis, the professional revolutionary can be recognized by his absolute subordination to the revolutionary sect. The communists are "special types of people," whose ideal is absolute regeneration, installing the kingdom of heaven on earth. Their revolutionary education has "divorced them from humanity in a more permanent and monstrous form,"[108] and they have learned to attach every fiber of their being to the party and its ideals. The revolutionary sect, continues Djilas, exercises a massive psychological violence on its adherents. It oppresses them and morally uproots them; it exposes them to refined and brutal torture. Finally, it teaches them to justify even the most ferocious crimes in the name of a "higher ideal." Communists have to internalize "mystical unity," that is, a system of moral rules and regulations conceived to stop them from leaving the group. They have renounced the pleasures of *this world* to give themselves entirely to the sect and they cannot lose its support without falling into despair.

---

104. *Leaflet commemorating the four militants killed on via Fracchia, Genoa.* Red Brigades document of 29 March 1980. It refers to the raid of the special antiterrorism squad in the apartment. After the shoot-out, Annamaria Ludmann, secretary, Riccardo Dura, Piero Panciarelli, and Lorenzo Betassa, factory workers, were dead. The entire text is available at www.brigaterosse.org.

105. Guagliardo, *Di sconfitta in sconfitta,* 65. Italics added.

106. Braghetti, *Il prigioniero,* 41.

107. M. Djilas, *La società imperfetta,* 22.

108. M. Djilas, *La nuova classe,* 164.

Djilas's conclusion is that *the success of a communist movement mainly depends on its psychic-moral unity:* "But this very psychic and moral unity—for which no statutes or laws have been written, but which spontaneously occurs, and goes on to become a conscious habit and tradition—more than anything else makes communists into an indestructible family, incomprehensible and impenetrable to others, inflexible in the solidarity and identity of its reactions, its thoughts, and its feelings. More than anything else, the existence of this psychic-moral unity... is the surest sign that the communist movement has become homogeneous and irresistible for its followers and for many others, strong because it is fused into one piece, one soul, and one body."[109] As the revolutionary Ernesto Che Guevara, so beloved of the Red Brigades, said: "Each one of us, alone, is worth nothing."[110]

The birth of a revolutionary sect has the same features that Francesco Alberoni defined for the "nascent state." It is "a state of transition and appears when social solidarity fails. Solidarity is then restructured on the basis of some very particular points of the social system. Generally speaking, we can say that the nascent stage appears as a part of the social system's reconstructive response. By creating an *alternative solidarity,* it unites participants and opposes the existing order. The nuclei formed in the nascent state have an experience sui generis, prompting them to reach an alternative interpretation and, on this basis, they attempt to make a whole again."[111] In Durkheim's words, in states of collective effervescence, that is, in periods of creation and renewal: "society wrenches the individual from himself and puts him in a circle of higher life."[112]

In the DRIA model, the route toward bloodshed starts with a feeling, a state of mind, that changes into an authentic existential drama. The aspiring brigadist is above all someone full of frustration and resentment caused by his or her marginal state.

The brigadist Mario Ferrandi rejected the values of material well-being. He despised the goal of success in the labor world; he felt repulsed by traditional family values. He found his life "intolerable" and considered it "not worth living." He felt he was slowly going crazy. He wanted to free himself from this terrible existential condition, but society offered him no alternatives. His feeling of extraneousness from the world is a "cancer that is gradually devouring me." Ferrandi's words describe the solitude and lack of

---

109. Ibid., 170–71.
110. E. C. Guevara, *Lettera ai figli* (1965), in *Leggere Che Guevara,* 431.
111. F. Alberoni, *Movimento e istituzione,* 30.
112. E. Durkheim, *Le forme elementari della vita religiosa.*

communication that afflicts the marginal individual: "In a certain sense, it's even forbidden to talk about how you feel, about your tensions. If the idea of progress or material well-being or success at work or an edifying family environment *doesn't in my eyes make my life worth living, if I feel it's unbearable*—or that socially there's no space to deny it or to find an alternative—*I will gradually go mad, because I feel this dissimilarity grow within me and I can't find an outlet, any possibility of communication, for this cancer that is slowly devouring me.*"[113]

The brigadist Gianluca Codrini describes the mental condition that prompts the marginal individual to seek the revolutionary sect. Faced with his "depersonalization and identity crisis," he saw the choice of the armed struggle as an answer to "the final resignation to absolute nothingness."[114] At the time he joins the Red Brigades, Codrini feels assailed by a "boundless desperation."[115] His alternatives are "rampant sociopolitical corruption or terrorism."[116] Entering the Red Brigades was the response "to my sense of frustration and my dreadful inner emptiness."[117] Brigadists, continues Codrini, have an "unhealthy taste for underground life commensurate with their sense of failure and consequent eagerness to achieve satisfaction."[118]

Of all the testimonies we have on the aspiring revolutionaries' existential drama and on the *life space* in which they move, Codrini's is one of the most significant. We should pay special attention to it.

Once, the streets in my town used to speak to me with their odors, their colors, their moods: they were streets that were *alive,* full of voices and sounds, with living people passing through them.

All around me I only saw faces, eyes, hair, and feet moving in every direction, one after the other, driven by an unhealthy frenzy.

As I wandered around during my impromptu evening surveillance, I discovered a dull, colorless, and tasteless town: I'd never seen it like that before.

I felt its vital breath to be short, wheezy, and painful.

Although there were hordes of people hustling here and there, the town seemed empty, deserted, and silent.

The walls of its houses bore the mark of a painful, incurable melancholy *and endless desperation.*

---

113. Brigadist Mario Ferrandi talking to S. Zavoli, *La notte della Repubblica,* 372. Italics added.
114. Codrini, *Io, un ex brigatista,* 9.
115. Ibid., 68.
116. Ibid., 10–11.
117. Ibid., 12.
118. Ibid., 26.

What kept my town alive was the piercing hiss of hundreds of cars ripping up and down, incessantly and frenziedly.

Metallic sounds, wild clanking, the sound track *of the daily massacre of our identity*. Frequent howls of sirens (I'd never heard so many) rent the atmosphere of that *dark spell*.

At a certain point I was shaken by an indescribable dismay that froze my blood.

I'd suddenly realized that my town was now nothing else but the place where I was walking that evening like a man adrift, without a past, without a future, and, what is worst, without a present.

An ordinary place, a place like any other, here, there, up, down, in this beat-up world.

I felt my thoughts spin wildly in my brain . . . in an endless vortex.

I continued to walk aimlessly, without knowing where I was going, who I was meeting, what to say, what to do, today, tomorrow, and all the tomorrows to come.

People came, people went, with their inexpressive faces, tense, as if awaiting the last judgment, as if under a terrifying, inexplicable evil spell.

A mass of shadows, of wraiths. . . . I couldn't understand why my beloved town had changed so radically. . . . All at once I realized why I was feeling such uneasy anxiety. What I thought was my town no longer existed; who knows how long it had been like that. It had been ruined forever by turning into a metropolis. At that moment everything became clear, terribly clear.[119]

In the DRIA model, the Red Brigades are "proletarians"—as understood by Arnold J. Toynbee and not by Marx. They are members of a "psychological class," composed of individuals who live on the outskirts of *this world* and who because of this have declared war on its established values. Toynbee has explained that "the true hall-mark of the proletariat is neither poverty nor humble birth, but a consciousness—and the resentment that this consciousness inspires—of being disinherited from their ancestral place in society."[120] For Marx, the proletariat is an economic-social category; it is all the wage-earning workers exploited by the capitalists. For Toynbee it is instead a sociopsychological category. When the social fabric undergoes an intense disintegration process, those individuals who are less "equipped" to tackle the challenge of change—and who are condemned to live on the margins of the community—turn into "shock troops," full of anger and

---

119. Ibid., 67–69.
120. A. J. Toynbee, *A Study of History,* 5:63.

frustration. It is a dissatisfaction that has a "spiritual" and not "material" origin. As such, it unites "rich" and "poor" in a single pantoclastic plan. Toynbee helps us understand how the Red Brigades came from such different social backgrounds.

Some are factory workers who feel unable to break free of their wretched condition. They are like "condemned people at liberty." Their feeling that there is no possibility of redemption in the future—because of a social system considered unfair and classist—is extremely significant. As a leader of the armed struggle asserts: "I rejected the logic of a system that had already decided my future, as earlier it had decided my father's, disabled by his work, and before that his father, killed by silicosis."[121] Others were high-school teachers, such as Maria Rosaria Roppoli, or university professors, such as Enrico Fenzi and Gianfranco Faina, or rich businessmen, such as Giangiacomo Feltrinelli. Men and women with high social status but who did not identify with the values of the world they lived in. (See table 1.)

For in addition to men, women were ready and eager to sacrifice everything, as the figures on the gender distribution of the 911 members of the Red Brigades under investigation demonstrate. (See table 2.)

Factory workers or not, the Red Brigades are fighting the world. Their lives are in constant danger. They are conscious of the risk of prison or death every moment of the day. The choice to go underground requires a strong motivation. Hatred for the enemy is the fundamental trigger: "Anger tormented me. Anger, anger, anger,"[122] explains Anna Laura Braghetti. However, even members of the Red Brigades are capable of calculating the costs and benefits of the revolutionary choice. Their pantoclastic fury does not stop them from wondering: "Is it worth it? What do I gain?" The answer of the working classes is not different from anyone else's: you join the Red Brigades to get away from a "crappy life";[123] you enter in the hope of a better future, for you and for your children. Fighting for others, sacrificing yourself for the weakest, is the banner of every member. The world has to be broken down and then rebuilt on completely new foundations.

---

121. This is the testimony of a brigadist called "Claudio" given to *Panorama*, 6 June 1978, 159.

122. Braghetti, *Il prigioniero*, 36.

123. P. Gallinari, *Un contadino nella metropoli*, 84. Prospero Gallinari, born in Reggio Emilia in 1951, became involved in politics when very young. After training in the Federazione Italiana Giovani Comunisti (FGCI), he was a militant in the Red Brigades until they disbanded in 1988. First arrested in 1974, he escaped in 1977, and was again arrested in 1979. He was given three life sentences. After eighteen years in prison, mostly in special sectors, he has for years been under house arrest for health reasons.

Table 1.   Red Brigades membership by profession

PROFESSION	NUMBER	PERCENT
Artisans	14	1.54
Blue-collar workers	214	23.49
Clerical workers	81	8.89
Outlaws	12	1.32
Farmers	5	0.55
Lecturers and researchers	6	0.66
Military members	10	1.10
Politicians and trade-union members	7	0.77
Professionals	35	3.84
Service workers	53	5.82
Students	111	12.18
Teachers	36	3.95
Technicians	20	2.20
Temporary workers	6	0.66
Tradespeople	23	2.52
Unemployed	26	2.85
Miscellaneous	11	1.21
Data missing	241	26.45
Total	911	100.00

Source: Progetto memoria, 62.

Table 2.   Red Brigades membership by gender

GENDER	NUMBER	PERCENT
Males	683	74.97
Females	228	25.03
Total	911	100.00

Source: Progetto memoria, 59.

Instead, the intellectual class mainly feels a fierce sense of impotence. These are people who hold themselves in high regard; they have devoted their life to knowledge and aspire to a role of spiritual guide. But this aspiration often clashes with the organization of the capitalist society, dominated by purely prosaic material and economic values. This helps us understand why the greatest enemies of the capitalist system come precisely from the marginal sectors of the modern intellectual class.

In a world dominated by the logic of profit, the humanistic culture that reflects on the great issues of human existence (the meaning of life and death, tolerance, war, etc.) is a nonspecialist culture and there is no demand for it on the professional market. Humanists feel as if they possess a knowledge that, in their eyes, has a very high value but which has no audience. Their values are not of *this world*. This gap between status and legitimate expectations causes a relative deprivation that in turn triggers a series of psychological mechanisms that can prompt intellectuals to take radical positions.

Intellectuals devise—or embrace—ethical-political utopias in which profit and competition have been banned. Their marginality is a painful condition that prompts them to imagine a world in which everyone is merged in a single, loving embrace. As Ernesto Che Guevara wrote: "Socialism cannot exist without a change in conscience to a new fraternal attitude toward humanity, not only within the societies which are building or have built socialism, but also on a world scale."[124]

Capitalism is the "mortal enemy," begrudged by those who are socially alienated and culturally rootless. For the professional revolutionary—these are again Guevara's words—nothing can eliminate "the immoral character of the exchange."[125] Those who profit from their business are corrupt and morally despicable. The Red Brigades, whether intellectuals or proletarians, tremble with indignation. In their previous lives they yearned for money, success, and power like everyone else. But now they have been "regenerated." They have completed an "inner" journey that has rendered them "different" and allows them to judge and condemn. They are "better" than the others; they are "cleaner," more generous, more honest. The Red Brigades are "inquisitors." In another life they were afflicted by an intense "spiritual vacuum" that was filled only after undergoing a painful procedure. They have become "pure." As we have seen, their materialistic concept of history has a religious character. With the absolute certainty of the believer, they are convinced that history is "inevitably" steered toward the revolution of the proletariat.

The Red Brigades are political men with a religious vocation and they consider the choice of militancy absolutely consistent with the necessary development of history. Their choices cannot be understood by using the "paradigm of power."[126] They are not the "Machiavellians."[127] Their lives, as happens with any self-respecting people of "faith," are mainly dominated by feelings and passions. For them, politics is a "salvific mission." They look around and see only misery and desperation; humanity is on the brink of an abyss and is waiting to be saved. No defeat can discourage gnostic activists.

---

124. E. C. Guevara, "Al secondo seminario economico sulla solidarietà afroasiatica di Algeri" (24 February 1965), in *Leggere Che Guevara,* 385–86.

125. Ibid., 386.

126. See G. Sola, *I paradigmi della scienza politica.*

127. J. Burnham, *Machiavellians.*

This is Che Guevara's oft-repeated lesson: "What do the dangers or the sacrifices of a man or of a nation matter, when the destiny of humanity is at stake?"[128] New uprisings "shall continue to grow in the midst of all the hardships inherent in this dangerous profession of being modern revolutionaries. Many shall perish, victims of their errors, others shall fall in the tough battle that approaches; new fighters and new leaders shall appear in the warmth of the revolutionary struggle."[129]

The revolution demands the blood of its sons no less than that of its enemies. Espousing the communist ideal implies "the immense sacrifice of the people, sacrifices that should be demanded beginning today, in plain daylight,"[130] because the survival of capitalism marks the triumph of the "society of wolves."[131] This is why, the professional revolutionaries assert, "we cannot harbor any illusions, and we have no right to do so, that freedom can be obtained without fighting. And these battles shall not be mere street fights with stones against tear-gas bombs, or pacific general strikes; neither shall it be the battle of a furious people destroying in two or three days the repressive scaffolds of the ruling oligarchies; the struggle shall be long and harsh,"[132] requiring a suitable spiritual preparation. It is hatred, explains Che Guevara, that is the professional revolutionaries' most powerful weapon. Those who do not hate fight a losing battle. The aim of the revolutionary education is to program people to deliver death without betraying any emotion. They have to whip up "hatred as an element of the struggle. A relentless hatred of the enemy, impelling us over and beyond the natural limitations that man is heir to and transforming him into an effective, violent, selective, and cold killing machine. Our soldiers must be thus."[133] They have to "carry the war into every corner the enemy happens to carry it: *to his home, to his centers of entertainment; a total war.* It is necessary to prevent him from having a moment of peace, a quiet moment outside his barracks or even inside; *we must attack him wherever he may be, make him feel like a cornered beast wherever he may move.*"[134]

---

128. E. C. Guevara, "Creare due, tre, molti Vietnam…Questa è la parola d'ordine" (April 1967), in *Leggere Che Guevara,* 408. This is also known as "Message to the Tricontinental," referring to the Tricontinental Conference of Solidarity with the peoples of Asia, Africa, and Latin America, held in January 1966 in Cuba.

129. Ibid., 403.

130. Ibid., 405.

131. E. C. Guevara, "Lettera a José Medero Mestre" (26 February 1964), in ibid., 425.

132. E. C. Guevara, "Creare due, tre, molti Vietnam," 405.

133. Ibid., 406.

134. Ibid. Italics added.

Shedding Blood and the Role of the Revolutionary Sect

The acquisition of the "binary code" mentality is a pillar of the revolutionary concept of the world. It enables "an all-embracing and ultra-determined reading of reality," which, the brigadist Nitta recounts, mainly comes from the "simplified and emotive" reading of Marx and Lenin's works.[135] We have seen that this approach to reality—the binary code mentality—has a very important function in fostering the gnostic activist's deployment of political violence. Society is divided into two areas: the area of revolution and the area of reaction. Those who militate in the opposite area merit hatred and contempt, two fundamental components of the Red Brigades' action. Illustrating the more complex aspects of reality makes it easier to identify the enemy.

Ezio Tarantelli, economics professor at the University of Rome "La Sapienza," was killed on 27 March 1985 because he was judged responsible for all humanity's evils. He is an abettor "at the highest levels of proletarian exploitation in the countries with advanced capitalism as well as in Western imperialism's robbery, starvation, and oppression of three-quarters of the global population."[136]

The pedagogy of intolerance and the binary code mentality enable hatred and anger to channel themselves toward a specific target. The unleashing of these feelings plays a fundamental role not only in political homicide but also in the kneecapping technique.

As the brigadist Peci explains, the shots fired at the victim's legs are not a casual act. They are proportionate to the shooter's anger. Peci's words constitute a *lectio magistralis* on revolutionary education: "You have to be very careful. When the targets are standing, you first of all have to shoot them a couple of times in their legs so that they fall down. You wait for them to fall to the ground because if you shoot while they're falling, there's the possibility you might kill them. So you stop and let them fall; they usually fall backward with their legs toward you. At that point you mustn't start shooting again immediately; you have to go around and stand beside them because if you shoot from the front—even if you shoot low—the bullet can rebound and end up in their stomach or head. Or you just have to aim a centimeter higher,

---

135. Novelli and Tranfaglia, *Vite sospese,* 195. I quote the brigadist Nitta's testimony in full: "In this kind of context, the simplified and emotive reading of Marx, Lenin, Giap, and Che Guevara did the rest to consolidate my reading of an all-embracing and ultra-determined reality."

136. Red Brigades document *claiming responsibility for the homicide of the political economy lecturer— Ezio Tarantelli* issued on 27 March 1985. This is their "judgment" against Tarantelli: "Who was Ezio Tarantelli? Someone whom the bourgeoisie, with great imagination, calls a 'professor,' an 'expert' in industrial relations, is in reality one of the most authoritative technical-political advisers of big capital." The document is available at www.brigaterosse.org.

in your emotion, to get them directly in the head. Standing beside the target, they are not at risk, and moreover, from that position you can hit their legs better; at that point you empty the magazine: three, five, six shots depending on the caliber, your precision, and *your anger*. It is important to shoot many times so as to be sure of hitting the bone, although from a political angle the action can be considered successful with any kind of wound."[137]

Social marginality and binary code mentality are not enough in themselves to guarantee the shift to revolutionary violence. They are necessary but still insufficient conditions. Alienated and frustrated individuals with a dichotomic vision of the world can take three routes before opting for revolution: (a) passive and resigned acceptance of reality; (b) withdrawal from the world to construct an isolated community for "establishing an exemplary system of social relations";[138] and (c) simple rebellion or "intermittent protest," possibly violent, against the established order, without, however, a plan for social change.

You need more to create a revolutionary.

You have to belong to an organized group, driven by the same "pantoclastic" fury, able to provide (a) the necessary psychological support for the "massive" plan for violently destroying the world and rebuilding it on completely new foundations; and (b) organizational tools (accommodation, food, false documents, money, weapons, etc.) to change a spiritual need into political action.

The group, explains the brigadist Prospero Gallinari, creates "what we called the superman. The superman was someone who focuses on the revolution and who is ready for any type of action."[139]

From the testimony of brigadist Angela Vai, one of those responsible for the murder of the "State lackey"[140] Fulvio Croce, president of the Turin Bar Association (28 April 1977): "Knowing that you have an organization of comrades behind you who are ready to take your place and who share your responsibilities is an important moral support for those who have to perform the task.... We are all aware, all involved, all responsible."[141]

---

137. Peci, *Io, l'infame*, 127. Italics added.

138. E.g., anarchic communities. See Alberoni, *Movimento e istituzione*, 261.

139. Prospero Gallinari talking to P. Pergolizzi, *L'appartamento: Br*, 176. Gallinari's testimony refers to the period in which he became a member of Corrado Simioni's underground group, in the years immediately prior to his entry in the Red Brigades.

140. This is the expression the Red Brigades used in the communiqué claiming responsibility for Fulvio Croce's murder (1 May 1977). The document was found in Turin, at the Red Brigades' indication, in a telephone book in a booth in Corso Vittorio.

141. G. Bianconi, *Mi dichiaro prigioniero politico*, 79.

In these sociopsychological conditions, giving and receiving death becomes a "routine job." The person who kills the "enemy" isn't a murderer but a benefactor of the exploited. So political homicide, to echo the brigadist Paolo Zambianchi, is nothing else but a "stage in the political debate."[142]

The Red Brigades' "criminal code" specifies different punishments. Kneecapping by shooting, for example, is considered a "mediation," a form of dialogue and "opening."

This is what we read in the document claiming responsibility for the murder of Guido Rossa, the communist worker killed on 24 January 1979 for having reported a work colleague discovered distributing Red Brigades material: "Although the proletariat has always, on principle, executed any spies found within it, the nucleus wanted just to disable the spy *as* the first and only *mediation* with these wretched people: but the spy's brainless reaction made any mediation impossible and so he was executed."[143]

Even when a "technical" error causes a worker's death, the Red Brigades have no reason to blame themselves because, as we read in a document of December 1980, "the communists fight not to assert themselves as a 'Party,' but to assert the interests of the proletariat and its dictatorship."[144] The conviction, reiterated in the *Strategic Management's Resolution of October 1980,* that the "capitalistic method of production has historically arrived at its final crisis, after which it becomes extinct," is a more-than-sufficient reason to continue the "political debate" as the Red Brigades understand it.

It is inside the revolutionary sect that the pedagogy of intolerance carries out its "dehumanization of the enemy" procedure. It is here that the final metamorphosis occurs; it is in the revolutionary sect that a person becomes a killer. Political homicide requires a very strong ideological motivation, supplied only by membership in a gnostic group: "To call people to arms you need a great and terrible enemy,"[145] explains Valerio Morucci. Militancy in a political group, driven by the same "armed utopia,"[146] is decisive. For the

---

142. Novelli and Tranfaglia, *Vite sospese,* 319–20. In Zambianchi's words: "In the autumn of that year I became a member of the Formazioni Comuniste Combattenti, and thus finally chose the armed struggle in a combatant organization. . . . My entry in that organization is thus also a statement of my willingness to perform political homicide, as a stage in the political debate and my life during those months."

143. *Document claiming responsibility for the murder of the communist Italsider, Genoa worker—Guido Rossa (24 January 1979).* Underlining in text; italics added. The entire document is available at www.brigaterosse.org.

144. *Brigate rosse, Le venti tesi finali.* Red Brigades document of December 1980. Available at www.brigaterosse.org.

145. Morucci, *La peggio gioventù,* 127

146. G. Pansa, *L'utopia armata.*

Red Brigades, "*it is important to act inside an armed organization that has a plan. It serves to exonerate yourself and to find the strength to continue.*"[147] The sect is everything. Outside the sect, the Red Brigades are nothing. They would be only rebels without any possibility of survival. As the brigadist Mario Moretti puts it: "Each of us entrusted our survival to the comrade who stood beside us."[148]

The sect confers a meaning on the Red Brigades' actions; it encourages and ennobles them. The sect is the only link between the individual and reality. Everything is mediated by the sect; everything has to be referred back to its logic. Relations with your comrades, sharing a great plan and ties of solidarity, take on an absolute value that transcends the meaning of the individual existences.

The links forged within a revolutionary sect can be difficult for someone outside that universe to imagine. The identification with the sect can be very profound. The absolute-revolution community gratifies and feeds a need for dependency that can last a lifetime.

Before going underground, Maria Rosaria Roppoli taught literature and philosophy in a high school. After becoming a regular militant in the Red Brigades, she had an intense affair with Patrizio Peci. The latter became a *pentito,* causing dozens of the Red Brigades to be arrested, but not his woman, whose name he never disclosed. Roppoli could have gone into exile abroad, but her deep emotional bond with the "sect-party" made her give herself up. The fear of benefiting from her man's "repentance"—thus losing her comrades' respect and trust—makes her prefer a lengthy imprisonment to an "ideological wound" that for her would have been worse than a life sentence.[149]

With the typical language and mentality of a professional revolutionary, a brigadist describes supporting the communist ideal as a choice that covers every aspect of his life. The socioaffective tentacles of the gnostic group are so powerful that the simple desire to contravene its regulations causes him great psychological distress: "Sometimes I felt schizophrenic," Morucci recounts, "because another part of me was kicking against the rules."[150]

Entering a terrorist group means sharing a new way of looking at reality. The aspiring revolutionary is asked to embrace a new culture that, in

---

147. Bianconi, *Mi dichiaro prigioniero politico,* 75. Italics added.
148. Moretti, *Brigate rosse,* 94.
149. See Peci, *Io, l'infame,* 99.
150. Morucci, *Ritratto di un terrorista da giovane,* 227.

J. M. Levine and R. L. Moreland's scheme, implies religiously abiding by a set of customs, such as:[151]

1. Routines—daily practices in which group members engage
2. Accounts—stories that group members tell about the group and one another
3. Jargon—words and phrases that mean something special to group members but not to outsiders
4. Rituals—ceremonies that mark important events in the life of the group
5. Symbols—objects that mean something important to the group's members

Berger and Luckmann would say that aspiring terrorists must internalize the group's "institutional sub-universes," a process that includes the acquisition of a specific vocabulary with meanings accessible only to its members. At the end of the "probation period"[152]—during which novices learn the group's fundamental rules while the same group assesses them—the terrorists are involved in a radical redefinition of their identity. Exactly as occurs in some religious orders, they are required to take another name to acknowledge they are "new" people who no longer have a past. This is an authentic "initiation" rite (from the Latin word *inire,* meaning "to enter, to commence") that aims to change the neophytes' way of perceiving reality.

The religious historian Mircea Eliade has found the ritual symbolism of *death* and *rebirth* in initiation rites. The initiation symbolizes a primordial event in creation. Everything the neophytes possess has to be eliminated, to be replaced by the values that the group wants to forge in their spirit. In the *upanayan,* a ceremony of the Vedic religious tradition, the neophyte presents himself to his guru and, after being covered with an antelope skin, is required to beg to live and to observe the vow of chastity. Once the initiation rite is terminated, the novice takes the name of *dvi-ja* ("born twice"), indicating a radical break from his previous identity. In the *dîksa* rite, again in the Vedic tradition, the novice, after being sprinkled with water (symbol of the male seed) is wrapped in a blanket and isolated in a cave. At the end of his isolation,

---

151. See J. M. Levine and R. L. Moreland, "Socialization in Small Groups." A valuable overview of the main studies in social psychology on passing from the condition of aspiring member of a group to that of new member is G. Speltini and A. Palmonari, *I gruppi sociali,* 80–92.

152. R. Brown, *Psicologia sociale dei gruppi.*

he is immersed in a bath from which he is extracted as the midwife extracts the newborn baby.[153]

Since an error in selecting an aspiring revolutionary could have devastating effects on a terrorist group, the "entry test" has to be demanding. R. P. Clark, in his study of members of the ETA terrorist group, saw the "strict initiation" practice as a way of discouraging less determined candidates.[154]

As Raffaele Fiore testifies, the Red Brigades were well aware of the importance of initiation rites: "To become a 'regular' in the Red Brigades you had to carry out an action of proletarian expropriation, signifying rejection of a consolidated political logic. Carrying out a theft . . . was a kind of initiation rite for the organization in which some social walls and conventions were demolished."[155]

In some cases, strict initiation can cause the revolutionary sect to destroy itself. This occurs when the obsession with purity reaches its zenith. In winter 1972, twelve members of the Rengo Sekigun (United Red Army) were horribly mutilated and then killed by their own members during a chilling reeducation therapy. It happened in Nagano, not far from Tokyo, where Hiroko Nagata and Tsuneo Mori—the two Rengo Sekigun leaders—brought followers to a remote mountain lodge to train them in the use of weapons. Before distributing the arms, Tsuneo Mori explained that the military drill would be preceded by a radical purification of the spirit from the encrustations of bourgeois society.

A radical "communization" (*kyosanshugika*) process was thus initiated, with the aim of picking out the members less willing to face sacrifice and suffering. Sexual relations were forbidden and everyone had to publicly declare their shame for how they had led their lives before entering the revolutionary sect. You had to admit your sins, repent, and abase yourself. These collective confessions soon turned into an authentic sacrificial rite. The first victim was Ozaki Mitsuo, a twenty-one-year-old student, whom Tsuneo Mori accused of having revealed to friends the place where the sect's weapons were hidden. Savagely beaten, bleeding, and badly wounded, Ozaki Mitsuo was left tied to a pole all night in arctic conditions. The next day he underwent a second beating and died. In another purification rite, Koojima Kazuko and Kato Yoshitaka, a boy and a girl, were forced to write their self-criticism on their knees. Both were given the same treatment as Ozaki Mitsuo. The former survived; the latter died. It was then the turn of Toyama Mieko, accused

153. See M. Eliade, *Initiation, rites, sociétés secrètes,* and J. Ries, ed., *I riti di iniziazione.*
154. See R. P. Clark, "Patterns in the Lives of ETA Members," 423–54.
155. Grandi, *L'ultimo brigatista,* 66.

of having sexual relations with another militant. The girl and her presumed lover had to exhume Koojima Kazuko's body and mutilate his face to get rid of, so they said, "the expression of death caused by failure." After this gruesome ritual, Toyama Mieko was forced to punch her own face repeatedly to ruin her looks, considered a source of narcissism. She was then killed together with her lover. But the most macabre episode concerned Yoshino Masakuni, a woman eight months pregnant who was tortured for lacking a proper revolutionary spirit. Yoshino Masakuni was killed as she gave birth, but the child was saved because the sect wanted to give him a revolutionary education without his parents' influence.[156]

The Detachment from the Surrounding World

Going underground is the indispensable condition for the final detachment from the world. "Going underground cuts off everything. It's a one-way road," explains the brigadist Morucci.[157] This "detachment"—physical and mental—completes the sociopsychological process that leads the Red Brigades to murder. It is no coincidence that the most ferocious actions against their enemies are performed only by the "regular," or clandestine, members.

Losing contact with reality is thus the decisive moment. It marks the final maturation of the gnostic activist. This explains why professional revolutionaries pursue their target independently of the conditions they are operating under. Even if everything seems to suggest that the mission is impossible, they don't stray from the path. "I had my own idea of the world," Morucci tells us, "to assert against anything that opposed it."[158]

It is again Peci who illuminates the point in his autobiography, one of the most valuable documents for illustrating the mental and sociological processes characterizing this stage of a revolutionary education.

Being "out of the world" is a key to understanding the mental process leading to murder. This phrase is found throughout Peci's autobiography. This "detachment from the world" concerns the individual but it occurs through merging into a gnostic group, conceived as something "totally

---

156. P. Steinhoff, "Death by Defeatism and Other Fables," 195–224. As Patricia Steinhoff wrote: "The raw, face-to-face brutality of the purge lends itself readily to pseudo-explanations that portray the perpetrators as monsters, fundamentally different from normal people. Yet the real horror of the Rengo Sekigun purge is that its bizarre outcomes resulted from very ordinary social processes enacted by quite normal individuals" (195). See also C. Camoriano, *Nihon Sekigun,* 79–86.

157. Morucci, *La peggio gioventù,* 106.

158. Ibid., 107.

other." It is certainly the individual who thinks and acts, but his thoughts and actions are shaped by the group, which rigidly disciplines the smallest aspect of its members' lives. The Red Brigades' physical and psychological survival depends entirely on the solidarity and support of the group, to which they owe everything. Outside the group they can find only prison or death.

Peci describes his alienated condition as an "outsider" very eloquently:

> Where did our error basically lie? In believing that Italy was a country ready for a communist revolution. We never considered for a moment that Italy is a highly developed capitalist state, that is, a society completely different from all the countries where the communist revolutions have been successful. In Italy the fundamental element was missing: there was no hunger. Without hunger, without a great majority of poor people, you can't have a revolution. Our error was in believing that, even without hunger, we could manage to make a revolution simply with people who didn't want to be economically exploited. We thought that people would risk everything, even their lives, for a principle. We lived out of the world. I had gradually realized this during the end of my clandestinity, then I understood it fully when I started my time in prison. But I only received the devastating effect, the physical sensation of being outside any logic, after my release, in March 1983. I was finally free and I went to the seaside. I hadn't seen the sea for years, and those who have lived in a coastal town know what that means. After three years of being underground and three in prison, it felt incredible to be free, to live like a normal person. Normal...I know that I can never live like a *normal* person. The memory of what has been done will always remain inside you. And I would always have to be watchful with regard to the world outside. Out of the world. It's as if, as punishment for being outside the world in the Red Brigades, I had to remain outside the world forever.[159]

Political militancy, Peci explains, takes on an all-embracing dimension, deforming every aspect of reality. Every point of reference with the outside world disappears, and it takes second place to the ideology. Ideas no longer have to take reality into account. It is reality that has to adjust to an idea of total regeneration. The world has to be demolished and rebuilt in the image and likeness of the professional revolutionaries: "When you're in the Red Brigades all the parameters change, your cultural education is

---

159. Ibid., 47.

no longer any use to you, because the terms of reference are missing. You might know the writings of Marx, Marcuse, and Mao by heart, but there you are, out of the world, you talk about things never broached before, and you don't know where they'll lead."[160]

No less significant is the description that Morucci has left us of underground life. In the Red Brigades, "the rules were very strict and you had to follow a sort of vade mecum of clandestinity. The Executive Committee commanded everything and you obviously weren't meant to know who belonged to it or where it met. . . . Everyday life also changed. No more contact with your family or old friends outside the organization. In fact, on this last point there was an absolute ban, for fear of 'contamination.' If you were having a relationship with a female comrade, it was taken for granted that you would end up in two different sectors, not so much to avoid promiscuity, but so that the revolutionary sacrifice did not weigh on your spirit."[161]

There is nothing heroic about life in the Red Brigades. Living apart from the world makes people frustrated and their daily life distressful. Hatred and detachment from society make even the smallest problems seem worse.

The brigadist's first problem, explains Peci, is a psychological one. He lives in limbo, halfway between the real world and the utopia of the perfect one: "People imagine that life in the Red Brigades is all violence, suspense, and adventure. That's rubbish. Those moments occur very rarely, a tiny minority compared to the rest. The rest is made up of everyday problems and anonymous banality. Problems of the heart, of sex, of the house, of money, of holidays, of family ties. *But above all psychological problems,* because all the others are *aggravated by the fact of being out of the world, against the world.*"[162]

With the detachment from reality, the Red Brigades complete their education. They are ready to give and receive death. They are a community capable of meeting all the needs of their members' existence. This is what Peci means when he says that you "leave the world" when you enter the Red Brigades. In the revolutionary sect, the militants' minds and outlooks are molded around a new credo, one that stops them from committing any "error." The Marxist-Leninist doctrine rids the militant of the encrustations of bourgeois morality.

The Leninist principle, which says that reality can be changed only through violence, explains Morucci, "is the key to everything and it is worth

---

160. Ibid., 54.
161. Morucci, *Ritratto di un terrorista da giovane,* 227.
162. Peci, *Io, l'infame,* 75. Italics added.

repeating."[163] The point, he specifies, is not violence, which is everywhere, but the "ideology of violence,"[164] or Leninism.

A Red Brigades multiple killer says that his problem with death was reconciled by a "great ideology" that allowed him to strip the victim of his humanity and to act without any emotional involvement. He saw the world as divided into friends and enemies. This extremely simplified reading of reality enabled him to view political homicide as a simple "routine job" because, and these are his words, "the enemies are not people." The only time that death caused anguish was when a comrade was killed. It's a concept we have already come across: a man is only such if he is a revolutionary, that is, a member of the community of absolute revolution. These are the consequences of the subversive-revolutionary feedback and of the alienation it produces.

A brigadist recounts that she had killed a man, but this action did not weigh on her. The revolutionary sect has transformed her into a perfectly trained machine. She kills without batting an eye. She emerges from the "catacombs" only to kill. Her relationship with this world is solely that of destruction and annihilation. This document merits extensive citation:

> We dealt with the problem of death inside a great ideology, so that, for example, I found I had to kill people directly. . . . In reality, death, experienced as a moment of anguish, only affected me when . . . it involved the death of my comrades. . . . The issue of death within the ideology is exactly this. For example, when you kill a person—I was one of the two people who shot the agent Lo Russo in Turin. I killed him. I remember it as if it were now. But I swear that I didn't really experience this event, the first murder I was directly involved in. . . . I still experienced that murder inside the logic of the function, because he was a guard, because he was known as a torturer, as we said then, and so I had all the justifications of the ideology. For me . . . it was like performing a routine task. This is the aberration, the dreadful thing about the ideology, because you have an ideology in which you are on one side, there are your friends, and on the other, your enemies, and your enemies are a category, that is, they're functions, they're symbols, they're not people. And so treating these people symbolically as absolute enemies means that you have an entirely abstract relationship with death.[165]

---

163. Ibid., 69.
164. Ibid., 70.
165. This is the testimony of a leader of the armed struggle given to D. Della Porta, *Il terrorismo di sinistra*, 181–82.

CHAPTER 4

The Genesis of the Red Brigades

> The "dregs" of society are the vanguard of the revolution.
>
> —Renato Curcio

The Red Brigades' Social Roots

To understand the desire to become brigadists, we need a theory for individual motivation. The DRIA model is programmed to meet this need. To understand how a revolutionary sect takes root and becomes successful, a broader theory of social change is required.[1] These two problems need different types of information.

Debating about the genesis of the Red Brigades means asking ourselves how a capitalist civilization that has generated unprecedented wealth and freedom among the working classes has aroused such hatred. This is a question that Joseph A. Schumpeter has tackled and which deserves to be recalled.[2]

The lesson of capitalism's main actors is clear: economic transformations are never just an economic issue.[3] Capitalism is "a gigantic process of commodification involving everyone and everything."[4] Anything opposing it must be swept away in the name of profit. The capitalistic economy is "an

---

1. See J. A. Geschwender, "Considerazioni sulla teoria dei movimenti sociali e delle rivoluzioni," 127–35.
2. See J. A. Schumpeter, *Capitalism, Socialism and Democracy* and *The Theory of Economic Development*.
3. See A. Orsini, *Le origini del capitalismo.*
4. L. Pellicani, *La genesi del capitalismo e le origini della modernità,* 24.

immense cosmos into which individuals are born and which they, as individuals, see as an unalterable order of things in which they must live."[5] Religion, family, traditions, every aspect of life in society is subjected to its logic. The workers are themselves commodities. They have to adjust to the pace of a frenetic and complex society in continuous competition.

The fact that the market controls the economic system, Karl Polanyi explains, means that society finds itself as an "accessory" to the profit logic.[6]

Capitalism—to use a famous expression of Marx's—is a "permanent revolution." Its expansion brings about very rapid changes and always creates, according to its intensity, problems of psychological and institutional readaptation. Hence economic growth changes people's lives, accentuating the individualistic and atomistic aspects of social organization.[7] These transformations can take on the aspect of a "collective trauma."[8]

A proof of this is Italy's rapid economic development after the war. Industrial development and its new needs overturned the system of rules and values that had regulated the lives of thousands of individuals for generations.

At the time the first Red Brigades were being formed, Italy was facing the problems of an intense modernization process. The logic of business and competition was involving all aspects of society, individualism was being asserted and traditional bonds eroded, the weaker social groups were being exploited, and there were widespread migratory movements.

In less than a decade (1955–63), Italy passed from having a mostly agricultural economy to being one of the world's major industrial powers. The process was rapid and sudden, but it was also marked by "profoundly contradictory elements."[9]

Men and women from the south moved to the towns of the north, where they had to adjust to the rhythm of the assembly line. Men accustomed to the values of a rural life, to a patriarchal concept of the family, lost contact with their roots.[10] They found themselves thrown into an unfamiliar situation.

---

5. M. Weber, *L'etica protestante e lo spirito del capitalismo,* 77.

6. K. Polanyi, *La grande trasformazione,* 74.

7. See L. Pellicani, *Il mercato e i socialismi.*

8. The expression is from J. Sémelin, *Purificare e distruggere,* 11.

9. A. Graziani, *Lo sviluppo dell'economia italiana,* in particular 77–78, in which the author dwells on the "negative" aspects of the Italian economic miracle. For a study of this period and the relative imbalances, not only economic but also political and institutional, see F. Barca, ed., *Storia del capitalismo italiano.* Barca observed that the so-called economic miracle involved a continuous compromise between Italy's leading actors (industry, trade unions, political parties, economic managers, intellectuals proclaiming conflicting ideologies) without the necessary reforms to ensure that the development of the market economy favored all social classes.

10. On the social, urban, and cultural impact of the migratory movement in the Italy of the economic boom, see, among others, P. Ginsborg, *Storia d'Italia dal dopoguerra a oggi,* 283–319; S. Lanaro,

Women were also entering the world of work, subjected to its relentless pace and forced into a life of sacrifice. The rural family, founded on strong bonds of solidarity and kinship, was profoundly affected by its collision with factory life. Some social groups had a swift ascent; others rapidly declined. The origins of the Red Brigades are to be found in the disintegration of Italy's social fabric in the years of the so-called economic boom. "The Red Brigades' initial group," the brigadist Raffaele Fiore writes, "consisted of a vanguard from the provinces, like the hungry poor surrounding the megalopolises."[11] It is thus not surprising that the Red Brigades came into being in the richest and most industrialized area of the country. They were a messianic response to the trauma caused by the modernization process that was to change the face of Italy in the space of a few years.

In attempting to find the reasons for this revolutionary choice, it is again the brigadist Fiore who stresses the social and political consequences of alienation and anomy. He describes the living conditions of that army of southerners forced to move to the industrialized areas in northern Italy to find work. In his words: "Those who haven't lived through those years, who don't remember or don't want to remember our country's profound economic crisis, those who forget the galloping inflation and the devaluation of the lire, who haven't felt the fear of losing their jobs and becoming unemployed, cannot understand what was really happening at that time."[12]

Fiore continues by indicating the responsibilities of the Italian political class, which was incapable, according to him, of responding with the right reforms to the new needs of a society in rapid change:

The big cities of the north were full of men and women migrating from the southern regions. The people had left the south because there was a huge demand for labor, with the big factories in particular needing great numbers of unskilled workers. The assembly line standardized the workers. Immigration started as always with a flow of men, with women coming later. They all had different values, closely bound to the rural life, with a patriarchal concept of the family in a dimension of time linked to the seasons and to the southern heat. None of them had experienced the skilled-worker phase, the struggle to become trained, with women moving from the land to the factories. These are some of

Storia dell'Italia repubblicana, 223–52; F. Compagna, "L'esodo dal Sud e la ricettività del triangolo industriale," 690–704; L. Libertini, *Capitalismo moderno e movimento operaio,* 82–92.

   11. A. Grandi, *L'ultimo brigatista,* 64.

   12. Ibid., 49.

the issues behind the great conflicts between the northern and southern communities. Only a few families from the north were squatters, and those few were terrorized by the southern lifestyle, with noisy, half-naked children playing in the dusty courtyards among the garbage, the women's vulgar language, and their welfare-state mentality.... The southerners also started to send their women to work in the factories, first their daughters and then also their wives. *The social transformations in those years were the result of a cultural melting pot that had vomited out a new magma.*[13]

Fiore's testimony provides a faithful representation of the sociopolitical earthquake that struck the Italy of the "economic miracle." Over a few years, Italian society adapted to the new needs of industrial production, whose added value between 1962 and 1963 was seven times that of 1913, the year that the first Italian industrial revolution concluded. In 1962, the Italian rate of per capita production rose 5.6 percent (second only to the Germans), much greater than the growth rates of every other country in western Europe. Between 1950 and 1960, Italy enjoyed a 5.9 percent average annual growth in its gross product against the 4.9 of the Netherlands, the 4.4 of France, the 3.5 of the Scandinavian countries, and the 2.6 percent of Great Britain.[14]

The change occurred with an intense and profound rhythm: "Besides production relations and methods, the type of settlement, the forms of co-existence and communication among people, habits, customs, the role of religion, values, consumption trends, social relations, the perception and distribution of time, and lifestyles all changed."[15] Thousands of men without any previous industrial and trade-union socialization[16] had to face the "brutal entrance into a degrading and oppressive work environment."[17] Between 1955 and 1971, 9,140,000 Italians were involved in interregional migration.[18] And for many of these families it was an "absolute disaster."[19] The countryside emptied. Seventy percent of those who immigrated to Milan between 1953 and 1963 came from rural communities. Between 1951 and 1964, those

---

13. Ibid., 50–51. Italics added.

14. See V. Castronovo, *L'industria italiana dall'Ottocento a oggi*, 275ff.

15. R. Petri, *Storia economica d'Italia*, 210.

16. See E. Reineri, "Il 'maggio strisciante.'"

17. B. Trentin, *Autunno caldo*, 15. See also Trentin, *Da sfruttati a produttori*, 253ff.

18. Ginsborg, *Storia d'Italia dal dopoguerra a oggi*, 2:295. For a historical reconstruction of migratory movements in Italy, see F. Barbagallo, *Lavoro ed esodo nel Sud;* Barbagallo, "L'emigrazione"; F. Barbagallo and G. Bruno, "Espansione e deriva del Mezzogiorno."

19. Ginsborg, *Storia d'Italia dal dopoguerra a oggi*, 2:293.

employed in agriculture in the northwest regions fell from 25 to 13 percent. The drop was even more drastic in the northeast. Over the same period, agricultural workers fell from 47.8 to 26.1 percent. In Lombardy, 109,000 women were employed in agriculture in 1959, falling to 36,000 in 1968.[20] The "agricultural exodus"[21] also involved central Italy, where those employed in the sector dropped from 44.3 percent to 23.3 between 1951 and 1964.

The decline was slower for agricultural population in the south, dropping from 56.7 percent in 1951 to 37.1 percent in 1964. However, though on a smaller scale, this had more dramatic aspects. The southern rural workers, instead of moving to towns in their own regions, left for remote and hostile places. For thousands of people it was a migration without group solidarity, "as painful as it was ancient, always difficult and often risky, sometimes tragic."[22]

From 1958 to 1963, migration from south to north totaled 1,637,512 persons by the end of the decade: 85,175 in 1958; 79,829 in 1959; 135,018 in 1960; 240,723 in 1961; 226,904 in 1962; and 204,589 in 1963.[23]

The population of Milan had a staggering increase, rising from 1,274,245 inhabitants in 1951 to 1,681,045 in 1967. Immigrants from Lombardy-Veneto were responsible for 70 percent of this demographic swell, with 30 percent from the southern regions. Turin's population rose from 719,300 in 1951 to 1,124,714 in 1967.[24] Its percentage of southern immigrants was so high that Paul Ginsborg could assert that, in those years, "Turin had become the third-largest 'southern' city after Naples and Palermo."[25] These internal migrations were very expensive for the municipalities of arrival, with urgent measures needed for low-cost housing, public utilities (transport, lighting, water), schools, vocational training, and social and hospital care.[26] However, the responses were inadequate.

Arriving in the metropolises of the north, the immigrants had the problem of finding accommodation. Where were they going to sleep? In Milan, the answer was the so-called Koreas, illegal housing erected by night, probably named after similar buildings appearing during the Korean War.

20. See M. Paci, *Mercato del lavoro e classi sociali in Italia,* 110.

21. P. Corsi, "L'esodo agricolo dagli anni '50 agli anni '70 in Italia e nel Mezzogiorno," 737, table 5.

22. F. Compagna, *I terroni in città,* 17.

23. G. Mottura and E. Pugliese, "Mercato del lavoro e caratteristiche della emigrazione italiana nell'ultimo quinquennio," 238.

24. See L. Meneghetti, *Aspetti di geografia della popolazione,* 178, table 48, for Milan; 174, table 47, for Turin.

25. Ginsborg, *Storia d'Italia dal dopoguerra a oggi,* 298.

26. G. Galeotti, *I movimenti migratori interni in Italia,* 178.

In this case the political responsibilities are all too clear.

In Milan, the building market was literally devastated by the city plan approved in 1953. A third of the entire area covered by this plan belonged to the municipality. In a few years (1951–55), the global value of the area tripled, without the municipal administration implementing any low-cost building policy;[27] the ground was prepared for intense building speculation. Already in 1955, experts were pronouncing "immediately with drastic and summary judgment that in Milan the speculation was triggered by the city plan constraints and by the lack of supervision of the same city plan implementation.... The disorderly city planning, that is, the accumulation of buildings along the sides of the region's arterial roads, unplanned proliferation of private houses without utilities, even inserted into courtyards and internal streets, the arbitrary location of these settlements and the consequent further strain on the transport system, the high-handed assertion of industrial over any local interests—this is the first effect to combat."[28]

The design of the Koreas is not without significance. These cement blocks are arranged so that their doors and windows do not face those of the neighbors. There is a refusal to socialize and to share one's "drama" with the others. The "terrible living conditions"[29] are endured in an entirely private dimension. Problems are kept under wraps, in an atmosphere that increases uncertainties and the sense of loneliness. In a world without a sense of solidarity, "you have to learn how to live and suffer by speaking as little as possible..., not letting the others know what you're thinking."[30] For the numerous immigrants living in basements, "this is a life that can't go on."[31] Under street level, humidity is one of the most serious problems. Everything gets covered in mold. There is not enough air or light. Rainwater continually filters through the walls, producing permanent rheumatism.[32] "Where once

---

27. F. Alasia and D. Montaldi, *Milano, Corea,* 57.

28. This is what we read in Dott. Ing. Lucio Stellario D'Angiolini's paper at the fifth Conference of the Istituto Nazionale di Urbanistica, Florence, 4–6 November 1955. Quoted by F. Alasia and D. Montaldi, *Milano, Corea,* 58, n. 1.

29. U. Ascoli, *Movimenti migratori in Italia,* 146.

30. This is the testimony of someone who had migrated from Naples to Turin, and he continues: "It's certainly awful to be in someone else's house, but I just would like to know this: 'What have we done that you have to treat us so badly? Don't we have the right to a crust of bread just like you? It's true it's easier to hit out at us southerners... it's easier to get angry with us, it doesn't cost anything, eh?' But we can't say these things, we have to keep them inside us, we have to shut up since we're guests." In C. Canteri, *Immigrati a Torino,* 60–61.

31. C. Commare and G. Commare, eds., *Presenti e invisibili,* 95. This is the testimony of "Nardo," age thirty-three, two children, builder. In 1972, he lost three fingers in a work accident.

32. See L. Diena, *Borgata milanese,* 78. The book also offers a reconstruction of the immigrants' accommodations in Milan, with some useful descriptions (68–84).

rabbits played," explains the sociologist Franco Martinelli, groups of six or more people live in "absolutely unhygienic" conditions.[33]

There are no "Koreas" in Turin, but the situation is no less dramatic. In the early sixties, forty-six thousand people were living in attics, basements, in old farmhouses, and in houses destined for demolition. Ninety-eight thousand lived in overcrowded housing. In the attics the facilities—toilets and basins— were in the corridors. Sometimes one facility served forty to fifty people.[34] In 1951, at the time of the census, there were seventy-two families living in shacks. Four years later, they rose to 140 families, a total of 589 people, of whom 56.7 percent came from the south. The lack of public intervention in the Turin building sector had also aggravated the housing problem in an "abnormal"[35] manner. Immigrants were unable to see a rosy future for their children. The food "burned their stomach" and "to be able at least to eat, a boy had to leave school to earn his crust of bread, and, since he didn't earn it every day, he ended up by dropping out of school, unemployed and uneducated."[36]

It wasn't only the factory that changed the face of the nation. Television also played an important role in modernizing Italy, which "would have been impossible without the great technological and cultural advances in the media industry."[37] Television was to become the "dominant medium," "one of the main long-term factors that was to mold our society's moral and mental attitudes."[38]

And while the Italians' cultural universe was changing and the economy experienced "a prodigious growth unprecedented in the country's history,"[39] their institutions came under fire, considered incapable of leading the social change and subjected to "aggressive and categorical criticism."[40] The working masses were losing faith in the trade unions, considered too accommodating to the employers, responsible for "repressive harshness inside the factory walls."[41] The trade-union representatives were criticized and booed,

---

33. F. Martinelli, *Contadini meridionali nella riviera dei fiori.* The book gives the results of a survey of the Unified Service Contributions on Internal Migrations. Neither the date of publication nor the publisher is given.

34. G. Fofi, *L'immigrazione meridionale a Torino,* 180.

35. Ibid., 185.

36. Canteri, *Immigrati a Torino,* 58. The testimony of an immigrant from the south in Turin.

37. F. Monteleone, *Storia della radio e della televisione in Italia,* 424.

38. L. Gorman and D. McLean, *Media e società nel mondo contemporaneo,* 175.

39. M. Magnani, "La vera occasione mancata degli anni '60," 163.

40. G. Martinotti, "Le caratteristiche dell'apatia politica," 297. For a survey of the principal research into political participation in Italy during the "economic boom" years, see R. Biorcio, *Sociologia politica,* 35–39.

41. Lanaro, *Storia dell'Italia repubblicana,* 234.

their proposals rejected. In brief, "civil society had become more political while the political institutes were declining."[42] Individualism was taking over. Careerism, blatant ambition, and "rampant consumption"[43] were accompanying what Vera Zamagni called the "Americanization process"[44] of Italian industry. Social bonds were weakening, spreading a sense of despondency and isolation that in some cases turned into fear. For the workers, the factory was "a prison"[45] and "those who entered Fiat could give up all hope, because when you work on an assembly line, you have no possibility of doing anything else.... 90% of us slept on the tram, arrived home, and prepared for work the next day ... we felt fear ... there was the desert in Fiat during the sixties and you were there alone, abandoned. Either you left or you gave up all hope, you had everyone against you, you couldn't even trust your workmates."[46] The workers were well aware that they were subjected to a staggering work pace. And very soon they had to reckon with a "very unequal"[47] income distribution: their wages had not increased in line with company profits.[48] All this provoked an explosion of conflicts with "generally devastating effects."[49] In 1967, 28 million hours were lost to strikes in industry, rising to some 50 million in 1968 and to over 230 million in 1969.[50] These are years in which "the police hit out fiercely."[51]

The reformist parties had to reckon with "powerful destabilizing forces."[52] These included an openly neofascist culture,[53] which saw the alliance between Christian Democratic and Socialist parties as a risk to be avoided by

---

42. M. Teodori, *Storia delle nuove sinistre in Europa (1956–1976)*, 536.

43. T. Veblen, *The Theory of the Leisure Class*.

44. V. Zamagni, "Un'analisi critica del 'miracolo economico' italiano"; also Zamagni, *Storia economica dell'Italia*, 128.

45. Testimony of a temporary worker to C. Canteri, *Immigrati a Torino*, 64.

46. Luciano Parlanti's testimony in G. Polo, *I tamburi di Mirafiori*, 57.

47. G. Federico and R. Giannetti, "Le politiche industriali," 15:1148.

48. See A. Graziani, *Lo sviluppo dell'economia italiana*, 83. In 1953, employees earned just under 70 percent of the manufacturing industry output; in 1961, their share had fallen to 57 percent; in 1963, it had risen again to 65 percent. Over the next years the trend reversed in favor of wages. See L. Ammassari, *I salari di fatto in Italia*; C. Dell'Aringa, *Occupazione, salari e prezzi*. According to Michele Salvati, the political power of left-wing parties had constituted a "problem" for the Italian economy. Their excessive demands did not take any account of the Italian economy's domestic and international constraints. This "extremist" stance of the left was accompanied by the ruling class's attachment to immediate profit and its incapacity to provide the necessary concessions on the social terrain already in place in other countries (M. Salvati, "Effetti reali o nominali della svalutazione?").

49. P. Scoppola, *La Repubblica dei partiti*, 383

50. See G. Crainz, *Il paese mancato*, 322, 325.

51. G. Pansa, "Annarumma," 18.

52. C. H. Maier, "Conti e racconti," 266.

53. For a reconstruction of Italian neofascism, see R. Chiarini and P. Corsini, *Da Salò a Piazza della Loggia*.

all possible means: "For those who...no longer acknowledge the predominance of the beast within them,...who would like to believe...in order and discipline..., who want a true civilization where all the healthy forces of the nation live in harmony,"[54] the first center-left government (December 1962) represented the "collapse of a world and of a system."[55]

"Right of fascism"[56] were those who, following the teaching of Julius Evola, denied that the Italian Constitution had any ethical or political legitimacy, because of the "complete dissolution of our social structure."[57] People, "escaping from freedom,"[58] openly supported the Nazi experience and its model of society, in which they saw the only instrument for guaranteeing "order, harmony, and discipline of the spirit."[59] The *Introduzione ad Adolf Hitler* (1966) by Salvatore De Domenico, appointed secretary of the Brescia section of the MSI (Italian Socialist Movement) in 1962, praised the legacy of Nazism. Hitler was even preferred to Mussolini, judged too moderate.[60] It was in this scenario that the first steps were taken by those who, "by arming themselves," would spread death and desperation in the Italian streets.

Between 1969 and 1985, there were fifty-one victims of right-wing terrorism in Italy,[61] and 150 died during bombings.[62] In April 1969, the Squadre d'azione Mussolini (Mussolini Action Squads) entered into action. Their leaflets proclaimed: "I swear to serve with all strength and, if necessary, with my blood the cause of the fascist revolution for the rebirth of Italy."[63] The "excluded pole,"[64] with its neofascist thugs ready to attack Italian democracy and its constitutionally guaranteed freedoms, could count on the "best demagogical outbursts"[65] of the MSI secretary, Giorgio Almirante, and of its president, Augusto De Marsanich. On 20 November 1970, at the Ninth National Congress of the MSI, these two men stated that "we do not owe either obedience, trust, or respect to this regime."[66] For Cesare Mantovani, secretary

54. S. De Domenico, *La battaglia è vicina,* 8.
55. M. Mainardi, *L'ultima battaglia per la libertà,* 18.
56. F. Cassata, *A destra del fascismo.*
57. M. Mainardi, "Costituzione impossibile," 1.
58. E. Fromm, *Fuga dalla libertà.*
59. S. De Domenico, *Il lavoro nell'Ordine nuovo,* 11.
60. S. De Domenico, *Introduzione ad Adolf Hitler.*
61. See L. Manconi, *Terroristi italiani,* 23.
62. A. Colonna Vilasi, *Il terrorismo.*
63. Quoted from G. C. Marino, *Biografia del Sessantotto,* 400.
64. P. Ignazi, *Il polo escluso.*
65. The expression is that of Giuseppe Carlo Marino, *Biografia del Sessantotto,* 395.
66. Ibid., 396. This extract from Almirante's speech is taken from the proceedings of the first day of the MSI Congress (Rome, 20 November 1970) prepared by the Rome police chief (Parlato) and transmitted the same day to the Police General Command.

of FUAN, the movement of young MSI university followers: "It is possible to reopen a revolutionary discourse on the institutions, and thus our battle stops being in waiting and starts to act; it stops restraining and starts to attack."[67] In the extreme-right circles there were those who proposed "isolating and confining the democratic state as you confine lepers in a leprosarium."[68]

Between 1969 and 1971, 160 members and sympathizers of the MSI and official youth organizations are arrested.[69] Between 1969 and 1973, 95 percent of the episodes of beating, aggression, and damage are attributed to right-wing militants; over half of the attacks for which responsibility was claimed is attributed to extreme-right movements.[70] It was to be Almirante also who acknowledged the presence of violent young people in his party: "Do we also have violent members? I had to admit that many young people close to us or members are unsatisfied and rebel against my orders and my directives."[71] During a press conference in June 1976, Almirante was to justify his party's acceptance of the violent young as an attempt to stop right-wing subversives from establishing their own organization: "For years I have strived, without much success I think, ... to ensure that the so-called right extremism—that exists as a state of mind, a kind of wishful thinking— does not become properly organized. ... The greatest madness for men of the right in Italy would be to consider that a violent right could block the left."[72] The MSI was engaged in "empowering the youth organizations, since the young represent the moral guarantee of a fight against the regime from an anti-Marxist, anticommunist revolution platform."[73] The MSI has educated hundreds of young people "in an antisystemic and extremist culture whose key themes are the alternative to the regime, the final battle, the fascist revolution."[74] According to Almirante, it has recruited young subversives as an "antisubversive" move, although aware that "the FUAN considered itself to be a particular, autonomous movement of a global revolutionary battle."[75]

---

67. Ibid.

68. Ibid., 400. The expression is that of Giacomo De Sario, president of the National Federation of Combatants of the Italian Social Republic and ex-MSI member.

69. See E. Pisetta, "Per una storia del terrorismo nero," 738–70.

70. See D. Della Porta and M. Rossi, *Cifre crudeli*, 20–25; see also R. Minna, "Il terrorismo di destra," 21–72.

71. *Il Secolo d'Italia*, 31 January 1975.

72. *Il Secolo d'Italia*, 1 June 1976.

73. This comes from the final motion of the Eighth SMI Congress, "Mozione finale dell'viii Congresso del Msi," in *L'alternativa in movimento*, 184.

74. Ignazi, *Il polo escluso*, 174.

75. *Documento del Consiglio Nazionale del FUAN* (23 December 1966), in G. Tagliente and S. Mensurati, *Il FUAN*, 25.

But the enemies of democracy were not only to be found in the streets. On 24 September 1969 in Grosseto, the prefect of police Marchione declared his sympathies for the subversive campaign run by the weekly *Il Borghese* that, he said, "wanted to restrain the extreme left's propaganda and action and to give a valid moral and material support to the police" (24 September 1969).[76] The democratic institutions also included the prefect of Palermo, Puglisi, who was prepared to absolve some fascists suspected of various bomb attacks: "Although they show a certain party spirit in carrying out their extreme-right political credo, I don't consider them a danger to the state's democratic order; they all come from good families and it seems they are well behaved and don't have a criminal record."[77] Again in 1960, sixty-two of the sixty-four highest-ranking prefects came from the fascist ranks, as did all the 241 vice-prefects, the 135 police chiefs, and the 139 vice–police chiefs.[78]

In the eyes of the correspondent of *Le Monde,* the Italian situation "seem[ed] to presage civil war." This statement does not seem so exaggerated after the facts of Battipaglia (9–10 April 1969), where the situation in the industry and the workers' exasperation started up "an authentic revolt: two dead, hundreds of wounded, the town hall in flames, the station cut off, the main roads impassable, the Autostrada del Sole blocked by tree trunks and iron girders, hundreds of police fleeing, disarmed, besieged in the barracks, dozens of coaches and buses lying across the streets downtown, fifteen police cars overturned and set on fire."[79]

From 1968 to 1973, Italy had the highest rate of unrest in Europe.[80] In 1968, 4,862,000 workers were involved in labor conflicts.[81] Besides the Battipaglia events, on 2 December 1968, two laborers were killed by the police during a strike in Avola. A general strike followed with impressive demonstrations nationwide. On 27 October 1969, a student was killed by the police during a demonstration against the colonels' regime in Greece. On 19 November, during a general strike for housing, sixty-three demonstrators were wounded in Milan. A policeman also lost his life.[82]

---

76. This is from the prefect Marchione's report to the minister (24 September 1969), in Marino, *Biografia del Sessantotto,* 405.

77. Ibid.

78. C. Pavone, "La continuità dello Stato," 282–83.

79. L. Longo, "Tumulti a Battipaglia."

80. See L. Bordogna and G. C. Provasi, "La conflittualità," 224.

81. See I. Regalia, M. Regini, and E. Reyneri, "Conflitti di lavoro e relazioni industriali in Italia," 69.

82. See N. Magrone and G. Pavese, *Ti ricordi di Piazza Fontana?* vol. 1.

Between 3 January and 12 December 1969, 145 bomb attacks took place (one every three days), ninety-six of which were traced back to extreme-right terrorism, both because of magistrates' investigations and because of the targets (left-wing parties, synagogues, partisan monuments, etc.). On 15 April, a bomb exploded in the rector's office of the University of Padua; on 25 April, powerful explosive devices wounded twenty people at the Milan Fair: in August, eight bombs wounded twelve passengers on Italian trains (two devices did not explode); on 12 December, in Milan, a bomb in the Banca Nazionale dell'Agricoltura in Piazza Fontana caused the death of sixteen people.[83]

For Sabino Acquaviva, the political violence in Italy is caused by the disintegration of the social fabric triggered by the sudden changes in the socioeconomic situation; in brief, *disintegration, aggregation, armed struggle*. For an armed revolt to happen, explains Acquaviva, the values of society have to be at least partly rejected. When this occurs, the power structure no longer enjoys the consensus of the governed (*disintegration*). Values opposing the dominant ones are also needed for individuals to group around (*aggregation*). If this condition is met—and if individuals are ready to use violence—we arrive at the armed struggle.[84]

The political socialization of the first Red Brigades occurred in a context of extreme anomic breakdown, with wretched living conditions, radical inequalities, exploitation, discrimination, and collective distress, in which there were also episodes of harsh repression against the working classes, prompted by the continuous obsession of a fascist military coup d'état.[85] An army of culturally alienated and morally uprooted individuals was ready to make its voice heard: "The modern revolution," writes the brigadist Curcio in

---

83. Fundamental on the role of right-wing terrorism in the bombings of republican Italy is F. Ferraresi, *Minacce alla democrazia*. On 1969–70 in particular, see 164ff.

84. S. Acquaviva, *Guerriglia e guerra rivoluzionaria in Italia*, 16–17. Umberto Melotti is the first Italian sociologist to perform an in-depth analysis of the revolutionary phenomena, with his *Rivoluzione e società* (1965). However, it is Luciano Pellicani who hinges his scientific study on it. The year in which the Red Brigades carried out their first homicide (Padua, 17 June 1974), Pellicani published *Dinamica delle rivoluzioni*. Over the next two years he published *I rivoluzionari di professione* (1975) and the edited volume *Sociologia delle rivoluzioni*, containing his study on the relationships between social distintegration processes and revolutionary ruptures ("Capitalismo, modernizzazione e rivoluzione," 1976). On 17 June 1974, during a raid in the MSI offices on via Zabarella in Padua, the Red Brigades killed the MSI militants Giuseppe Mazzola and Graziano Giralucci.

85. "Plan Solo"—involving taking control of the RAI and telephone and telegraph exchanges as well as the arrest of numerous political and trade-union leaders—dates back to the summer of 1964. See *Dossier "Piano solo."* In the memories of the first Red Brigades, the violence of the state against the workers and peasants is described as one of the main sources of hatred for bourgeois society. The book cited contains the Parliamentary Commission on the events of June–July 1964: minority report of the Honorables Terracini, Spagnoli, D'Ippolito, Galante Garrone, and Lami.

January 1971, "gathers up its elements by fishing in turbid waters and venturing into side streets and it finds allies in those who have no power over their lives and who know it."[86]

It was in this "turbid" basin that the Red Brigades were to find the base of their consensus. The first militants were to be forged in this "new magma." Now, as then, the Red Brigades—the title of Prospero Gallinari's autobiography, *Un contadino nella metropoli,* is very apt—live like peasants in the metropolis. They reject the dominant values of a society that they feel oppresses and humiliates them. They live in this world, but they are not a part of it. They set political militancy against the values of careerism and personal success, which—especially in the extreme forms of the armed struggle and clandestinity—is also a socioaffective process that satisfies a fierce need for solidarity and cohesion: the need to rebuild truer and deeper social bonds.[87] All the Red Brigades felt this need, not only the founding members but also those who were to join after their baptism of fire in Milan, the evening of 17 September 1970.[88]

Adriana Faranda, in recalling why she entered the Red Brigades, states: "I feel that the choice of the Red Brigades is the last of possible choices.... I'm looking not only for organizational solidity but for a *feeling of community, of sharing, of solidarity.* Much more important, I think, than pure efficiency."[89] No less significant is the way in which Mario Moretti recalls his communal experience in 1969 in Milan ("Commune of Piazza Stuparich") shared with eighteen young people from various backgrounds (members of student movements, anarchists, Catholics, orthodox Marxists).

Moretti had moved from Porto San Giorgio—a small town in the Marche—to Milan, a city he defines as a "horrible and extraordinary termites' nest."[90] He is homesick and, to escape the solitude of the metropolis, feels the need to construct a community with strong bonds of solidarity.[91]

---

86. R. Curcio in *Nuova resistenza,* January 1971, in D. Settembrini, *Il labirinto rivoluzionario,* 2:277–78. This same extract appears in A. Silj, *Mai più senza fucile,* 120–21.

87. For an "identity-making" approach to the study of political phenomena and for a criticism of the economic theory of democracy, see A. Pizzorno, "Sulla razionalità della scelta democratica," in Pizzorno, *Le radici della politica assoluta,* 145–84; also Pizzorno, "Mutamenti nelle istituzioni rappresentative e sviluppo dei partiti politici," 961–1031.

88. At eight thirty p.m. on 17 September 1970, in Milan, on via Moretto da Brescia, a peaceful residential street in the Città Studi district, two bombs exploded against the garage of Giuseppe Leoni, personnel manager in Sit-Siemens. The Red Brigades symbol was painted on the door of the garage. See M. Clementi, *Storia delle Brigate rosse,* 25.

89. Testimony of Adriana Faranda to S. Mazzocchi, *Nell'anno della tigre,* 70–71. Italics added.

90. M. Moretti, *Brigate rosse,* 4.

91. Ibid., 4–5. Moretti recalls: "I lived in a beautiful town in the Marche called Porto San Giorgio. It's on the Adriatic coast, and on one part there's the countryside and Leopardi's famous

It was an exhilarating experience, he recounts, in which "there was no separation between political life and personal life."[92] Moretti was not to find "that
vitality pervading through everything" ever again.

In Moretti's commune, individuals are merged into a single body: "Only
the bedrooms were separate. There was a big common room whose walls
were covered in posters and notes, everyone left their messages there, almost
always containing caustic words against someone. I think they served as an
outlet, or to create a real tolerance, something I've never found again any-
where.... There were couples naturally, but inserted in a structure that served
everyone. At a certain point, almost as if we'd given ourselves a signal, the
couples started having children. I think that the vitality that pervaded everything we were doing needed to project itself into the future.... The outcome
was that the commune became full of babies...and we organized a proper
kindergarten."[93] This need for solidarity, for merging, accompanies every
moment of the Red Brigades' life.

In an anonymous interview given at the time to the journalist Walter
Tobagi, Moretti justifies the choice to live in a commune with these enlightening words: "A family that lives in an immense apartment block is
confused, isolated, and scared. We feel nostalgia for the old patriarchal family, with everyone living in an enormous house. Our communes meet this
need, they re-create a shared life, they save the single person from individual
alienation."[94] Alberto Franceschini defines the experience of the commune
as an authentic "life choice."[95] Patrizio Peci, after describing the anger and
frustration of his job as a factory worker, writes: "Thank God there was the
Organization. I had an appointment twice a week with the Organization.
When you're alone, when you make holes in plastic all day, eat in a trattoria,
and sleep with strangers, you either go mad or do something. If you have
a goal, an important goal, then it's all more bearable. Some have the soccer
team, some have their wives, some their automobiles. I had the Organization,
and through the Organization I was convinced I was also working for the
good of those who thought only of their wives, their soccer team, or their
automobiles."[96]

---

hills, on the other, the sea.... Countryside, sea, castle—in a place like this, childhood is never sad.
I remember it as a happy time. My family was poor, at home we ate mostly bread and mortadella,
but we were okay."

92. Ibid., 15.
93. Ibid.
94. Quoted from S. Flamigni, *La sfinge delle Brigate rosse,* 34. The author does not give the
source.
95. G. Fasanella and A. Franceschini, *Che cosa sono le BR,* 61.
96. P. Peci, *Io, l'infame,* 53.

The first Red Brigades members were united by having shared the same condition of marginality and uprootedness. Their entry into the Red Brigades represented the chance to re-create their lost solidarity. Sociologists know that "those who participate in a movement, who constitute a sect, who are active members of a progressive party, do not do it out of personal interest, they do not have an egoistic and utilitarian purpose. They are prompted by solidarity with the others, their brothers and comrades, and their action is anti-utilitarian."[97] Like every "true believer," the Red Brigades accept the sacrifice to give "a value and a significance to their futile and empty existences."[98]

Renato Curcio, Mario Moretti, Prospero Gallinari, Raffaele Fiore, Patrizio Peci, and Valerio Morucci, to cite just some of the more famous names, were typically alienated individuals. Without the necessary means, or, at any rate, not prepared to accept the continuous challenges of a self-propelled economy, they developed a profound revulsion from and a visceral hatred of the world around them. Their defense was a strategy of attack.

The Red Brigades—to recall Friedrich Nietzsche's admirable lecture on the slave revolt in morality—are *men of resentment:* "Impotence generates in them a hate that becomes monstrous and sinister, extremely spiritual and poisonous to the highest degree. . . . The man of *ressentiment* is neither upright nor honest and straightforward with himself. His soul *squints;* his spirit loves hiding places, secret paths and back doors, everything covert entices him as *his* world, *his* security, *his* refreshment. He understands about remaining silent, not forgetting, waiting, temporarily diminishing himself, humiliating himself."[99]

The Red Brigades do not act, they react. To come out of the marginality affecting them in *this world,* they define themselves and their actions as "good," "just," in antithesis to everything considered "bourgeois" and thus corrupt. Once again, it is in the revolutionary sect that we find the roots of this *metamorphosis of morality* that enables professional revolutionaries to see themselves as "totally diverse" and to claim they belong to "a higher rank."

The revolutionary group possesses what we could define as the "culture of the catacombs."

Outside the community of absolute revolution there is only pain and unhappiness. You have to leave the world because any contact with bourgeois society attacks the purity of the elect. Gnostic activists live hidden

97. F. Alberoni, *Movimenti sociali e società italiana,* 114.
98. E. Hoffer, *The True Believer,* 24.
99. F. W. Nietzsche, *Genealogia della morale,* 59.

underneath Western civilization. They come out only to strike. This is a hard-and-fast rule and no exceptions can be made. The relationship with *this world* can only be one of profound hatred and absolute loathing. Everything has to perish for everything to be regenerated.

The "Cultural Lag" Theory

Prospero Gallinari also came from the "magma" that the brigadist Fiore spoke about.

In 1954 Prospero moved from Villa Ospizio to Villa Mancasale (Reggio Emilia), where his family's living conditions got drastically worse. Gallinari recounts that "I was only three and I wasn't able to understand the change that occurred in my family's fortunes. To go from renting a farmhouse to the *mezzadria* (share-cropping) state meant a fall in status. Our poverty increased; although it had existed before, it was better supported in the other house. In the *mezzadria* system the landowner got half of everything. So killing a chicken or a rabbit meant you had to share it with the landowner, as well as eggs, milk, and anything else produced on the farm. In the end not much remained, and we often ate polenta and vegetables, a lot of vegetables. . . . I ate vegetables for years because there wasn't anything else. . . . We didn't even know what meat was. . . . We were in a wretched condition, even if you couldn't actually say we went hungry: in spring we started with tomatoes, salad, and green beans . . . till I was sick of them; and then winter with beans and potatoes; and the season of pears, apples, grapes."[100]

Gallinari also came from that incandescent basin of men and women incapable of living in this world, or anyway not prepared to do so. A world that Gallinari didn't like, which he deeply hated and which he would have liked to do away with: "All the memories I managed to collect about my ancestors showed that the Gallinaris had always been farmworkers. Poor peasants who, from generation to generation, worked the land owned by others. Hence the most significant element of their lives was the struggle against hunger."[101]

While other social groups rose rapidly thanks to the economic boom, Prospero Gallinari can see only a life of sacrifices in front of him. He is a farmworker, and his family tradition forces him to work the land. Clashes with his parents are inevitable: "Being a farmworker," he explains, "is the pits." He wants a different life. He is well aware that "earth and manure are

---

100. P. Gallinari, *Un contadino nella metropoli*, 18.
101. Ibid., 10.

dirty and stick to you, and in the winter you have to prune and take care of the plants even if they're wet and cold. . . . The dirt . . . sticks to your hand, gets ingrained in your skin. A special kind of dirt because you can't get rid of it either with soap or other detergents. It's a mixture of wrinkled and stained skin, a strange color that gets into the lines and cuts on your hands. A color that tells the whole world that you're a peasant. *At that time, among the young, being a farmworker is the pits.* For the girls it's *as if you were a bearer of the plague.* There was a saying then, used mostly by mothers for their daughters: '*En spusar mai un cuntadein!!*' (Never marry a hick)."[102]

Renato Curcio is an emblematic figure. Besides having theorized and founded the Red Brigades, he fully embodies the typical traits of the marginal and alienated individual who finds an answer to his existential drama in revolutionary politics. His life is full of "radical breaks."[103] He is born in Monterotondo, a town near Rome, on 23 September 1941, to eighteen-year-old Jolanda Curcio. Jolanda is a maid in the house of an old lady. Here she meets Renato Zampa, with whom she has a brief relationship, enough to conceive the future architect of the Red Brigades (Curcio was to learn his father's identity when he was about twelve). Jolanda does not have the means to bring up her son, and when he's just a few months old, she hands him over to a family from Torre Pellice, a hamlet in the Piedmontese mountains. Curcio remains with the Paschetto family until he is ten.

After elementary school, he is faced with a "dramatic decision,"[104] to leave Torre Pellice for a priests' college in the Rome suburbs, Don Bosco of Centocelle. He rebels, closing up into an "almost autistic sphere of silence and refusal."[105] He doesn't talk, he doesn't study. He runs away various times, in search of his uncle Luigi Zampa, the only family link. After failing his exams, he has to move from Rome to Imperia, where he is taken in by another family until he's fifteen. He continues his revolt. He doesn't study and is failed again. A professor threatens to send Curcio to a reformatory. He's panic-stricken and seeks an escape. He decides to study the minimum necessary to become independent. He leaves school at fifteen and is employed as an elevator operator in the Hotel Cavalieri of Milan. He takes up his studies again and obtains a diploma. In the autumn of 1961 he is hired by Pirelli in Milan.

---

102. Ibid., 42. Italics added.

103. R. Curcio, *A viso aperto,* 14. Arrested on 8 September 1974, he is liberated by an armed nucleus of the Red Brigades on 18 February 1975. He is again arrested on 18 February 1976. He has spent eighteen years in prison.

104. Ibid., 18.

105. Ibid.

Curcio had tremendous psychological difficulties adapting to Milan and the city had a huge effect on him. They take him to a "black smoke" section, which he describes as a "foggy black nightmare"[106] from which he wants only to escape. He wants to burn his bridges and start another life. He is walking alone along a street in Milan and suddenly, out of the blue, he decides to hitchhike. By chance he finds himself in Genoa, the first town encountered along the way. Here he spends a "rather absurd and vagabond" year in which he lives "on the edge."[107] He sleeps on a bench, he hasn't got any means of support. One night he meets a young man who has run away from home after quarreling with his family. The man invites him to stay in the house of his girlfriend, a prostitute. Curcio delivers papers to the newsagents, works as a docker in the port and a waiter. He slowly slips into alcoholism. He takes methedrine. He's miserable, his life is falling about his ears: "It was a hellish period and I was about to fall into extreme mental confusion."[108] His friend, also an alcoholic, collapses and is admitted to the hospital. Curcio realizes that his life in Genoa is a one-way street. Sometime before, in a bar near the port, a man had talked to him about the imminent opening of the Faculty of Sociology in Trento. He remembers that fact. He likes the idea. He says good-bye to his friend in the hospital and, "light as a feather,"[109] takes the train to Trento.

Curcio confesses—and this is an extremely important detail—that when he starts his new life in Trento, he doesn't know anything about politics. Thanks to his educational qualifications, he obtains a scholarship.

In the autumn of 1963, he starts to attend his first lectures in sociology, which were to have a profound effect on his future life choices.[110] Like Moretti in Milan, Curcio also founds a commune. He sets up in a "half-ruined" house on the banks of the river Adige. Three sleep there at night, but the house is open to everyone during the day.

For many, acceptance of the Marxist-Leninist ideology—with its ability to respond to every query about human existence[111]—and membership in the

106. Ibid., 21.
107. Ibid., 23.
108. Ibid., 25.
109. Ibid., 26.
110. Vincenzo Tessandori has attributed great importance to the Trento university experience in the birth of the Red Brigades: "The Red Brigades' story started in the university corridors in Trento, where in 1962, a Higher Institute of Social Sciences (ISSS) was created, soon transformed into a public university." V. Tessandori, *Br. imputazione,* 28.
111. Through Marx's and Lenin's categories, the Red Brigades explain every aspect of social life, including the inefficiency of automobile alarms. See, for example, *Risoluzione della direzione strategica* of April 1975, where it is asserted that "capitalism" would have a real interest in encouraging

Red Brigades represented a form of compensation. They procured an incredible satisfaction of a need they would never have been able to find in civil society. Curcio removed himself from the world, in which he felt an outsider, to enter a group with very close bonds of solidarity and in which everyone could have a "heroic" function. The Red Brigades felt part of a "great plan" that transformed them all into "martyrs" of the revolution.

This brings to mind Émile Durkheim's lesson: if left to themselves, people are incapable of self-regulation. Human needs and desires are potentially unlimited. This is why our impulses can be restrained only by shared values (this is what Durkheim means by society's "moral authority[112]"). Values, regulations, and institutions (understood as models of behavior with coercive power) stop us from falling into the vortex of our passions. Society is a "safety net." When it is affected by sudden and radical changes, its members' lifestyles, sentiments, and expectations are shaken. This initiates a "crisis" that makes the most solid certainties and customs waver. Alternative visions of the world are developed; there is no longer consensus on principles that had seemed unshakable. Society's moderating role is weakened and individuals plummet into "anomie" (literally, "absence of rules"), or into a condition of disorientation and abandonment, which can also lead—these are Renato Curcio's words—"to the brink of an extreme mental confusion."

Durkheim writes that "life is said to be intolerable unless some reason for existing is involved. Some purpose justifying life's trials. The individual alone is not a sufficient end for his activity. He is too little. He is not only hemmed in spatially; he is also strictly limited temporally. When, therefore, we have no other object but ourselves, we cannot avoid the thought that our efforts will finally end in nothingness, since we ourselves disappear. But annihilation terrifies us. Under these conditions one would lose the courage to live, to act, and to struggle, since nothing would remain of our exertions."[113]

---

criminality, which would help make the middle classes even richer and happier. Fiat, we read, could build thief-proof automobiles, but it prefers for them to be stolen. Car thefts are in its interest. In this *Resolution* we read: "Marginal individuals are a product of the capitalistic society in its current stage of development and they are continually increasing in number. They are used by the capitalistic society, since it is a consumer society, as consumers. But they are consumers without wages. Hence 'criminality' is born. Capitalism's 'economic' use of criminality lies in the fact that it helps destroy the goods needed to continue the cycle. *To make it clearer, it is entirely possible to produce thief-proof cars, but this is not in Fiat's interest*" (italics added). *Risoluzione della direzione strategica* in *Dossier Brigate rosse,* 1:355.

112. Durkheim's expression "moral authority" needs explaining. For Durkheim, individuals live in harmony as long as society is based on the respect of shared values. But this does not mean that these values have to be "imposed." Durkheim explains that "society's power" lasts only if obeyed "through respect and not fear." It comes from consensus and not force. E. Durkheim, *Il suicidio.*

113. Ibid., 259.

When society is shaken by unexpected changes, whether favorable or not, individuals have to carry out a "cultural conversion" to enable them to respond suitably to the new challenges. But changes involving the cultural sphere are much slower and more difficult than economic ones. Culture and economy do not advance at the same pace. For some individuals, changing their values and models of behavior can require an intolerable effort. So the "conversion" fails, creating a feeling of rejection. Love for "tradition" becomes an obsession, increasing the mistrust, or even rejection, of the surrounding world.

The lesson of the American sociologist William F. Ogburn is just as valuable as Durkheim's.

Ogburn's theory of the *cultural lag* starts with the distinction between *material culture* (technological and industrial know-how) and *nonmaterial culture* (ideas, values, sentiments). The material culture is much more dynamic than the nonmaterial one, which has continuously to adapt to the former (it is also called "adaptive culture"). In Ogburn's words: "Changes in the material culture force changes in other parts of culture, but these latter parts of culture do not change as quickly. They lag behind the material culture changes."[114]

Using an opposite approach to the Marxist one—which tends to conceive nonmaterial culture (ideology) as a reflection of the underlying economic structure—Ogburn finds a *tension* between the *rapidity* with which the material culture changes and the *slowness* of the adaptive culture. An example of cultural lag is technological development that demands greater participation of women in the labor force and families' consequent difficulty in accepting their new role in society.[115]

Durkheim and Ogburn's contributions are summarized and further developed in Gino Germani's social mobilization model.

Germani also agrees that social change, especially when rapid and deep, always involves a certain disintegration in the social fabric. When this happens, a very complex process is triggered that changes relationships among the classes.

---

114. W. F. Ogburn, *Social Change with Respect to Culture and Original Nature,* 196. A summary of Ogburn's thinking can be found in Ogburn, *Tecnologia e mutamento sociale.* See also A. Izzo, *Storia del pensiero sociologico,* 269–70.

115. Another example regards the development of nuclear weapons. They are potentially capable of extinguishing the human race, but a culture that can prevent such a danger has not yet been developed (see N. J. Smelser, *Manuale di sociologia*). Various factors can cause the cultural gap, among them simple habit, the strength and endurance of traditional values, and the existence of interests in maintaining the established order.

Germani breaks down this process into six stages:

1. Individuals are inserted in a certain social order.
2. A *rupture* alters the harmony of the system.
3. Some individuals and groups are first "uprooted" and then projected into a new social-relations network (*dislocation* stage).
4. The groups most affected by the consequences of the social change react, preparing themselves to embrace new models of behavior (*reaction* stage).
5. A constructive stage starts, during which the marginal groups work out responses and possible solutions to their problems.
6. The cycle of social mobilization closes with the *reintegration* stage, in which the social groups reconstruct new social bonds and harmony is restored to the different parts of the system.[116]

The Red Brigades were created, first of all, as a "rejection" of the "dislocation" processes affecting Italy during the economic-boom years. It was an economic, political, and psychological trauma that produced a sensation of uprootedness, always accompanied by a feeling of desertion and isolation. Thus formed what Arnold J. Toynbee (1889–1975) called the internal proletariat, that is, a "psychological class" that includes individuals of very different social extraction, but all united by their resentment toward a social order that handicaps them. They have lost any bond of loyalty toward the institutions and dominant models and are ready to support radical solutions against the existing order.

To understand the genesis of the Red Brigades, Toynbee's theory can be very instructive. He helps us shed light on the stage we are interested in, that of *dislocation*. To clarify the consequences of this phenomenon, social scientists make use of the concept of *relative deprivation,* which can be defined as the difference between our expectations and their satisfaction. In Ted R. Gurr's words, relative deprivation is the "actors' perception of discrepancy between their value expectations and their value capacities. Value expectations are the goods and conditions of life to which people believe they are rightfully entitled. Value capabilities are the goods and conditions they think they are capable of getting and keeping."[117]

---

116. G. Germani, *Sociologia della modernizzazione,* 94.

117. Particularly instructive is T. Gurr's definition of relative deprivation in *Why Men Rebel,* 24. Also important are studies by S. A. Stouffer, *The American Soldier,* vol. 1; R. K. Merton, *Social Theory and Social Structure;* W. G. Runciman, *Relative Deprivation and Social Justice.*

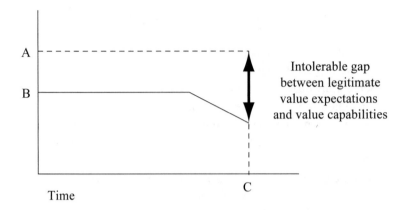

FIGURE 2. Decremental deprivation. L. Pellicani, *Dinamica delle rivoluzioni,* 135, adapted from a figure in J. C. Davies, "Toward a Theory of Revolution," 135.

According to Gurr, political, rebellious, and revolutionary violence comes from the discrepancy between what an individual or group consider they have the right to obtain and what they believe they can effectively obtain.[118] Relative deprivation can be caused either by increasing expectations concerning an actual unchanged situation (*aspirational deprivation*); or by the fact that the group's perceived situation worsens over time (*decremental deprivation*); or, finally, by the presence of both conditions, that is, expectations rise and the perceived situation deteriorates (*progressive deprivation*). The greater and more extensive the perception of relative deprivation by the members of a group, the greater possibility that these will use collective violence against other groups or against the political regime in force.[119]

James C. Davies has drawn a graph of the relationship between the dissatisfaction of the governed and revolutionary ruptures (see figure 2).

The *decremental deprivation* diagram indicates the dissatisfaction caused by a worsening of the real situation compared to stable value expectations.

Line A represents value expectations; line B, value capabilities. Point C indicates the moment at which the insurrection explodes. Decremental deprivation is typical of jacqueries, who do not want to upset the fundamental

---

118. As Davies wrote: "Our desires and pleasure spring from society; we measure them, therefore, by society and not by the objects which serve for their satisfaction. Because they are of a social nature, they are of a relative nature" (J. C. Davies, "Toward a Theory of Revolution," in *When Men Revolt and Why,* ed. J. C. Davies, 135).

119. See T. D. Gurr, *Why Men Rebel.* For a summary of Gurr's contribution, see M. Stoppino, *Potere e teoria politica,* 83, 84. Stoppino's bibliographic references are also useful at 66, n. 4. Part of the relevant literature is also present in L. Bonante, ed., *La violenza politica nel mondo contemporaneo.*

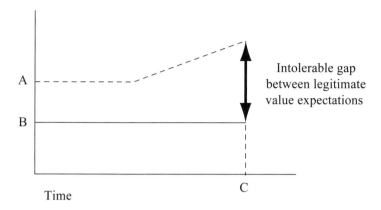

FIGURE 3. Aspirational deprivation. L. Pellicani, *Dinamica delle rivoluzioni*, 135, adapted from a figure in J. C. Davies, "Toward a Theory of Revolution," 135.

values of society but rebel against abuses that have become particularly intolerable. This is a revolt that proposes to reestablish customs that have been crushed. It is a violence that looks to the past and not to the future. Its effects are therefore contained. The established order is not challenged.

The *aspirational deprivation* diagram (see figure 3) indicates the dissatisfaction caused by a rise in expectations (line A) in a stable situation (line B). It is a phenomenon typical of capitalistic societies characterized by intense social mobility processes. In a continually changing world, social groups start to compare their position with that of the reference groups. The improvement in the conditions of group x can cause group y to retaliate. This signifies that the propensity to protest against the existing order can also occur when a country's wealth is growing, after some individuals improve their social position, arousing resentment in those who have the impression of not advancing.

The case of *progressive deprivation* is the most explosive, because the increase in expectations is accompanied by the deterioration of real conditions (see figure 4). In this case what Neil J. Smelser calls "structural propensity to violence" is created.[120] When progressive deprivation strikes wide bands of the population, even a relatively insignificant event can trigger revolt against the authorities. On condition, however, that there is an ideology capable of steering the masses' dissatisfaction toward a specific political target. Left to themselves, the masses are incapable of defining the causes of their frustration. They need someone from outside to work out a new plan for social change, pointing out the "friends" and "enemies" of the revolution. This

120. N. J. Smelser, *Il comportamento collettivo.*

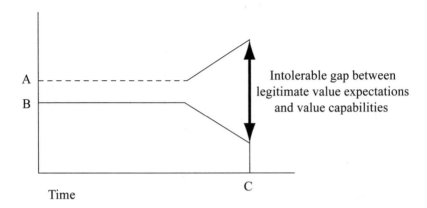

FIGURE 4. Progressive deprivation. L. Pellicani, *Dinamica delle rivoluzioni*, 135, adapted from a figure in J. C. Davies, "Toward a Theory of Revolution," 135.

is the task of the intellectuals, who provide the new representations of the world so necessary to the masses.

For the sociologist of revolutionary phenomena, the way in which individuals perceive their role in the world is very important. As Maurice Duverger has written: "In sociology nothing is really natural, everything is cultural."[121] There is always a gap between the objective reality and how it is perceived. From this angle, political ideologies are themselves agents of social change because they represent the medium between the individual and reality, affecting our "scale of values." What is desirable for some is not so for others. Members of revolutionary sects have no use for economic success. This aspiration of some social groups is disdained by those who have embraced the utopia of the "total revolution."

This leads us to conclude that it is not hunger in itself that makes the masses revolt but the conviction that they are victims of injustice. Without the support of an ideology of protest, poverty can distance people from politics, driving them toward fatalism and superstition.[122] Someone whose vision of the world justifies exploitation will never be a rebel. Trotsky wrote that "the mere existence of privations is not enough to cause an insurrection: if it were, the masses would always be in revolt. It is necessary that the bankruptcy of the social regime, being conclusively revealed, should make these privations intolerable, and that new conditions and new ideas should open the prospect of a revolutionary way out."[123]

---

121. M. Duverger, *Sociologia della politica*, 89.
122. See D. Bell, *The End of Ideology*, 31.
123. L. Trotsky, *Storia della rivoluzione russa*, 651.

As Tocqueville explains in his analysis of the change in public opinion in revolutionary France, what drives some social groups to protest is not the impossibility of achieving all their desires, but just those considered "legitimate" on the basis of a given system of rules.[124] Every individual works out his or her goals in relation to their environment. It follows that "a group will be and will feel integrated in society only to the extent to which it obtains what it believes is due to it, that is, only if its culturally defined expectations are at least partly satisfied. Its behavior will be laid down by the normative system and made possible by environmental circumstances."[125] So—this is the lesson of the main theorists of relative deprivation—those who believe they have the right to possess more than they already have are potential rebels.

So far we have examined the role of the masses and the intellectuals. The former provide the violence needed to demolish the established order, the latter the plan for social transformation. But there is a third actor in revolutionary processes: the elite in power. Frustrated masses and radical intellectuals are not enough, in themselves, to guarantee the success of a revolution. The group controlling the coercive apparatus has to have lost its creative abilities. Ideas trigger revolutions; ideas can stop them. A revolutionary crisis is, first of all, a challenge to the governance capabilities of the minority leading society. Revolutions are sudden, but revolutionary processes are gradual. The violence of the governed is unleashed when the political elites show they are incapable of responding adequately to the changes under way. Failure after failure, they lose the faith of the governed. The frustration that the "dislocated" groups feel, if ideologically directed, has repercussions on the political system, which is asked to tackle the new requirements of a rapidly changing society. The demands of the governed increase, in quantity and quality. The ensuing pressure becomes unsustainable, causing an authentic "decisional collapse." No society is able to satisfy all the legitimate expectations of its members. This means that the social mobilization process, producing what David Easton has called the "failure of the outputs,"[126] exposes the political elite to the risk of losing their authority, that is, losing the consensus of the governed.

The genesis of the Red Brigades was a consequence of the social mobilization process and of the accompanying dislocation. Their foundation was a declaration of war on an entire system of values (competition, individualism, etc.) carried by the wave of modernization in postwar Italy. In other words,

---

124. See A. de Tocqueville, "L'antico regime e la rivoluzione," in his *Scritti politici,* 1:764–65.

125. Pellicani, *Dinamica delle rivoluzioni,* 130.

126. D. Easton, *A Systems Analysis of Political Life,* 403.

the Red Brigades were the "victims of the great transformation."[127] They were suffering from a psychological unease that had a social origin.

This is what Curcio writes in November 1969: "We are deeply scarred by an alienated social life.... A weak, neurotic, alienated, egoistic, individualist, and manipulated ego is a fact to reckon with: it is a fact of our revolution."[128] We know that this "fact" existed in Curcio, because he had been well aware of this "ego" during his experience in Genoa. And it is the same "ego" that marks the youth of Valerio Morucci, who recounts with these dramatic words the mental condition with which you approach the armed struggle: "After drifting for a bit, because I had some money that was no longer any use, *I started to be ashamed of myself. The world continued to be a disaster.* Violence after violence and abuse after abuse. It couldn't go on. I had an urge inside, a commotion that brought me to tears, but which wasn't even ideological anymore. It came before. From far away. I couldn't ignore it."[129] The brigadist Maurizio Rotaris also sought an escape in politics from "that state of mental debilitation and breakdown"[130] caused by heavy drugs.

The first members of the Red Brigades saw their present condition as a nightmare and were firmly decided to change it. The prospect of spending all their lives "working for someone else" seemed no less "terrifying." They felt victims of injustice, abandoned to a painful and hopeless fate. "Emptied" of value, uprooted from their original communities, subjected to the "merciless" laws of capitalism, they felt like outsiders in the hated and despised "new world." This helps us understand Renato Curcio when he says, in an article from January 1971, that "the 'dregs' of society are the vanguard of the revolution."[131] Curcio realized that an army of rootless and frustrated individuals had been created by the "mobilization" process affecting Italy, ready to embrace new radical ideas of revenge and emancipation.

When Were the Red Brigades Born?

It is with this "lack of meaning," and the relative need for something significant, that Curcio arrives in Trento. Here he encounters the student movement and starts out on the political path that will lead him to found the Red

---

127. The expression refers to professional revolutionaries and is from L. Pellicani, "Capitalismo, modernizzazione, rivoluzione," 22.

128. *Social Struggle and Organization in the Metropolis,* in *Dossier Brigate rosse,* 1:57.

129. V. Morucci, *La peggio gioventù,* 108. Italics added.

130. Testimony of Maurizio Rotaris to L. Guicciardi, *Il tempo del furore,* 237.

131. R. Curcio in *Nuova resistenza.*

Brigades. In September 1969 he founds, with Corrado Simioni, the Collettivo Politico Metropolitano—CPM (Metropolitan Political Collective). In November 1969 the CPM meets in Chiavari, where Curcio gives a long address, *The Social Struggle and Organization in the Metropolis,* mentioned earlier. The meeting discusses moving to a new political stage, as well as to a better and more efficient organizational structure.

Contrary to what Alberto Franceschini claimed in an interview of 1988, we regard Curcio's address as the manifesto of the armed struggle in Italy.

Franceschini has played down the importance of the Chiavari "congress," stating that "we discussed only how the newborn Collettivo Politico Metropolitano should move. We didn't talk about the armed struggle, and 'going underground' was rejected as a political stance."[132] The step toward the armed struggle, Franceschini concludes, was decided later, at Pecorile, in August 1970. There are two things that cast doubt on this testimony. The first is the contradiction present in Franceschini's words. If it is true that the armed struggle entails going underground, it is difficult to understand how Franceschini could state that "we didn't talk about the armed struggle" at Chiavari and then immediately after claim that the proposal to go underground was rejected. If the hypothesis of going underground was examined, this means that the possibility of passing to the armed struggle was also agreed. Furthermore, the "22 October 1969" group—the first to have embraced the armed struggle—was active in Genoa and it is very likely that some of its members went to Chiavari (forty-four kilometers from Genoa), both to follow the CPM developments and to spread their ideas and seek new militants. Nor were the "22 October" ideas traveling alone in that period. In July 1969, Giangiacomo Feltrinelli had already published his article "Summer 1969: The Impending Threat of a Radical and Authoritarian Shift to the Right, of an Italian-Style Coup d'État." In his conclusions, the author decreed that capitalism could not be eliminated through "a bottom-up peaceful revolution,"[133] announcing the "closing stages not only of revisionism, but also of the idea of a socialist revolution *without the critical support of weapons.*"[134]

The second element is decisive. It concerns the address that Curcio read in Chiavari, the entire text of which is available today.

---

132. A. Franceschini, *Mara, Renato e io,* 23.

133. G. Feltrinelli, *Estate 1969,* 19. Italics added. Another two papers preceded this: "Italy 1968: Theories and Proposals for a Communist Vanguard" (probably written in Cuba in January 1968) and "The Threat of a Coup d'État in Italy Persists" (April 1968). Only two typewritten copies of the first text were issued. The second was published, with slight variations, by the periodical *La Sinistra,* no. 3, 1968. See G. Galli, *Il partito armato,* 16, n. 1.

134. Feltrinelli, *Estate 1969,* 9.

The document contains the following words of the Brazilian revolutionary Marcelo De Andrade: "Today, given that the possibility of an interimperialist war is historically excluded, an alterative proletarian power must be, *from the beginning*, political-military, given that the armed struggle is the main form of the class struggle."[135] Curcio follows this with: "The bourgeoisie has already chosen illegality. The long march in the metropolises is the only adequate response. It has to begin *here and now*."[136]

The document is clear.

My conclusion is that at Chiavari, in early November 1969, the idea of the armed struggle was tackled because it was already on the agenda. It was debated, and not all were in agreement. We are left even more perplexed when, in an attempt to describe the impact of the Piazza Fontana bombings on the decision to move to armed struggle, Curcio states that "in the Collective, located in an old abandoned theater on via Curtatone, we sang, we put on plays, we organized graphics exhibitions. It was a continual explosion of playfulness and invention. The atmosphere changed after the bombings."[137] But, as the paper that Curcio gave in Chiavari—which contains a violent declaration of war against the bourgeoisie and the entire world—proves, the atmosphere in the Collettivo Politico Metropolitano was anything but "lighthearted" before the Piazza Fontana bombing.[138]

Franceschini confesses that his first reconstruction is disingenuous. In an interview given in 2004 (sixteen years after his first version of the facts) he admits, after an initial evasive answer, that "our armed struggle was being planned before Piazza Fontana, independently of the killings. However, in our eyes, Piazza Fontana constitutes the proof that our plan was necessary and sound, and it hastened its implementation."[139] It is obvious that these words belie Franceschini's first version and confirm my thesis that the step toward armed struggle was decided before 12 December 1969. Even more incredible is what Franceschini said when interviewed by Sergio Zavoli (1992), where he categorically denies that he had ever believed in a coup d'état being carried out in Italy: "We never believed in the possibility of a right-wing coup in Italy. In our opinion, coups were simply put-up affairs by political bodies

---

135. *Social Struggle and Organization in the Metropolis*, in *Dossier Brigate rosse*, 1:49.

136. Ibid. Italics added.

137. Curcio, *A viso aperto*, 49.

138. Danilo Breschi, after studying Italian society in the year before the Red Brigades came on the scene, concluded that already in 1968 some left-wing groups were ready to take the route of the "flight forward" by minorities who spoke about "profound injustices" and terrible repressions inside and outside the universities of republican Italy. D. Breschi, *Sognando la rivoluzione*, 251.

139. Fasanella and Franceschini, *Che cosa sono le BR*, 56.

inside the state to support its reorganization along authoritarian lines."[140] However, it was a Red Brigades member, Valerio Morucci, who demolished the thesis of the armed struggle as a "reaction" to the nameless bombings. He reckoned this was "bullshit."

Morucci's words are important because they indirectly attack the thesis of the "system block." Morucci writes that "if anyone tries to say—and some whiners have already tried—that we did all this because the generals passed their time planning coups d'état and internment camps in Sardinia, and because the fascists were organizing bombings, then they are very mistaken. Certainly, that whole atmosphere fed our hate for the bosses. . . . *But we couldn't have cared less if the PCI had managed to achieve 51 percent:* we wanted to make a revolution against the capitalists who were plundering the social wealth produced by the proletariat. That's all."[141]

Prospero Gallinari, in an interview from 2006, does not ascribe much importance to the strategy of fascist bombings in the genesis of the Red Brigades. He thought that people needed to be convinced that there were actually the conditions for a revolution to pass to the armed struggle. In the end, Morucci and Gallinari explain, the "revolutionary illusion" was the trigger that started the process. In Gallinari's words: "There are some who say that it was after the Piazza Fontana bombings that a part of the movement chose to pass to the armed struggle. It's true that this inflamed the debate, but it wasn't the main reason for our choices. I think it was because the great international revolutionary movement made us think there was an actual possibility of revolution here. Just think, for example, of what was happening in China at that time. All the analyses prompted us to assess the hypothesis of a revolution."[142]

Why—we have to ask ourselves—did Franceschini want people to believe that the possibility of the armed struggle was discussed only in August 1970? The reason is only too evident: if Franceschini and company were advocating the armed struggle after the Piazza Fontana bombings (Milan, 12 December 1969), it could have been prompted by the "strategy of tension" launched by the fascist and deviated secret services. This version is still widely accepted in Italian left-wing circles. If instead the decision to espouse the military-political cause was taken before the Milan deaths, this means that the roots of the armed struggle have to be sought in the Red Brigades' ideology.

This is a delicate topic and needs to be clarified.

---

140. S. Zavoli, *La notte della Repubblica,* 119.
141. Morucci, *La peggio gioventù,* 169. Italics added.
142. P. Pergolizzi interviewing Prospero Gallinari, *L'appartamento,* 172.

I have no interest—nor would I find it interesting—in establishing who were the "good" or the "bad" among fascists, Red Brigades, and deviated secret services. I am reconstructing this particular moment in the Red Brigades' story to defend a methodological principle, namely, that an ideology can change the course of history. Or—if you prefer—that our representation of the world and its future development can be a very powerful instrument of social transformation. Political ideas influence and, in some cases, decide the lives of millions of people. They can be the authentic independent variables of social change. And I think they were for the Red Brigades. As Crane Brinton has so rightly said: "No ideas, no revolution."[143] This does not mean that there is a cause-effect link between ideas and revolutionary ruptures. The simple literary circulation of ideas is not enough to make a revolution. You need individuals and social groups who are prepared to fight for them. And this is exactly what the Red Brigades did when, overwhelmed by the *dislocation* processes, they found the answer to their new problems as marginal individuals in the "revolutionary message."

The Red Brigades: "Imbeciles" or Real Revolutionaries?

I believe that ideology is very important for the Red Brigades.

The time has now come to reconstruct its origins.

Strictly speaking, the term "Red Brigades ideology" is incorrect since all the interpretive categories they used came word for word from the works of Marx and Lenin. Which signifies that the Red Brigades' vision of the world was Marx's and Lenin's vision of human history and coexistence. The numerous political experiences triggered by Marx's and Lenin's writings also included that of the Red Brigades, one of the chapters in the history of Marxism-Leninism. This is the basis of their ideology and it would be arbitrary to remove them from this tradition, although some communist intellectuals are still trying to do so. According to Luciano Canfora, the Red Brigades were neither revolutionaries nor communists but "a few imbeciles, uneducated and maybe even mercenaries."[144]

The fact that they were "uneducated" is open to discussion, because a revolutionary education is measured by the extent of the militant's hatred of society (and cannot therefore be assessed according to "scholastic" guidelines). Also because, even using an "academic" parameter, the educational

143. C. Brinton, *Anatomy of Revolution,* 49.
144. Luciano Canfora in *La Stampa,* 10 May 2008.

Table 3.   Red Brigades membership by level of education

LEVEL OF EDUCATION	NUMBER	PERCENT
Elementary	37	4.1
Lower secondary school	244	26.8
Upper secondary school	188	20.6
University	198	21.7
Missing data	244	26.8
Total	911	100.0

Source: *Progetto memoria,* 60–61.

levels at the time of the arrest and/or questioning of the Red Brigades members submitted to trial (911 in all) demonstrate varying situations that do not fit Canfora's description (see table 3).

As for Canfora's statement that the Red Brigades were "a few imbeciles" and "maybe even mercenaries," the opposite is true. The police authorities are well aware that the Red Brigades "are all loyal, cogent, indoctrinated, and competent militants, neither corrupt nor corruptible."[145] The Red Brigades were really pure and incorruptible. They were to sacrifice their own lives on the altar of communism, prompted by the sincere desire to succeed in an "immense" undertaking: the construction of a "perfect society." Exactly what Marx and Lenin had in mind. I realize that this kind of statement can arouse understandable distress (perhaps even disgust) in the relatives of the Red Brigades' victims. As Andrea Casalegno has written: "You can be an ex-terrorist, but you can't be an ex-killer. You can't give back life because killing is and remains killing."[146] Any academic who tries to understand the causes of political violence is open to misunderstanding and manipulation. Therefore I would ask readers to suspend judgment until they have learned what I offer to support my theories.

Before entering the Red Brigades, Enrico Fenzi was a respected lecturer in Italian literature at the University of Genoa. He was first arrested in 1979. After a few months, he was fully acquitted. He could have gone back to his academic life or fled abroad. Instead, despite his dramatic prison experience, he decided to go underground and continue his struggle with the Red Brigades: "I did it because I wanted to fight for a better world, a different society, because I believed in the revolution."[147]

---

145. These words were spoken by Federico Umberto D'Amato (head of the Ministry of the Interior's Office of Classified Affairs), after Judge Mario Sossi's kidnapping (18 April 1974). *L'Espresso,* 28 April 1974, in S. Flamigni, *La tela del ragno,* 103.

146. Andrea Casalegno talking to A. Grandi, *L'ultimo brigatista,* 101.

147. E. Fenzi, *Armi e bagagli,* 22.

Only a pure spirit, a man driven by an intense ideal of redemption, can renounce his life and say: "I was ready to follow them [the Red Brigades] along a road soaked in blood. Why them? Why in that way? Why was I so cruel to those who loved me? First of all because they were there, in flesh and blood. Perhaps that's the only explanation. Even the strongest ideal needs to become real to be loved, to arouse devotion. I felt it. And what I felt most was that I wanted to merge with the function assigned me. . . . For me it was fundamental—politically and personally fundamental—to accept everything, because they had accepted it. This was the concrete, possible form of being a communist for me. I was ready for anything they would ask of me. This was the sense of my membership in the Red Brigades."[148]

These are the words of Fenzi, who was neither uneducated nor an imbecile nor a mercenary. He was a follower of Lenin, a real revolutionary. He was a man who wanted to demolish capitalism to install the communist society. Lenin had taught him that, to be able to hope for this, you had to create a vanguard of revolutionaries prepared to use violence against their enemies; and you needed fierce ideological determination.

Fenzi read, learned, and put into practice. So did Giovanni Senzani. A literature graduate from Bologna, Senzani specialized in sociology, publishing various studies on the prison system.[149] He won scholarships abroad. He was a lecturer in education in Florence and a researcher for the CNR (National Research Council). He was first arrested in March 1978 for having a brigadist, Salvatore Bombacci, in his house. Freed after a few months, he went underground, researching a new strategic line to respond to the crisis that was to have struck the organization at the beginning of the eighties.[150]

It is certainly true that "the Red Brigades had nothing to do with the Italian communists,"[151] but not in the sense that Canfora meant. I mean that the only true communist revolutionaries in Italy were the Red Brigades and certainly not the followers of Berlinguer.

The Red Brigades imbibed Marx's and Lenin's lesson that capitalism is born from violence, feeds off violence, and can be destroyed only with violence. The capitalist is always an exploiter, and his allies—we read in a Red Brigades document of 23 December 1980—are "parasites."[152] The history of capitalism is the story of a barbarism that cries for revenge. As long as there is even

---

148. Ibid., 43–44.
149. See G. Senzani, *L'esclusione anticipata*.
150. See Clementi, *Storia delle Brigate rosse*, 272.
151. Luciano Canfora in *La Stampa*, 10 May 2008.
152. *Communiqué no. 4—D'Urso Campaign*. Red Brigades document of 23 December 1980 (www.brigaterosse.org).

one bourgeois on earth, humanity can never be redeemed. This mentality is at the roots of the Marxist-Leninist doctrine. It is summed up best in an article by Antonio Gramsci appearing in *Ordine nuovo* in 1919. We read here that the bourgeoisie represents a "repugnant" class. The communists have the task of eliminating it from society with the same determination with which you eliminate "noxious insects." Only in this way, concludes Gramsci, can society be "purified." In his clear prose: "The lower and middle bourgeoisie are the barrier of corrupt, dissolute, and putrescent humanity with which capitalism defends its economic and political power—a servile, despicable humanity, a humanity of hit men and lackeys. They have become the servant-turned-master, who want to take higher cuts from production—not only from the wages of the working class, but also from the capitalists' share. To expel them from the social field with iron and fire, as if they were a swarm of locusts infesting a semi-destroyed field, means cleansing the national manufacturing and trade system of its oppressive trappings, which suffocate it and prevent it from functioning. It means purifying the social environment."[153]

Antonio Gramsci and the "Hour of Redemption"

Gramsci also had a strictly gnostic concept of progress. He believed that he possessed a superior knowledge and thus felt the right/duty to impose his "truth" with every means. His vision of the world is inspired by the same radical pessimism we find in the Red Brigades' writings.

Gramsci was convinced that he was the victim of a sick world that forced people to the brink of schizophrenia. We are all victims of an "evil power," we are immersed in a "terrible asphyxiating bourgeois reality that is driving society to indiscipline, frenzy, and homicidal chaos. We are bound in a straitjacket that makes us angry and exasperated."[154] For Gramsci, "the proletarian revolution is the greatest revolution" that will make a clean sweep of the present world to build a society that is the "irrevocable fruit of the fatal process of human civilization."[155] The Party has a duty to educate and organize. It must carefully select its members, closing its doors to those who do not show they are driven by a fierce ideological determination. The masses need education and discipline. They cannot see and they need to be guided: "It is necessary to give a permanent form and discipline to these chaotic energies, absorb

153. A. Gramsci, *L'ordine nuovo*, 61.
154. A. Gramsci, "La sovranità della legge," 1 June 1919, in Gramsci, *L'ordine nuovo 1919–1920*, 48.
155. A. Gramsci, "La taglia della storia," 7 June 1919, no. 5, in ibid., 59.

them, arrange them, and empower them."[156] Without the Party, Gramsci writes, the proletariat is "nothing."[157] "The communist revolution is essentially a problem of organization and discipline."[158] Without an "enlightened" minority, everything is lost, "and chaos, disorder, unemployment, and hunger will swallow up and crush the finest and most vigorous proletarian forces."[159] The world is immersed in slavery, but the communist revolution will mark "the hour of redemption."[160] Redeem and purify: this is a religious language to which Gramsci proudly laid claim.

In an article appearing on 4 September 1920 in *L'ordine nuovo,* Gramsci explains that the Communist Party is like the early Christian religious communities and adds that the spirit of its adepts is like that of the Christians who hid in the catacombs. It is a style steeped in mystic-religious categories. The following passage is extremely interesting:

> In the present period the Communist Party is the only institution that can seriously be compared with the religious communities of primitive Christianity. Within the limits of the Party's international presence, one can attempt a comparison between the militants for the City of God and those for the City of Man. The communist is certainly not inferior to the Christian of the catacombs. The ineffable goal that Christianity offered its champions is, in its evocative mystery, a validation full of heroism, of the thirst for martyrdom, for sanctity; it is not necessary for the great human strengths of character and will to enter into play to arouse the spirit of sacrifice in those who believe in the heavenly prize and in eternal beatitude. From a historical point of view, the communist worker...is greater than the slave and the artisan who risks everything to attend the clandestine prayer meeting. In the same way, Rosa Luxemburg and Carlo Liebknecht are greater than the greatest saints of Christ. Because the aim of their militancy is concrete, human, and limited, hence the fighters for the working class are greater than the fighters for God....This miracle of the worker who takes charge each day of his own intellectual autonomy...is expressed in the Communist Party.[161]

156. A. Gramsci and P. Togliatti, "Democrazia operaia," 21 June 1919, no. 7, in ibid., 88.

157. A. Gramsci, "La conquista dello Stato," 12 July 1919, no. 9, in ibid., 129.

158. A. Gramsci, "Operai e contadini," 2 August 1919, no. 12, in ibid., 160.

159. A. Gramsci, "Lo sviluppo della rivoluzione," 13 September 1919, no. 18, in ibid., 207.

160. A. Gramsci, "Ai commissari di reparto delle officine *fiat* centro e brevetti," 13 September 1919, no. 18, in ibid., 211.

161. A. Gramsci, "Il Partito comunista," 4 September 1920, no. 15, in ibid., 659–660.

The Communist Party thus possesses a "magical-sacral" power. It is composed of "martyrs" and is able to perform "miracles."

In his article "Socialists and Anarchists," Gramsci dwells on the importance of the revolutionary education. He explains that the communists' identity and their historic function is based on a particular doctrine. It is through this doctrine that the communists interpret reality and define the immediate goals of their historic "mission." Being a communist involves first of all a "mentality," a way of regarding the world. In his words: "The socialists, or critical communists, have a steadfast and systematic doctrine and they have a method, the dialectic method. Since they have a doctrine, they have a distinct personality and their own well-defined dominion."[162] Gramsci would never have agreed with those who want us to believe that ideologies are never the true decisive factors for collective behavior. According to him, people are only really free when their thoughts are "ordered" and "their inner self is perfectly organized."[163]

Gramsci has a healthy contempt for the reformists, who are "the petty bourgeoisie and bourgeoisie. This is why their men are the most worthy representatives of these classes."[164]

In an article of 18 October 1919—which has all the appearance of a necrology—the enemies are "skeletal corpses" to be removed as soon as possible "because there are in Europe many hundreds of thousands of living corpses, hundreds of bodies that contain a fossil brain, a fossil intelligence, a fossil heart…alongside millions and millions of skeletal corpses covering plains and mountains, in Europe there are many hundreds of thousands of living corpses."[165]

The article that shows the extent of Gramsci's radical pessimism dates back to October 1920. It has a significant title, "The Company of Jesus," and the same language (and the same analysis) we encountered in *Drops of Sun in the City of Ghosts* by the brigadists Curcio and Franceschini.

The world is described as a "gruesome" place, inhabited by "corpses," populated by the walking dead. Gramsci, in the guise of a moralizer, denounces luxury, wealth, and profit. Like any self-respecting "priest" he speaks to "men of goodwill." He urges them to fight to free the world from the depths into which it has fallen. The shadows are encroaching. He sees bourgeois society as an "atrocious panorama" defining "a building without human

162. A. Gramsci, "Socialisti e anarchici," 20–27 September 1919, no. 19, in ibid., 217.
163. Ibid.
164. A. Gramsci, "Chiarezza, democrazia, ordine," 17 October 1919, in ibid., 247.
165. A. Gramsci, "Cronache dell'Ordine nuovo,'" 18 October 1919, no. 22, in ibid., 249.

inhabitants."[166] The Communist Party has the task of defeating "evil" and establishing the kingdom of eternal happiness. The workers "face a mission superior to any human force":[167] the destruction of *this world,* because every possibility of human freedom and development has been rendered impossible by the "system,"[168] which suffocates and oppresses everything. The working class "is the guardian of the future, the living force of history."[169] What does Gramsci want? He wants humanity to be "reintegrated in its essential values." This is why, he writes—and these words are far from a materialistic concept of history—*"Bolshevism is especially a reaction of the spirit."*[170]

Gramsci hated the "lukewarm." Since he had an "extremist" concept of politics, he considered it intolerable that men would not act in a rigorously "partisan" spirit. The binary code mentality produces these effects: "I hate the indifferent. I believe like Federico Hebbel that 'living means taking sides.' Those who really live cannot help being citizens and partisans. Indifference and apathy are parasitism, perversion, not life. That is why I hate the indifferent."[171] In a capitalist society, this is Gramsci's message, "shadow zones" are not tolerated. Everyone must line up, on one side the forces of reaction, on the other that of the revolution. In this article of 11 February 1917, Gramsci has a concept of the world "that wants everyone to be active in life, that allows no kind of agnosticism and indifference," and he sums up—with these disturbing words—the real meaning of the pedagogy of intolerance: "I also hate the indifferent because their whimpering as eternal innocents annoys me. I make them responsible, asking them how they've tackled the task that life has given them, and gives them every day, what they've done, and especially what they haven't done. *I feel I've the right to be inexorable and not to squander my compassion, not to share my tears with them.* I'm a partisan, I'm alive, I feel in the virile consciences of those on my side the pulse of the future city that they're building.... No one in it is standing at the window looking out.... I'm alive, I'm a partisan. This is why I hate those who don't take sides. I hate the indifferent."[172]

One can question the "technique" for demolishing bourgeois society (the Red Brigades had a macabre imagination in such matters), but the basic idea—the design—had been developed before they came on the scene: to raze

166. A. Gramsci, "La compagnia di Gesù," 9 October 1920, no. 258, in ibid., 706.
167. A. Gramsci, "La forza della rivoluzione," 8 May 1920, no. 1, in ibid., 520.
168. A. Gramsci, "L'organizzazione capitalista," 7 September 1920, no. 226, in ibid., 673.
169. A. Gramsci, "Il problema della forza," 26 March 1920, no. 74, in ibid., 475.
170. A. Gramsci, "Valori," 13 June 1919, no. 163, in ibid., 77. Italics added.
171. A. Gramsci, "Indifferenti," 11 February 1917, in Gramsci, *Le opere,* 23.
172. Ibid., 24–25. Italics added.

to the ground every aspect of the present society "swallowed up"—these are Gramsci's words—"by bestial barbarism."[173] It's a funereal litany with which we are now familiar: *this world* is a lurid and nauseating "morass." It has to be destroyed and purified. Togliatti and Berlinguer knew the Marxist-Leninist lesson by heart, but they had no intention of putting it into practice. Forced to restrain their revolutionary impetus because the international scenario was unfavorable for a communist revolution in Italy, they did not on principle deny the possibility of "an even violent socialist transformation in Italy."[174]

I'm well aware that this will arouse contrasting emotions, but I have to ask the question: Did the Italian Communist Party have any responsibility for the genesis of the Red Brigades? My answer is that most of the founding members of the Red Brigades paid the price for basing their political practice on the revolutionary education received in the Communist Party.

The Italian Communist Party had a very evident "pedagogical" responsibility in the genesis of the Red Brigades.

As Rossana Rossanda acknowledges in an article published on 28 March 1978 in *Il Manifesto,* there is an undeniable link between the indoctrination received in the Communist Party and the Red Brigades' ideology: "In fact," Rossanda writes, "anyone who was a communist in the fifties is struck by the BR's new language. *It's like looking into a family album: there's everything we imbibed during the Stalin and Zdanov courses of happy memory.* The world, we learned then, is divided into two: on one side imperialism, on the other socialism."[175]

Rossanda wrote something similar after reading the second communiqué on the Moro kidnapping, issued by the Red Brigades on 25 March 1978 in Turin, Milan, and Genoa. She wasn't wrong: the new Red Brigades communiqués on the Moro case faithfully reproposed Marx's and Lenin's teachings. The Red Brigades expressed the fear that a "false conscience" could move the proletarian movement away from the goal of the revolution (communiqué 1);[176] the concept of reformism as an instrument to inhibit the proletariat's revolutionary potential (communiqué 2);[177] the implacable

---

173. A. Gramsci, "La settimana politica," 4 October 1919, no. 20, in Gramsci, *L'ordine nuovo 1919–1920,* 231.

174. Aldo Natoli is speaking in the interview cited in P. di Loreto, *Togliatti e la "doppiezza,"* 68.

175. R. Rossanda, "Il discorso sulla Dc," *Il Manifesto,* 28 March 1978. Rossanda is referring to the second communiqué on the Moro kidnapping, issued by the Red Brigades on 25 March 1978 in Turin, Milan, and Genoa. Italics added. An excellent historical reconstruction of the Aldo Moro kidnapping is A. Giovagnoli, *Il caso Moro.*

176. *Moro Kidnapping. BR Communiqué no. 1.* Document issued in Rome on 18 March 1978. Attached to the document, a photo of Moro with the BR symbol behind him. *Dossier Brigate rosse,* 2:296.

177. *Moro Kidnapping. BR Communiqué no. 2.* Document issued by the Red Brigades on 25 March 1978 in Turin, Rome, Milan, and Genoa. *Dossier Brigate rosse,* 2:298.

contraposition between the bourgeoisie and the proletariat; the dialectics between the development of productive forces and relations of production as a tool for interpreting historical development (communiqué 3);[178] the category of exploitation constructed through plus-labor and plus-value concepts (communiqué 4);[179] the idea that politics is nothing but the reflection of the underlying economic interests (communiqué 5);[180] the state understood as the "business committee of the bourgeoisie" (communiqué 6);[181] the idea that the violence of those who act in the name of the proletariat is lawful and the only justification they need is their faith in the communist ideal: "We answer only to the proletariat and the revolutionary movement, taking responsibility for the execution of the sentence issued by the People's Tribunal" (communiqué 7);[182] the state as guarantor of the relations of production and the sole interests of the dominant class: "The Christian Democrats not only respect the laws of the imperialist State but, choosing from time to time their accomplices, make the laws, impose them, and apply them at the risk of the proletariat's life" (communiqué 8);[183] and the concept of "formal democracy," where the freedom of the workers is only apparent. There is also the idea of the revolution as an "inevitable" event (communiqué 9).[184]

Rossanda also agreed that the Red Brigades were always "incurably materialistic,"[185] viewing the world through the same eyes as many communist militants.

---

178. *Moro Kidnapping. BR Communiqué no. 3.* Document issued by the Red Brigades in Rome, Genoa, Milan, and Turin on 29 March 1978. Attached to the communiqué, three letters from Moro addressed to Nicola Rana, his assistant at Sapienza University of Rome; to his wife; and to the Interior Minister Francesco Cossiga. *Dossier Brigate rosse,* 2:304.

179. *Moro Kidnapping. BR Communiqué no. 4.* Document issued by the BR on 4 April 1978 in Milan, Genoa, Rome, and Turin. Attached to the communiqué a letter from Moro to the Christian Democratic secretary Benigno Zaccagnini, in which Moro urges negotiations for an exchange of prisoners. *Dossier Brigate rosse,* 2:309.

180. *Moro Kidnapping. BR Communiqué no. 5.* BR document issued in Rome, Milan, Turin, and Genoa on 10 April 1978. Attached to the communiqué was part of the "minutes" of the Moro interrogation, where the statesman speaks polemically about Paolo Emilio Taviani. *Dossier Brigate rosse,* 2:312.

181. *Moro Kidnapping. BR Communiqué no. 6.* BR document issued on 15 April 1978. *Dossier Brigate rosse,* 2:315.

182. *Moro Kidnapping. BR Communiqué no. 7.* BR document issued on 20 April 1978. Attached to the communiqué was a photo of Moro with a copy of the daily *La Repubblica* of 19 April. *Dossier Brigate rosse,* 2:322.

183. *Moro Kidnapping. BR Communiqué no. 8.* BR document issued on 24 April 1978. Attached is a letter from Moro to Zaccagnini. *Dossier Brigate rosse,* 2:324.

184. *Moro Kidnapping. BR Communiqué no. 9.* BR document issued on 5 May 1978 in Rome, Milan, Turin, and Genoa. Four days later Moro was killed. *Dossier Brigate rosse,* 2:333.

185. *Communiqué no. 5. D'Urso Campaign.* BR document issued on 28 December 1980. The entire text is available at www.brigaterosse.org.

Let us now return to our debate on the Italian Communist Party's (PCI) pedagogical responsibilities in the genesis of the Red Brigades.

The Italian Communist Party's Role in the Genesis of the Red Brigades

The documents at our disposal show that, in the history of republican Italy, the relationship between the PCI and political violence went through two stages. In the first, ending with the advent of the Red Brigades, revolutionary and subversive violence was exalted, whereas a "political-ideological short circuit" occurred in the second. Although rigidly defending Italian democracy and its institutions, the PCI never on principle denied the possibility of using political violence to establish socialism.

In his final address to the party's central committee on 10 October 1947, Togliatti asked: "Is there any immediate prospect of insurrection?" His answer was that "a communist cannot exclude forever this possibility."[186] A few days before the elections, in a very tense atmosphere, Togliatti had asked for a secret meeting with Ambassador Kostylev to gauge the possibility of seizing power with an armed insurrection in the event of an electoral defeat. They met on 23 March 1948 in a forest near Rome. Togliatti told Kostylev that the PCI central committee was preparing the masses for insurrection, but that it would only have acted in extreme circumstances and after having obtained Soviet authorization.[187]

Moscow's response arrived swiftly on 26 March. Molotov telegraphed Kostylev informing him what the Soviet Central Committee had decided for the PCI: the Italian Communists would have to take up arms only if the Christian Democrats were to attack the party offices. The possibility of seizing power with weapons was categorically denied: "With regard to gaining power through an armed insurrection, we consider that the PCI cannot in any way implement it at this time."[188]

---

186. Meeting of 7–10 October 1947, cited in R. Martinelli and M. L. Righi, eds., *La politica del partito comunista italiano nel periodo costituente,* 524, 526.

187. See E. Aga-Rossi and V. Zaslavsky, *Togliatti e Stalin,* 239–40.

188. Ibid., 240. On the Soviet decision to discourage the PCI from undertaking any initiative for insurrection, see also S. Pons, *L'egemonia impossibile,* 189–227. Pons writes: "In the extremely bitter climate created around the elections, Togliatti believed in the possibility of a civil war with dramatic international consequences: an event whose implications directly involved the USSR leadership" (223).

Besides Stalin's opposition, Togliatti's revolutionary ambitions also had to come to terms with two serious defeats, one electoral in April 1948, and the other military in July 1948.

On 14 July 1948, Togliatti was wounded by a Sicilian student from the Far Right; news of the attack spread swiftly, prompting the immediate protest of the Communist Party's grass roots, at that time numbering 2.5 million. The response of the government and Interior minister Mario Scelba was extremely harsh. Italy underwent three days of civil war with thirty deaths, over eight hundred wounded, factories occupied, barricades in the cities, partisan war weapons unearthed, police stations attacked, carabinieri and police taken as prisoners, telephone and telegraphic communications interrupted.[189]

Defeated at the polls and in the streets, "Togliatti's ideology started to carry out that profound and constant function of delegitimizing the State that prepares, perhaps even unknowingly, the most suitable terrain for bringing to flower the seeds of terrorism."[190]

The first reaction to the electoral results was to attribute the Christian Democrats' victory to pressures, blackmail, and fraud. A delegitimization campaign was launched that, from 1948 to 1953, adopted increasingly furious tones. Thousands of militants were convinced they had been the victims of a "coup d'état," an insufferable abuse that would have justified, should favorable conditions be created, resorting to violence.

For the PCI, the Christian Democrats were a "party without scruples, better than anyone else in the art of duplicity, of deceit, of lying, and of corruption" (April 1948).[191] Its victory is only to be put down to the "policelike intimidation"[192] typical "of men of a totalitarian regime."[193] The Christian Democrats govern "with religious terror and with the threat of hunger, suffocating the worker's most elementary and vital aspirations."[194] For Luigi Longo, De Gasperi wanted to do away with Italian democracy, governing in a "totalitarian and fascist" manner thanks to the support of his Christian Democratic followers who, besides being "enemies of the workers and of national interests,"[195] are "accustomed to kissing the slippers and shining the shoes of priests and fascist leaders" (August 1948).[196] De Gasperi is leading

189. See C. M. Lomartire, *Insurrezione.*

190. D. Settembrini, "Il Pci e la violenza rivoluzionaria," in Settembrini, *Socialismo, marxismo e mercato,* 118.

191. "Considerazioni sul 18 aprile" in *Rinascita,* April–May 1948, 138.

192. Ibid.

193. F. Platone, "Stato di polizia," *Rinascita,* June 1948, 187.

194. Ibid.

195. L. Longo, "La risposta del popolo," *Rinascita,* July 1948, 236.

196. L. Longo, "Il nostro capo," *Rinascita,* August 1948, 281.

"a party that has snatched a parliamentary majority with illicit and immoral pressures, with fraud and with the help of foreigners" (October 1948).[197] Italy has a "police State,"[198] in which constitutional freedoms are daily trampled (May 1949).

Togliatti is certain that the Christian Democrats are attempting to implement a reactionary plan, which "is presented as a dreadful adventure for the entire nation" (June 1949).[199] They are responsible for "one of the most flagrant injustices."[200] Hence, getting rid of the Christian Democratic government is a matter of political "hygiene." In other words, "it is the first task of civilization, of honesty, of *cleanliness*" (March 1950).[201]

In a speech of 1950, Togliatti denounces "the threat of the return of a regime of tyranny and corruption similar to, if not exactly the same as, the fascist one."[202] The communists are described as the "victims of violent persecutions."[203] The PCI is engaged in a "crusade for freedom," because the Christian Democrats want to "gag their opponents, denounce them and persecute them" (February 1951).[204] For the communists, the Christian Democrats' international agreements are a "blank check for blood and ruin."[205] If they are not stopped, asserts Luigi Longo, they will bring Italy to "economic ruin, open tyranny, war, and disaster" (April 1951).[206]

On 29 June 1952, the PCI Central Committee asserts that "the majority party... shamelessly proposes and wants to implement a program gradually to destroy constitutional freedoms." Its aim is to "found an authentic clerical totalitarian regime."[207]

Lelio Basso went further than anyone else in his article of September 1952, "De Gasperi's Coup d'État." After having claimed the merit "of being one of the first in Italy to denounce the danger of a Christian Democratic totalitarianism that is formally different but actually a continuance of fascist totalitarianism,"[208] he states that there is really no difference between the Christian Democratic regime and that of the fascists. In fact, *the Christian*

---

197. "Sulla nostra politica," *Rinascita,* September–October 1948, 330.
198. "Distensione," *Rinascita,* May 1949, 195.
199. P. Togliatti, "Tentazioni e minacce," *Rinascita,* June 1949, 247.
200. P. Togliatti, "Piano del lavoro," *Rinascita,* February 1950, 58.
201. P. Togliatti, "Governo anticomunista," *Rinascita,* March 1950, 114. Italics added.
202. Cited in G. Vacca, *Saggio su Togliatti,* 293.
203. F. Platone, "Trent'anni," *Rinascita,* January 1951, 1.
204. C. Negarville, "Crociata per la libertà," *Rinascita,* February 1951, 58.
205. A. Donini, "Avanti nella lotta per la pace," *Rinascita,* March 1951, 113.
206. L. Longo, "Ai cittadini italiani," *Rinascita,* April 1951, 161–62.
207. "Contro il totalitarismo clericale," *Rinascita,* June 1952, 326. The article bears the signature of the PCI Central Committee.
208. L. Basso, "Il colpo di Stato di De Gasperi," *Rinascita,* September 1952, 467.

Democratic government is essentially illegal and thus less lawful than the fascist one. Basso continues: "I consider that it is right and proper to say clearly to the country that not only is this regime basically continuing fascist politics...but that, on a level of respect of legality, *De Gasperi's government is even more illegal than Mussolini's.*"[209] Basso claimed the right of resistance, sanctioned by the French Declaration of 1793, against an illegal government guilty of an abuse of power. In his words: "This is a right implicit in the legal system, since no citizen can have the obligation to obey a power that has been usurped through an authentic coup d'état."[210] The Christian Democratic government is a daily usurpation that justifies the destruction of the system.

In June 1958, Togliatti spoke these words to the PCI Central Committee: "Remember that as long as power is in the hands of the bourgeoisie, it is prepared to commit any crime against democracy, any offense against the will of the people to solve its own contradictions. We have to be ready to see the enemy and to fight against it with suitable weapons."[211] A few months later (October 1958), he would be stressing that "it is no longer possible to think, after forty years of socialist building, of a parliamentarianism of the type that exists here, or of a multiplicity of parties, or of political-economic debates like those we are urging and conducting, and so on."[212]

On 25 January 1959, Amendola specified that the communists have no intention of being content with a simple alternation in government, so that "the socialist revolution means the end of the bourgeois State...the developments of this last forty years have confirmed the validity of the Leninist theory of the State.... We ask this: Does democracy consist in the possibility of an alternation in power? But the alternation of parties is one thing and the alternation of classes another. When the working class takes power in its hands...it has the duty to defend the conquests of the socialist revolution."[213]

To shed light on the "pedagogic" role of the Italian Communist Party in the genesis of the Red Brigades, I point out the conceptual categories and the lexicon the Red Brigades used in their first communiqué on the Moro kidnapping (18 March 1978).

In this document, Moro is described as a "tyrant." He is the main heir of a party that for thirty years has been "oppressing the Italian people." He

---

209. Ibid.
210. Ibid.
211. *L'Unità*, 12 June 1958.
212. *Rinascita*, October 1958, 609–17.
213. G. Amendola, *Tra passione e ragione*, 47–48.

is responsible for a "bloodthirsty" policy that goes hand in hand with the interests of the multinationals.

The communiqué reads as follows:

> Thursday 16 March, an armed nucleus of the Red Brigades captured *Aldo Moro,* leader of the Christian Democratic Party, and placed him in a people's prison.
>
> His armed escort, comprising five agents of the famous Special Corps, was completely annihilated.
>
> It is easy to explain who *Aldo Moro* is. After his worthy accomplice De Gasperi, until now he has been the most authoritative leader, the "theoretician" and the undisputed strategist of the Christian Democratic regime that has been oppressing the Italian people for thirty years. For every stage of the imperialist counterrevolution that the Christian Democrats have carried out in our country, from the bloodthirsty policies of the fifties to the "center-left" turning point and to the current "six-party agreement,"[214] *Aldo Moro* has acted as its political godfather and most faithful executor of the directives imparted by the imperialistic centers.[215]

No less significant is the Red Brigades communiqué no. 7 (20 April 1978), which reads: "The first to come to trial is this corrupt party, this lurid organization of the State's power. As for Aldo Moro, we repeat…that he is a political prisoner condemned to death because responsible to the greatest degree for thirty years of Christian Democratic government of the State and for everything that has meant for the proletarians."[216]

The PCI's responsibility does not only concern the revolutionary education given for *identifying evil.* The "educational package" contains not only the daily delegitimizing of the Italian institutions and the demonization of the enemy but also the exaltation of revolutionary violence. Because the PCI never excluded, on principle, the possibility of using it to defeat the "bourgeois State" represented by the Christian Democratic Party.[217]

In February 1961, the African leader Lumumba was assassinated. *L'Unità* celebrates his revolutionary feats "in the awareness that the Africans' fight to

---

214. The "six-party agreement" refers to the understanding for the composition of the government between the Christian Democrats, the Communist Party, the Socialist Party, the Liberal Party, the Social Democratic Party, and the Republican Party.

215. *Moro Kidnapping. BR Communiqué no. 1,* in *Dossier Brigate rosse,* 2:293.

216. *Moro Kidnapping. BR Communiqué no. 7,* in ibid., 2:322.

217. See Settembrini, "Il Pci e la violenza rivoluzionaria," 115.

free themselves of European capitalism is inseparable from ours." Lumumba "is one of the most generous sons of the revolution." "Lumumba was part of the best heritage of all of us." The PCI tells its militants not to cry "for the murdered hero," while encouraging them to nurture hatred and revenge against the "system." Tears are useless. He has to be "avenged": "This is the duty of people of our time . . . with the clear awareness that the Africans' fight to free themselves of European capitalism is inseparable from our fight to shake off the dominion of the forces that know how to produce only poverty, oppression, and injustice."[218]

The PCI does not always disapprove of physical aggression against political "enemies." In some cases it is even encouraged. Following the parliamentary debate on the killing of left-wing student Paolo Rossi (28 April 1966) by some far-right students, *L'Unità* reports, almost exulting, the news of the attacks on the MSI deputies in which the communist leaders Veronesi, Pajetta, Ingrao, Chiaromonte, Bronzuto, and Pellegrini "hurled themselves against the fascists."[219] During the parliamentary session, the Communist deputy Melis addresses the MSI deputies, saying: "We were too kind to you, don't take advantage of the freedom we've given you." For *L'Unità* these words were pregnant with "very noble antifascist sentiments."[220]

There is no need to stress the "pedagogical" effects of similar episodes on young militants of the Far Left, who saw their "pursuit of the fascists" justified (which was, however, "generously" reciprocated in an equally violent manner).

The eulogy of Ernesto Che Guevara's revolutionary trajectory arrived punctually on 20 October 1967. In an article with a significant title, "Fallen in a Battle without Frontiers," Petruccioli states: "Every revolutionary movement must be prepared for guerrilla warfare, to tackle the changing conduct of the enemy you're fighting. . . . The guerrilla warfare line, as Guevara has described it to us . . . has . . . an international justification and dimension." The Italian communists should have learned how to "consider the armed struggle as the continuation . . . of a revolutionary political strategy."[221]

As these words show, the armed struggle, far from being condemned in principle, was even considered a possible strategic resource.

---

218. *L'Unità*, 15 February 1961, 1.
219. *L'Unità*, 30 April 1966, 2.
220. Ibid.
221. C. Petruccioli, "Caduto in una battaglia che non ha frontiere," *Rinascita*, 20 October 1967.

On 13 July 1968, twenty years after the attempt on Togliatti's life, the PCI's official historian Paolo Spriano stresses that the communists have never abandoned the idea of using violence to achieve power. The PCI abandoned the attack on the institutions created after World War II because the world was divided into zones of influence, something that eliminated the possibility of "holding onto a power that had been seized."[222] After the attempt on Togliatti, a strike was announced that "had elements of a pre-insurrectional nature." However, explains Spriano, the PCI refused the prospect of civil war because the balance of powers would have made them lose it.

There is no need to dwell on the communists' delegitimizing campaign against the state and its institutions, since there is a full archive on it. We should just recall that, in 1968, Luigi Longo was still asserting that "it is we who, with our political and social action, with our fight against the political monopoly of the Christian Democratic Party and its arrogance,... it is we, I was saying, who are the defenders of freedom and democracy in Italy and of those constitutional principles that the Christian Democrats have been trampling on for twenty years" (February 1968).[223]

Togliatti died in 1964, but communist propaganda, with its revolutionary rhetoric, did not falter. It is in this guise as a revolutionary and antisystemic party that the PCI tackles the unprecedented explosion of student protests in Italian universities, an explosion that the communist leaders were to consider a response to the "mortifying limits that the current structure of society imposes."[224] For the PCI, the students react to a "society that tries to hide, behind a mask of apparent calmness and superficial optimism, the reality of class oppression, of exploitation, of the mortification of the best civil and intellectual forces, and of the growing crises of the same democratic institutions."[225]

As the student movement takes on a violent and subversive aspect, the PCI, instead of distancing itself from the more-radical fringes, decides to organize the youth protest for the transformation of society.[226] This is the long-term strategy. In the short term, there are the political elections of 19 May 1968. Electoral competition is aggressive and the student movement can become an important element.

---

222. P. Spriano, "L'Italia disse no," *L'Unità,* 13 July 1968, 1.
223. L. Longo, "Risposta alla Dc," *Rinascita,* 9 February 1968, 3.
224. G. Chiarante, "Università '68," *Rinascita,* 9 February 1968, 24.
225. Ibid.
226. The student protest trend has been analyzed by S. Tarrow, *Democrazia e disordine,* 71ff.

In the months prior to the opening of the polls, the PCI press is a daily hymn to the revolution.

If it is not to become a minority and break up, the student movement has to let itself be guided by the PCI, which proposes to "define the new organizational models" (16 February 1968).[227] And since the "the lead-up to the elections is unclear, confused, and full of obscure dangers,"[228] it is advisable to greet the student movement as a "great new and positive fact... to which we are, either as communist students and teachers or as the party as a whole, wholly committed."[229] The aim is a shared one: to enable "the vanguards to be increasingly real vanguards, leaders and guides of the masses"[230] toward the revolution (1 March 1968). But the students must moderate their antiparty impulse or, better, save it for counterrevolutionary efforts. Putting the PCI on the same level as the other parties is a mistake; "it's a discourse that denies the political and revolutionary battle" (15 March 1968).[231]

In the meantime, the declaredly nonviolent student movement had demonstrated that it could start real urban guerrilla warfare. It happened on 1 March 1968 in Rome, on the via di Valle Giulia, near the Villa Borghese, in the Faculty of Architecture. Students threw stones and incendiary bombs against police armed with nightsticks and hoses. Hundreds were wounded. A magazine, *La Sinistra,* had issued an illustrated manual for making Molotov cocktails. According to *L'Unità,* "the police attacked the University of Rome."[232] The rioting students' leaders were described as victims of the government's "irresponsibility" by the PCI's official organ. According to the PCI, the Christian Democrats had offered the occupying students "only insults and threats, often carried out forcefully, as happened yesterday in Rome." On the other hand, "the sense of responsibility on the part of the student organizations" was praised.[233] Another article speaks of the "brutal

---

227. C. Petruccioli, "Dentro le aule e fuori," *Rinascita,* 16 February 1968, 1. Petruccioli writes: "We've always been and are now even more, faced with the real possibility that the movement will expand to new and consistent masses... but we are also—and I say this bluntly—watchful and interested in its strength, its consistency, its possibility to develop, because we consider the students an important component that can and must flow, with their goals and their organization, into the general struggle for the transformation of society conducted by a block of social forces directed by the working class."

228. G. Amendola, "Vigilia elettorale," *Rinascita,* 23 February 1968, 1.

229. P. Bufalini, "Il Partito e gli studenti," *Rinascita,* 1 March 1968, 1.

230. Ibid.

231. A. Natta, "Università da cambiare," *Rinascita,* 15 March 1968, 2.

232. *L'Unità,* 1 March 1968.

233. M. Ferrara, "Responsabilità democratica, irresponsabilità governativa," *L'Unità,* 1 March 1968.

police raid on the Roman university."[234] *L'Unità* does not mention that the more extreme fringes of the student movement attacked some of the police vehicles. The next day, the PCI's newspaper informed its readers of three police vehicles upturned and burned (but without stating by whom), while the PCI Central Committee met to offer "its indignant protest against and condemnation of" the police.

The issue is not the condemnation of police violence (which did occur) but the unconditional support without an "if" or "but" of the entire student movement, although it was already very clear that there were violent and uncontrolled elements in it (to set fire to the vehicles you needed Molotov cocktails!). However, the PCI assured, the students conducted a "great, civil battle for renewal." "For hours they resisted and counterattacked" (2 March 1968).[235]

In the days following the Valle Giulia clashes, the PCI praised the students' "rebellion" that had spread to all the Italian cities "with the unstoppable force of a river" (3 March 1968).[236] The student movement "never stops surprising us with its vitality" (8 March 1968).[237] In an article of 17 March 1968, "A New Generation," Achille Occhetto hears "the memory of an entire revolutionary tradition" echoing in the students' words and invites them to "leave a system founded on the exploitation and depersonalization of people."[238]

On 11 March 1969, Professor Pietro Trimarchi of the University of Milan, after having failed a student in Civil Law, was spat at and held prisoner from eleven thirty in the morning to four thirty in the afternoon. He was freed by some one hundred policemen. The next day *L'Unità* reported in indignation the news of a law professor imprisoned in Barcelona. It is Jordi Sole-Tura, translator of Antonio Gramsci's *Notebooks from Prison.* Not a word about the Trimarchi affair.[239] One can understand why: "We are fighting to create a new world in which there will be no more violence and oppression or destruction and massacres. Our violence creates order and freedom. Theirs is the blind anger of the impotent."[240]

On 19 November 1969, the policeman Antonio Annarumma dies in Milan while driving his jeep during clashes between the police and young

---

234. M. Ro, "La brutale irruzione poliziesca nell'ateneo romano," *L'Unità,* 1 March 1968, 3.
235. *L'Unità,* 2 March 1968, 3.
236. A. Rodari, "La rivolta degli studenti," *L'Unità,* 3 March 1968, 3.
237. *L'Unità,* 8 March 1968, 3.
238. A. Occhetto, "Una nuova generazione," *L'Unità,* 17 March 1968, 1.
239. *L'Unità,* 12 March 1968.
240. P. Togliatti, *Opere,* 1:163.

protesters. Born in Avellino, twenty-two years of age, he was the son of a farmworker.[241] For *L'Unità*, the police are entirely responsible for the tragedy: "The police provocation during which the officer Annarumma died followed a design that clearly shows who was responsible." According to the PCI version, the policeman hit a police vehicle. On impact he shattered the windshield with his head and died. According to the forensic report of professors Caio Mario Cattabeni, Raineri Luvoni, and Romeo Pozzato: "Annarumma was killed by a blunt object used as a lance. The object... hit him with violence in the right parietal area, just above the eye, causing an extensive wound with the exit of cerebral matter."[242]

The PCI's aim at that time was to guide the student protest "according to the vision of hegemony that Gramsci and Togliatti indicated to us" (29 March 1968).[243] The best way to succeed in this undertaking is to convince the new generations that the Communist Party is truly revolutionary. The young trust it: "Since the communist organization is a revolutionary one, it does not live before and alongside the struggles, but in them and through them."[244] It considers "the student struggle as the antechamber, the apprenticeship to a revolutionary struggle"[245] involving society as a whole (12 April 1968). Obviously the students cannot think that the revolution will take place tomorrow. The Communist Party needs time to create the favorable conditions for overthrowing capitalism. For this to occur, Occhetto explains, the PCI has to obtain the votes necessary to govern in the political elections. Only in this way can the "unsustainable human condition of the workers, of the farmers, and of the students"[246] be remedied (26 April 1968).

The PCI would have to make greater efforts to render its role as a revolutionary vanguard more credible in the eyes of the young. Although the way forward is uncertain and obscure, decisive action has to be taken. The violence raging in the streets is always the fault of the state, which uses the fascist thugs' aggression to defend an order based on the mortification of human life. For the PCI, the division of power in Italy consisted of the fact that "there are those who bludgeon (fascist action squads and plainclothes police) and those who arrest" (3 May 1968).[247]

---

241. See R. Lumley, *Dal '68 agli anni di piombo*, 208.
242. Quoted in I. Montanelli, *Storia d'Italia. 1965–1993*, 11:60.
243. L. Pavolini, "La via di Togliatti," *Rinascita*, 29 March 1968, 1.
244. C. Petruccioli, "Studenti," *Rinascita*, 12 April 1968, 18.
245. Ibid., 17.
246. A. Occhetto, "Cambiare o continuare?" *Rinascita*, 26 April 1968, 2.
247. F. di Giulio, "Lotta sindacale e svolta politica," *Rinascita*, 3 May 1968, 8.

The political elections are imminent, and Longo stresses that the student movement is "an aspect and a moment" of the Italian revolutionary movement, which aims to construct a new society. The students must be encouraged in this revolutionary impulse. The PCI is "a workers' and communist movement... that aims at profound political and social upheaval."[248] The battle will be harsh, but in the end the communists will win. Until then, the students will have to hold fast. The PCI is well aware that violence is always triggered by the police, under the direction of the Christian Democratic Party—the source, according to Amendola, of "corruption, despotism, and provocation."[249] Also for Massimo D'Alema, violence is always a unilateral aggression that represents "a clear confirmation of this relentless repressive violence by the government and ruling classes" (10 May 1968).[250] Occhetto feels no need to address paternalistic appeals to the students because the PCI's electoral marketing helps them choose the model of socialism they find most attractive. He has no doubts: the vote for the PCI is a foregone conclusion, "because we have asked the young only to fight, to construct in Italy *a socialism made to their measure, according to their needs* of complete freedom of the human person."[251]

Even on the eve of the elections, with last-minute attempts to intercept its opponents' votes, the PCI does not lose the rhetoric of the subversive party.

It is again Occhetto who points out that the PCI is the "party of the revolution" because "*it has not been integrated in the system.*" This article by Occhetto, published in *Rinascita* on 17 May 1968, merits extensive citation:

A few hours from the vote, we trust in the knowledge that a new generation is appearing in the country's political life. A new generation that realizes that in Italy an offensive stage has begun in the struggle to develop democracy and come out of a system founded on the depersonalization of people. We are thus offering the young a party different from the others; we say to the young: *Ours is the only true protest against a humiliating system of human relations,* because it is a protest against exploitation.... But we are not asking the young only for their vote but for a general commitment and choice: we are asking them to become protagonists, to fight, to want to change things at the roots...; *we are asking them because we are the party of the partisans, we are the party of Ho Chi*

---

248. L. Longo, "Il movimento studentesco nella lotta anticapitalistica," *Rinascita,* 3 May 1968, 14.

249. G. Amendola, "Dietro il polverone," *Rinascita,* 10 May 1968, 2.

250. M. D'Alema, "Sedicenti rivoluzionari," *Rinascita,* 10 May 1968, 30.

251. A. Occhetto, "Il voto comunista," *Rinascita,* 17 May 1968, 2. Italics added.

Min and of Giap, and finally we are asking because we are the party of the Italian revolution. We are asking the young to come with us because we have never bowed our heads, because we are a party with clean hands, a party that is fighting against corruption, that has not been integrated into the system. (17 May 1968)[252]

Judging by the electoral results, the PCI had not missed the target. On the "unforgettable nineteenth of May,"[253] the PCI obtains 26.9 percent of the vote compared to the 25.3 percent attained in the previous elections of 1963. Instead, for the PSU (United Socialist Party) it was an "electoral disaster."[254] Created from the merger of the PSI (Italian Socialist Party) and PSDI (Italian Democratic Socialist Party), the PSU lost a quarter of the electorate that had voted for the two parties in 1963 (PSI 13.8 percent and PSDI 6.1 percent). Their total votes should have given the two parties around 20 percent, but the 14.5 percent result was much lower than expected, bringing the reunification to an end.

It was not only the socialists who were experiencing a disaster but the country as a whole, which was heading toward permanent mourning. What was happening? Once the subversive forces present in the youth movement had been ignited, the PCI could no longer control them, to the extent that the PCI had very soon to transform itself from a revolutionary party to a party of legality and uncompromising defense of institutions. The tactics were successful (the conquest of the youth vote in '68), but the strategy was a disaster (the conviction of being able to guide the protest to establish socialism). It was Amendola who realized it, in an article of 16 May 1972, "The PCI and the Young," in which, reversing his party's approach, he warns against the danger of "flirting with the extremism of the young.... *This attitude might have been useful for the elections (those of '68), but it hasn't helped clarify the political struggle.*"[255]

In 1972, the Red Brigades are fully operative and the PCI urges "a strongly critical attitude" toward "extremist outbursts,"[256] denouncing the "flurry of inconclusive and rousing slogans...; and the choice of the most violent form of struggle, of guerrilla warfare in the cities."[257]

But let us proceed in order, because during the early years of student protest when left-wing terrorism is still incubating, the PCI is always the party

---

252. Ibid. Italics added.
253. A. Coppola, "L'indimenticabile diciannove maggio," *Rinascita*, 24 May 1968, 3.
254. S. Colarizi, *Storia dei partiti nell'Italia repubblicana*, 386.
255. G. Amendola, "Il Pci e i giovani," *L'Unità*, 16 May 1972, 3. Italics added.
256. Ibid.
257. Ibid.

that wants to do away with the existing system. During these months, it is involved in recruiting young militants from the protest movement, not to guarantee a simple alternation in those governing but to ensure "dedication to a stirring mission, *the practical verification of the revolutionary will.*"[258] This verification is urgent because the communists have the challenging mission of putting an end to "the workers' rapid destruction in the modern factory, the liquidation of their qualifications, the urban chaos, the suffocation of scientific research, and the medieval university system."[259] Because in Italy—don't forget—the Christian Democratic government corrupts every aspect of community life. Hence the PCI continues to play with words, convinced of being able to obtain everything with its "duplicity" policy: the votes of the youth movement, the guidance of the protest, and perhaps even the government of the country. Amendola is "flirting" heavily during this time. He never stops repeating that the PCI has the task, as a party organized by the working class, "to gather up these feelings of rage and anger and change them into a political conscience."[260]

For Occhetto, then a young member of the party's leadership, the aim remains the demolition of capitalism. The young have an important role in this battle for establishing a new type of society. In his words: "The young have been activated because we're now moving ahead in the struggle to demolish capitalism and to construct a new organization of power; and, as always occurs in the decisive moments of history, the new generations assume a leading role in the clashes, in the unrest, and in the movement. The sansculottes of the French Revolution were young, the revolutionaries who attacked the Winter Palace were young, the Italian partisans and FNL combatants in Vietnam were young" (21 June 1968).[261] For Occhetto, the system has to be brought to its critical point, only then will insurrection be possible, considered as "compulsory in the revolutionary struggle."[262] During these years, Occhetto has a firmly military-political view of the political contest: "There is no doubt that, for a party that wants the revolution, that wants to do away with the capitalist society, it is necessary to maintain the crisis in bourgeois society, never to give up, to pass from trench to trench and demolish the adversary's strongholds."[263]

---

258. C. Petruccioli, "La spinta dei giovani," *Rinascita,* 31 May 1968, 2.

259. L. Pavolini, "Francia all'opposizione," *Rinascita,* 7 June 1968, 1–2.

260. G. Amendola, "I comunisti e il movimento studentesco," *Rinascita,* 7 June 1968, 4.

261. *Rinascita,* 21 June 1968.

262. Cited in Settembrini, "Il Pci e la violenza rivoluzionaria," 146.

263. Cited in E. Bettizza, *Il comunismo europeo,* 155. Bettizza does not give either the source or the complete date.

However, the party's leadership had always been certain of one thing: that a revolution in Italy is not even remotely imaginable. They know it because Togliatti is "present with us every day with his political theory and with practical, political, and organizational indications."[264] And what of the revolutionary spark ignited in the hearts of the young rebels? The promises to get rid of the widespread corruption, repression, and exploitation in Italy? The invitations to destroy a regime considered even worse than Mussolini's? We'll see. For the moment, Amendola explains: "There's a speech we have to make [to the young], and that we often neglect because we take our raison d'être for granted. *We have to tell the young that the communist ideal answers their need to condemn the society they're living in,* and that appears to them to be absurd, unjust, and founded on exploitation. And we have to tell them that... we will build together, in a new and necessarily original way, socialism in our country as well."[265]

Before tackling the issue of the revolution (it will come, obviously, when the time is ripe, as Longo explains in an article of 14 June 1968[266]), consensus has to be obtained. And, as we have seen, the votes arrive.

Meanwhile, the Socialist Party remained alone in keeping the show of Italian reformism on the road, with a performance that would have been grotesque if it had not been so tragic. The successors of Filippo Turati, who continued to indicate reforms as the only way either to improve the workers' conditions or to defend Italian democracy from subversion (both right and left), lost the elections and had to listen to the PCI derisively explain the "ideological and political errors, both old and new" of "those socialists who do not want to resign themselves to a subordinate role" (31 May 1968).[267]

Unlike the PCI, the PSI immediately made a distinction between the democratic students who fought for a modern university and the more violent ones who, starting with schools, wanted to overturn the entire social order.

After the Valle Giulia clashes, Gian Piero Orsello advised against representing Italian institutions as entirely negative.[268] The Socialist deputy Tristano Codignola, speaking in Parliament, reproached the PCI for its revolutionary demagogy: "We're not students, we're politicians, and our function, our duty with regard to the students is not to come here, repeat what they say, and applaud them. Our function is to interpret what is legitimate in the students'

264. G. Amendola, "Il posto di Togliatti," *Rinascita,* 12 January 1968, 21.

265. Amendola, *I comunisti e il movimento studentesco,* 4. Italics added.

266. L. Longo, "Riflessioni sugli avvenimenti di Francia," *Rinascita,* 14 June 1968, 6.

267. G. Amendola, "La crisi del Psu. Analisi del significato e della portata di una sconfitta," *Rinascita,* 31 May 1968, 3.

268. G. P. Orsello, "I socialisti e l'università," *Avanti!* 1 March 1968, 1.

requests and to transform it into law."[269] It is the first of March 1968 and Codignola fears that the student movement could degenerate and become uncontrollable. He thinks that "the student movement risks going up a blind alley, if it hasn't already done so... because it lacks, or hasn't properly prepared, the political channel of unrest."[270]

The PSI urges dialogue with the students, in the attempt to transform their more rational requests into reforms and to warn against the danger of revolutionary rhetorics. It defends the institutions, which they also want to reform, from being brutally delegitimized by the masses. The PCI realizes that it is facing an "explosive stage that evidently opens a different dialogue."[271] Codignola ends his speech by addressing the PCI deputies with these words: "I told you at the start that I wouldn't always have said what you wanted to hear and I'm not sorry because I have the duty to say what I consider is the truth, so bear with me! Because it's all too easy to come to Parliament to express solidarity with the student movement... without offering any political possibilities... for a legislative outcome. I want to say to my communist colleagues that, if at first they thought—not without reason, because all the parties have done so—they could somehow take control of and politically exploit student dissatisfaction, then they, like us, have had to think again. We're now facing this situation. I ask myself, honorable colleagues, if we shouldn't, in this final part of the legislature, tackle those few issues of university reform that we can tackle."[272]

On 3 March 1968, it is Gaetano Arfé who calls attention to the fact that part of the student movement has taken a dangerous turn for Italian democracy, and he urges the PCI not to agitate the masses with demagogy, which has produced the "brilliant result" of making the political parties lose control of the protest. "When things reach a certain stage of deterioration," concludes Arfé, "it's too late to put them right."[273] On 5 March, the socialist Aldo Visalberghi tells the PCI it should act more responsibly to "avert disaster."[274] The next day, the PSI national secretary intervenes and, although condemning police violence, refuses to "accept inane episodes of meaningless violence, which badly conceal half-baked schoolboy notions and degenerate into trite and hackneyed extremist rhetoric."[275]

---

269. *Avanti!* 2 March 1968, 8.
270. Ibid.
271. Ibid.
272. Ibid.
273. G. Arfé, "Costruire insieme un destino nuovo," *Avanti!* 3 March 1968, 1.
274. A. Visalberghi, "Cosa fare per l'università," *Avanti!* 5 March 1968, 1.
275. *Avanti!* 6 March 1968, 1.

The Socialists intensify their appeals but to no effect. The PCI continues its attacks against Italian society, the "system," capitalism, exploitation, corruption, the Christian Democratic Party, and anything that can be used in "the dramatic dialogue on the basic issues of *a life that is becoming not worth living.*"[276] But the students insist on asking about the revolution. Longo replies that the successes of the proletariat, even with the prospect of democratic progress, "can neither be forecast nor programmed in the abstract: they will be the result of the movement's situation, which will include sudden leaps ahead, momentary pauses, and even violent clashes with the forces that want to oppose the masses' democratic will."[277] In other words, wait. The revolution will come, but the PCI will say when. This speech of Longo's is one of the most ambiguous ever pronounced by the PCI leadership during the years of student protest.

This is what he says in *Rinascita* on 14 June 1968: "The democratic struggle can and must be enriched with new forms of struggle, because it is not only through the traditional methods of trade-union struggle that one can influence the political situation and force the institutions and authorities to satisfy the needs of the workers and of the people. There is a whole series of struggles, of pressures, that has to be seen in the prospect of an *escalation* of political and social conquests."[278] The effect of such vagueness on the masses of young people in full mobilization is easy to imagine.

Longo was certainly not including the armed struggle among the "new series of struggles." However, if we accept Max Weber's avowal that a sense of responsibility is one of the qualities for judging a professional politician,[279] many historic judgments on the leading players of those "formidable" years[280] would have to be revised. In June 1968 Occhetto explains that the PCI's problem is that of "preparing and defending a consistently revolutionary line" (21 June 1968).[281]

Longo could be even more radical than Occhetto when singing the praises—in full student mobilization—of the youth rebellion. In a long article published in *Rinascita* on 3 May 1968, Longo sheds any kind of ambiguity. After acknowledging that the student movement has undertaken

276. L. Barca, "Il balletto di Rumor," *Rinascita,* 14 June 1968, 2.
277. Longo, "Riflessioni sugli avvenimenti di Francia," 6.
278. Ibid.
279. See M. Weber, *La politica come professione,* 96. For Weber: "In the end there are only two types of mortal sin in politics: the absence of a cause and—what is often but not always the same thing—the lack of responsibility."
280. M. Capanna, *Formidabili quegli anni.*
281. A. Occhetto, "Insurrezione e via democratica," *Rinascita,* 21 June 1968, 3.

"a certain type of struggle against the system," the PCI secretary concludes with these words: "We have to recognize that, essentially, it [the student movement] has shaken the Italian political situation and *has had a mainly positive value, because it has shown itself to be a subversive movement*."[282] A few weeks later, Longo points out before the Central Committee that overturning the system remains the aim to achieve and stresses that the French protesters are "puerile" in thinking that they can obtain this result solely by occupying the prefectures, the police, radio, and television. The revolutionary objective "requires a broader struggle process, more convoluted, sometimes with unexpected leaps ahead."[283]

An Oxymoron: The "Leninist-Reformist" Party

This was the PCI propaganda until the Communists decided to reconsider the Christian Democrats with the hope of flanking them in the country's government.

After the bloody coup of 11 September 1973 in Chile, during which the Socialist president Salvador Allende was killed, Berlinguer started to fear that something similar could occur in Italy with the help of the U.S. secret services. He thought that the coup d'état in Chile was "an event of global range"[284] that would have repercussions on the PCI's political strategy. At the end of a series of three articles published in *Rinascita* (28 September, 5 and 12 October 1973), Berlinguer concluded that it would be "entirely misleading" to believe that the Communists could have governed the country, even if they were to win the elections. To guarantee the good of Italy, the PCI would have had to ally itself with the Christian Democrats.

The "turning point" is first of all only in words.

The term "revolution" disappears, replaced by expressions such as "renewal process," "democratic renewal," "democratic progress."[285] From then on, the Christian Democratic Party is no longer the "party of the corrupt" but a "reality not only varied but extremely changeable."[286] It's a real coup de théâtre. The PCI's leaders start to rap the knuckles of all those "who didn't

---

282. Longo, "Il movimento studentesco nella lotta anticapitalistica," 15. Longo's article appeared in *Contemporaneo,* a monthly supplement to *Rinascita.*

283. *L'Unità,* 21 June 1968.

284. See E. Berlinguer, "Imperialismo e coesistenza alla luce dei fatti cileni," *Rinascita,* 28 September 1973, 3.

285. E. Berlinguer, "Via democratica e violenza reazionaria," *Rinascita,* 5 October 1973.

286. E. Berlinguer, "Alleanze sociali e schieramenti politici," *Rinascita,* 12 October 1973, 5.

condemn the first episodes [of violence]. And who still today refuse to accept responsibility for the actions triggered by their virulent unrest."[287] The PCI shakes with indignation toward those who played with words, arousing facile revolutionary enthusiasm for which the whole country now has to pay the price. And it doesn't save anyone, because "the discourse on violence has to be free of any ambiguity, clear and consistent, so that all are forced to shoulder their responsibilities."[288]

With the change in political conditions, the relationship between the PCI and revolutionary violence becomes profoundly inconsistent.

Giorgio Amendola, intervening in a debate on the relationship between the Left and violence, offers a harsh tirade against "verbal violence" that is now condemned for its culturally "pernicious" effects. In Amendola's words: "The main responsibility of the extreme groups is that of having consciously given a pernicious political example that culturally prepares the terrain for the use of violence... because there is verbal violence, consisting of partisan judgments, erroneous political analyses, and offensive invectives... that opens the road to material violence... *now who has taught the young that the DC and fascism are the same thing?* How can the subtle strategies of the 'Manifesto' support such a statement...? Who has taught the young that the resistance was 'red' and not 'tricolored'?"[289] Amendola concludes that "by dint of shouting 'Revolution,' you end up obscuring any concrete prospect of socialist progress. You don't make revolutions with shouts and chatter."[290]

In the same pedagogic tone, Ferdinando Adornato—forgetting the appeals to the "party of the resistance" and the fact that the Christian Democrats were equated with the fascists—claims that "when you use concepts like 'authoritarian state' or 'fascistization,' it's as if we were in the Resistance, the only way out is inevitably that of the last resort, the desperate and hopeless struggle of violence."[291]

On 16 May 1972, Amendola reproves young left-wingers for having uncritically praised Che Guevara's political lesson, which instead requires critical reflection. In his words, one has to move away from the "uncritical exaltation of Che Guevara's tragic experience, not in its enduring human significance of consciously sought sacrifice, but as political teaching."[292] But not everyone manages to "convert" with the same rapidity, because the PCI

---

287. G. Amendola, "Il discorso sulla violenza," *L'Unità,* 11 May 1976, 3.
288. Ibid.
289. Ibid. Italics added.
290. Ibid.
291. F. Adornato, "Se la violenza sostituisce la politica," *L'Unità,* 26 January 1978, 3.
292. Amendola, "Il Pci e i giovani," *L'Unità,* 16 May 1972.

has no intention of launching an ideological revision process. Its bonds with Marxist-Leninist traditions remain firm. The Italian Communists consider themselves to be "Leninists" but aim to flank the Christian Democrats in the government of the country. This "Leninist reformism" produces a "politico-ideological short circuit" that is never to be repaired. Three months before Amendola's words on Che Guevara, *L'Unità* (1 February 1972) refuses to condemn Irish terrorism—one of the most ferocious—justifying its logic: "We can talk about violence from State institutions or what people ineffectively want to describe as 'terrorism,' but it really *involves a broad response, at various levels, through popular resistance* and the campaign for work, social justice, and civil rights."[293] In the same article, *L'Unità* also accuses the British of having provoked the attacks by infiltrating their own people into the IRA.

In November 1976, Occhetto has a much more ambitious plan than the simple conquest of power. He aims at the transformation of society. In his opinion, "it is entirely legitimate for a party bringing new social and ideal values to pursue a hegemony founded on consensus and to aim, not at an alternation of progressive and conservative governments, but at the historic objective of the transformation of society."[294]

There is impressive documentation of the PCI's "politico-ideological short circuit." Of the numerous documents that could be quoted, there is one that deserves particular attention. It is an interview that Enrico Berlinguer gave to *La Repubblica* in July 1981, in which the PCI secretary manages, in the same speech, to radically criticize the "system," source of every evil, and to praise its essential "pillars" (market, individual initiative, and private enterprise). We can understand why: criticizing the "system" is useful as long as the Communists are in the opposition; on the other hand, praising the market economy could become constructive if the government doors should open to them.

Berlinguer's position fully embodies Leninist morality, according to which everything is legitimate that at any given moment is useful to the party. The principles of this morality have been very clearly described in Antonio Gramsci's *Prison Notebooks,* where we read that "the modern Prince, by developing, revolutionizes the whole system of intellectual and moral relations, since it means that any *given act is seen as useful or harmful, as virtuous or as wicked, only insofar as it has as its point of reference the modern Prince itself,* and helps to strengthen or to oppose it. In people's consciences, the Prince takes the place of the divinity or the categorical imperative, and becomes

---

293. *L'Unità*, 1 February 1972. Italics added.
294. *L'Unità*, 21 November 1976.

the basis for a complete laicization of all aspects of life and of all customary relationships."[295]

This kind of thinking pervades the entire history of the PCI and Berlinguer, who during the cited interview gives a picture of Italian society "that makes your flesh creep" (the words of the interviewer, Eugenio Scalfari). The poor, the marginalized, and the disadvantaged are defenseless, they have no voice and no weight in decisions. What is even more important, they have no possibility of improving their conditions because the government parties, lacking any morality, have taken over the state and all its institutions. The local authorities, the insurance bodies, the banks, the public companies, the cultural institutions, the hospitals, the universities, the television, and the press are all in the hands of corrupt and unscrupulous people. The Italians can hope to save themselves in only one way: by entrusting themselves to the Communist Party, that is, to the party of the "honest," who are fighting, completely alone, against widespread corruption. However, changing Italy isn't easy, Berlinguer tells us, because the Italians are not free to choose. They "are well aware of how the State is being prostituted, of the abuses, of the favoritisms, of the discriminations. But most of them are being held ransom. They've had advantages... or they hope to receive them, or they fear they won't have them anymore."[296] At the center of everything there is always "the system," responsible for every evil. It "creates growing masses of the unemployed, of the marginalized, and of the exploited." It is also responsible for "the circulation of drugs, the refusal to work, for distrust, tedium, and desperation." Wherever you look it's a permanent disaster.

After such an analysis, the Red Brigades should have expected praise from the proletarian revolution. But instead there is Berlinguer's "political-ideological short circuit," which, after having condemned the "system," praises its "pillars": "We think that the market can maintain an essential function, that individual initiative is irreplaceable, that there is room for private enterprise to maintain its important role." This continual "political-ideological short circuit" of the PCI has had significant repercussions on the history of republican Italy. It has helped create a mass of "morally alienated" militants, or individuals who, although living in Italian society, feel culturally extraneous to it. The Communist militants are absolutely convinced that only what comes out of their party is "just" and morally correct; whatever was corrupt in Italian society came from excluding the Communists from power.

---

295. A. Gramsci, *Quaderni dal carcere,* 1561. Italics added.
296. *La Repubblica,* 28 July 1981.

The "system block" has in fact performed exactly this function, an ideological and self-exonerating function. Vacca has recently stated that the insurgence of terrorism in Italy was mainly prompted by the decision to exclude the PCI from the government together with the Christian Democratic Party's relations with the murkiest reactionary groups. In his words: "I believe that the block of the political system has played a determining role. The double 'centrality' of the DC in the government and the PCI as opposition did not enable the political system to alternate." Vacca comes down heavily on the Christian Democrats' responsibilities: "The uninterrupted exercise of power and the impossibility of alternate governments fostered its collusion with the subversive Right and the 'double State' mechanism."[297] As if to say it was the Christian Democrats' fault because they "colluded" with neofascist subversive movements and because the Communists were excluded from the government.

All this supports what the Red Brigades have always claimed, that the birth of red terrorism in Italy had its deepest roots in the contradiction between the Italian Communist Party's revolutionary ideology and its moderate political action.

In his autobiography, *Una vita in Prima Linea* (A Life in Prima Linea), the brigadist Sergio Segio recalls the words that Pietro Ingrao pronounced on 12 September 1973 to the PCI's leadership. It was Ingrao, who was to become speaker of the Chamber of Deputies from 1976 to 1979, who asserted that "with regard to our line we have to make it clear that the *'democratic route' does not mean the 'peaceful route,'* that we realize there will be harsh battles. Hence the problem of how to equip ourselves.... The prospect of a clash with armed corps also raises specific problems that have to be tackled."[298]

"The PCI," recounts the brigadist Gallinari, recalling the years of his militancy in that party, "lives on the myth of the Resistance and past struggles, but in its actual activities, in its daily political work, it always tends to govern the local situation through continual compromises. I instead chose Che Guevara's line: 'To build 10, 100, 1,000 Vietnams.' There's a contradiction in terms."[299]

The route that led Gallinari to leave the Italian Communist Party is extremely emblematic and similar to that of Alberto Franceschini, Roberto

297. G. Vacca, "Il problema storico del terrorismo in Italia," preface to P. Pergolizzi, *L'appartamento*, 13.

298. PCI leadership of 12 September 1973. Sergio Segio quoted by G. Crainz, *Il paese mancato*, 450. Italics added.

299. Gallinari, *Un contadino nella metropoli*, 46.

Ognibene, Attilio Casaletti, Fabrizio Pelli, Tonino Paroli, Lauro Azzolini, and Franco Bonisoli. The future leaders of the Red Brigades came, to a significant extent, from the FGCI (Young Italian Communists Federation) of Reggio Emilia. Hence Franceschini's opinion that the Red Brigades were "the fruit of a political culture and tradition of the Italian Left"[300] should also be carefully analyzed.

Gallinari is stirred by the myth of the betrayed Resistance, debated in the local branches of the Communist Party, and is enraptured by proclamations praising the revolution of the proletariat. But he very soon realizes that the party line is not consistent with its revolutionary objectives.

In late 1968, Gallinari, as a militant in the Communist Party's youth movement (FGCI), is asked to participate in a demonstration in Florence on the Indochina situation. The PCI's Central Committee decides that young Communists will be mobilized alongside young Catholics. The order is to march in silence, with lit candles and without party flags. Gallinari and his comrades are indignant: "The world is protesting... and we are sent... to trim candles!"[301] Dissent grows. The FGCI Provincial Committee of Reggio Emilia votes against the Central Committee's line. The protest is expressed publicly. It is an insult to the party, which replies by appointing an external commissioner.

A few months after the protest against the Florentine appointment, the news spreads that the U.S. president Nixon will be visiting Italy. Prompted by the party slogan "Italy out of NATO, NATO out of Italy," Gallinari, with some of his comrades, decides to participate in a demonstration against NATO at Miramare, near Rimini, where there is a U.S. base. The aim is ambitious: to reach the entrance of the base "and express all our anger against the United States military installation."[302]

Thanks to political training received in the Communist Party, Gallinari and his friends are well organized: "There's a strong emotional charge with many young people present. Demonstrators are coming from Trento, Pisa, Milan, Turin, Rome.... The slogans are extremely one-sided and not at all conciliatory. Vietnam, the events in Latin America, from the Bay of Pigs to the death of Guevara, are all facts that give us no reason to soften our relationship with the Yankees, the world's police."[303]

---

300. Fasanella and Franceschini, *Che cosa sono le BR*, 4.
301. Ibid., 50.
302. Ibid., 52.
303. Ibid.

When Gallinari arrives on the scene, the prefect is very clear: no offensive banners against the Americans because the national highway flanking the base is half Italian and half NATO territory. The demonstrators revolt. The clashes begin with insults, shoves, and bludgeons. The police are hit with marbles shot from catapults. "But, with equal velocity, the local party leaders consider the marchers' violent reaction as *fomented by troublemakers surreptitiously inserted in the demonstration.*" As the clashes increase in violence, the demonstrators furiously extract their party membership cards "to highlight to what *family* the agitators belong. . . . In a minute dozens of cards are brought out, flourished as if they were *Mao's little books* to the rhythm of anti-NATO slogans."[304] The officials are having a very difficult time and, after a negotiation, obtain an agreement to meet in a local theater to reach an understanding.

Gallinari understands that the Italian Communist Party is not acting in accordance with the revolutionary teaching with which it stirred the young militants' hearts. The PCI speaks of revolution but actually follows a moderate line. "The words that continued to be uttered in the rank and file," explains Franceschini, "were that you couldn't trust the middle classes and the institutions, that democracy was only a deceit: if you didn't annoy them they let you survive; but if you tried truly to change things, they would shoot you. To transform society it was necessary to disrupt the power relationships. And the only way to change the power relationships was to start the revolution, to use violence. In Reggio Emilia, during those years, this was what the Communist rank and file thought."[305]

Gallinari is not alone in feeling this. Other young militant communists would have chosen to be true to the revolutionary education they had received. The Italian Communist Party's leaders had exalted the myth of the proletarian revolution, knowing, however, that the international situation was unfavorable to insurrection (the fact that Italy had fallen under U.S. influence was obviously important). Although Palmiro Togliatti was among the first to realize that the idea of gaining power through violence (something not entirely repugnant to his political morality) had to be rejected,[306] many communist militants were still waiting for the "salvific" event, with all the frustration and resentment that a great disillusionment always causes.

Referring to the early seventies, Morucci recalls that "the working class was strong and angry in those years, the PCI grass roots were still waiting to

---

304. Ibid., 53.
305. Ibid., 27.
306. A. Agosti, *Togliatti,* 313.

see the promised fruits of the 'Republic born from the Resistance.'. . . The PCI
rank and file were still expecting that for once machine guns would be bran-
dished instead of olive branches, as Togliatti had promised in order to keep
them quiet. . . . I remember certain discussions with the PCI grass roots' militants: they weren't about whether violence was needed or not, but only when
it should be used. We were adventurists who used it irresponsibly, but then
they would have arrived to put everything right, when the time was ripe.
Only the time was never ripe. So we took things into our own hands."[307]

307. V. Morucci, *Ritratto di un terrorista da giovane*, 130–31.

CHAPTER 5

The Masters of the Red Brigades

> We are ruthless and ask no quarter from you. When
> our turn comes we shall not disguise our terrorism.
>
> —Karl Marx

Illustrious Predecessors: Thomas Müntzer

The Red Brigades' allegory of a joyful kingdom until the end of time has deep
roots. It is a yearning for transcendence with respect to *this world* that tends to
reappear during moments of great collective tension. The times and manner
of its appearance can vary, but the story is always the same: the world is a place
inhabited by demoniacal presences that are taking humanity toward destruction. But all is not lost because a handful of men know the way to salvation. To
expel "evil" from history one has to undergo a very harsh discipline. Thoughts,
gestures, and words must be purified to lead the war of extermination against
the "infected" elements that are attacking eternal happiness. An immense clash
is looming on the horizon. On the day of the "end," the "elect" will lead the
forces of "light" to victory. Then everything will be completed and finally a
joyful kingdom will liberate humanity from pain and suffering.

  The Red Brigades have illustrious predecessors. They belong to a politico-
religious tradition that, in its most complete form represented by the Jacobin
revolution, boasts at least two centuries of history. Although the core event
was Robespierre's ascent to power, the historic rise of revolutionary gnosticism started with the Protestant theologian Thomas Müntzer, the first to
accomplish a revolution in the attempt in install paradise on earth. He represents an "anthropological type" that still exists today.

As Tommaso La Rocca observes, Müntzer was a revolutionary through and through. He gives us an analysis of the social and political situation of Müntzer's time, including the radical plan for social transformation; the organization of a popular insurrection to be achieved by an alliance of peasants, miners, and other marginalized poor classes; the formation of vanguards; the careful selection of professional revolutionaries; the attempt to coordinate the various bands of insurgents as well as the importance attributed to propaganda in the form of leaflets, appeals, and letters.[1]

Müntzer is born around 1489–90 in Stolberg in the Harz Mountains, a village with its share of social and political tensions. Germany is involved in a stage of intense capitalistic development. The peasants' attempt to defend themselves from the "great transformation" provokes a chain of revolts that crosses Germany between 1513 and 1517, from the Hungarian border to southern Swabia.[2] Alongside the introduction of the first rudimental means of capitalist production, the serf system and church levies continue. Müntzer is the "son of these contradictions, that is, of the old that wants to preserve and the new that wants to assert itself."[3]

Unlike Luther, Müntzer has no vocation for the monastic life and meditation.[4] He is driven by the desire to tackle the problems of a society full of tensions. *This world* enthuses him more than the kingdom of heaven. His writings are concerned with the artisans and peasants who have migrated to the cities, with the exploited and the oppressed.

In 1512 he graduates in philosophy and theology at the University of Frankfurt on the Oder. In 1519—the year the emperor Maximilian I dies—he goes to Wittenberg, whose university is famous throughout Europe thanks to Luther, Carlostadio, and Melanchthon and their theological interpretation of the Bible. Müntzer supports Luther in denouncing the corruption of the Roman Church. From May 1519 to May 1520, he withdraws to the monastery of Beuditz near Weissenfels, where he devotes himself entirely to his studies. He molds his ideas into a revolutionary plan. At the end of his brief retreat, everything seems clear to him: the world is a corrupt place full of wicked people. The rich, the famous, the princes are all godless, and a relentless battle must be fought against them. The humble and the oppressed,

---

1. T. La Rocca, *Es ist Zeit*, 8.

2. For an analysis of the Peasants' War, see I. M. Battafarano, *Da Müntzer a Gaismair*, 11–27.

3. E. Campi, introduction to *Scritti politici*, by Thomas Müntzer, 13. See also Campi, "Thomas Müntzer," notebook no. 5.

4. For an analysis of Luther's and Müntzer's doctrinal differences, see E. Bloch, *Thomas Müntzer teologo della rivoluzione*, 120; M. Miegge, *Il sogno del re di babilonia*, 15–47; J. Lortz and E. Iserloh, *Storia della riforma*, 86–91.

guided by the will of God, have a mission to purify society. They will establish a kingdom based on love and solidarity. Egoism, self-interest, and money
will be eliminated.

In May 1520, Müntzer leaves Beuditz and goes to Zwickau, center of the
textile industry, where he finds a society undergoing intense proletarianiza-
tion. Capitalism has started to erode community bonds, creating an army of
alienated individuals in desperate search of "meaning." Müntzer becomes
immersed in the industrial proletariat's world, which is surrounded by a fe-
verish climate of religious exaltation. Numerous chiliastic sects, who believe
in Christ's imminent return, are active in Zwickau. This is where Nikolaus
Storch, Thomas Drechsel, and Markus Stübner, called the "Zwickau prophets," preach, bearing apocalyptic messages and convinced they are directly
inspired by the Holy Spirit. The working-class environment and the mystic-
religious exaltation radicalize Müntzer's preaching, and he is one of the main
promoters of a revolt in 1521. Because of this, he is "retired," accused of
instigating hatred. He flees the city and finds shelter in Bohemia, where the
memory is still alive of Jan Hus, theologian and religious reformer, excom-
municated in 1411 by the Catholic Church and burned at the stake. He
writes the *Prague Manifesto* in which he fulminates against priests and against
the Wittenberg theologians, accusing them of taking people away from the
word of God. He announces that the church of the elect will arise in Bohemia, where he intends to "sound the brazen and melodious bugles with the
new praises of the Holy Spirit."[5] His adversaries "are creatures of the devil,"[6]
"wicked men."[7] On Judgment Day, "the elect will clash with the wicked and
the latter's strength will fail before him."[8] To his beloved Bohemians he says,
"For love of the blood of Christ help me fight these enemies of the faith!"[9]

His incitement to insurrection is unsuccessful, and in December 1521
he leaves Prague. It is an eventful year. In April the Diet of Worms meets.
Luther refuses to recant his beliefs before Charles V: "*Hier stehe ich, ich kann
nicht anders*" (Here I stand, I cannot do otherwise). On Christmas in 1521,
Karlstadt, professor of theology at Wittenberg and ex-colleague of Luther,
celebrates Mass in the vernacular without holy vestments, omitting to el-
evate the consecrated host and inviting the faithful to receive Communion
by themselves. The population grows fervid with excitement. The peasants

5. T. Müntzer, "Manifesto di Praga," in *Scritti politici,* 75.
6. Ibid., 77.
7. Ibid., 78.
8. Ibid., 83.
9. Ibid., 86.

are threatening to revolt, and Luther openly takes the side of the German princes. In his *Faithful exhortation to all Christians not to become involved in disturbances and rebellion,* Luther condemns every form of violent protest against the established order. For Müntzer, this is a betrayal. His wanderings continue until he manages to be elected pastor in the small Saxony village of Allstedt (March 1523). He abolishes the Latin Mass and introduces a new liturgy. His preaching attracts new proselytes among the peasants and miners. He founds the "League of the Elect," a vanguard of believers, whose motto is "*Omnia sunt communia*" (All things are in common). Every man has to share what he has with his neighbor. The princes or counts who refuse to do so will be hanged or beheaded, because "not only are they acting against the faith, but against natural law, and *they must be killed like dogs.*"[10] On 24 March 1523, some "elect" of Allstedt lead an armed action against a Marian chapel containing an image of the Madonna considered miraculous.

For Luther, Müntzer is the "Satan of Allstedt."

Magister Thomas does not let himself be intimidated and exhorts his followers to exterminate without pity the enemies of his doctrine. It is a colossal plan of collective purification: "*For the ungodly have no right to live, save what the Elect choose to allow them.*" "Don't let them live any longer, the evildoers who turn us away from God." The sinners must be brought back to the straight path, "*and if they resist, let them be slaughtered without mercy.*" "Not only godless rulers, but priests and monks must be killed who call our holy Gospel a heresy and claim to be the best Christians themselves." "Christ has significantly ordered us to bring his enemies before him and to shake them. For what reason? Because they have damaged his plan."[11] Power on earth belongs to God, and Müntzer considers himself God's only interpreter: "The very stuff of usury, theft, and robbery are our lords made of. Fish in the water, birds in the air, the fruits of the earth—they want to take everything." "It would be a wondrous church in which the elect would be separated from the godless."[12]

The Saxon authorities react immediately. Under the threat of a bloodbath, Müntzer is forced to leave Allstedt. He takes refuge in Mühlhausen, where his preaching becomes even more radical. Mühlhausen is a small town of around seven thousand souls, where a furious conflict is already raging between the authorities and the urban proletariat. The former monk Heinrich Pfeiffer heads the people's protest. Contemporary chronicles speak of

---

10. Quoted by I. Šafarevič, *Il socialismo come fenomeno storico mondiale,* 90. Italics added. On this point, see also, for a rich bibliography, P. Blickle, *La riforma luterana e la guerra contadina,* 267–70.

11. Müntzer, "Manifesto di Praga," 90.

12. Ibid., 96.

repeated assaults on monasteries and churches and the destruction of images, statues, and religious objects.

Müntzer arrives on 24 August 1523. In September an insurrection leads to the dissolution of the town council and the foundation of the "Eternal League of God," a military organization that Müntzer eagerly supports with the compilation of the "Eleven Mühlhausen Articles." Once again, Müntzer is forced to flee (27 September 1524). This time he goes to Nuremberg, where he prints two of his works: *Explicit Unmasking of the False Belief of the Faithless World* and *Well-Founded Confutation.* He is censured and once more sets off. Arriving in Switzerland, he receives news that the popular front led by Pfeiffer has yet again seized power in Mühlhausen (February 1525). He turns back and becomes promoter of a "new order" founded on collectivism and on the people's direct control over government bodies. Ernst Bloch calls his preaching a "source of fire."[13]

In April 1525, armed peasants spread throughout Thuringia. Frankenhausen becomes the center of action, and eight thousand rebels arrive, but the princes have superior forces. Five thousand peasants die in the battle, with another thousand killed in the now conquered city. On 17 May, Müntzer writes to the Mühlhausen insurgents. He claims responsibility for the choices made, but urges them to surrender. In Igor Šafarevič's reconstruction, Müntzer ran from the city, found an empty house, and got into bed, feigning illness. A looting soldier who had entered the house recognized him by chance. Once arrested he was horribly tortured and, to discredit him, was forced to write a retraction (Manfred Bensing has judged it to be "false"[14]). He was beheaded, and his head exhibited on a stake.

Emidio Campi maintains that Müntzer worked "with the real intuition of a great revolutionary." For him, Mühlhausen represented "a hope for all the exploited and a continual threat to feudal power."[15] Campi has defended Müntzer from those who, with "false" documents, have tried to stain his reputation. He is also defended by Friedrich Engels, who, besides recalling the courage with which Müntzer faced the scaffold,[16] thought his program was an "inspired forerunner"[17] of the communist revolution.

---

13. Bloch, *Thomas Müntzer teologo della rivoluzione,* 166.

14. See M. Bensing, *Thomas Müntzer und der Thuringer Aufstand.*

15. Campi, introduction, 39.

16. F. Engels, "La guerra dei contadini in Germania," in *Opere complete,* by K. Marx and F. Engels, 10:482.

17. Ibid., 10:427–28. Engels writes: "For Müntzer the kingdom of God is an organization of society in which there are no longer any social differences, nor private property, nor extraneous and independent state authority, conflict with members of society."

It is difficult to deny that Müntzer constituted a threat to the privileged classes. There is no doubt that the peasant "was treated as a thing, a beast of burden and even worse."[18] However, it is not at all certain that the society of the "elect" would have been the salvation of the oppressed, as Engels would have us believe. Müntzer was a fundamentalist, a religious fanatic. Driven by a millenarian concept of history, he considered himself to be the guardian of absolute knowledge that would open the doors of heaven on earth to the oppressed.

Müntzer was an explosive mixture of both gnosticism and messianism.

Messianism can be studied either as a religious, psychological, or political phenomenon. As a religious phenomenon, messianism is waiting for the Messiah to bring salvation. In psychology, it is the delirious state of someone convinced of having a mission of fundamental importance for the destiny of humanity. In politics, it is the expectation of a profound political and social upheaval that will free people from unhappiness and suffering.

Müntzer possessed all three aspects of messianism. The Devil is everywhere in his preaching.[19] People have to be vigilant to prevent the Evil One entering merciful hearts. The society he planned had no individual freedom. Individuals would have had to breathe together, merged in a single body. Thoughts, gestures, and words would all be strictly disciplined, forbidden, and condemned—in fact everything that displeased Müntzer, the intermediary between God and people, the only guardian of absolute, incontestable truth, because of divine origin. For Italo Michele Battafarano, he was "firmly convinced that, because of its divine descent, the community of the elect could never fail. Müntzer, thinking of himself, denied that a bad preacher could pervert the soul of true Christians—he did not even consider it a theoretical possibility."[20]

His community was a permanent pyre. Horrendous tortures, hangings, and beheadings awaited those who dared to express even the mildest doubt about his ideas. The "godless" would be exterminated because the word of God, we read in one of his works, must be listened to "with the greatest fear and trembling."[21]

---

18. Ibid., 10:412.

19. See L. Parinetto, *La rivolta del diavolo*, 103–21.

20. Battafarano, *Da Müntzer a Gaismair*, 39. Battafarano's book is also useful for its reconstruction of Michael Gaismair's revolutionary path and for its observations on the relationship between the revolutionary spirit and the capitalist adventures that were to change the face of the Tyrol between the fifteenth and sixteenth centuries (90ff.).

21. *Esplicita messa a nudo della falsa fede del mondo infedele mediante la testimonianza del vangelo di Luca esposto alla misera compassionevole cristianità per rammentarle i suoi falli*, in Müntzer, *Scritti politici*, 138.

The princes will disappear, but the hierarchical principle and exploitation will not disappear because of this. In Müntzer's society, where the opponents were normally decapitated,[22] the "elect" speak, teach, and explain, and all the others listen, learn, and carry out: "Thus you, man of the people, must learn your knowledge directly from the mouth of God so that you are no longer seduced."[23] "Thus someone is needed to turn men toward the revelation of the divine lamb, in accordance with the eternal word that comes from the Father."[24] In such a society, "we carnal, earthly men shall become gods through the incarnation of Christ as man. And we will be pupils of God with him, being taught and deified by God himself. Yes indeed, even more, we should be completely and totally transformed into him so that earthly life revolves around into the heavenly."[25] No more laughter, jests, or amusements of any kind. Every demonstration of joyfulness or merriment must be repressed, because it is only in suffering and mortification of the flesh that the message of God can be understood: "In short, it cannot be otherwise. Man must smash to bits his stolen, contrived Christian faith through powerful, *enormous suffering* of the heart, through painful grief, and through an amazement that cannot be rejected."[26]

These are some extracts from his work *Explicit Unmasking of the False Belief of the Faithless World* (1524): "Should someone wish to be filled with the eternal divine gifts, *then after long chastisement, through his suffering and his cross,* he must be emptied for revelations, so that he may be filled according to the measure of his faith, by the greatest treasures of Christian wisdom."[27] "Man with all his carnal desires must turn to God."[28] "A servant of God, rich in grace, must step forward in the Spirit of Elijah and he must bring all things into the right momentum. *Truly, many of these servants must be awakened, so that, with the greatest zeal and with passionate rigor, they cleanse Christendom of godless rulers.* First of all, *the people must also be sternly reprimanded on account of their disorderly desires,* who so luxuriously while away their time without any steadfast interest in a rigorous consideration of the faith."[29]

---

22. F. Engels recalls it in *La guerra dei contadini in Germania,* 482.
23. Müntzer, *Esplicita messa,* 136.
24. Ibid., 158.
25. Ibid., 145.
26. Ibid., 159. Italics added.
27. Ibid., 158. Italics added.
28. Ibid., 161.
29. Ibid., 160. Italics added.

John of Leiden, King and Revolutionary

The Anabaptist Jan Beukelszoon, better known as John of Leiden, had no better fate than Müntzer. The name "Anabaptist" was coined by their adversaries to indicate those who rejected infant baptism, claiming that a "second" baptism was needed in adult life.

John of Leiden also believes that the world is corrupt and corrupting and lives under the constant influence of Satan. Between 1534 and 1535, accompanied by the Dutch baker Jan Matthys, he took control of the city of Münster, in Westphalia. The Anabaptists established a theocratic-communalistic republic, based on the massive and systematic use of totalitarian terror. The history of this experiment starts with Matthys's mystic-religious delirium and his prediction of the imminent reign of Christ on earth before the final judgment.

Armed rebellion broke out on 9 February 1534 following the decision of Münster's town council to expel some Anabaptists who had plundered and set fire to churches and convents. Hordes of fanatics ran through the city, shouting, "Repent, or God will punish you! Father, Father, annihilate the godless." The Lutherans were in the majority and could have crushed the rebels, but the mediation of burgomaster Tilbek (who sympathized with the Anabaptists) brought about an agreement for religious peace. Power relations were reversed on 21 February, when the Anabaptists obtained the majority in the town council. On 24 February they undertook their first punitive expedition. Churches were destroyed, religious objects smashed, and saints' relics thrown into the streets. Their pantoclastic fury was also turned on the statues decorating the marketplace.

Since the world is "infected" and fire purifies, the bonfires arrived soon after. A valuable collection of Italian manuscripts belonging to Rudolf van Langen was burned in the public square. The paintings of the Westphalian school, famous at the time, were destroyed so thoroughly that this school is now known only by reputation. Even musical instruments were smashed. On 27 February, the Anabaptists started to carry out one of the major items of their "electoral program": the expulsion of the godless. Matthys, inspired by God's will, insisted that they all be put to death. Burgomaster Knipperdolling was more realistic, albeit sharing in principle his master's approach. Fearing the revenge of their enemies, he proposed their expulsion. An armed meeting of Anabaptists was called. Matthys closed his eyes and fell into a trance. At the end of his tête-à-tête with the Eternal Father, he exclaimed: "Down with the sons of Esau! The inheritance belongs to the sons of Jacob." It was a very cold winter. The Anabaptists forced their way into the citizens' houses. Hundreds of men and women, old people and children, were dragged out into the snow and their homes sacked.

Another item in the "divine program" was the socialization of property. Silver, gold, and money had to be handed over and terror was used to overcome any resistance. Matthys gathered three hundred people in the town square and said to them, "The Lord is wrathful and calls for sacrifice."[30] For hours the desperate prayers could be heard of those who, locked in a deserted church, were sure they would die. Entering the church behind a group of armed men, Matthys watched the victims grovel before him on their knees, imploring him to intercede for them. There was great joy when they learned that Matthys had obtained pardon for them from God.[31]

The blacksmith Hubert Rüsher, who had spoken against the actions of the prophets, was dragged in front of the citizens' meeting. Matthys demanded his death. Some of those present asked for him to be pardoned. John of Leiden shouted, "To me the power of the Lord is given so that by my hand everyone who opposes the commands of the Lord will be struck down!"[32] He hit Rüsher with a halberd, and the wounded man was led away to jail. While the assembly continued to dispute his fate, Rüsher was again brought to the town square, where Matthys killed him with a single thrust in the back.

Münster's theocratic republic was not a peaceful community, threatened only by outside enemies. The establishment of polygamy, for example, was resisted by the same insurgents. Thus John of Leiden announced that polygamy was a divine order. Anyone who opposed it would be condemned to death.

This was the law introduced in Münster:[33]

1. All previous marriages are declared null.
2. All women have to take a husband. This also applies to old and barren women.
3. The woman in a "sterile" marriage shall be given another husband.
4. A man who has already conceived a child with a woman is immediately allowed to take another and, after having made this one pregnant, has the right to take a third wife, a fourth, and so on.
5. Both husband and wife are allowed to request and obtain divorce.
6. Foreigners are also held to observe these rules.

---

30. Quoted from Šafarevič, *Il socialismo come fenomeno storico mondiale,* 104.
31. See N. Cohn, *I fanatici dell'apocalisse,* 351.
32. Quoted from Šafarevič, *Il socialismo come fenomeno storico mondiale,* 105.
33. See F. P. Reck-Malleczewen, *Il re degli anabattisti,* 101–2.

7. An assembly of elders would resolve any conflicts between husband and wives.

8. The nonobservance of these laws carries the death penalty.

The blacksmith Mollenhecke opposed the oligarchy of the "elect." Supported by two hundred citizens, he organized a rebellion to put an end to the prophets' reign of terror and fury. Discovered, the rebels barricaded themselves in the town hall, declaring their surrender from its windows. Out of two hundred, forty were pardoned.

The others were massacred, but without haste.

John of Leiden called his faithful men and ordered them to dig a great ditch in the cathedral square. A rebel who had managed to escape was torn from the arms of his wife and children and quartered, still alive, with halberds. The executions were performed in small doses so that the pedagogic effect would be more lasting. Each day ten rebels were killed. For weeks, the victims' cries of pain echoed through the city. After the repression, matrimonial legislation was no longer questioned and neither was the harem of John of Leiden, containing sixteen women.

John of Leiden's coronation is worth recording.

In September 1534, a goldsmith called Dusentschur appeared in Münster. According to his prophecy, announced in the city square, John of Leiden would have established, by God's will, a new kingdom that would have held dominion over the sovereigns of the earth. On hearing these words, John of Leiden threw himself face down on the ground and invoked the aid of the Lord. Then he shouted: "In just such a manner was David, humble shepherd, consecrated by the prophet, by order of God, as king of Israel. God often acts in this way; and anyone who resists the will of God calls down his anger on himself. Now I receive the power over all the nations of the earth, and the right to use the sword to mortify the wicked and to defend the just. May no one in this city stain himself with sin and resist the will of God, or otherwise he will be put to death by the sword."[34]

Not everyone was won over by these prophecies. John of Leiden replied to the signs of protest from the people with these words: "Shame on you, who murmur against the decree of the heavenly Father! Even if you all come together against me, I would reign, despite you, not only over this city but over the entire world, because it is the Father who wants it; and my reign, which begins now, will last and will never be overturned."[35]

---

34. This speech can be read in Cohn, *I fanatici dell'apocalisse,* 361.

35. Ibid., 361–62.

Münster had a new king who wore clothes studded with gold and fine rings worked by the best craftsmen of the city. His wife Divara was proclaimed queen. A court of two hundred people was created that strolled through the city streets showing off precious apparel. A bodyguard was organized and a magnificent throne was erected in the marketplace. John of Leiden said he gained no benefit from the splendor surrounding him since he considered his earthly body to be dead.

And yet in a propaganda pamphlet of October 1534, he had written: "Everything that has served the purposes of self-seeking and private property, such as buying and selling, working for money, taking interest and practicing usury—even at the expense of unbelievers—or eating and drinking the sweat of the poor (that is, making one's own people and fellow creatures work so that one can grow fat) and indeed everything that offends against love—all such things are abolished among us by the power of love and community. And knowing that God now desires to abolish such abominations, we would die rather than turn to them. We know that such sacrifices are pleasing to the Lord. And indeed no Christian or saint can satisfy God if he does not live in such community or at least desire with all his heart to live in it."[36]

Münster capitulated on 14 June 1535, after an eighteen-month siege. John of Leiden had to surrender to the bishop prince Franz von Waldeck. Attached to a pole by an iron-spiked collar, his body was ripped with red-hot tongs for the space of an hour. He died after his heart was pierced with a red-hot dagger. Yet his revolutionary spirit long survived him.[37]

The English Revolution and the Puritan Movement

The idea of the purification of the world, to be accomplished by subverting its foundations, reappears "after a century of hibernation"[38] in the leaders of the Puritan revolution. For Vittorio Mathieu, the first "real revolutionaries"[39] were the Puritans. They transferred the revolution from heaven to earth, transforming a religious attitude into a political force. In seventeenth-century England, "so modern and so emblematically remote from the ducal fortress

---

36. Ibid., 353.
37. For an analysis of the political myth of a kingdom with no more conflict and of its most recent "incarnations," see M. G. Pelayo, *Miti e simboli politici.*
38. L. Pellicani, *Revolutionary Apocalypse.*
39. V. Mathieu, *La speranza nella rivoluzione,* 193.

of Allstedt, a religious game is again being played whose actors consider it to be above human capacities."[40]

Revolutionary gnosticism is a "karstic" phenomenon. It "creeps" under the surface of Western civilization, ready to reemerge at times of great political and social upheaval.

Michael Walzer, in a historical and sociological study of Calvinist politics during the hundred years before the English Revolution of 1640, considered the Puritan conscience to be a response to the social tensions caused by the modernization process.[41]

The contest for political power, explains Walzer, has always existed, whereas revolutionary politics has appeared only in recent times. The idea of "remaking society" according to God's word does not come into Machiavelli's thinking. Here, the *Prince* is the driving force of historical change; all the others are condemned to political passiveness. But modern revolutions have not been the work of a sovereign or a state but of radical groups driven by an extraordinary ideological determination. The Puritans considered themselves "divine instruments" and thought any opposition was an example of the Devil's ingeniousness. Calvin himself urged believers to fight to establish the kingdom of God on earth. His preaching exhorted action and not passiveness.[42] With Puritanism, a "new" idea of politics asserts itself that—for Walzer as well as Sternberger—is no longer the art of governing the city (Aristotle), nor the fight to gain power (Machiavelli). It is the attainment of heaven on earth, the systematic attempt to transform the world to glorify God. Puritan politics are typically "eschatological." They shift the problem of salvation from the hereafter to the here and now.

In Oliver Cromwell's vision, politics and religion are inseparable. Driven by a "providentialistic" view of history—according to which God deals directly with earthly affairs—Cromwell regarded his victory as the direct result of the will of God. On 4 July 1653, he spoke to Parliament: "I confess I never looked to see such a day as this—it may be nor you neither—when Jesus Christ should be so owned as He is, at this day.... And you manifest this, insofar as poor creatures can do, to be a day of the Power of Jesus Christ.... Therefore hold steady your vocation: it is extraordinary and comes from God and has neither been designed nor thought by you or me."[43]

---

40. Miegge, *Il sogno del re di babilonia,* 138.

41. See M. Walzer, *La rivoluzione de santi (The Revolution of the Saints).*

42. See J. Calvin, *Istituzione della religione cristiana (Institutes of the Christian Religion),* 1:1076–78.

43. The quotation is from *The Writings and Speeches of Oliver Cromwell,* ed. W. C. Abbott. See also O. Cromwell, *Discorsi e lettere della rivoluzione.* On this extract, see Miegge, *Il sogno del re di babilonia,* 178.

Thanks to this "ideology of redemption," to be achieved through politics, Cromwell managed to create an army of men upheld by the conviction that they were the instrument of Christ's will. His followers marched to free the world of evil and sin. It was the desire to glorify the Lord more than the lust for power that transformed them into a feared and disciplined army, capable of defeating Charles I: "What are all our histories," Cromwell once asked, "and other traditions of the past, if not God who manifests himself?"[44] In his speeches and his letters, people are the instrument of divine will. It is God who instills courage or cowardice in their hearts. There is no human thought or action that does not follow his plans.

Religious fanaticism played a key role in the English Revolution. The people's movements were created around radical religious sects. Their preaching against simoniac clergy, the pope, feudal privileges, and the corruption of earthly institutions was all inspired by the model of early Christianity, aimed at achieving a strictly communal kingdom. They pursued the dream of a perfect society, based on justice and universal brotherhood.[45] They promised that evil would disappear and the destitute would finally receive justice. This revolutionary utopia incited the masses, calling the deprived to action by providing new visions of the world and fomenting a climate of collective exaltation focused on the expectation of the end.[46]

Thomas Harrison, a prominent Fifth Monarchist, was certain that the return of Christ to earth was imminent. His followers were convinced that they had to gain power to remove the obstacles to his advent. For this work of redemption, Christ would have called them to him on the day of the last judgment. All would have had to recognize the government of the saints. Those who opposed it would have been considered servants of the Antichrist.[47] "In an atmosphere of millenarian and apocalyptic expectations, the crowds were harangued by all kind of preachers, who spread with words and pamphlets great hopes and terrible fears: fears of plots and betrayals, hopes of renewal of the world and the return of Christ on earth."[48] In this context, the "Antichrist" category bursts into the political debate with devastating force. Between 1640 and 1660, the English Parliament acted as a sounding board for the millenarian blaze that inflamed the multitudes. The enemies

---

44. Quoted from H. N. Brailsford, *I livellatori e la Revoluzione inglese,* 1:195.
45. G. Schiavone, *Winstanley,* 11.
46. On the role of religious sects and on "waiting for the end" in English revolutionary history, see A. Colombo and G. Schiavone, eds., *L'utopia nella storia.*
47. See G. Garavaglia, *Storia dell'Inghilterra moderna,* 746.
48. A. Prosperi and P. Viola, *Storia moderna e contemporanea,* 2:35.

are "the followers of the Beast," and the king's armed supporters are "the party of the Antichrist."

In a sermon to the Commons in 1641, William Bridge announced that: "This moment of Parliament is the moment of the start for good or for evil...down with Babylon."[49] In June of the same year, Henry Burton warned the deputies against "the slavery of the Antichrist's hierarchy," announcing its imminent end. In September it was the turn of Jeremiah Burroughs, who described the peace concluded with Scotland "as the greatest blow ever made against the Antichristian power of prelacy, ... God's revenge against the Antichrist." And added: "God has started a work that He will never leave until He has completed it. The Antichrist will no longer prevail as he has in the past....It was the moment that God spurred his servants to tackle the ways of the Antichrist, solely to bear witness to His truth, and to exercise their graces; but He let the Antichrist prevail....But now...God has decided to ruin him....Thus all you who love Jerusalem take courage in setting yourselves against the Antichristian party."[50]

Other members of Parliament warned: "It has been prophesied in the *Apocalypse* that the Whore of Babylon will be destroyed with fire and with the sword....It is said in the *Apocalypse* that also the people, the multitude and the nations have to bring her down."[51] On 23 February 1642, the theologian Stephen Marshall preached the following sermon to the House of Commons: "The powerful often oppose the Lord....The followers and servants of the Lamb are often poor and the dregs of the world, whereas kings and captains, merchants and sages...give the Beast all their strength."[52] This sermon is remembered for a particularly brutal passage: "If the work were that of avenging God's church against Babylon, he is a blessed man that takes and dashes the little ones against the stones."[53] Two months later, Marshall added in that same arena that "many of the nobles, judges, knights and gentlemen and people of great quality are infamous traitors and rebels against God, allied with men and wicked causes against truth."[54]

The English Revolution had its "mystic" in Gerrard Winstanley, the leader of the Diggers (so called because they proposed to dig up the enclosures

---

49. Quoted by C. Hill, *L'Anticristo nel Seicento inglese,* 63.
50. Ibid., 64.
51. Ibid., 61.
52. Ibid., 62.
53. Ibid.
54. Ibid., 63.

around private property).[55] In his book, *The New Law of Righteousness,* 1649, Winstanley recounts that during a mystic trance he had heard the voice of God telling him: "Work together. Eat bread together." Winstanley organized a community founded on the common cultivation of land on Saint George's Hill. On 20 April 1649, the Diggers published a kind of manifesto, the *True Levellers Standard Advanced,* with fifteen signatories. It challenged the hierarchical organization of society and the authoritarianism on which it is founded: the king has been deposed, but people have still not yet been liberated from oppression. They are born equal and they should aspire to behave like Jesus' apostles. Hence the institution of private property is an aberration that offends the will of the Lord.

The public authorities and the residents of Cobham, the district that they had chosen as their base, were both hostile to the Diggers who, pacifist and hardworking, were often forced to leave their settlements because of harassment. They represent a typical example of the "passive sect." They were obsessed by the idea of "purity" but did not adopt the idea of "purification." As seen earlier, the identification of "evil" is only typical of "active sects," who follow up the rejection of the world with the desire to destroy it and to re-create it in a completely new way.

The identification of evil was the characteristic trait of the Jacobin movement. It did not stop at exterminating its enemies but practiced a "philosophy of terror" that was to find its best interpreters in the twentieth century.

The English Revolution overturned the ancient regime, beheaded the king, declared it wanted to establish the kingdom of God on earth, and launched a rigid dictatorship. However, Cromwell's experiment did not create a revolutionary tradition because the English elite were extremely wary of the consequences of violence. They considered the Puritan revolution as something never to be repeated and best forgotten. It is no coincidence that they called the revolution of 1688 "glorious" since, unlike the former, it had occurred without bloodshed.

The Jacobin revolution of 1793 was a very different experience. After having created the myth of revolutionary violence as an instrument for "remaking" the world, it was exported worldwide. A myth—it has been said—

---

55. On the Diggers movement and Winstanley, besides Schiavone, *Winstanley,* see also E. Bernstein, *Cromwell and Communism,* 105–32; *The Works of Gerrard Winstanley,* ed. G. H. Sabine; G. H. Sabine, *Storia delle dottrine politiche,* 393–97; G. E. Aylmer, "England's Spirit Unfolded; or, An Incouragement to Take the Engagement"; C. Hill, *Il mondo alla rovescia,* 97–140; G. Fiaschi, *Potere, rivoluzione e utopia nell'esperienza di Gerrard Winstanley;* O. Lutaud, *Winstanley;* G. Gabriella, *La lingua inglese e la rivoluzione puritana.*

that was to have profound repercussions on the history of the twentieth century.

The French Revolution and the Jacobin Experiment

With the French Revolution, the idea of rebellion broke away from its religious origin. History is guided not by God but by people.

Cromwell's experiment had its intellectual roots in Puritan preaching. Robespierre's political mission was inscribed in that tradition that sees society—and no longer people—as the source of every evil: "Man by nature is good," wrote Rousseau, "and it is only our society that has corrupted him,"[56] or, to quote from his most famous work: "Man is born free, but everywhere he is in chains."[57]

Rousseau, Morelly, Mably, and Deschamps entrust the task of ridding history of evil to a profound social upheaval.[58]

Morelly's *Code of Nature* appeared in 1755 in an anonymous form. This work—which Babeuf claimed inspired him—contained, according to Engels, "an authentic communist theory." It had an enormous influence in the history of revolutionary thought and was superseded only by Marxist doctrine, which absorbed its fundamental ideas. Morelly's thesis is that property is the source of all human woes. Where no property exists, none of its pernicious consequences could exist: "Take away property, I will repeat tirelessly, and you will eliminate forever the thousand events that lead men to desperation. I say that, if freed from this tyranny, it is absolutely impossible for man to be driven to commit crimes, whether he be a thief, murderer, or conqueror."[59]

Gabriel Bonnot de Mably reached the same conclusion, seeing in private property the source of "all the vices of wealth, all those of poverty, the brutalization of souls, the corruption of civil customs... unjust and tyrannical governments, partial and oppressive laws, in fact this mass of disasters, under which the people groan.... Establish the communality of goods and it will

---

56. Quoted by W. Durant, *Rousseau e la rivoluzione,* 198. From a letter Rousseau wrote to Malesherbes dated 12 January 1762.

57. J.-J. Rousseau, *Il contratto sociale,* 52.

58. A fundamental discussion of Rousseau's transposition of the debate on evil from the theological to the political field is E. Cassirer, "Il problema Gian Giacomo Rousseau," in his *Tre letture di Rousseau.*

59. Morelly, *Codice della natura,* 51.

become easier to establish the equality of conditions and to found on this double base the happiness of men."[60]

Deschamps also wanted to relieve humanity from moral corruption through the same "antienlightenment" recipe. By making private property communal, "there would be no more religion, or subordination, or wars, or politics, or jurisprudence, or finance, or taxes, or trade, or fraud; no bankruptcies, nor judges, no thefts, no murders, no moral evil, no criminal laws."[61]

Rousseau did not theorize communism, but he uncompromisingly criticizes the institutions supporting capitalist society. Starting from the assumption that "the majority of evils is our work and we could have prevented almost all of them by preserving the simple, uniform and solitary life that nature prescribed,"[62] he condemns individualism, profit, representative democracy, and the market. In his *Constitutional Project for Corsica,* he would like the state "to own everything, and for each individual to share in the common property only in proportion to his services."[63] However, considering it impossible to destroy private property absolutely, he proposes to "confine it within the narrowest possible limits; to give it a measure, a rule, a rein which will contain, direct, and subjugate it, and keep it ever subordinate to the public good." His aim is to ensure that "the property of the state be as large and strong, that of the citizens as small and weak, as possible."[64]

It is the triumph of the Spartan ideal over the Athenian one; the community over the individual. The philosophes have the task of shaping society according to the categorical imperatives of "disembodied reason." Philosophy is not only a method for knowing the world, it is the instrument for radically transforming it. The masses must become responsible for their own destiny, but they need to be guided because, as Rousseau writes, "often they do not know what they want because they rarely know what is good for them."[65] These succinct words contain the "manifesto" of all the demoted intellectuals who want to assume the right/duty to guide humanity toward harmony and universal concord. This helps us understand how Ernst Cassirer, in a justly famous essay, stressed "the detachment between Rousseau and his century,"[66] a conclusion shared by Lucio Colletti, who dwelled on the

60. G. Bonnot de Mably, "Dubbi proposti ai filosofi economisti sull'ordine naturale delle società politiche," in his *Scritti politici,* 2:47–49 and 51.

61. D. Deschamps, "Le vrai systeme," in *Illuminismo e utopia,* ed. S. Bartolomei, 211.

62. J.-J. Rousseau, *Origine della disuguaglianza,* 44.

63. J.-J. Rousseau, "Progetto di Costituzione per la Corsica," in *Scritti politici,* 1113.

64. Ibid.

65. Rousseau, *Il contratto sociale,* 751.

66. E. Cassirer, *Filosofia dell'illuminismo,* 368.

"rupture between Rousseau and liberalism."[67] Rousseau was not the "spiritual father of modern democracy"[68]—as Galvano Della Volpe tells us—but its staunch enemy.

Rousseau's general will, Guido De Ruggiero has written, cannot err: "It is thus an infallible and irresistible power, against which the individual can neither complain nor appeal: who would he complain to if not to himself, to whom could he appeal against the truth?"[69] On the other hand, it was Rousseau who proved the illiberal nature of his key idea of the "general will," pillar of a rigorously anti-individualistic society. In his words: "The Sovereign, being formed wholly of the individuals who compose it, neither has nor can have any interest contrary to theirs; and *consequently the sovereign power need give no guarantee to its subjects, because it is impossible for the body to wish to hurt all its members.*"[70]

The principle on which a liberal democracy is founded, however, is the opposite of that announced by Rousseau. This principle asserts that individuals must be continuously "protected" by the "sovereign power" through a series of political-juridical guarantees, without which the public powers would be "free"—they alone—to give themselves up to abuse and prevarication at any time. Liberal democracy, to echo Giovanni Sartori, is a system for controlling and limiting power.[71]

Rousseau, Morelly, and their imitators rejected what the dominant values of the Enlightenment had extolled. They conceived the history of humanity as a continual regression and defended a model of collectivistic society—the "virtuous" Sparta against the "corrupt" Athens—whereas the Enlightenment thinkers had reformist and never revolutionary aims.

Condorcet (1743–94), mathematician and philosopher, a student of d'Alembert, contributed to the *Encyclopédie* and took an active part in the revolutionary events of his time. After having been president of the National Assembly, he was overthrown by the Jacobin Terror. Branded a traitor, he committed suicide a few days after his arrest in March 1794. Convinced that violent and sudden upheavals were worse than the evils people wanted to cure, Condorcet preached in favor of a gradual change in French society. In his fundamental work, *Progress of the Human Mind,* he distinguished between the equality established by institutions and that existing among individuals.

---

67. L. Colletti, "Rousseau critico della 'società civile,'" in *Ideologia e società,* 229.
68. G. Della Volpe, *Rousseau e Marx,* 11.
69. G. De Ruggiero, *Storia del liberalismo europeo,* 67–68.
70. Rousseau, *Il contratto sociale,* 66. Italics added.
71. See G. Sartori, *Democrazia,* 155.

He also pointed out that equality must be considered a "guiding idea" of political action and not a principle for precipitating the world into chaos, because assassinations are "freakish atrocities, humiliating and vile in the eyes of nature and staining with indelible opprobrium the country or the age whose annals record them."[72] The causes of inequality in wealth and education, explained Condorcet, "must constantly diminish without, however, disappearing altogether: for they are the result of natural and necessary causes which it would be foolish and dangerous to wish to eradicate and one could not even attempt to bring about the entire disappearance of their effects... without striking more direct and more fatal blows at the rights of man."[73]

Condorcet had learned Voltaire's lesson that social changes should occur in a continuous and gradual manner: "There are many countries," Voltaire wrote, "in which the laws are more uniform, but there is not one which does not need a reform; and once this reform is carried another is needed.... Finally, when one comes to live under a tolerable law, war arrives that confuses all the limits, that ruins everything; and you have to start again like ants whose house has been crushed."[74] Holbach's "proposal" was no less hostile to sudden and radical changes: "No, not by means of dangerous upheavals, not by means of struggles, assassinations and useless crimes can the people's wounds be healed. The remedies are always worse than the evils they want to treat. The voice of reason is neither seditious nor bloodthirsty. The reforms it proposes are slow, but no less secure because of this."[75]

Voltaire's and Rousseau's contrasting philosophical traditions inspired two French revolutions with divergent means and ends: the revolution of 1789, which was to have reconciled the monarchic principle with the emerging classes' right to representation; and the one of 1793, which proposed to *make a clean sweep of this world* by eliminating all those who had compromised themselves with the aristocratic regime. The leading actors of 1789 opted for a gradual transformation of the French institutions; those of 1793 were inspired by a pantoclastic concept of historic development.[76]

With the Jacobin revolution, the religious sphere is absorbed in the political one.[77] Here virtue triumphs over "the will of God." The revolutionary Jacobin addresses the people, calling them to action in the name of a "higher" truth, fruit of philosophical reflection. The Jacobin "story" goes

---

72. N. de Condorcet, *I progressi dello spirito umano,* 205.
73. Ibid., 192.
74. Voltaire, *Saggio sui costumi e lo spirito delle nazioni,* 4:531.
75. Quoted by Pellicani, *Revolutionary Apocalypse,* 35.
76. See G. Ferrero, *Le due rivoluzioni francesi.*
77. See F. Furet, *Le due rivoluzioni,* 37.

as follows: the world is "infested" with the corrupt aristocratic presence. To save it from the depths into which it has fallen, the harmful elements have to be found and exterminated. This idea has its most famous formulation in Robespierre's *Report*, presented to the Convention on 25 December 1793: "The revolution is the war of liberty against its enemies. . . . The revolutionary government needs extraordinary acts precisely because it is in a state of war. If virtue be the spring of a popular government in times of peace, the spring of that government during a revolution is virtue combined with terror: virtue, without which terror is destructive; terror, without which virtue is impotent. Terror is only justice—prompt, severe and inflexible; it is then an emanation of virtue; it is less a distinct principle than a natural consequence of the general principle of democracy, applied to the most pressing wants of the country. . . . The government in a revolution is the despotism of liberty against tyranny."[78] On 5 February 1794, Robespierre was to assert: "We wish, in a word, to fulfil the intentions of nature and the destiny of man, realize the promises of philosophy, and acquit providence of a long reign of crime and tyranny."[79]

The Jacobins never actually proposed the abolition of private property, but the idea of purifying the world through the extermination of their enemies is fully theorized and consistently applied. The same idea of purification and regeneration returns in the words of Fouquier-Tinville, public prosecutor of the revolutionary tribunal:

> If we purge ourselves, it is because we want the right to purge France. We will not leave any foreign body in the Republic: the enemies of freedom must tremble because the club is raised; it will be the Convention that wields it. Our enemies are not so numerous as they want us to think; they will soon be exposed and will appear on the theatre of the guillotine. It is said that we want to abolish the Convention; no, it will remain intact; but we intend to prune the dead branches of this great tree. The great measures we have taken are like gusts of wind that make the rotten fruit fall and leave the good fruit on the tree; afterwards you will be able to pick those remaining and they will be ripe and tasty; they will carry life into the republic. I don't care if there are many branches, if they are rotten. It's better that a smaller number remain, as long as they are green and sturdy.[80]

---

78. M. Robespierre, *La rivoluzione giacobina*, 160.
79. Ibid.
80. Quoted by L. Trockij, *Giacobinismo e socialdemocrazia*, 424.

The gnostic-Manichaean Weltanschauung returns: the world is a putrid and nauseating marsh. The revolutionaries have the task of reclaiming it, whatever the cost. What Robespierre wants, as revealed by his letter to Baumetz in 1790, is no different from what the apostle Paul announced in his second epistle: "A new land in which justice will reign."[81] The Jacobin Carrier's intentions are clear: "We will make France a cemetery," says Carrier, "rather than not regenerate it our own way."[82] The words of Saint-Just are no less instructive: "The incorrigible supporters of tyranny dream of nothing else but our defeat, and every day they create new enemies of freedom.... Thus we must purge the country of its declared enemies.... There is no hope of prosperity if the last enemy of freedom would breathe. *You have to punish not only the traitors, but even those who are indifferent;* you have to punish whoever is passive in the republic, and who does nothing for it; since the French people have manifested their will, everything opposed to it is outside the sovereign body. Whatever is outside the sovereign body is an enemy."[83]

As we have seen, one of the typical traits of the "active sects" is the identification of evil, always accompanied by the idea of purifying through the extermination of entire social categories. Revolutionary violence continually changes the boundaries between "good" and "evil." Since these are established by the minority in power, they are liable to continual variation. It follows that the political activity of a revolutionary sect has necessarily to be terroristic because its "friends" cannot be clearly distinguished from its "enemies." The world is "infected," hence there is a continual risk of contamination. Anyone could be accused of coming to terms with *this world* or of having had a friend, a relative, or even only an acquaintance "contaminated." The Terror is not only a "warning" for future actions. It is a permanent nightmare that has deep roots. The "Law of Suspects," approved by the Convention on 17 September 1793, also made the relatives of monarchists prosecutable unless they had demonstrated their support for the Revolution. On the basis of the Jacobin Terror, Michelet writes that "not one innocent person would be found. All those from the monarchy, all more or less corrupt because of this single fact, in virtue of this strange doctrine, were all traitors."[84]

According to the Law of Suspects, the following had to be arrested and beheaded:

---

81. H. Guillemin, *Robespierre politico e mistico,* 383.
82. Quoted by H. Taine, *Le origini della Francia contemporanea,* 4:55.
83. L. A. de Saint-Just, *Terrore e libertà,* 207. Italics added.
84. J. Michelet, *Storia della Rivoluzione francese,* 4:130.

1. Those who, in assemblies of the people, arrest its energy by crafty discourses, turbulent cries, and threats.
2. Those, more prudent, who speak mysteriously of the misfortune of the republic, who are full of pity for the lot of the people and are ready to spread bad news with an affected grief.
3. Those who have changed their conduct and language in line with events: who, silent regarding the crimes of royalists and federalists, declaim emphatically against the trifling faults of the patriots; who, in order to appear republican, affect an austerity, a studied severity, and then yield as soon as it is a question of judging a moderate or an aristocrat.
4. Those who pity the farmers and greedy merchants against whom the law is obliged to take measures.
5. Those who have the words "liberty," "republic," and "fatherland" constantly on their lips, but who consort with former nobles, counterrevolutionary priests, aristocrats, Feuillants, moderates, and show concern for their fate.
6. Those who have taken no active part in revolutionary matters and who, to exonerate themselves, make much of their payment of taxes, their patriotic gifts, their service in the National Guard.
7. Those have received the republican constitution with indifference and have given credence to false fears concerning its establishment and duration.
8. Those who, having done nothing against liberty, have also done nothing for it.
9. Those who do not attend the meetings of their sections, and give as excuses that they don't know how to speak or that their occupation prevents them.
10. Those who speak with contempt of the constituted authorities, the symbols of the law, defenders of liberty.
11. Those who have signed counterrevolutionary petitions, or frequented antidemocratic societies and clubs.
12. Those who have notoriously acted in bad faith, the partisans of Lafayette, and the assassins who followed him to the Champ de Mars.[85]

Similar guidelines, making almost everyone presumed enemies of the Revolution, enabled the Jacobins to guillotine, without any trial, some sixteen

---

85. Quoted by A. Thiers, *Storia della rivoluzione francese*, 5:225–26.

thousand people over thirteen months (the duration of the Jacobin government). Prey to maniacal delirium, the same Revolution started to exterminate hundreds of their own members.

Robespierre was truly convinced that he was "pure," one of the "elect," a
man "morally superior" to all his opponents. "Those who criticize me," this
was the argument he used, "hide wretched passions." By shifting the focus
of attention to the "morality" of his opponents, he avoided discussion. Exemplary of this kind of "intellectual" conduct is the argument with which
he defended himself from Camille Desmoulins, one of the most famous
revolutionary writers. Desmoulins, although enjoying Robespierre's support,
launched a courageous criticism of the potentially devastating effects of the
Law of Suspects. To prevent France from plunging into a bloodbath, he decided to speak of ancient Rome with the intention of depicting a terrifying
picture of Paris.

Once upon a time in Rome, Desmoulins explained from his paper *Vieux
Cordelier,* there was a law that defined crimes against the state. Under the
republic, treasons were reduced to four kinds: abandoning an army in the
country of an enemy, exciting sedition, the maladministration of the public
treasury, and the impairment by inefficiency of the majesty of the Roman
people. But the Roman emperors needed more clauses in order that they
might place cities and citizens under proscription. Augustus was the first to
extend the law of lèse-majesté to include writings that he called counterrevolutionary. At that point, explained Desmoulins, extensions were made
until none was exempt: "As soon as words had become state crimes, it was
only a step to transform into offenses mere glances, sorrow, compassion, sighs,
silence even. . . . It was necessary to display joy at the death of a friend or of a
relation if one did not wish to run the risk of perishing oneself."[86]

The uncompromising revolutionaries came out against Desmoulins, who
was called before the Convention to justify his writings and his speeches.
Le Père Duchesne called him "a wretched intriguer, a reprobate to send to
the guillotine,...a little donkey with long ears." The extremely violent
Hébert, the leading force behind that paper, instead of debating the merit of
Desmoulins' criticisms, accused him of having married a rich woman and
of sitting with the aristocrats. The fight between the two was ferocious.
Robespierre intervened and, although accusing Desmoulins of having been
led astray by aristocratic circles, granted him pardon. He asked, however, that
his writings be burned. Desmoulins cried out indignantly: "Burning is not
answering!"

---

86. Ibid., 6:72.

Robespierre's response was terse. He followed a pattern by now well-known to the reader: Desmoulins deserves to be treated with contempt. He is a corrupt man who plots in the "shadows." He is a writer for hire; his works are at the service of the counterrevolutionary forces. Robespierre's arguments are entirely constructed on moral categories. His speech to the Convention is a masterly illustration of the gnostic revolutionary's typical mentality, with all its particular features: (a) the "binary-code mentality" that reduces everything to the conflict between the forces of "good" and the forces of "evil"; (b) "radical catastrophism" in which the world is besieged by perfidious and corrupt people, who act deceitfully; (c) "the identification of evil," that is, of an "enemy" to blame for human unhappiness; and (d) the salvific concept of the revolution.

We are in December 1793. These are Robespierre's words to Desmoulins: "So be it. We will answer, then, instead of burning, since Camille still defends his writings. If he wishes it, let him be covered with ignominy; let the society restrain its indignation no longer, since he is obstinate in maintaining his diatribes and his dangerous principles. I was evidently mistaken in believing that he was merely misled; if he had been in good faith, if he had merely written in the simplicity of his heart, he would not have dared to uphold works that are proscribed by patriots and welcomed by counterrevolutionaries. His courage is only borrowed; it betrays someone concealed, who has dictated what he has written in his journal; it betrays that Desmoulins is the organ of a rascally faction that has borrowed his pen to spread its poison with all the more audacity and sureness."[87]

According to some historians, the Law of Suspects imprisoned over 100,000 people; others put the number closer to 300,000. Overall, Donald Greer estimated the number of deaths at 35,000–40,000 (also counting the executions without trial, as in Nantes and Toulon). On the basis of Greer's statistics, the revolutionary tribunal pronounced 16,594 death sentences. There were 518 executions from March to September 1793; 10,182 from October 1793 to May 1794; 2,554 from June to July 1794; and 86 in August 1794.

Seventy-eight percent of the sentences were pronounced for rebellion or treason; 19 percent for crimes of opinion; 1 percent for economic offenses (false checks, extortion). As for the victims' social background, 84 percent came from the old Third State (bourgeois 25 percent, peasants 28 percent, and sansculottes 31 percent); only 8 percent came from the nobility, and 6.5 percent from the clergy.[88]

---

87. Ibid., 6:87.

88. See D. Greer, *The Incidence of the Terror during the French Revolution*. On the "insanity" of the Jacobin Terror, see L. Colin, *The Structure of the Terror*; N. Hampson, *The Life and Opinions of*

Desmoulins was beheaded on 5 April 1794.

For the Marxist historian Albert Soboul, the Jacobins had tried to contain the homicidal fury of the sansculottes by gratifying, to a limited extent, their thirst for blood. According to him, the Terror was triggered by the popular movement, but this interpretation is debatable. Although the role of popular fury in unleashing the "first Terror" is not debated, it is not enough to explain the political violence that beleaguered Jacobin France. For the physical elimination of your adversaries to become "routine work," you need an ideology that encourages and justifies, that incites and absolves.

The guillotine was in use before the Jacobins come on the scene, but it was with them that it replaced political debate. We find the best interpreters of the *doctrine of purification* in the Jacobin clubs, where the number of French people to exterminate is discussed passionately, in the name of a "total and unyielding subversion."[89] Inspired by the *clean slate* principle, Jeanbon proposed to eliminate half of the population; Bo concluded that at most 12 million lives could be saved; Antonelli was more conservative and proposed that "only" a third of the French should go to the guillotine; Gouffroy, instead, said he was sure that 5 million survivors would have been more than enough to build a "better" society; Catherine Théot wanted to be more specific and, broadening the horizons of the debate, proposed to leave only 140,000 "elect" in the entire world.[90]

Soboul, asserting that the Public Health Committee should have been "forced" to adopt extreme measures to appease the masses' thirst for blood, wrote that "the Terror [was] a fundamentally political phenomenon."[91] This removes the focus from the revolutionary mentality. It induces one to believe that the Terror—to recall the words of another Marxist historian, Albert Mathiez—was "a necessary response to the circumstances."[92]

Both Soboul and Mathiez want to make us believe that the Jacobin Terror was a fortuitous event.

Permit me to disagree: the Jacobin Terror had deep roots. It was an essentially cultural phenomenon that found in politics the means to deploy all

---

Maximilien Robespierre, 223–90. I do not agree with Hampson's thesis that the Jacobin Terror "did not have an ideological base" (258). The revolutionary violence that shook France during Robespierre's government was not random at all. History confirms, with macabre punctiliousness, that an obsession with purification and identification of evil systematically leads to the dehumanization of your political enemies and their physical elimination. When an active revolutionary sect gains power, society is tipped into a continuous nightmare. The Terror and its "insanity," which Hampson thinks has no precise logic, are a constant of all gnostic revolutions.

89. See M. Vovelle, *La mentalità rivoluzionaria,* 97.

90. Quoted by J. Servier, *Le terrorisme,* 20–21.

91. A. Soboul, *La rivoluzione francese,* 270.

92. A. Mathiez and G. Lefebvre, *La rivoluzione francese,* 2:19.

its pantoclastic power. The obsession with purification is inherent in revolutionary sects; it is a typical trait of gnostic revolutionaries. As we shall see later on, in those countries where the purifiers of the world have taken over the state apparatus, the extermination of their enemies is no longer an "extraordinary" fact but a normal "practice." It has happened both in times of war and in times of peace; in periods of recession and in periods of economic prosperity. Robespierre saw the world as a place to "cleanse" of egoism and bourgeois passions: "From whence does evil come? From the bourgeois," he asserts on the eve of 2 June 1793. On 21 July 1794, he signs a message to Herman, with Barère and Billaud, stating that there has to be "a clean sweep of the prisons to free the land of liberty from these scum, these rejects of humanity."[93] As François Furet has so aptly said: "For Robespierre and Saint-Just, the bourgeois revolution they have created has brought about the absolute evil, luxury, affluence, atheism, and individualism of interest that they detest."[94]

It is true that the first two outbursts of terrorism occurred under the threat of foreign invasion (August 1792; summer 1793). But the "great Terror" (spring 1794) took place under decidedly favorable conditions for the French army.

Furet fiercely criticizes Soboul, denouncing "[his] poverty-stricken schema, this resurrection of scholasticism, this dearth of ideas, this passionate obstinacy disguised as Marxism."[95] He pointed out the autonomous role of Jacobin ideology that, in his opinion, should be conceptualized and analyzed as such: "*In the main, Jacobin and terrorist ideology functioned autonomously, unrelated to the political and military circumstance.*"[96] Furet concludes that Soboul's interpretation is the "product of a confused encounter between Jacobinism and Leninism, this mixed discourse is unsuitable for discovery."[97] And, above all, it conceals the fact that the Terror is "the product, not of real struggle, but of the Manichaean ideology that would separate the good from the wicked and of a pervasive social panic."[98]

On this point Furet's criticism is invaluable, but it stops there. He stigmatizes the ideological and instrumental aspect of the Marxist rendering of the Jacobin Terror, but does not explain why the historiographic reading conflicts with historical experience.

---

93. Quoted by Hampson, *Robespierre*, 259.
94. F. Furet and D. Richet, *La rivoluzione francese*, 1:270.
95. Ibid., 1:146.
96. F. Furet, *Critica della rivoluzione francese*, 143. Italics added.
97. Ibid., 146.
98. Ibid., 143.

For the guardians of Marxist tradition, revolutionary violence is never intentional. The revolutionaries are generous men who are forced to kill. Their enemies are always waiting in ambush. Hidden in the "shadows," they're plotting to prevent humanity's regeneration. It is they who force the "pure" to commit political homicide. Moreover, in the attempt to distract attention away from Robespierre's political culture, which Lenin was to proudly support, Soboul only questions the "external" circumstances of Jacobin politics (the war and the sansculottes' fury). There is no thought about how the Jacobin Terror influenced international actors. Nor is there any question about how Robespierre's Manichaean vision incited popular hatred of the presumed enemies of the Revolution. For Soboul, Robespierre is "forced" to the Terror by the irrational passions of the masses. Hence Robespierre has no responsibility for the Terror. Once again we hear the familiar justification: "terrorist despite myself." According to Soboul, the Jacobin Terror had only two causes: the war and the popular fury that Robespierre had indulged for "contingent" reasons. The idea that a particular political culture could have had an independent role in inciting violence is not considered.

The absolving intention of revolutionary violence is even more explicit in Albert Mathiez's works. This Marxist historian establishes a premise before touching the issue of "revolutionary justice": "It is almost unheard of that, in a country at war with another country, complicated by civil war, the governors are not obliged to summary and hasty justice in order to repress any spies, plots, and rebellions."[99]

As if to say: I will speak to you about atrocious crimes, about massacres and beheadings, but don't blame the executioner, because he was carried along by events. He didn't want to; he was forced to do it: "In general," Mathiez writes, "the revolutionaries struck so as not to be struck."[100]

Soboul and Mathiez provide a classic example of the so-called thesis of circumstances, condemned by sociologist Augustin Cochin with these words: "It wasn't the Revolution that 'started' everything. It has always acted under the impulse of unpredictable external circumstances: this is the thesis of all its defenders. It is a thesis that tends to prove, first, that the ideas and sentiments of the men of 1793 have nothing abnormal in themselves; if we are shocked by their acts, it's because we forget the dangers that beset them, that is, the 'circumstances'; and that in their place anyone with good sense and heart would have acted like them. And second, that such natural sentiments

---

99. Mathiez and Lefebvre, *La rivoluzione francese,* 2:10.
100. Ibid., 2:20.

are shared by many, and that terrorism is the fact not of a minority but of all France."[101]

Guglielmo Ferrero has highlighted the practice of Terror, analyzing its effects on the developments of the Jacobin revolution. In a book containing one of the most important interpretations of the French Revolution, Ferrero has attributed revolutionary violence with the power to influence the course of events, according to a logic independent of its protagonists. Those who unleash Terror, explains Ferrero, end up by being overwhelmed themselves. Even the most bloodthirsty government is forced to live in permanent fear of being overturned. To prevent this from happening, it increases its ferocity, provoking new grief that augments its fears.

Ferrero writes:

> Revolutionary governments are always afraid because their power has been acquired with force—by nature unstable and transient—and because they do not rely on any legal principle recognized by those who have to obey them. . . . The Convention was a revolutionary government that was afraid. To understand it we have to start from here. . . . This is explained with psychological reasons that belong to revolutionary governments, which distrust their subjects because the majority contests their right to command. Thus for them fear is an instrument of dominion, which they use frequently. . . . *And this is the key point of all revolutions.* The unlawful government is struck by fear. Fear drives it to abuse force. And since it fears the victims of this abuse, instead of being cured, its fear increases, plunging it into even greater abuse. A vicious circle is created where fear causes abuse of force and abuse of force aggravates fear.[102]

The French Revolution is a history of economic crises and budgets to be balanced, but it is also a history of ideas and words that break completely with the past. Customs, traditions, and lifestyles were called into question by the conviction of being able to found a human community without historic precedents. Politics and its "new" symbols invaded every aspect of daily life and became in themselves the "causes" of collective behavior. On the

---

101. A. Cochin, *Lo spirito del giacobinismo,* 122. It should be noted that, in Marxist historiography, the thesis of circumstances is applied only to the "friends" of the revolution. In this case, revolutionary violence is a "necessity" of the class war. As such, it has to be put in its proper historical context. The violence of those who do not espouse the revolutionary ideal is instead always carried out by petty, corrupt men who operate underhandedly to oppress humanity.

102. Ferrero, *Le due rivoluzioni francesi,* 87, 91, 107, 131. Italics added.

evening of 6 October 1790, a crowd of men and women, followed by the National Guard, marched to Versailles, killing the Swiss Guards and bursting into the royal apartments. They were driven by what was considered an insupportable insult. During a banquet, in the presence of the royal family, the royal guards had trampled on the tricolor cockade, symbol of the Revolution. The crowd was appeased only by the promise to take the king to Paris, to the Tuileries.

In recalling this episode, Lynn Hunt has emphasized the causal power of revolutionary symbols and culture.

At the end of a survey that includes literary criticism, art history, anthropology, and the quantitative methods of social history, Hunt arrived at the conclusion that the revolutionary language, far from being a simple "reflection" of the underlying material interests, is itself the cause of social change. The rhetoric of the "clean slate," the pantoclastic fury, and the identification of evil shape the perception of reality and thus change the revolutionaries' scale of values. Waiting for the end upsets every aspect of their daily life. Their clothes, their thoughts, their eyes become "smeared" with ideology. The "interests" of the revolution become their "interests." As Hunt writes, the revolutionary language "was itself transformed into an instrument of political and social change."[103]

The Terror, far from being a "causal" episode of the French Revolution, was the characteristic trait of the Jacobin culture, of which Robespierre and Saint-Just were the main interpreters. The idea of extermination as an instrument to purify society from corruption and egoism played a critical role in the history of the French Revolution. The Reign of Terror cannot be considered as something "that just happened." A political idea is never born "by chance." And even less a doctrine of extermination, so succinctly expressed by the Jacobin Barère: "*But humanity consists in exterminating our enemies.*"[104]

Before the Jacobin revolution of 1793, terror had been conceived as a "means" to gain power or to maintain it. Machiavelli, fascinated by the figure of Cesare Borgia, had advised princes not to disdain the possibility of using "evil and deceitful means"[105] in the fight for power. In this case, terror is seen as a "technique" for domination. Instead, with Robespierre, terror rises to the rank of "doctrine," becoming an integral part of a political philosophy that denies its adversaries the right to exist. "You can say," writes Andrew Sinclair,

---

103. L. Hunt, *La rivoluzione francese,* 31.
104. Quoted by N. Hampson, *Storia sociale della rivoluzione francese,* 242.
105. N. Machiavelli, *Il principe,* 103.

"that a history of Terror could be dated, in the manner of the history of Europe, not Before or After Christ, but Before and After Robespierre."[106]

Babeuf: "The world has plunged into chaos"

Robespierre's revolutionary spirit was alive in an even more radical form in Babeuf.

François-Noël (Gracchus) Babeuf was born in Saint-Quentin on 23 November 1760 to a petit bourgeois family that was plunged into poverty after the death of his father, when he was sixteen. In 1782, he married a domestic servant. Besides his wife, he also had to provide for his mother and siblings. Ambitious and seeking a position worthy of his education, he was frustrated in his aspirations by a society in which feudal titles still counted for much. He became convinced that the world was too corrupt to recognize his talent. His aversion to the nobility soon turned into hate. Reading Rousseau's letter, he learned that "nature made man happy and good but society depraves him and makes him miserable."[107] The idea that man was corrupted by institutions increased his rebellious spirit. He came to the conclusion that private property was the source of every evil. Maurice Dommanget has asserted that "there is no doubt about the originality of Babeuf's communist ideas."[108] But what is really "original" in Babeuf is not his communist ideology, already theorized before him, but the fact of having taken the "decisive step" from theory to practice. His was not pure speculation, but a genuine social and economic doctrine to guide the revolutionary enterprise. He organized a rebellion, "the Conspiracy of the Equals," to implement communism against the Thermidorian Reaction that had overturned Robespierre. The men flanking him were true revolutionary professionals—Antonelle, Maréchal, Lepeletier, Darthé, Buonarroti, and Debon, who were members of the secret Directory. They met almost every evening, studying their insurrectional strategy in detail and the legal provisions to adopt after the Revolution. Babeuf's agents distributed the organization's instructions all over Paris. Its propaganda was also well organized. Newspapers, manifestos, and pamphlets reached the proletariat in clandestine form. The conspirators did methodical, well-coordinated work underpinned by a deep hatred for the society in which they lived. They were discovered and arrested on 10 May 1796. On the night between 9 and 10 Fructidor (26–27 August 1796) the conspirators

---

106. A. Sinclair, *Storia del terrorismo*, 63.
107. J.-J. Rousseau, "Rousseau giudice di Jean-Jacques," in *Opere*, 1284.
108. M. Dommanget, *Babeuf e la congiura degli uguali*, 9.

were taken to the Vendôme in iron cages. Their trial was held at the end of February 1797 and lasted three months. After their death sentence was read out, on 7 Prairial of the year V (26 May 1797), Babeuf and Darthé attempted suicide; the next day they were led bleeding to the scaffold. The other conspirators were instead deported.

The *Manifesto of the Equals,* written by Sylvain Maréchal, is one of the world's most valuable testimonies of the revolutionary concept.

There is a direct filiation between this work and the numerous Red Brigades documents encountered during the first part of this book. The vision of the world is identical, as is the waiting for the end, the conviction that the greatest happiness for all is around the corner, the identification of evil, and the pantoclastic vocation. There is even great similarity in the style and terms used.

Maréchal writes:

We want this real equality or death; that's what we need. And we'll have this real equality, at whatever price. Unhappy will be those who stand between it and us! Unhappy will be those who resist a wish so firmly expressed. *The French Revolution was nothing but a precursor of another revolution, one that will be bigger, more solemn and which will be the last.* What do we need besides equality of rights? We need not only that equality of rights is written into the Declaration of the Rights of Man and Citizen; we want it in our midst, under the roofs of our houses. *We consent to everything for it, to make a clean slate so that we hold to it alone.* Let all the arts perish, if need be, as long as real equality remains! *We reach for something more sublime* and more just: the common good or the community of goods! No more individual property in land: the land belongs to no one. We demand, we want, the common enjoyment of the fruits of the land: the fruits belong to all. We declare that we can no longer put up with the fact that the great majority work and sweat for the smallest of minorities. Long enough, and for too long, less than a million individuals have disposed of that which belongs to 20 million of their like, their equals. Let it at last end, this great scandal that our descendants will never believe existed! Disappear at last, revolting distinctions between rich and poor, great and small, masters and servants, rulers and ruled. . . . *The holy enterprise* that we are organizing has no other goal than to put an end to civil dissension and public misery.[109]

---

109. S. Maréchal, "Manifesto degli eguali," in *Cospirazione dell'eguaglianza detta di Babeuf,* by F. Buonarroti, 312–13. Italics added.

For Babeuf's followers, the world is full of desperation and unhappiness. Everything is corrupt. Thus everything has to be destroyed and remade. The aim is to make a clean sweep of every aspect of present life to build the society of concord and universal harmony. The world has to plunge into chaos in order to be regenerated. The masses are not to know what will come after. However, what is certain is that *this world* has to perish. A handful of the "elect" knows the right remedy. Humanity has fallen into the abyss. Everything that is real is corrupted, degenerated, and perverse. The world is in a terrible predicament; it has to be razed to the ground. *Chaos—destruction—regeneration* is the apocalyptic schema with which Babeuf announced the revolution.

In his words: "*Evil is at its height; it cannot become worse, the only remedy is total subversion! Let all return to chaos, and from chaos let a world arise new and regenerated.*"[110]

Babeuf and his group were democratic in revolutionary rhetoric, elitist in revolutionary practice. In the *Conspiracy of the Equals,* Buonarroti proposes a well-known lesson: the masses are blind and have to let themselves be guided by those with superior knowledge. In his words: "But the ways of truth and justice are with difficulty perceived by the multitude, who cannot be persuaded by the same motives that determine minds accustomed to reflect."[111] It is legitimate, explains Buonarroti, for the "elect" to deceive the masses because the latter do not have access to revolutionary knowledge and are often hostile to change. The destruction of the present society is the premise for the creation of paradise on earth. It is an "immense" enterprise that justifies any means: "It is difficult to convince the multitude of the advantages of innovations, without the aid of that experience which can happen only after they have been acted on. Accordingly, the wisest legislators of antiquity have been obliged to have recourse to religious fictions, by which they astonished the multitude whom they could not persuade. This expedience, which in any case is dangerous, cannot be employed at all with success among a people who (whether fortunately or unfortunately I cannot say) cultivate science and philosophy: with these you can accomplish nothing, unless by the attractions of pleasure, or with force."[112]

For Buonarroti, the world is divided into those with "corrupt hearts" and those with "pure hearts."[113] The former are led by egoism; the second by love

110. Babeuf, *Il manifesto dei plebei,* in *Il tribuno del popolo,* 152. Italics added.
111. F. Buonarroti, *Cospirazione dell'eguaglianza,* 61.
112. Ibid., 61, n. 1.
113. Ibid., 14.

for their neighbor. Minos, Plato, Lycurgus, Thomas More, Mably, and Rousseau are the "masters" he refers to in his work. They are the theorists of the "perfect society"; they are all prompted by the desire to "melt" the individual into a fusion model; they want to purify people by eliminating egoism; they want to expel "evil" from history.

Karl Marx's Pantoclastic Dream

This was Karl Marx's aspiration, after being profoundly influenced by reading Babeuf.

Marx's well-known "recipe" for remedying the evils of capitalism was to eliminate every aspect of the present world through a violent and radical upheaval. Just like Babeuf, he wanted to build a "new world," where men would have been free and happy forever. This was the project to which he devoted his life.

In the *Jewish Question* (1843) Marx had identified the source of the typical egoism of bourgeois society in the separation between the state and civil society; that is, in the separation between the public and private spheres. The egoistic man, for Marx, "is a man as a member of civil society; that is, an individual withdrawn into himself, into the confines of his private interests and private caprice, and separated from the community." What drives individuals in such a society "is natural necessity, need, and private interest, the preservation of their property and their egoistic selves."[114] It is this individual, "a monad enclosed in his work, interests, calculations, and pleasures, separated from his fellow man and indifferent to the community and its concerns"[115] whom Marx criticizes. This criticism firmly sets him, with no hope for reconciliation, against the liberal tradition. A tradition that, by tackling the fundamental issue of "marking a boundary between private life and that of public authority,"[116] had made the separation between public and private spheres the dividing line between the "liberty of the ancients" and the "liberty of the moderns."[117] Marx, under Rousseau's decisive influence,[118] hoped for the advent of "the *real and total* man," continuously engaged in exercising his right as a citizen. The "new man" would be completely politicized, ready

---

114. K. Marx, *La questione ebraica,* 31.
115. F. Furet, *Marx e la rivoluzione francese,* 27.
116. I. Berlin, *Due concetti di libertà,* 15.
117. B. Constant, *La libertà degli antichi paragonata a quella dei moderni* (1819).
118. See Della Volpe, *Rousseau e Marx,* 67–68.

to surrender his interests to those of the collectivity,[119] since—we read in *The German Ideology*—"as long as a cleavage exists between the particular and the common interest . . . , man's own deed becomes an alien power opposed to him, which enslaves him instead of being controlled by him."[120] To build the "true democracy"—this was Marx's conclusion—the individual must no longer oppose the political community.[121]

Marx's vision of *this world* can be summed up as follows: the bourgeoisie has built a world in its image, based on egoism, private property, and exploitation. In *this world,* the interests of the community are completely subordinated to those of the individual. Egoism and alienation triumph. Those who are joyful, who believe they are happy, are victims of an illusion, because in the bourgeois society all men are alienated. All except those who have embraced the Marxist doctrine, the only source of truth and liberation. It is the Platonic myth of the cave. The common man is like a slave locked in an underground place. His legs and neck are chained from birth and he is forced to remain still and look in front of him. At his back, the light of a distant fire throws the shadows of real objects on the walls of the cave. Since the slave cannot turn around, his reality is nothing but senseless emptiness. What would happen if just one of these slaves were to be freed and taken to the surface? Arriving in the light of the sun and seeing the real world, he would feel pity for his companions and would fight desperately to preserve the freedom gained. When he returned to the cave, the other slaves would ridicule him, not believing a word of his story, and would try to kill whoever tried to free them from their chains.[122]

In Marxist doctrine, bourgeois ideology deforms the common man's perception of reality. The revolutionary gnosis has the task of liberating man from "blindness" and leading him to a "higher" knowledge. Only in this way will the world appear for what it really is: a horrible and putrescent place. To get out of this condition of suffering and slavery, a band of revolutionaries would have to lead a total upheaval that, by destroying the bourgeoisie, would transform man and society.

Marx's criticism of the French Revolution is very helpful in understanding his mental universe. He takes it to task for failing to bring about human emancipation, since it was "only" a political revolution and thus, in his words,

119. N. Bobbio, *Il futuro della democrazia,* 35.
120. K. Marx and F. Engels, *L'ideologia tedesca* (1845–46), 24.
121. A. Giddens, *Capitalism and Modern Social Theory.*
122. Plato, *La Repubblica,* in Plato, *Opere,* 2:341–42.

a "partial revolution."[123] For the transformation that Marx had in mind, the French Revolution was only a very small foreshadowing of the apocalyptic event that would have overturned the world. Its historic function was to foster the ascent of the bourgeoisie, leaving the proletariat in chains.[124] It claimed to speak on behalf of humanity but it just defended the interests of a small minority.[125]

It is by now clear that Marx did not know what to do with the "egoistic" liberal freedoms advocated by the Revolution of 1789. For him, "true" liberty meant "real equality," that is, equality with regard to material goods. Economic equality, therefore, and not legal or social equality,[126] which performs the sole function of ensuring the bourgeoisie's privileges and leaves the proletariat in chains.[127]

We are familiar with Marx's "version of the facts" because the Red Brigades took it in toto: bourgeois society is a corrupt and nauseating place that deserves only to be destroyed. People are alienated and unhappy there. However, there are a few "elect" who, because of their superior knowledge, will guide humanity toward a radiant, conflict-free future.

Marx—besides having devoted the most important part of his life to "implementing, with all the means of propaganda and political struggle, the dismantling of the old society and the overthrow of the bourgeoisie, the spiritual, political and economic freedom of the proletariat, the communist revolution"[128]—believed that hatred against their enemies was to be encouraged. His incitement to "popular revenge" is very clear. Even after victory—he writes in March 1850—you should show no mercy for your defeated enemies. Because a pure and simple instinct of destruction and hate has to be appeased.

This is what he writes: "Above all things, the workers must counteract, as much as is at all possible, during the conflict and immediately after the struggle, the bourgeois endeavours to allay the storm, and must compel the democrats to carry out their present terrorist phrases. Their actions must be so aimed as to prevent the direct revolutionary excitement from being suppressed again immediately after the victory. On the contrary, they must keep it alive as long as possible. *Far from opposing so-called excesses, instances of popular revenge against hated individuals or public buildings that are associated only*

---

123. See N. Bobbio, *Né con Marx, né contro Marx*, 106.
124. K. Marx, *Il 18 brumaio di Luigi Napoleone* (1852), 46.
125. K. Marx, introduction to *Per la critica della filosofia del diritto di Hegel* (1843), 59.
126. See N. Bobbio, *Eguaglianza e libertà*, 27.
127. H. J. Laski, *The Rise of European Liberalism*.
128. K. Marx, "Statuti della Lega dei comunisti," in Marx and Engels, *Opere complete*, 10:635.

with hateful recollections, such incidences must not only be tolerated, but the leadership of them taken in hand."[129] This is why the world would soon be devastated by a duel to the death between the "conservative party" and the "*destructive party,*"[130] and why this latter, once in power, would have made "*a clean slate of the old spectral world.*"[131]

In Marx's political ethics, the proletarian fury against one's enemies, albeit defenseless, has nothing reprehensible about it. In fact it should be encouraged. These are the instructions that Marx and Engels sent to Köttgen, who was told that, for revolutionary violence to be effectively deployed, you must "proceed Jesuitically, put aside Teutonic probity, true-heartedness and decency. . . . In a party one must support everything which helps towards progress, and have no truck with any tedious moral scruples."[132]

For Marx, the path that leads to revolution can only be taken "with ruthless terrorism." This is what he asserts in his *Victory of the Counter-Revolution in Vienna:* "There is only one way in which the murderous death agonies of the old society and the bloody birth throes of the new society can be shortened, simplified and concentrated, and that way is revolutionary terror."[133] In an article of 19 May 1849, Marx invited people to be unfaltering in using terror: "We are ruthless and ask no quarter from you. When our turn comes we shall not disguise our terrorism."[134]

Engels even came to consider the elimination of "entire populations" as "progress." The leitmotif is always the same: the enemy has to be destroyed. The "impure" do not deserve any clemency: "The next war will not only make reactionary classes and dynasties disappear from the face of the earth but also whole reactionary peoples. And that is also progress."[135] It is again Engels who states, in another work: "To the sentimental phrases about brotherhood which we are being offered here on behalf of the most counter-revolutionary nations of Europe, we reply that hatred of Russians was and still is the primary revolutionary passion among Germans; that since

---

129. K. Marx, "Indirizzo del Comitato centrale alla Lega [comunista] del marzo 1850," in Marx and Engels, *Opere complete,* 10:283. Italics added.

130. K. Marx and F. Engels, "La sacra famiglia," in Marx and Engels, *Opere complete,* 4:37.

131. K. Marx, "Il diciotto Brumaio di Luigi Bonaparte," in Marx and Engels, *Opere complete,* 11:115.

132. K. Marx and F. Engels, "Lettera a G. A. Koettgen," in Marx and Engels, *Opere complete,* 7:14.

133. K. Marx, "Vittoria della controrivoluzione a Vienna," in Marx and Engels, *Opere complete,* 7:519–20.

134. K. Marx, "La soppressione della *Neue Rheinische Zeitung,"* in Marx and Engels, *Il quarantotto,* 290.

135. K. Marx and F. Engels, "La lotta delle nazioni," in Marx and Engels, *Opere complete,* 8:237.

the revolution hatred of Czechs and Croats has been added, and that only by the most determined use of terror against these Slav peoples can we, jointly with the Poles and Magyars, safeguard the revolution.... Then there will be a struggle, an 'inexorable life-and-death struggle,' against those Slavs who betray the revolution; an annihilating fight and ruthless terror—not in the interests of Germany, but in the interests of the revolution!"[136]

Marx and Engels awaited with trepidation "the universal conflagration which will burn up the old institutions of Europe, and light the victorious nations to a future—free, happy, and glorious."[137] Given these assumptions, one can understand Marx's and Lenin's hatred for any kind of reformism. The idea is always the same: society has to be destroyed not reformed. The attempt to mitigate the exploitation of the workers lessens anger and inhibits its revolutionary potentiality. No compromise would have been possible with the bourgeois world. Hence Marx claimed that "the clashes that spontaneously arise out of conditions of bourgeois society must be fought to the bitter end."[138] The reformist parties would like to reconcile the interests of the workers with those of the capitalists, but we must always beware of reformists. They are unscrupulous. They seek in the proletariat the force to gain power, but immediately after having gained control of the state apparatus they will be ready to betray the proletarian cause. Thus: "The workers must be armed and organized. The arming of the whole proletariat with rifles, muskets, cannon and ammunition must be carried out at once.... Arms and ammunition must not be surrendered under any pretext. Any attempt at disarming must be frustrated, if necessary, with force."[139]

For Marx, the establishment of communism would have meant the end of history. If communism is the greatest happiness for all, no one would have been able to desire anything else. (The brigadist Patrizio Peci recounts that, before going to sleep, he used to imagine that once the revolution had come he would have been able to enjoy the rest of his days in a country house, immersed in a happy and joyful world: "We saw everything in terms of tranquillity, that was our aim.")[140]

Often exiled for his radical ideas, Marx is a typical example of the marginal individual, an outsider who profoundly hates the society of his time. He is dominated, wrote Arnold Künzli, "by pride, contempt, envy, revenge,

136. F. Engels, "Il panslavismo democratico," in Marx and Engels, *Opere complete,* 7:381.
137. F. Engels, "Lettere della Germania," in Marx and Engels, *Opere complete,* 10:16.
138. Quoted by I. Berlin, *Karl Marx,* 161–62.
139. Ibid., 284.
140. P. Peci, *Io, l'infame,* 102.

hatred, desire for destruction and self-destruction, but also the desire to re-create the world starting with himself, accompanied by an evident aspiration for self-deification."[141]

Particularly indicative of Marx's personality are some of his youthful poems, written between 1836 and the beginning of 1837. I quote from four of them:

Worlds my longing cannot ever still,
Nor yet gods with magic blest;
Higher than them all is my own Will,
Stormily wakeful in my breast.

Drank I all the stars' bright radiance,
All the light by suns o'erspilled,
Still my pains would want for recompense,
And my dreams be unfulfilled.

Hence! To endless battle, to the striving
Like a talisman out there,
Demon-wise into the far mists driving
Towards a goal I cannot near.[142]

Heaven I would comprehend,
I would draw the world to me;
Loving, hating, I intend
That my star shine brilliantly.

All things I would strive to win,
All the blessings Gods impart,
Grasp all knowledge deep within,
Plumb the depths of Song and Art.

Worlds I would destroy for ever,
Since I can create no world,
Since my call they notice never,
Coursing dumb in magic whirl.[143]

---

141. Quoted in E. Topitsch, *Per una critica del marxismo,* 160.
142. K. Marx, "My World," in Marx and Engels, *Opere complete,* 1:579.
143. K. Marx, "Sensations," in Marx and Engels, *Opere complete,* 1:581. Italics added.

So a god has snatched from me my all
In the curse and rack of destiny.
All his worlds are gone beyond recall!
Nothing but revenge is left to me!

On myself revenge I'll proudly wreak,
On that being, that enthroned Lord,
Make my strength a patchwork of what's weak,
Leave my better self without reward![144]

With disdain I will throw my gauntlet
Full in the face of the world,
And see the collapse of this pygmy giant
Whose fall will not stifle my ardor.

Then I will be able to walk triumphantly
Like a god, through the ruins of their kingdom.
Every word of mine is fire and action.
My breast is equal to that of the Creator.[145]

Unaware of what the future had in store for him, Marx anticipated the drama of his marginality in a high-school essay of 12 August 1835. In this work Marx writes about the piercing frustration of those who cannot manage to be recognized by others. Every man, writes Marx, seeks his place in the world. Those who fail in this undertaking are condemned to despair, which can be relieved only by the capacity to deceive and betray ourselves. In his words: "But if we have chosen a profession for which we do not possess the talent, we can never exercise it worthily, we shall soon realize with shame our own incapacity, and tell ourselves that we are useless created beings, members of society who are incapable of fulfilling their vocation. Then the most natural consequence is self-contempt, and what feeling is more painful and less capable of being made up for by all that the outside world has to offer? Self-contempt is a serpent that ever gnaws at one's breast, sucking the life-blood from one's heart and mixing it with the poison of misanthropy and despair." Sometimes, continues Marx, to get out of a condition that degrades us, "then

144. K. Marx, "The Prayer of a Desperate Man," in Marx and Engels, *Opere complete,* 1:620. Italics added.

145. K. Marx, "Human Arrogance," in Marx and Engels, *Opere complete,* 1:643. Italics added.

we have no recourse but to self-deception, and what desperate salvation is that which is obtained by self-betrayal!"[146]

In the attempt to solve his existential drama, Marx worked out a concept of the world that would have saved him from unbearable frustration and that would have changed the course of history. As a prophet, he comes second only to Jesus and Muhammad. His ideas were to rule over 40 percent of the world population. He was arguably the most important gnostic revolutionary in history, as well as one of the leading theoreticians of the pedagogy of intolerance.

Marx was always violent and intolerant with his critics. He called Lassalle a "Negro Jew"; Moses Mendelssohn, instead, was a "scumbag."[147] Marx considered neutrality in ideological disputes on a par with infectious disease. Choleric and vindictive, he never distinguished ideas from those who pronounced them. He expected absolute loyalty from his friends. Referring to the poet Ferdinand Freiligrath, who had lacked conviction in supporting him in his dispute with Karl Vogt, he wrote in a letter to Engels on 7 June 1859: "Between you and me, he's a shit. . . . May the devil take this corporation of cantors."[148] Frank E. Manuel—author of one of the best biographies of Marx—wrote that "in Marx's life aggression against a host of former friends and newborn enemies was a constant preoccupation that used up as much of his energy as his study of capitalist development at the British Museum. Whether the enemies were primarily doctrinal or whether they were potential rivals for the leadership of the First International, the release of affect was similar. Marx's outbursts extended from the attack on Bruno Bauer and company in the *Holy Family,* through the critique on Feuerbach, Bauer, Stirner, Grün, the Saint-Simonians, Cabet and the Fourierists in the *German Ideology,* and the derision of Proudhon's economics in *Misère de la philosophie.* His anger culminated in the wholesale assault in the *Communist Manifesto* on the entire catalogue of social doctrines—feudal socialism, petty-bourgeois socialism, German or 'True' socialism, conservative or bourgeois socialism, utopian socialism, and sectarian communism."[149]

During an argument with Wilhelm Weitling on 30 March 1846, Marx humiliated his adversary to the point of making him stutter. When Weitling— bastard son of a German laundrywoman and without Marx's education—said

146. K. Marx, *Considerazioni di un giovane sulla scelta di una professione,* in Marx and Engels, *Opere complete,* 1:5–6.

147. See F. E. Manuel, *Requiem per Carlo Marx,* 29–30.

148. Ibid., 232.

149. Ibid., 234.

he shouldn't be so mortified after having devoted his life to helping the cause of the exploited, Marx leaped on the seat and, after striking the table so violently that the lamp on it shook, shouted, "Ignorance has never yet helped anyone."[150] Pavel Annenkov, an admirer of Marx, recounts that "he spoke only in the imperative, brooking no contradiction, and this was intensified by the tone, which to me was almost painfully jarring, in which he spoke. This tone expressed the firm conviction of his mission to reign over man's minds and dictate their laws. Before my eyes stood the personification of the democratic dictator such as might appear before one in moments of fantasy."[151]

Both admirers like Annenkov and adversaries like Bakunin were united in their judgment of Marx: "There is no lie, no calumny, which he is not capable of using against anyone who has incurred his jealousy or his hatred; he will not stop at the basest intrigue if, in his opinion, it will serve to increase his position, his influence and his power."[152]

This should not surprise us, since communist materialism has an exclusive and all-embracing vision of the world that prevents its supporters from harboring any other opinion. Those who do not espouse the Marxist doctrine must also be despised. Not only do they live in error but they also refuse to take the part of the oppressed because they want to defend their own class interests that, according to the Marxists, are always based on exploitation and abuse. It is no coincidence that the pedagogy of intolerance advocated by Marx produced the same effects wherever it gained power.

Marx and Engels's most fanatic and exclusive theory—from which communism took its ideological intolerance—is that the value of the work of a scientist or an artist is inseparable from his or her political ideas. This means that the value of a scientific discovery or a work of art is judged exclusively by the political use that can be made of it. In other words, any intellectual contribution that comes from the other side can only be ignored, dismissed, or destroyed.

Certain of having achieved the highest peak of human and philosophical thought, Marx believed that it was impossible to obtain anything important or significant outside his system. He was also convinced that only what would foster the progress of the revolutionary movement was worthy of consideration, thus subordinating the value of scientific knowledge to its political usefulness. Marx imposed an authentic "tyranny of thought" that

150. See F. Wheen, *Marx*, 91.
151. Ibid., 90.
152. M. Bakunin quoted by I. Berlin, *Karl Marx*, 101–2.

also affected those who tried to protect their independent judgment within the socialist movement.

Those who, like Milovan Djilas, managed to free themselves from this mental universe, could write that "the assertion that Marxism is a universal method, an assertion that the communists are forced to observe scrupulously, must in practice lead to tyranny in all sectors of intellectual activity. What can the unfortunate physicists do if the atoms don't behave according to Hegelian-Marxist dialectics or according to the identity of the opposites and their development in higher forms? And what should the astronomers do if the cosmos is indifferent to communist dialectics? And the biologists, if the plants don't agree with the Lysenko-Stalinian theory on harmony and on the cooperation of classes in a 'socialist' society? Since it isn't possible to lie, these scientists must undergo the consequences of their 'heresies.' If their discoveries are to be accepted, they must serve to 'confirm' the formulas of Marxism-Leninism. The scientists are in a constant dilemma: Will their ideas and discoveries offend the official dogma? They are thus forced to opportunism and compromise in the scientific field."[153] Under the Soviet regime, continues Djilas, there was no great scientific discovery. This is explained by a particular diktat that makes the "discoverer's" life impossible. The social sciences were the most abused forms of knowledge. Marx and Lenin defined and solved all the problems concerning human existence. Where Marxist ideology became a state doctrine, concludes Djilas, every "new" thought was suffocated.

The Revolutionary Tradition of Russian Populism

In the historical rise and fall of revolutionary gnosticism, populism occupies a leading role. This political-cultural movement had the function of channeling Marx and Engels's ideas into the Russia of the late nineteenth century. Its leading interpreters were Alexander Herzen (1812–70), Mikhail Bakunin (1814–76), and Nikolay Chernyshevsky (1828–89).

Herzen, the father of populism, was profoundly influenced by the Decembrist revolt of 14 December 1825, where a group of intellectuals—inspired by the Enlightenment and the French Revolution—tried to overturn Czar Nicholas I and establish a constitutional regime. The defeat of the Decembrists

---

153. M. Djilas, *La nuova classe*, 144–45.

taught the future revolutionary movement that, without popular support, any struggle was destined to fail.

In voluntary exile from 1847, Herzen lived in France, moving to Switzerland and Italy. In 1852 he finally settled in London, where he founded the review *Kolokol* (The Bell) opposing czarist authoritarianism. He was the friend of Giuseppe Mazzini and Giuseppe Garibaldi. He also knew some of the leading Italian revolutionaries of his time, including Felice Orsini, Aurelio Saffi, and Carlo Pisacane.

In Russia, Herzen preached a mystic-religious concept of revolutionary practice, which he was convinced would open the way to an era of peace and happiness. Also for Herzen, inflamed by the Paris uprisings of 1848, "there's nothing to adjust...the first task is to demolish what exists."[154] One of the most interesting aspects of his preaching is the invitation to perform an "inner revolution." This was to have transformed people, liberating them of every bond to *this world*. In his thinking, political practice requires a proper revolutionary education; the first leads on from the second. Before attacking the institutions, aspiring revolutionaries must learn to look at the world with "new" eyes.

The spiritual formation of the aspiring revolutionary is the most important element when developing the socialist society. Without a proper spiritual education, the socialist ideal would have no possibility of being achieved. Herzen ordered revolutionaries to be "implacable" with themselves and to "guillotine" within them every aspect of the current society. This was the only way to "unmask" the supporters of *this world* and to take the road that leads to the "new world." His "obsession with purity" is summed up in these words: "Inside each man there is a revolutionary tribunal, there is an implacable Fouquier-Tinville and—what is essential—there is a guillotine."[155] When the guillotine becomes blunt, he continues, all society feels it dramatically. We have to be inflexible, since "reason is implacable, like the Convention, [it] is severe and without hypocrisy."[156] The reference to the Jacobin tradition is explicit.

The mystic-religious nature of Herzen's preaching is best illustrated in a paper written after the defeat of the Paris uprisings of 1848. We read that the people are waiting for a "revelation" and that their salvation is entrusted to a band of men driven by an unshakable faith. These "apostles" of the revolution—who do not come from the people but who have the task of guiding

---

154. Quoted by F. Venturi, *Il populismo russo,* 1:50.
155. Ibid., 1:53.
156. Ibid.

them from outside—have first of all to perform an "inner transformation." They must purify themselves by destroying their emotional bonds with the surrounding world. Nothing extraneous to the revolutionary cause must live inside them. Loving the people means hating the present society.

Herzen thus also sees the world as a corrupt place that needs a radical upheaval. After having announced that "soon there will be a change," he continues with these words: "The people suffer greatly, their life is onerous, they hate intensely. . . . They are waiting not for ready-made works but the revelation of what is secretly passing through their minds. They are waiting not for books but apostles, people in whom faith, will, conviction, and strength coincide, people who will never leave them, people who do not come from them but who act in them and with them, with open and unshakable faith, with a dedication that nothing can distract. Those who feel so close to the people that they have liberated themselves from the artificial civilization after having reworked and defeated it within themselves, who have achieved the unity and intensity we are speaking about, these will be able to speak to the people and must do so."[157]

Waiting for the end, hatred of the present world and the desire to sacrifice oneself to redeem humanity are typical traits of Bakunin's revolutionary spirit, summed up in a letter of 14 November 1835: "There is only one misfortune that can affect man, a single disaster: to lose the aspiration, the desire, and the strength to act, and to be without an aim. Then man not only can but must shoot himself."[158]

Bakunin's revolutionary ideal is driven by a pantoclastic extremism, fed by the expectation of a radical upheaval that announces the imminent "end" of *this world:* "The air is suffocating, pregnant with a storm!" "We are on the eve of a great revolution . . . that will have not only a political nature but also one of principle and religion."[159] Bakunin was one of the most uncompromising "destroyers" of *this world,* whose every aspect he rejected. His mission was to "devote himself immediately to the holy cause of the extermination of evil, of the purification and cleansing of the Russian soil with iron and fire."[160]

Although Marx and Bakunin had different ideas about the step that should lead to the "new world,"[161] they shared the same hate for *this world,* the same pantoclastic passion and thus the same revolutionary education:

157. Ibid., 1:58.

158. Ibid., 1:73.

159. Ibid., 1:85.

160. M. Bakunin, "I principi della rivoluzione," in *A un vecchio compagno,* by A. Herzen, 45.

161. See E. H. Carr, *Bakunin,* 328.

"The passion for destruction," Bakunin always insisted, "is a creative passion." Marx and Bakunin were united by their faith in the possibility of man's total liberation and by their adherence to a "definitive" choice of destruction/ regeneration.

Like any revolutionary worth his salt, Bakunin also defended "the most humane, the most just, the most magnificent cause ever produced on earth."[162] He was interpreting the "inexorable" laws of historic development, which would have led to the "inevitable triumph" of the revolution. In a work of October 1864, Bakunin explains that the task of regenerating the world is in the hands of a "tiny minority of intelligent, sincere people, profoundly dedicated to the cause of humanity." The alliance of these men of rare and extraordinary virtues forms a "small invisible church,"[163] without which the world would be condemned to desperation and slavery.

In another work, he asserts that human life will begin only with a revolutionary apocalypse marking the death of *this world*. In expectation of this salvific event, Bakunin—with a typically monastic spirit—invites men to abstain from the pleasures of bourgeois society and not give in to enticements. In language full of mystic-religious references he speaks of a "sentence" hanging over this world and exhorts people to prepare themselves spiritually for the day of the "end." This is not delirious raving, it is the mental universe of gnostic activities: "You want to escape the sentence hanging over the world in which you were born? Do you want finally to live, think, invent, act, create, and to be men? Give up the bourgeois world forever, its prejudices, its sentiments, its vanity, and put yourselves at the head of the proletariat. Embrace its cause, dedicate yourselves to this cause, give it your thought, and it will give you force and life."[164]

These words demonstrate the gnostic activists' psychological dependency on the masses. Professional revolutionaries have given themselves a grandiose function. They consider themselves to be "saviors" and they believe that humanity's destiny depends on their "deeds." In truth, they need to feel in the service of the "oppressed" to fill the "emptiness" provoked by their condition as rootless and marginal individuals. The gnostic activists are "saviors" asking for help; they are redeemers waiting to be redeemed. They want to give the "blind" back their sight, but they cannot discover the profound causes of their pantoclastic fury. With the relentless drive of the believer, Bakunin asserts that the world is about to fall headlong into a regenerating

---

162. M. Bakunin, *La teologia politica di Mazzini e l'internazionale*, in his *Scritti editi ed inediti*, 11.
163. M. Bakunin, *Organizzazione anarchica e lotta armata (lettera a uno svedese)*, 22.
164. M. Bakunin, "La rivolta," in Arvon, *Bakunin*, 161.

chaos. The "elect" are preparing themselves: looming on the horizon is the final battle between the forces of Good and Evil. It will be terrible because "the revolution is war, and those who declare war declare the destruction of men and things."[165] To promote the greatest happiness for all people: "this is the true, the great aim, the supreme end of history."[166]

Bakunin agrees with Herzen's principle that revolutionaries should first of all fight themselves. Since the world is corrupt, Bakunin explains, everyone is to some extent contaminated. Bourgeois society insinuates itself into hearts in a devious and imperceptible manner. You have to beware because "it envelops people right from their birth, influences them, penetrates them, and forms the very base of their existence, so that everyone in some way is acting against him or herself and often without even suspecting it. Thus, to rebel against this influence that society naturally exercises on them, people have at least partly to rebel against themselves."[167]

Among those who formed the nineteenth-century Russian intelligentsia and revolutionary movement, Lenin's favorite was indubitably Chernyshevsky. At the age of twenty he was already one of the most erudite critics and theorists of Russian culture. His subversive activity took place during the so-called epoch of reforms, starting after Alexander II succeeded Nicholas I (1855). His revolutionary spirit found its sounding board in the review *The Contemporary.* He maintained that the "mir" was the ideal model of labor organization that would have eliminated every form of exploitation. By jumping the capitalist stage, the mir would have guaranteed a cooperative type of production with an egalitarian distribution of profits.

In 1861, Chernyshevsky founded the revolutionary secret society Zemlia i Volia (Land and Liberty) in Saint Petersburg that was to earn him a fourteen-year (later reduced to seven) sentence of exile and forced labor in Siberia in 1862. Imprisoned in the Peter and Paul Fortress, he wrote his first novel, *What Is to Be Done?* (1863), read in clandestine copies until 1905, when it was published. This "social novel" profoundly influenced the revolutionary spirit of subsequent generations.[168] Kropotkin called it "the breviary of every young Russian." It was also praised by Nadezhda Konstantinovna Krupskaya, Lenin's wife, who said, "Lenin loved no one as much as Chernyshevsky." Lenin titled the pamphlet in which he outlined his theory of the revolutionary party organization *What Is to Be Done?* in honor of Chernyshevsky.

---

165. M. Bakunin, "La rivoluzione è la guerra," in Arvon, *Bakunin,* 162.
166. M. Bakunin, "La società e la libertà individuale," in Arvon, *Bakunin,* 171.
167. M. Bakunin, *Le vie della libertà,* in Arvon, *Bakunin,* 183.
168. See T. Szamuely, *The Russian Tradition,* 214.

In his novel, Chernyshevsky critically analyzes social conventions and tackles issues such as equality of the sexes and the organization of labor. His heroes and heroines do not actively participate in subversive actions but are presented as "models of revolutionary choice." The main character is Rakhmetov, a revolutionary leader who—like the author—is prepared to abase himself for the revolutionary cause: "We demand that men may have a complete enjoyment of their lives, and we must show by our example that we demand it, not to satisfy our personal passions, but for mankind in general; that what we say we say from principle and not from passion, from conviction and not from personal desire."[169] Rakhmetov's austere spirit makes him dissatisfied with himself. He tries to eliminate everything that has been compromised by this world from his life. He wants to be like the people and is tormented by having continually to confirm his spirit of abnegation. He eats black bread and even gives up sugar and fruit: "I have no right to spend money on a whim which I need not gratify....I must not eat that which is entirely out of the reach of the common people. This is necessary in order that I may feel, though but in a very slight degree, how much harder is the life of the common people than my own."[170] He renounces love in favor of his mission as liberator of the oppressed. To a rich nineteen-year-old girl who had been attracted to him and his revolutionary passion he uses the same words as the terrorists (whether red or black): "I must stifle love in me.... No, I must not love."[171] Men like Rakhmetov have the task of giving new life to humanity. They are the "elect" who teach people to "breathe." Chernyshevsky praises his hero's virtues with these words: *"They are few in number, but through them the life of all mankind expands; without them it would have been stifled. They are few in number, but they put others in a position to breathe, who without them would have been suffocated....They are strength, spirit, and aroma. They are the best among the best, they are the movers of the movers, they are the salt of the salt of the earth."*[172]

Starting again, making a clean slate of their country's history: this was the political ideal of the Russian populists. Chernyshevsky demonstrated that he was well aware of the dramatic consequences of revolutionary violence but was prepared to accept them because the end would have purified the means. Even if "for a long and perhaps even very long time nothing good comes of [the revolution], in spite of all the evil that revolutions cause at their outset,

---

169. N. G. Chernyshevsky, *Che fare?* 177–78.
170. Ibid., 178.
171. Ibid., 181.
172. Ibid. Italics added.

you must not be frightened. You know that you cannot expect anything else from people and that a peaceful, calm development is impossible."[173]

Chernyshevsky's revolutionary ideology—although he never suggested using terrorism—found an enthusiastic admirer in Nikolai Ishutin. This latter founded the "Organization" in Moscow (1863), a secret society of apocalyptic inspiration, containing a select group of thirty adherents who constituted "Hell" (1865). The task of this small nucleus was to control the work of the "Organization," punishing with death all those who left what its members called the "community of absolute revolution."

Ishutin proposed to abolish czarism through the massive and methodical use of terrorism. Herzen, Bakunin, and Chernyshevsky's "inner guillotine" was being set up to attack not so much the customs of bourgeois society but its flesh and blood representatives. This kind of undertaking required an organization based on very strict inner discipline that Ishutin described thus: "The members of Hell have to live under a false name and break off family bonds; they must not marry, they have to leave their friends and generally live with a single and exclusive aim: the infinite love and dedication to their country and to its good. For this they have to renounce any personal satisfaction and, in exchange, concentrating it in themselves, nourish hate against hate, wickedness against wickedness. They have to live feeling satisfied with this aspect of their lives."[174]

The final aim of the "Organization" was the assassination of the emperor. The killer, who would be drawn by lots, would have had to separate himself completely from his comrades and conduct a dissolute life. Besides getting drunk, he would have had to frequent dubious places and even inform the police. The day of the attack, he would have disfigured his face with acid so as not to be recognized, putting a revolutionary manifesto in his pocket giving the reasons for the assassination. The mission would be concluded with the suicide of the "chosen one" by poison, to guarantee the safety of the other members.

No less significant is *The Revolutionary Catechism,* a document written in 1869 by an anonymous author (probably Sergei Nechaev, a leading figure in Russian terrorism, former collaborator of Bakunin) in which the professional revolutionary is described as a man who has broken all the bonds that tie him to the social order. Every violent action against present society is lawful because those who love humanity can have no compassion for *this putrescent world.* Nechaev's revolutionary spirit can be summed up

---

173. Quoted by Venturi, *Il populismo russo,* 1:254.
174. Ibid., 2:234–35.

with two words used by all gnostic activists: *destroy and purify*. In his words: "We consider the work of destruction such an enormous and difficult task that we have to give all our strength to it and we do not want to deceive ourselves with the delusion that our strength and our capacity to build are enough. . . . By concentrating all our strength in destruction, we have neither doubts nor illusions; we will pursue our only vital aim in a constant, uniform, and cold manner."[175]

The gnostic activists can attack their own "brothers" with the same ferocity they use for the enemies of the revolution. The student Ivan Ivanov left the "Popular Justice" organization after criticizing its authoritarian methods. He was not a "traitor"; he wanted to found a new revolutionary sect. Nechayev killed him, involving another four adherents in the act to cement their membership in the group (21 November 1869). The gnostic groups saw adherence to the revolutionary ideal as a total and final choice without any possibility of criticism.

During a search, the police discovered the second edition of the review *Narodnaya rasprava* (The People's Will), containing an outline of the future communist society founded on compulsory work and on the principle that everyone "must produce as much as possible for society and consume as little as possible." Nechaev, who said he was inspired by Marx and Engels's *Communist Manifesto,* was inflexible. Arrested in 1872, he was imprisoned in the Peter and Paul Fortress, where he managed to win over even his warders to his cause. Although in prison, he made contact with the members of *The People's Will.* Betrayed by an informer, his prison conditions became even harsher. He died in 1882.

Vittorio Strada emphasizes that Lenin admired Nechaev. Particularly significant is the testimony of the historian and ethnographer Vladimir Bonch-Bruyevich—Bolshevik and friend of Lenin—who recalls that "hitherto we had not studied Nechaev, whose works Lenin frequently referred to. When the words 'Nechaevism' and 'Nechaevian' sounded like insults even among the political immigrants, when this term was adopted by those who wanted to publicize the proletariat seizing power, to organize the armed revolt and establish the proletariat dictatorship, when Nechaev—almost as if it were something bad—was called the 'Russian Blanquist,' Vladimir Ilyich [Lenin] often said that the reactionaries had carried out a clever trick thanks to Dostoyevsky and his repugnant but brilliant book *The Devils,* in which even revolutionary circles had started treating Nechayev negatively, entirely

---

175. Quoted in V. Strada, *Etica del terrore,* 25.

forgetting that this titan of the revolution possessed such a powerful will, such enthusiasm, that in the Peter and Paul Fortress he had managed, in those terrible conditions, to influence the soldiers so as to completely win them over to him."[176]

Dostoyevsky, in his book *The Devils*, described the paradox accompanying every "revolutionary catechism": the idea that absolute freedom can come from absolute power. The total destruction of *this world*—and its replacement with the kingdom of permanent happiness—demands a great effort, which can be achieved only by concentrating immeasurable power in the hands of a small band of the "elect." Dostoyevsky illustrated this view through the story of Shigalyov, one of the heroes in the book. To achieve absolute equality, he works out a totalitarian plan that divides humanity into two groups: a minority that enjoys absolute freedom and a completely dominated majority, forced to work to redeem themselves. In Shigalyov's community, people have to spy on everyone else and denounce even the smallest infringement of the revolutionary rule: "Every one belongs to all and all to every one. All are slaves and equal in their slavery. In extreme cases he advocates slander and murder, but the great thing about it is equality. To begin with, the level of education, science and talents is lowered. A high level of education and science is only possible for great intellects, and they are not wanted. The great intellects have always seized the power and been despots. Great intellects cannot help being despots and they've always done more harm than good. They will be banished or put to death. Cicero will have his tongue cut out, Copernicus will have his eyes put out, Shakespeare will be stoned. . . . Slaves are bound to be equal. There has never been either freedom or equality without despotism, but in the herd there is bound to be equality."[177]

Dostoyevsky's words help us introduce the figure of Pyotr Zaichnevsky, one of the most radical populists. At the age of nineteen he issued an underground pamphlet, *The Young Russia,* that can be considered the founding document of terrorism in Russia.

Zaichnevsky's manifesto—which in breadth and depth goes beyond all the revolutionary programs circulating at that time—specified free education, the emancipation of women, the abolition of monasteries, the shortening of the period of military service, and the increase of soldiers' pay. The financial system would have had to weigh on the rich much more than on the poor and the Russian territory would be divided into regions, united in a federal republic. Each region would be made up of rural communities based

---

176. Ibid., 28.
177. F. Dostoyevsky, *I demoni,* 422.

on the equality of rights and economic cooperation. Before achieving social-ism, however, a transitory stage would be necessary, during which the revo-lutionary party would have centralized all power to achieve the immense plan of abolishing the present world and creating a new one: "It must seize power, set up a dictatorship, and stop at nothing."[178] All this implied an impla-cable struggle against the defenders of *this world,* whom he called "filthy cowards." On the day of the revolution, "he who is not with us is against us, and who is against us is an enemy, and enemies one must destroy by all possible means."[179]

Zaichnevsky's proclamation circulated around Saint Petersburg and Mos-cow in May 1862 and caused a great sensation in government spheres. One can understand why. The language used is full of violence and disgust for the present world. The solution to the evils of the world lies in a regenerating bloodbath: "There is only one way out of this terrible, oppressive situation that is ruining contemporary man and in the fight against it consumes all his best forces: revolution, a bloody and implacable revolution that will radically change all the foundations of contemporary society without exception and will destroy the defenders of the present order." Zaichnevsky is well aware that radical upheavals always reap innocent victims, but that doesn't stop him. The end he wants to achieve, he explains, purifies the means. It is right and proper to kill for the revolution: "We are not afraid of [the revolution], although we know that a river of blood will flow and that innocent victims will perish; we greet its coming, we are prepared to lay down our lives for the sake of it, the long desired!"[180]

Jacobin revolutionary violence has to be regarded as the timid anticipa-tion of a much more bloodthirsty and sensational change: "We have studied the history of the West and this study was not in vain; we will be more con-sistent, not only than the wretched revolutionaries of '48, but also than the great terrorists of '92. We will not be afraid if we see that, to demolish the present order, we have to shed three times the blood shed by the Jacobins in the nineties."[181] It is a violence that causes joy because it appeases a boundless rage. Besides the mass murders, the proclamation envisages that the revolu-tionaries will wash their hands in the blood of their enemies, who must be hunted down in the squares, in the streets, and in the houses. So "we will shout with one voice: 'Get your axes!' and then we will attack the Imperial

---

178. Quoted by Venturi, *Il populismo russo,* 2:164–65.
179. Ibid., 2:165.
180. Quoted by Strada, *Etica del terrore,* 17.
181. Ibid.

Party with no more mercy than they show us; we will kill them in the squares... kill them in the houses, kill them in the narrow alleys of towns, in the broad avenues of capitals, kill them in the villages and hamlets.... Who is not with us is against us, and who is against us is an enemy, and enemies one must destroy by all possible means."[182]

The "Young Russia" members were immediately arrested. Nevertheless, their ideas inspired the failed attack against Czar Alexander II (4 April 1866) by Dmitri Karakozov, former member of the "Organization" and cousin of Isutin.

In his love for the revolution, Zaichnevsky did not lack a certain disdain for the masses, "who are always on the side of the fait accompli." Pyotr Nikitich Tkachev (1844–85), the greatest theorist of red "Jacobinism," was of the same opinion.

Tkachev wanted absolute equality, but said one should not rely on the people, who he believed had no revolutionary initiative. The task of transforming the world was entrusted to a minority of the "elect" capable of imposing their will and of centralizing every decision. He considered terrorism the most suitable means for speedily liberating humanity from the evil afflicting it. In his article "Terrorism as the Only Means for the Moral and Social Regeneration of Russia," he writes that "in the present conditions of Russia's political and social life, there is only one possible way to achieve the ultimate aim of disorganizing and weakening the government power: by terrorizing the individuals who to the greatest degree embody government power."[183] Terrorism, he continues, makes those in government lose their heads, it weakens their power and throws them into panic.

Tkachev devoted his life to the revolution, seeing it as a "sacrificial gesture." He was in and out of prison numerous times without ever losing his revolutionary fire. He lived in conspiracy without managing to found a movement. In 1874 he wrote: "Almost every blow struck by the reaction has directly affected me or my comrades and closest friends. Since high school I have known no other society than young people who assiduously frequent student meetings, secretly conspiring.... I've always been with them and among them. I never left them until the walls of the Peter and Paul Fortress separated us."[184]

---

182. Ibid., 18.
183. Ibid., 33.
184. Quoted by Venturi, *Il populismo russo*, 2:329–30.

Tkachev was one of the first in Russia to disseminate historic Marxist materialism. He saw the works of Marx and Engels as the key to transforming the world. Absolute equality was his main inspiration: "The problem will be solved, the principle will be achieved when all people are unconditionally equal, when there is no difference between them from an intellectual, moral or physical point of view."[185]

185. Ibid., 2:342.

CHAPTER 6

The Purifiers of the World in Power

> This point is fundamental: the dictatorship of the proletariat can only be founded on Jacobin violence.
>
> —Lenin

Lenin and State Terrorism

Russian populism had a profound influence on the thought and political practice of Lenin, the greatest purifier of the world known to history.

The populists taught Lenin that the revolution is first of all an inner journey, focused on sacrifice and discipline. Unlike his predecessors, however, he was successful. He achieved power and set about regenerating humanity. His political actions have enabled the effects of the gnostic recipe to be verified "in the field." Thanks to the Bolshevik Revolution, we can now answer the question of what happens when professional revolutionaries actually gain power.

Respecting a tradition that sees political practice as a consequence of revolutionary education, Lenin defined his point of view about the road to take to build socialism. This is what he wrote in 1901: "In principle we have never rejected, and cannot reject, terror. Terror is one of the forms of military action that may be perfectly suitable and even essential at a definite juncture in the battle, given a definite state of the troops and the existence of definite conditions."[1] In another work, *The Lessons of the Moscow Uprising,* Lenin is

---

1. V. Lenin, "Da dove cominciare," in Lenin, *Opere complete,* 8:371. On the relationship between Leninism and terrorism, see L. Pellicani, *Miseria del marxismo.*

equally explicit: "We would be deceiving both ourselves and the people if we concealed from the masses the necessity of a desperate, bloody war of extermination, as the immediate task of the coming revolutionary action."[2]

Lenin admired Jacobin violence and claimed that the communist objective could not be achieved without it; the enemies of the proletariat must be "annihilated." The conversations with Valentinov are illuminating on Lenin's mental universe: "Jacobinism does not mean fighting with white gloves, but fighting without sentimentality, without being afraid of the guillotine; it means fighting without being discouraged by failure. Of course Bernstein and company would never be Jacobins because they supported democratic principles. Hostility for the Jacobin methods inevitably generates hostility for the concept of the dictatorship of the proletariat, namely violence, which is inevitable if the socialist revolution is to triumph and *the enemies of the proletariat be annihilated.* If the Jacobin purges are indispensable for the success of the bourgeois revolution, they are all the more indispensable for the successful outcome of a socialist revolution. A Jacobin spirit is essential to establish the dictatorship of the proletariat. This point is fundamental: the dictatorship of the proletariat can only be founded on Jacobin violence."[3]

Faithful to this approach, even after gaining power Lenin wanted to reassure his supporters that the only way really was "that of the ruthless struggle, of terrorism,"[4] adding that "terror and the CHEKA [secret police] are absolutely indispensable."[5] Because "the revolution is an intense, furious and desperate class struggle and civil war."[6] For Lenin, "the ruthlessly severe, swift and resolute use of force"[7] was necessary against those who had not joined the communist cause. He always swore that "we shall be merciless both to our enemies and to all waverers and harmful elements in our midst."[8]

The Red Brigades learned from Lenin that the world is divided into two camps. On one side are the supporters of the revolution; on the other all those who deserve only to be crushed: "We have lit the torch of socialism at home and all over the world. We shall fight ruthlessly against anyone who hinders this struggle in the slightest. He who is not for us is against us."[9] "We

2. V. Lenin, "Gli insegnamenti dei fatti di Mosca," in Lenin, *Opere complete,* 9:50–51.

3. Ibid., 9:125–26. Italics added.

4. V. Lenin, "Assemblea dell'attivo di partito di Mosca," in Lenin, *Opere complete,* 28:215.

5. V. Lenin, "Discorso conclusivo del VII congresso dei soviet," in Lenin, *Opere complete,* 30:207.

6. V. Lenin, "I bolscevichi conserveranno il potere?" in Lenin, *Opere complete,* 29:354.

7. V. Lenin, "Saluto agli operai ungheresi," in Lenin, *Opere complete,* 29:354.

8. V. Lenin, "Discorso al soviet di Mosca," in Lenin, *Opere complete,* 27:210.

9. V. Lenin, "Assemblea plenaria del Consiglio centrale dei sindacati," in Lenin, *Opere complete,* 29:267.

say: yes, the dictatorship of a party"[10] that "needs the State not for freedom but to crush the enemy."[11] And again: "The word dictatorship is a cruel, stern, bloody and painful one; it is not a word to play with."[12] "The revolutionary dictatorship of the proletariat is a power that rests on violence, it is not bound by any law,"[13] and "it does not renounce terror."[14]

Just as explicit was Lenin's disgust for all those who had not blindly submitted to Marx and Engels' doctrine. In his words, the critics of Marxism are "putrid corpses." During an encounter with Nikolai Valentinov, he announced: "We will know what attempts at revision of Marxism lead to. We need only to think of Bernstein and, here at home, of Struve and Bulgakov. With his revisionism, Struve has got bogged down in the most abject revisionism; as for Bulgakov, he's gone even lower. *Marxist doctrine is monolithic. There can be no way it can be diluted or its nature changed with the addition of other elements.* Of a person who criticised Marxism, Plechanov once said: 'Mark him with the ace of spades and then we'll see.' This is what a true revolutionary would say. *If you come across a dead body you don't have to touch it to know what it is and decide what to do. The stink is enough.*"[15]

The Red Brigades found these words of Lenin particularly apt: "By following the path of Marxist theory we shall draw closer and closer to objective truth (without ever exhausting it); but by following any other path we shall arrive at nothing but confusion and lies," because "Marxism is the objective truth."[16] Lenin said, "The Marxian doctrine is omnipotent because it is true. It is complete and harmonious, and provides men with an integral world conception."[17]

Lenin was not only a "theorist" of terror, he was also an "active militant." The enemies have to be "terrorized," that is, attacked *without any specific criterion,* so that the survivors live in constant fear of being killed.

In November 1917, he sent the following instructions on the "management" of some prisoners considered enemies and thus "harmful persons." Lenin writes: "In one place half a score of rich, a dozen rogues, half a dozen workers who shirk their work will be put in prison.... In another place they will be put to cleaning latrines. In a third place they will be provided with

---

10. V. Lenin, "Primo congresso dei lavoratori dell'istruzione e della cultura socialista," in Lenin, *Opere complete,* 29:491.

11. V. Lenin, "I compiti della Terza internazionale," in Lenin, *Opere complete,* 29:469.

12. V. Lenin, "Primo congresso per l'istruzione extrascolastica," in Lenin, *Opere complete,* 29:323.

13. V. Lenin, "La rivoluzione proletaria e il rinnegato Kautsky," in Lenin, *Opere complete,* 38:241.

14. V. Lenin, "Conferenza degli operai e dei soldati russi senza partito," in Lenin, *Opere complete,* 29:503.

15. N. Valentinov, *I miei colloqui con Lenin,* 170. Italics added.

16. Lenin, "Materialismo ed empiriocriticismo," in Lenin, *Opere complete,* 14:139.

17. Lenin, "Tre fonti e tre parti integranti del marxismo," in Lenin, *Opere scelte,* 475.

'yellow tickets' after they have served their time, so that everyone shall keep
an eye on them, as harmful persons.... In a fourth place, one out of every
ten idlers will be shot on the spot. In a fifth place, mixed methods may be
adopted.... The more variety there will be, the better and richer will be
our general experience, the more certain and rapid will be the success of
socialism."[18]

The instructions Lenin gave in July 1918 are the manifesto of the coher-
ence between his principles and his political actions. In this document, Lenin
reproves Zinoviev for not having practiced mass terror and tells him to use
the greatest determination in repressing his enemies: "Comrade Zinoviev,
only today we have heard at the Central Committee that in Petrograd the
workers wanted to reply to the murder of Volodarsky by mass terror and
that you (not you personally, but the Petrograd Central Committee members, or Petrograd Committee members) restrained them. I protest most
emphatically!... We must encourage the energy and mass character of the
terror against the counter-revolutionaries." "We must make every effort,
form a triumvirate of dictators, impose mass terror immediately... the mass
deportations of Mensheviks and the unreliable." "We must repress the kulaks'
uprising with the greatest force, swiftness and ruthlessness." "Act decisively
against the kulaks and the left revolutionary-socialist rabble that hangs out
with them. The blood-sucking kulaks have to be mercilessly crushed." "The
insurrection of the kulaks and the left revolutionary socialists has to be ruthlessly suppressed."[19]

For Lenin, the choice of terror was not an "extraordinary" fact determined by the civil war. It was a feature of his political culture. He saw terror
as an instrument on which to base the exercise of political power. Terror is
understood as a political and legal principle to be inserted in the penal code.
The revolutionary conscience will establish, each time, to what extent terrorist measures should be used. Lenin placed state terrorism, of which he
was a theorist as well as a zealous executor, over "individual" terrorism that
he considered "ineffective."[20] This was his argument: the terrorist actions of
single militants do not produce the desired effects. To build communism
you have to concentrate power in the hands of the party and conduct the
continuous, systematic, and coordinated extermination of all social categories
considered "harmful" for the achievement of the communist plan. Because

18. V. Lenin, "Come organizzare l'emulazione," in Lenin, *Opere complete,* 26:394.
19. V. Lenin, *Opere complete,* 35:241–43 and 249–51.
20. See R. Service, *L'uomo, il leader, il mito,* 53–57.

all those who do not support Bolshevikism—including intellectuals who are faint in praise of it, albeit not hostile—are pure and simple "crap."[21]

Lenin theorized—and put into practice—the extermination of his enemies with a zeal that was always to arouse the Red Brigades' greatest admiration. Once in power, he was meticulous in applying the principles he had so eagerly pronounced.

Read his letter of 17 May 1922, which makes it very difficult to agree with Roberto Massari when he asserts that terrorism and communism are "two antithetical terms."[22]

Lenin writes: "Comrade Kursky, further to our conversation, I herewith enclose the draft of an article supplementary to the Criminal Code. The main idea will be clear, I hope, in spite of the faulty drafting: to put forward publicly a thesis that is correct in principle and politically (not only strictly juridical), which explains the *substance* of terror, its necessity and limits, and provides *justification* for it. The courts must not ban terror—to promise that would be deception or self-deception—but must formulate the motives underlying it, legalize it as a principle, plainly, without any make-believe or embellishment. It must be formulated in the broadest possible manner, for only revolutionary law and revolutionary conscience can more or less widely determine the limits within which it should be applied."[23]

With these ideological claims, it is not surprising that the idea of purifying the world through the extermination of the "impure" elements found one of its most complete incarnations in the Bolshevik Revolution of 1917.

Lenin passionately and methodically pursued the purification of the world through the extermination of its enemies. His followers did not "add" any theoretical contribution to his pedagogy of intolerance. Despite Eric Hobsbawm, who would have us believe that Stalinism was a "degeneration" of the communist plan,[24] Stalin did nothing else but apply the teachings of the "master." The Stalin regime was not "the revolution betrayed,"[25] but a promise kept. Lenin's teaching had been very clear: the only possible relationship with your enemies is their extermination. This is what emerges from a secret document that Lenin wrote in August 1918.

---

21. Quoted in P. P. Poggio, "Il difficile rapporto tra intellettuali e popolo nel lungo Novecento," 10.
22. R. Massari, *Il terrorismo,* 420.
23. V. Lenin, quoted by A. Solzhenitsyn, *Arcipelago Gulag,* 1:356.
24. See E. J. Hobsbawm, *Il secolo breve,* 460–61.
25. L. Trotsky, *La rivoluzione tradita.*

Also here note the parasitological language, typical of the purifiers of the world. The enemies of Soviet power are "bloodsuckers" and "poisonous spiders." And as such they have to be mercilessly crushed.

Lenin writes:

> There is no doubt about it. The kulaks are rabid foes of the Soviet government. Either the kulaks massacre vast numbers of workers, or the workers ruthlessly suppress the revolts of the predatory kulak minority of the people against the working people's government. *There can be no middle course.* Peace is out of the question: even if they have quarrelled, the kulaks can easily come to terms with the landowner, the tsar and the priest, but with the working class never. That is why we call the fight against the kulaks the *last, decisive fight....* The kulaks are the most brutal, callous and savage exploiters.... These *bloodsuckers* have grown rich on the want suffered by the people in the war.... These *poisonous spiders* have grown fat at the expense of the peasants ruined by the war, at the expense of the starving workers. These leeches have sucked the blood of the working people.... *Ruthless war* on the kulaks! Death to them! *Hatred and contempt* for the parties which defend them—the Right Socialist-Revolutionaries, the Mensheviks and today's Left Socialist-Revolutionaries! The workers must crush the revolts of the kulaks with an iron hand, the kulaks who are forming an alliance with the foreign capitalists against the working people of their own country.[26]

The Bolshevik Revolution and the "Victims of the Victims"

The famous political scientist Rudolph J. Rummel has calculated that the Communist Party of the Soviet Union is directly responsible for the death of some 62 million people, of whom 54,800,000 were Soviet citizens: "In fact, we have witnessed in the Soviet Union a true egalitarian social cleansing: no group or class escaped, for everyone and anyone could have had counterrevolutionary ancestors, class lineage, or counterrevolutionary ideas or thoughts, or be susceptible to them. And thus, almost anyone was arrested, interrogated, tortured and, after a forced confession of a plot to blow up the Kremlin, or some such, shot or sentenced to the 'dry guillotine'—slow death

---

26. V. Lenin, "Alla lotta finale, decisiva!" in Lenin, *Opere complete,* 28:53–54. Italics added. L. Pellicani has drawn attention to this passage in his *Lenin e Hitler,* 38.

by exposure, malnutrition, and overwork in a forced labor camp."[27] Old and young, healthy and sick, men and women, even infants and the infirm, were killed in cold blood. They were not killed in a civil war; they were not rebels. Some were from the "wrong" class; some were from the "wrong" nation or race; some were considered "enemies" of the revolution. Finally, there were the "victims of the victims," the fathers and mothers, sons and daughters, eliminated for having been in contact with "infected" elements and thus for having been "contaminated" themselves.

As the Red Brigades explain, "infectious" ideas exist before "infected persons," who from time to time turn into "agents of evil." It is what Hannah Arendt has called the "simple and ingenious device of guilt by association" of totalitarian regimes.[28] Since "the citizen, in the communist system, is continuously tormented by conscience and fear of transgression,"[29] when people are suspected of plotting against the revolution, their friends become their merciless enemies. To save themselves from the Terror, relatives voluntarily inform on their dear ones, making use of entirely inconsistent evidence. It was no coincidence that Stalin's regime assessed allegiance to socialism on the basis of the number of reports made against comrades. Reporting your parents was considered the "noblest" gesture, demonstrating profound love of the proletarian cause. The device of guilt by association produces the effect of cutting off victims from their sentimental and emotional relations as the prelude to their physical elimination. "Dissidents" die before being killed. Society abandons them, leaving them without any psychological refuge.

This is the case of Sidorov Vasily Klementovich, an ordinary Soviet peasant, to whom an informer had attributed the following words: "Stalin and his gang won't give up power. Stalin has killed a whole mass of people, but he doesn't want to go. The Bolsheviks will hold on to power and go on arresting innocent people, and you can't even talk about that, or you'll end up in a camp for twenty-five years."

Klementovich lives in a wood house with a tin roof. He has no criminal record and has never taken part in subversive actions. We are not in a "particular" situation here. It is 1938 and there is no civil war raging, the fatherland runs no risk of being invaded by a foreign army. The document demonstrates the "normality" of the purification policy. In this case, the idea that politics always involves a fight for power does not help us understand the details of the revolutionary mentality; nor can the "thesis of circumstances"

---

27. R. J. Rummel, *Stati assassini*, 98.
28. H. Arendt, *Le origini del totalitarismo*, 447.
29. M. Djilas, *La nuova classe*, 147.

be of any help to us. Eschatological politics has a "very high" aim that cannot be reduced to the simple conquest of the coercitive apparatus. Its objective is to free the world of suffering, exterminating those who are seen as "the evil ones." Sidorov Vasily Klementovich is what the Red Brigades would call a "vile creature," a "pig," who "arouses absolute disgust." Lenin instead preferred to talk about "these survivals of accursed capitalist society, these dregs of humanity, these hopelessly decayed and atrophied limbs, this contagion, this plague, this ulcer that socialism has inherited from capitalism."[30]

This document is from the archives of the Soviet police, for a long time inaccessible to historical research:

Dossier no. 24260

1. Last name: Sidorov
2. First name: Vasily Klementovich
3. Place and date of birth: Sechevo, Moscow region, 1893
4. Address: Sechevo, Kolomenskii districts, Moscow region
5. Profession: cooperative employee
6. Union membership: cooperative employees' union
7. Possessions at time of arrest (detailed description): 1 wooden house, 8 meters by 8, covered with metal sheet, with a partially covered courtyard, 20 meters by 7, 1 cow, 4 sheep, 2 pigs, chickens
8. Property in 1929: identical plus 1 horse
9. Property in 1917: 1 wooden house, 8 meters by 8, a partially covered courtyard, 30 meters by 20, 2 barns, 2 hangars, 2 horses, 2 cows, 7 sheep
10. Social situation at moment of arrest: employed
11. Service in czarist army: 1915–16 foot soldier, second class, 6th Infantry Regiment of Turkestan
12. Military service in the White Army: none
13. Military service in the Red Army: none
14. Social origin: I consider myself the son of an ordinary peasant.
15. Political history: no party memberships
16. Nationality and citizenship: Russian, USSR citizen
17. Communist Party membership: no
18. Education: basic
19. Present military situation: reservist
20. Criminal record: no

---

30. Quoted by B. Brunetau, *Il secolo dei genocidi,* 97.

21. State of health: hernia
22. Family situation: married. Wife: Anastasia Fedorovna, 43 years old, *kolkhoz* worker; daughter: Nina, 24 years old

An excerpt from the interrogation protocol:

Question: Explain your social origins, your social situation, and your possessions before and after 1917.

Answer: I came originally from a family of small merchants. Until about 1904 my father had a small shop in Moscow, on Zolotorozhskaya Street where, according to what he told me, he did business but had no employees. After 1904 he was forced to close his shop, for he couldn't compete with the bigger shops. He came back to the country, to Sechevo, where he rented six hectares of arable land and two hectares of meadow. He had one employee, a man called Goryachev, who worked with him for many years, up to 1916. After 1917 we kept the farm but we lost the horses. I worked with my father until 1925, then after his death, my brother and I shared out the land between us. I don't think I am guilty of anything at all.

An excerpt from the charges drawn up:

Sidorov, hostile to the Soviet regime in general and the Party in particular, was given to systematically spreading anti-Soviet propaganda, saying: "Stalin and his gang won't give up power. Stalin has killed a whole mass of people, but he doesn't want to go. The Bolsheviks will hold onto power and go on arresting innocent people, and you can't even talk about that, or you'll end up in a camp for twenty-five years."

The accused Sidorov pleaded not guilty, but was unmasked by several witnesses. The affair has been passed on to the troika for judgment.

Signed: Salahaev, Second Lieutenant in the Kolomenskaya district police.

Agreed: Galkin, Lieutenant in the State Security, Chief of the State Security Detachment in the Kolomenskaya district.

An excerpt from the protocol of the troika's judgment, 15 July 1938:

V. K. Sidorov affair. Ex-merchant, he had previously kept a shop with his father. Accused of spreading counterrevolutionary ideas among *kolkhoz* workers, characterized by defeatist statements, together with threats against Communists, criticism of Party policies and of the government.

Verdict: Shoot Sidorov Vasily Klementovich.

Sentence carried out on 3 August 1938.

Posthumously rehabilitated on 24 January 1989.[31]

In many cases, the punishments inflicted on the enemies of Soviet power were much worse than shooting. This is the treatment that the purifiers of the world, once they have conquered the coercive apparatus, usually reserve for their political enemies, those "poisonous spiders," those "bloodsuckers" that Lenin hated so much:

In Kharkiv they went in for the "glove trick"—burning the victim's hands in boiling water until the blistered skin could be peeled off: this left the victims with raw and bleeding hands and their torturers with "human gloves." The Tsaritsyn cheka sawed its victims' bones in half. In Voronezh they rolled their naked victims in nail-studded barrels. In Armavir they crushed their skulls by tightening a leather strap with an iron bolt around their head. In Kiev they affixed a cage with rats to the victim's torso and heated it so that the enraged rats ate their way through the victim's guts in an effort to escape. In Odessa they chained their victims to planks and pushed them slowly into a furnace or a tank of boiling water. A favorite winter torture was to pour water on the naked victims until they became living ice statues. Many chekas preferred psychological forms of torture. One had the victims led off to what they thought was their execution, only to have blanks fired at them. Another had the victims buried alive, or kept in a coffin with a corpse. Some chekas forced their victims to watch their loved ones being tortured, raped, or killed.[32]

The Gulag, or The Promise Kept

Ten years after the revolution, Soviet prisons housed many more prisoners than under the czarist regime. There were 144,000 inmates in 1925, 149,000 in 1926, and 185,000 in 1927. In 1912, the czarist prisons housed 183,864 detainees,

---

31. Quoted by N. Werth, "Violenze, repressioni, terrori nell'Unione Sovietica," in *Il libro nero del comunismo,* 181–82.

32. O. Figes, *La tragedia di un popolo,* 775.

dropping to 142,339 in 1916.[33] The number of people in Soviet prisons and gulags increased to an astonishing degree. According to the Bolsheviks' central committee's statistics, in 1930 there were 179,000 prisoners in corrective labor camps and colonies. In the space of a few years, the number had tripled to 510,307 in 1934 and then 1,929,729 in 1941. The historic maximum occurred in 1950, with 2,561,351 detainees. The elimination of the well-off peasants (kulaks) provides equally consistent figures, especially with regard to their children. The decree of the OGPU (the secret police) of 2 February 1930 specified two types of sanctions for the kulaks: immediate elimination or deportation. In two years, 388,334 families, amounting to 1,637,740 people, were deported to desolate zones in the north or the steppes of Kazakhstan, with half a million children involved. Only 1,421,380 people reached their destination. Many of these were killed on the spot or died of hardship during their banishment. An immense number of children died[34] after Stalin introduced the death penalty for children of twelve years and over.[35]

One of the most interesting aspects of the historic trajectory of revolutionary gnosticism is the transformation of the sect into the church, according to the formula "the revolutionaries return home." The adventure of the "exterminating angels" had begun under the banner of purity. They had broken away from the "church-party" to found a community of "saints." But everything changed once they had conquered the coercive apparatus. The revolutionaries are now required to come to terms with the powers of *this world*. The main objective is no longer the retreat from the world to avoid "contamination" but that of increasing power to establish heaven on earth. The Red Brigades repeat it obsessively: the conquest of power is the first step toward the kingdom of absolute happiness. As Milovan Djilas has written: "Power is the main objective and also the main instrument of communism and every true communist. The thirst for power is insatiable and irresistible among communists. For them victory in the struggle for power represents almost elevation to God, defeat means the deepest humiliation and shame."[36]

With the conquest of the coercive apparatus, the purifiers of the world come out of the "catacombs," transforming the problem of "identifying evil" into the problem of its total elimination. When the revolutionaries cannot abolish the "horrors" of the "old world" they have sworn to raze to

---

33. See M. Heller and A. Nekrich, *Storia dell'Urss,* 257.

34. For the figures on the Soviet Terror, see F. Bettanin, *Il lungo terrore,* 27ff. According to Bettanin: "There are thus good reasons for concentrating on the political culture rather than on the personality of the leading actors of the terror" (43).

35. M. McCauley, *Stalin e lo stalinismo,* 78.

36. Djilas, *La nuova classe,* 185–86.

the ground, they turn to the "politics of words." Some are changed, others even prohibited. After the October Revolution, "prison" becomes "detention center" (*domzak*), whereas the term "punishment" is replaced by "social protection measure."

In some cases, however, the horrors of the old world are not so "terrible." In July 1922, the Bolshevik Party approved a decree "On the Improvement of the Living Conditions of Party Activists." This decree established a new wage scale for party officials who, besides receiving several hundred rubles, were also given additional money for their family and many other privileges. For example, high-ranking bureaucrats were given a car with driver, housing, health care, and clothing (in the same period a Soviet industry worker earned on average ten rubles). Lenin was the first to become the owner of a luxurious dacha; in October 1918, he occupied the estate of a czarist general in Gor'Kij, thirty-five kilometers south of Moscow. Besides the house, Lenin also had at his disposal six limousines with chauffeur. One of the most luxurious estates in Russia, Arkhangelskoye, belonging to the Yusupov princes, was handed over to Trotsky; Stalin instead took possession of an oil magnate's dacha in Zubalovo.[37]

Rather than criticize the cynicism in this behavior—condemning is not explaining—we should see a historical-sociological constancy that Robert Michels has described as follows: "Who says organization says a tendency to oligarchy. A profoundly aristocratic element is inherent in the very nature of the organization. While it creates a solid structure, the organization causes considerable changes in the organized masses, totally overturning the leadership's relationship with the masses and dividing every party or trade union into two parts: a minority with the task of governing and a majority governed by the former."[38] This is the so-called iron law of oligarchy. According to Michels, the workers' strength lies in organization. The "weak" can hope to beat the "strong" only if they march together. Thus the workers need a stable apparatus of officials who coordinate their protests according to their technical skills. The result is that all the decision-making powers of the masses are transferred to the leadership, making democratic exercise entirely illusionary. This creates a paradox: if the power of the organization increases, the power of the leaders also increases. These, distancing themselves from the work floor, become detached from the masses and accustomed to a life of privilege.[39]

---

37. See R. Pipes, *Il regime bolscevico*, 503.

38. R. Michels, *La sociologia del partito politico nella democrazia moderna*, 56–57.

39. Privilege does not mean idleness. In his analysis, Michels never broaches what we usually call "antipolitics." He states that the party leaders had "excessive work and fatigue, burdens and stress, and, for those with a weak constitution, a premature death." Ibid., 96.

The workers' conditions are not necessarily improved by a stronger organizational apparatus and leadership. But, as Trotsky stated in 1924, "None of us desires or is able to dispute the will of the party. The party in the last analysis is always right.... One can be right only with the party, and through the party, for history has no other road for being in the right."[40] It goes without saying that an "infallible" party cannot commit any crimes. This is why the metamorphosis of the revolutionary sect into the church-party inevitably transforms the community of absolute revolution into *the country of the great lie*.[41]

In the wake of the Ribbentrop-Molotov pact (23 August 1939), the Germans invaded Poland (1 September 1939), sparking off World War II. Two weeks later, the USSR occupied the other half of the country, according to its pact with the Nazis. Thousands of Polish soldiers were captured by the Soviet army. A politburo order of March 1940 condemned around 22,000 of them to be shot because they were considered "class enemies." The bodies of the victims were buried in the Katyn Forest. The Nazis reported the massacre after occupying the area. The Soviets blamed the Germans, orchestrating a disinformation campaign that lasted almost fifty years.

Victor Zaslavsky has published the documents proving Soviet guilt, hidden in the politburo's secret archives until Gorbachev's arrival. In a "very secret" letter of 3 March 1959, addressed to "Comrade Khrushchev," a senior Soviet manager, before reporting the numbers of the massacre, specifies that it involves "class enemies" and thus people whose lives have no value whatsoever.[42] They were—mark well—"bourgeois." This historic document has great sociological value. It enables us to observe at close hand the typical mentality of the purifiers of the world. The bureaucrat states that the files relating to the victims have no "historical value" and repeats that those who had not supported the revolutionary ideal can be eliminated with total confidence because they are entirely "irrelevant."

The letter runs as follows:

The Committee of State Security of the Council of Ministers, USSR, has held since 1940 case files and other materials regarding prisoners and interned officers, policemen, gendarmes, military settlers, landowners, etc., persons from former bourgeois Poland who were shot in the same year. In all, on the basis of the decision of a special Troika

---

40. Quoted by R. Conquest, *Stalin*, 137.
41. A. Ciliga, *Au pays du grand mensonge*.
42. See V. Zaslavsky, *Pulizia di classe*, 80.

of the NKVD USSR, 21,857 people were shot, of which: 4,421 at Katyn forest (province of Smolensk); 3,820 in the Starobelsk camp near Charkov; 6,311 in the Ostaskov camp (Kalinin province); and 7,305 at the hands of Belorussian and Ukrainian NKVD prison officials.

The entire operation was carried out on the basis of the decision of the Central Committee of March 5, 1940.

The prisoners were given the death sentence on the basis of their individual files in the archive regarding their status as prisoners of war interned in 1939.

Since 1940, no information from these files was released to anyone, and all of the files, numbering 21,857, have been stored in a sealed location.

To Soviet organs, all of these files represent neither operational interest nor historical value. It is also doubtful that they could be of any real value to our Polish friends. Quite the contrary, any unforeseen incident may lead to revealing the operation with all the undesirable consequences for our state. This is especially so because, regarding those shot in the Katyn forest, there is an official version supported by an investigation carried out on the initiative of the Soviet state in 1944 by the commission called the "Special Commission for the Investigation of the Shooting Carried Out by the Nazi-Fascist Invaders of Polish Officers Prisoners of War in the Katyn forest."

The commission concluded that all of the Poles liquidated there are considered to have been killed by the German invaders. The materials of the investigation of that time have been widely covered in the Soviet and the foreign press. The conclusions of the commission became firmly established in international public opinion.

On the basis of what has been presented, it seems appropriate to destroy all of the records regarding the persons shot in 1940 in the above-mentioned operation.

The President of the Committee of State
Security of the Council of Ministers, USSR.
A. Shelepin

It is not cynicism that corrupts the purifiers of the world, but the nature of revolutionary politics itself; underpinned by a highly demanding ideology, it realizes that it has to centralize power to be efficient. A subversive party needs a rigidly hierarchical structure if it is to make rapid decisions. But more organization means less democracy: "It is only a minority that participates in party decisions, and sometimes that minority is ludicrously small. The most important decisions taken in the name of an avowedly democratic party always emanate from a handful of members."[43]

Michels' conclusion is still relevant: "The power of decision and direction is inversely proportionate to the number."[44] The practical rendition of the revolutionary ideal has the form of a pyramid. At the summit, a small minority of the privileged who are in command; at the base, a mass of individuals completely subject to the will of the "Party."

Michels helps us understand that all revolutionaries have a democratic rhetoric and rigorously oligarchical practice. He shows us that the ideal of a society without social classes has never been achieved. And it is clear why not: the destruction of all the aspects of *this world* is an immense task that requires a gigantic process of political-administrative centralization and thus the formation of an omnipotent oligarchy. As the Red Brigades teach, everything has to plunge into *chaos* before being regenerated. School, kindergartens, collective habits, public festivals, family life, and work: every aspect of daily life has to be reshaped. This is how the Leninist Party is conceived. A "miracle" is needed to completely subvert the social order. It is no coincidence that Lenin's followers considered him to be "a miraculous man."

In 1928, Yuri Pyatakov—whom Lenin considered one of the six most promising and valuable communists and who was responsible for the success of Soviet industry in the early thirties—had an argument in Paris with an old Menshevik comrade, N. V. Volsky. Pyatakov explained that a "true Bolshevik," besides blind obedience to his party, must be ready to overcome any "moral limitation." Any action requested of him must be carried out without hesitation. A party based on such assumptions, he concludes, can succeed in undertakings that would be impossible for other groups.

In Pyatakov's words: "According to Lenin...the Communist Party is based on the principle of coercion, which doesn't recognize any limitations or inhibitions. And the central idea of this principle of boundless coercion is not coercion itself, but the absence of any limitation whatsoever—moral, political and even physical....Such a Party is capable of achieving miracles and of doing things which no other collective of men could achieve....He is a true Communist ... a man who has grown inside the Party and who has absorbed its spirit so profoundly that in a certain sense he has become a miraculous man."[45]

---

43. Michels, *La sociologia del partito politico,* 85.
44. Ibid., 88.
45. Quoted by R. Conquest, *Il secolo delle idee assassine,* 96.

For Pyatakov, the ideas of a Communist are the ideas of his party. The professional revolutionary has to cancel out his personality and be ready, at any time, to substitute even the most deep-rooted convictions with conflicting ones: "For such a Party," Pyatakov continues, "a true Bolshevik is ready to renounce at any moment the ideas in which he has believed for years. A true Bolshevik is a man who has drowned his personality in the collective dimension, 'in the Party,' until he obtains the capacity to separate himself from his opinions and his convictions, and to agree completely with the Party: this is what it means to be a true Bolshevik."[46]

In 1936 Pyatakov agreed to testify against his wife because of her Trotskyist sympathies and, so that he could regain the party's trust, to shoot her himself along with the other "traitors." His offer was rejected. Years later, Pyatakov fell into disgrace and was shot in turn after having been one of the leading figures of the second show trials in Moscow, celebrated in 1937.

The human journey of this man—and its tragic end—can be summed up in the words of Malevich, who, enthusiastic about the triumph of Bolshevism, proclaimed in 1920: "If we want to achieve perfection, the ego must be annihilated. Like religious fanatics who annihilate themselves in front of the divinity, the modern saint has to annihilate himself before the 'collective,' before that image that perfects itself in the name of unity, in the name of the community."[47]

Professional revolutionaries become convinced they belong to a species with a "superior" morality. Their enemies are "inferior" and the world has to rid itself of them. The objective of purification is achieved through "blood." Rivers of blood flow to "disinfect" the bourgeois scourge that afflicts humanity! This is what we read in the leading article of the first issue of *Krasnyi mech* (The Red Sword), newspaper of the Kiev Cheka on 18 August 1919: "We reject the old systems of morality and 'humanity' invented by the bourgeoisie to oppress and exploit the 'lower classes.' Our morality has no precedent, and our humanity is absolute because it rests on a new ideal. Our aim is to destroy all forms of oppression and violence. To us, everything is permitted, for we are the first to raise the sword not to oppress races and reduce them to slavery, but to liberate humanity from its shackles. . . . Blood? Let blood flow like water! Let blood stain forever the black pirate's flag flown by the bourgeoisie, and let our flag be blood-red forever. For only through

---

46. Ibid.
47. Quoted by T. J. Clark, *Addio a un'idea*, 216.

the death of the old world can we liberate ourselves forever from the return of those jackals!"[48]

It is thus not surprising if the Marxist-Leninist plan has always turned into its opposite. Created to guarantee everyone the greatest freedom in opulence, it has distributed misery and oppression in an "unequal" way by distinguishing the class of the bureaucrats from that of the workers.

For a paradox of history, it was a professional revolutionary, Mikhail Bakunin, who so clearly envisaged the results of the Marxist plan. In his *Statism and Anarchy* (1873), Bakunin had seen a new form of slavery in the centralization of power, based on the omnipotence of the Communist Party. According to him, the correct application of Marx's "recipe" would have created a "new caste" of the privileged. Society would not have lost its antagonistic nature, and the workers would have once again been dependent. Bakunin writes: "As soon as the proletariat seizes the State, it must move at once to abolish immediately this eternal prison of the people. But according to Mr. Marx, the people not only should not abolish the State but, on the contrary, they must strengthen and enlarge it and turn it over to the full disposition of their benefactors, guardians, and teachers—the leaders of the Communist Party, meaning Mr. Marx and his friends—who will then liberate them in their own way. They will concentrate all administrative power in their own strong hands, because the ignorant people are in need of a strong guardianship; and they will create a central state bank, which will also control all the commerce, industry, agriculture, and even science. The mass of the people will be divided into two armies, the agricultural and the industrial, under the direct command of the state engineers, who will constitute the new privileged political-scientific class."[49]

In such a society, the governed have no possibility of inspiring fear in the governors. As Moisei Ostrogorski has so aptly said, the peculiarity of a democratic regime lies in its "power of social intimidation" that controls everyone through the strength of law and public opinion. A community is not democratic because the people exercise the function of government. This will not happen because, in democracy as in autocracy, it is always a small minority that decides. A democracy is such if the laws in force permit the governed to intimidate the governors. The real issue is not that of establishing whether the people govern or not, but whether and to what extent they are capable

---

48. Quoted by N. Werth, "Violenze, repressioni, terrori nell'Unione Sovietica," in *Il libro nero del comunismo,* 95–96.

49. M. A. Bakunin, *Stato e anarchia,* 214.

of arousing fear in the class that controls the coercive apparatus.[50] Freedom of the press, the right to meet and form associations, and the guarantees of individual freedom are tools of "social intimidation," as are the fundamental principles regulating the organization of public powers (the system for electing state managerial positions, the separation of powers, the announcement of public authority acts, and so forth).

Analyzing the "Red Brigades sect," we have seen that militants of far-left terrorist groups consider the rule of law to be a product of bourgeois civilization, and as such something to be abolished. In the Red Brigades' society—identical to the Leninist one—freedom of speech has no need of any "constitutional" guarantee since the unique and infallible Marxist truth prevails and one has the problem only of eliminating those who refuse to think "correctly." Hence there are only two conclusions to the Red Brigades "political debate": kneecapping or peremptory execution. The Bolsheviks were in charge of the state apparatus and could thus extend the "debate" to three possible outcomes: forced labor camps, psychiatric clinics, and immediate shooting.

Lenin set up the camps to repress: "The concentration camps became, from the moment they appeared, the whip with which the Bolshevik Party wanted to thrash the rebels to paradise."[51] Soviet law provides for the "reeducation" and "correction" of prisoners. The motive is pedagogical. In the Soviet camps, the KVCh (Kulturno-Vospitatelnaya Chast), the cultural-educational section, provides newspapers, films, and reading rooms, but its function is purely symbolic because the inmates' physical and psychological conditions make education impossible. When first established, the Soviet camps had a high mortality rate, not only because of insufficient food and lack of hygiene, but also because of the torture and arbitrary killings by the guards. Solzhenitsyn recounts that some prisoners were burned alive for not respecting some rules.[52] In spite of this, the inmates had to be enthusiastic. The party works to reeducate the mind. "Harmful" thoughts prevent the love that supports the revolutionary reeducation: "In the Gulag," recalled a survivor, "you were expected not only to be a slave laborer, but to sing and smile while you worked as well. They didn't just want to oppress us: they wanted us to thank them for it."[53]

---

50. M. Ostrogorski, *Democrazia e partiti politici,* 616. However, Ostrogorski also criticized the characteristics of a society in which the "brutal pressure" of public opinion looms over everyone (618).

51. M. Geller, *Il mondo dei lager e la letteratura sovietica,* 7.

52. Solzhenitsyn, *Arcipelago Gulag,* 2:59.

53. A. Applebaum, *Gulag,* 265.

According to Jacques Rossi,[54] there were the following types of camps:

- *Closed camps,* in which those who were condemned to have no more contact with the outside world were imprisoned. It was the favorite place for summary executions.
- *Female camps*
- *Camps for the old and sick*
- *Special camps,* which served as a punishment and which had very harsh living conditions. They were reserved for enemies.
- *Camps for children,* who were included in the purification policies. From 1935 onward, children of twelve years and over, if offspring of the people's "enemies," could be sent to camps for three, five, or eight years. If under twelve, they were put in an orphanage.

Thus the camp, like the Red Brigades' kneecapping, constitutes an "opportunity"[55] that is not granted to the "unredeemable" elements who have to be eliminated. But reeducation never actually happens: "The Gulag is an entirely negative school of life, from every point of view. No one will ever obtain anything useful or beneficial from it. . . . In the Gulag the prisoner learns how to . . . grovel, how to lie and how to commit every kind of baseness. . . . When he regains his freedom, he realizes that the period of imprisonment not only has not matured him, but that all his concerns have been limited, impoverished and cheapened."[56]

Mao and the Myth of the "New Man"

Among socialist leaders, Mao Tse-tung was one of the most critical toward bureaucracy, the new state bourgeoisie, corruption, and betrayal. This aspect of his "preaching" prompted Marie-Claire Bergère to compare the Chinese Cultural Revolution with the Jacobin Terror: both Mao and Robespierre had claimed to install the kingdom of virtue.[57] Bergère makes an important point but ignores the essential fact. What makes Robespierre and Mao sons of the same cultural tradition is not the fight against corruption, which can be found in political regimes of the opposite side, but radical catastrophism,

54. See J. Rossi, *Le manuel du goulag.*
55. J. Kotek and P. Rigoulot, *Il secolo dei campi,* 104.
56. V. Shalamov, *Racconti di Kolyma,* 180–81.
57. See M.-C. Bergère, *La Cina dal 1949 ai giorni nostri,* 172.

the binary-code mentality, the obsession with purity, the identification of the Devil, and the doctrine of purification, according to which your enemies can only be exterminated. This helps us understand the Red Brigades' admiration for the figure of Mao and, more specifically, for the Cultural Revolution.[58]

The Cultural Revolution is generally said to have begun on 25 May 1966, the day on which Nie Yuanzi, a young philosophy teacher, put up a poster (*dazibao*) in which she accused the rector of Peking University, Lu Ping, of being a counterrevolutionary. Mao, enthusiastic, saw in the document the "manifesto of the *commune* of Peking"—that is, the start of a radical transformation of the state and of Chinese society. Between 1966 and 1969, China was plunged into a "fierce struggle for power,"[59] characterized by a wave of brutal repressions and violence aimed at removing any form of opposition to Mao's policy. The phenomenon was even more devastating since it involved masses of fanatical students (the "Red Guards"), to whom Mao gave the task of "cleansing" Chinese society of what he called "bad elements."

Thousands of young people demonstrated in Tiananmen Square between 18 August and 25 November 1966. The atmosphere was almost religious; during the first gathering (18 August), Mao appeared in public at sunrise and was greeted like a god. In his speeches, China is immersed in corruption and the young have the task of regenerating it. In his poster, "Fire on the Headquarters," Mao invites the students to attack the party leaders. The "Red Guards" are the "pure" who will defeat the forces of "evil."

For historians, Mao acted from the desire to free the party of its opponents. However, his propaganda is effective because it is based on the "success" of a mentality. The doctrine of purification has fully penetrated young minds and is now being used to strike the party members. After almost twenty years of state revolutionary education, a fuse has to be lit. Mao's "preaching" precedes his arrival in power, but after 1 October 1949, the year in which the People's Republic of China was proclaimed, the "doctrine of purification" becomes a state doctrine.

The Red Brigades' fascination for Mao is soon explained.

In a speech of 6 June 1950, Mao states that, to improve the country's economic and financial system, "we have resolutely to eliminate"[60] all those

---

58. See *Self-Interview.* Red Brigades pamphlet distributed in Milan in September 1971, in *Dossier Brigate rosse,* 1:127.

59. J. A. G. Roberts, *Storia della Cina,* 355.

60. Mao Tse-tung, "Lottiamo per un radicale miglioramento della situazione economica e finanziaria del Paese," in his *Rivoluzione e costruzione,* 25. Report written by Mao Tse-tung for the third plenary session of the Seventh Central Committee of the Chinese Communist Party (6 June 1950).

who do not support the revolution. We have to spark off, he says, a "relentless struggle without precedent in history" against our enemies.[61] On 25 September 1950, in a message of congratulations to the National Conference of Combat Heroes, the "model revolutionary" is he who perseveres "in the struggle to wipe out the enemy."[62]

On this point, Mao never had any doubts or hesitations.

In a speech given in October 1955 during a meeting of the party leaders, he reiterates that any violence against the enemy is lawful and appropriate. When building socialism, one has to be "heartless" and "cruel" and have "little mercy." "On this matter," Mao writes, "we are quite heartless! On this matter Marxism is indeed cruel and has little mercy, for it is determined to exterminate imperialism, feudalism, capitalism, and small production to boot. In this respect, it is better not to have much mercy. Some of our comrades are too kind, they are not tough enough, in other words, they are not so Marxist. It is a very good thing, and a significant one too, to exterminate the bourgeoisie and capitalism in China.... Our aim is to exterminate capitalism, obliterate it from the face of the earth and make it a thing of the past."[63]

Revolutionary education has no variations on the theme: it is good and just to wipe out our enemies because—these are the words of Kang Sheng, head of Mao's secret police, pronounced on 9 August 1958—"Communism is a paradise."[64] With very down-to-earth language, Mao gives an example of the pedagogy of intolerance, where other people's ideas are just "farts." In January 1957, Mao was speaking to a conference of party regional secretaries and invites them to publish openly works hostile to Marxism, to "vaccinate" people against "harmful" ideas. We have to give our enemies, explains Mao, the chance to come out into the open. Only in this way can their ideas be stamped out. In his words: "If [our enemies] want to fart, let them. For everybody can judge whether the smell is good or foul, and through discussion the majority can be won over and these types isolated."[65]

These words are followed by an extraordinary depiction of the binary-code mentality, which denies the right to err in the conviction that Marxism has already revealed the Truth, which is unique and unalterable: "Truth

61. Ibid., 28.
62. Mao Tse-tung, "Siete dei modelli per tutta la nazione." Message of greetings delivered on behalf of the Central Committee of the Chinese Communist Party to the National Conferences of Combat Heroes and of Model Workers in Industry, Agriculture, and the Army (25 September 1950), in *Rivoluzione e costruzione,* 36.
63. Quoted by P. Short, *Mao,* 380.
64. Ibid.
65. Ibid., 390.

stands in contrast to falsehood and develops in struggle with it. The beautiful stands in contrast to the ugly and develops in struggle with it. The same holds true of good and bad, that is, good deeds and good people stand in contrast to bad deeds and bad people and develop in struggle with them. In short, fragrant flowers stand in contrast to poisonous weeds and develop in struggle with them."[66] Revolutionary education does not admit gradations: either you live in the light of Marxist truth or you live in the darkness of bourgeois ideology. As Mao affirms in May 1957 during a meeting with delegates of the Youth League: "Any word or deed at variance with socialism is completely wrong."[67]

Han Suyin, in a celebratory biography of the Chinese dictator, asserted that there was a "symbiotic" relationship between Mao—who "had loving eyes"—and the Chinese Revolution.[68] Experts agree in considering that Mao Tse-tung's thought played an "extraordinary role"[69] in the transformation of Chinese society. However, Suyin ignores another "symbiosis," that between Mao and the laogai, or the "camps" reserved for those who were not "friends" of the regime, of which there is never any trace in the Chinese dictator's hagiographies.

We have seen that, in the Soviet camps, the presence of centers for revolutionary reeducation is purely symbolic. Instead, in the Chinese camps the violence to the victims' bodies is no less than that to their minds. Mao pursued the aim to forge a "new man" with fierce determination. Mao considered that the laogai were a necessary step toward building socialism. He didn't just theorize their existence; he looked after the details, establishing their aims and the methods to be used in the revolutionary "reeducation" process. In the closing address at the second session of the First National Committee of the Chinese People's Political Consultative Conference (23 June 1950), Mao explains what it means "to be true revolutionaries: toward the enemy, we use the method of dictatorship . . . it compels them to . . . engage in labor and, through such labor, be transformed into new men."[70] For Mao, "it is criminal to allow counterrevolutionaries to be unruly in word or deed. . . . This is our system. . . . They must behave themselves."[71] In his article of 24 May 1955,

---

66. Ibid., 389.
67. Ibid., 397.
68. H. Suyin, *Mao Tsetung.*
69. M. L. Salvadori, *Storia dell'età contemporanea,* 1067.
70. Mao Tse-tung, "Essere dei veri rivoluzionari," in his *Rivoluzione e costruzione,* 35. This is the closing address of the second session of the First National Committee of the Chinese People's Political Consultative Conference (23 June 1950).
71. Mao Tse-tung, "Confutare la cosiddetta 'uniformità dell'opinione pubblica.'" Article of 24 May 1955. *Rivoluzione e costruzione,* 200.

Mao says he is proud to have established a regime of terror without precedent in history. The following words merit the greatest attention: "*Yes, they [the opponents] tremble with fear, feeling 'like the miserable daughter-in-law always afraid of being beaten,' or worrying that 'a mere cough is being recorded.' We consider this excellent too. Nothing like this had ever happened in thousands of years. Only after the Communist Party led the people through a long and arduous struggle were these scoundrels made to feel so uncomfortable.*"[72]

In the *Resolution of the Third National Conference on Public Security,* Mao establishes the principle of terror by adopting the death penalty. Dying or surviving is a wholly random fact. Opponents must be terrorized until they are shattered. This document is very important because it shows that the horrors of the Chinese camps were the result of a carefully planned strategy. Mao is a purifier of the world and we are familiar with his mentality: "In particular regard to the counterrevolutionaries deserving death ferreted out in the Communist Party, People's Liberation Army, and organs of the People's Government, and in educational, industrial, and commercial and religious circles, democratic parties and people's organizations, 10 to 20 percent must be sentenced to death, while the policy toward the remaining 80 to 90 percent shall be one of granting a two-year reprieve and subjecting them to forced labor during this period to see how they behave" (May 1951).[73]

Martin Bernal has seen a condemnation of the excesses of the Stalin terror in Mao's directive.[74] We disagree: the document, rather than condemning that type of practice, attempts to institutionalize it for greater efficiency. For Mao, "it doesn't make much difference if a counterrevolutionary is put to death a few days sooner or a few days later."[75] Meaning there is no need to be rushed because what counts is to terrorize. On the other hand, Mao continues, "If some are beyond reform and continue their wrongdoing, they can be executed later on, as the initiative is in our hands."[76]

Thus the prisoners must be changed into "new men." To this end they have to realize that a life rejecting communist doctrine is a life not worth living.

---

72. Ibid., 201.

73. Mao Tse-tung, *Risoluzione della III Conferenza nazionale sulla pubblica sicurezza* (15 May 1951), in *Rivoluzione e costruzione,* 51.

74. M. Bernal, "Mao e la rivoluzione cinese," in *Storia del marxismo,* 3:1005.

75. Mao Tse-tung, "Nella repressione dei controrivoluzionari bisogna colpire con fermezza, precisione e durezza" (30 March 1951). Draft of some important directives on the movement to suppress counterrevolutionaries made by Mao Tse-tung for the Central Committee of the Chinese Communist Party, in *Rivoluzione e costruzione,* 53.

76. Ibid., 55. Draft of 8 May 1951.

One of the most popular means for purifying the mind is writing your autobiography. The "scoundrels" (the expression is Mao's) have to repent for having cultivated "impure" thoughts. They are not condemned for what they have done but for what they are. The obsession with purification is one of the gnostic activist's characteristic traits. The pedagogical motivation in the creation of the camps is proved by the fact that, before being subjected to forced labor, newly arrived prisoners have to undergo a "reeducational therapy" that can last from fifteen days to three months. According to Joël Kotek and Pierre Rigoulot, the "study sessions" for prisoners in the Chinese camps "constitute the great invention of the Chinese in penal theory"[77] and the main difference between their camps and the Soviet ones.

The prisoners' education is divided into three stages:

1. Recognition of crimes
2. Self-criticism
3. Submission to authority and teaching

Prisoners must demonstrate that they are repentant and ashamed of what they have been. Denouncing "traitors" is considered an important step in the "mental reform." The prisoners are obliged to spy on each other and report even the most trivial infraction of the camp regulations, transforming the victims into their own executioners. For Mao, "it is important to draw a clear-cut line between ourselves and the enemy.... Besides drawing a clear-cut line between ourselves and the enemy, there is the need to distinguish between right and wrong within our own ranks. Compared with the former," Mao states in his speech of 4 August 1952, "the latter is secondary."[78] In short, eliminating the "harmful insects" is the absolute priority.

To be effective, a "mental reform" has first to demolish human self-respect and dignity. Chained day and night,[79] reduced to skin and bone, the "new man" regularly eats the worms in cow or horse dung or in the feces of the camp officials or staff. "We ate everything," Jean Pasqualini relates in his book about his time in the Chinese camps, "even the most repugnant things: rotten vegetables, rats' winter stores, bones dug up in the fields, worms in the mouths of cattle ... we fought with the pigs if by chance we saw something edible in their feed. We had fallen even lower than the animals. And it was

77. Kotek and Rigoulot, *Il secolo dei campi,* 461.
78. Mao Tse-tung, *Rivoluzione e costruzione,* in his *Scritti e discorsi,* 86.
79. G. Fazzini, ed., *Il libro rosso dei martiri cinesi,* 37.

all deliberate, it was part of the 'reform' that strips people of the only thing remaining to them: their dignity."[80]

We find the same words in Harry Wu's account. He was twenty-three when he was arrested. A model student from a middle-class family, he had never opposed Mao's regime but had not shown the proper enthusiasm for the communist cause. Besides torture for the most futile reasons, the "counterrevolutionaries" are given the most terrible food: "After a week of that diet," Wu recounts, "my bowels stopped moving. Most of the other prisoners had the same problem. The sorghum had hardened in our intestines, causing acute pain. The weakness caused by our hunger compounded our distress. The only way to move the bowels was to reach inside the rectum and pull out the hardened sorghum lumps."[81]

During his education, the "new man" who had to be forged in Mao's labor camps is reduced to the following state. Prisoner Xing, at the sight of food transported in a bucket by some guards of the reeducation camp, "charged, butting his head between them. He plunged his face into the soup and started lapping it up like a dog. The study leaders began furiously beating him, but Xing ignored their blows and kicks. The bucket tipped over and soup spilled across the dirt floor. Xing, on all fours, put his face to the mud, and licked up every piece of pork fat. The study leader named Ling picked up the bucket and clubbed him, splitting his head open. Xing stood up, bean sauce, blood, and mud smeared across his face. He didn't shout or cry. He just stood there, blood trickling from the wound on his head."[82]

After a few months of "mental reform," the prisoners suffer atrocious punishments. The pedagogical aim is always very evident. Before being beaten, the victim is asked the following questions: "Have you reviewed your thoughts? Do you want to continue to alienate yourself from the people or are you ready to walk on the bright path of confessing and receiving leniency?"[83]

The Chinese concentration camps are divided into three sectors:

- *laogai,* abbreviation of *lao dong gai zao* (correction by prison labor)
- *laojiao* (reeducation by work)
- *jiuye* (compulsory assigned jobs)

---

80. Quoted by Kotek and Rigoulot, *Il secolo dei campi,* 468.
81. H. Wu, *Controrivoluzionario,* 122.
82. Ibid., 107.
83. Ibid., 268.

Those who have committed "crimes" are held in the laogai; those who have committed "errors" in the *laojiao.* Meanwhile, the jiuye is reserved for the so-called free prisoners who enjoy some "privileges." These include the possibility of spending one week a year with their families.

Established in 1957, the *laojiao* is conceived to reeducate those who have distanced themselves from the party orthodoxy. You arrive there without trial since police action is sufficient. On the basis of Mao's directive, the duration of the punishment is never certain and depends on entirely arbitrary guidelines. Trials are not always held, and when they are, the victim is not present. Pasqualini tells of the desperation of an elderly prisoner when he is told that his detention has been suddenly extended for another twenty years: "The answer arrived on 5 January 1961: twenty years of additional imprisonment. Old Lin fell to the ground and had to be carried to the infirmary. He returned after a month or so, but he was never the same again."[84]

For Mao, this system—in which even the students' hours of sleep are established on the basis of his personal directives[85]—is an integral part of "a revolution that will bury the capitalist system and all other systems of exploitation once and for all."[86]

The purifiers of the world do not attack the victims for what they do but for what they were before the revolutionary palingenesis. Once the party has pinpointed a "scoundrel," the victim has no possibility of avoiding punishment. Whatever he or she says or does is interpreted as an attempt to oppose the construction of socialism.

When Mao came to power, Chen Ming was forty-two years of age. Lecturer in history at the University of Nanjing, he had never shown any hostility toward the new regime, nor had he ever been compromised with the previous nationalist government. The sole fact of being a professor made him suspect. He was dismissed and subjected to continual police visits. During one of his numerous interrogations, a police agent asked him if his father

84. J. Pasqualini, *Prisonnier de Mao,* 218. Pasqualini, of Franco-Chinese origin, was released after nine years in prison, following General de Gaulle's recognition of the PRC.

85. Mao Tse-tung, "Nell'attività della Lega della gioventù bisogna tener conto delle caratteristiche dei giovani," in his *Rivoluzione e costruzione,* 105. Mao writes: "I would suggest that all students be given an additional hour of sleep. They are supposed to have eight hours of sleep, but actually they take only six or seven and generally feel they don't have enough.... Be sure to make nine hours of sleep a rule. An order to this effect should be issued and enforced, there should be no argument about it." Talk by Comrade Mao Tse-tung when he received the Presidium of the Second National Congress of the New Democratic Youth League of China (30 June 1953).

86. Mao Tse-tung, "Criticare le opinioni deviazioniste di destra che si discostano dalla linea generale," in his *Rivoluzione e costruzione,* 102. Speech at a meeting of the Political Bureau of the Central Committee of the Chinese Communist Party (15 June 1953).

had been a member of the Nationalist Party. Ming had to remind him that this party did not exist under the Qing dynasty. Questioned about the land his family had possessed, he replied that his father didn't even have a house and had found it difficult to procure food. The policeman found it very strange that someone who had come from such a poor background could have become a university professor. "I studied very hard," answered Ming. This statement was interpreted as a support of the previous regime: "If I understand you," replied the policeman, "under the Nationalist government the people were not oppressed, everyone could make their way in society thanks to their own labor and their own talents."[87] Ming was conducted, with another fifty people, into a police station. In a climate of terror, he heard the judgment that condemned him to forced labor for thirty years and permanent purification: "You are all criminals, you have to sincerely confess your crimes, extract the most hidden thoughts from your consciences. You have to examine your past actions, purify your minds, so as to be able to recount the story of your life in detail."[88] The Chinese authorities, not being able to accuse Ming of being a member of the Nationalist Party, established that he had been a "secret agent." This was published in the newspapers. Ming was arrested and locked for seven days in a cramped cell, without being able to sit down, immersed in excrement. Worn down, he was asked to write his autobiography. He recounted his life with the greatest candor, but the party, not finding any evidence for accusing him, continued to torture him: "We've read your report, we don't think you would have been able to succeed in life without the support of the Nationalist Party. Since you come from such a poor environment, you would never have been able to aspire to your level of education by yourself. You have to rewrite your autobiography."[89]

The purifiers of the world spare neither women nor children. Wang Xiaoling, arrested for her Catholic faith, spent twenty years in reeducation camps. One of the most significant documents in her autobiography is the speech of a party bureaucrat who invites the political prisoners to thank the "venerable President Mao" for his magnanimity. Mao has allowed them to live, but he could change his mind at any moment. The prisoners are "monsters and demons." The party's commitment is to transform them into "new people." On awakening and before going to bed, the prisoners have to acknowledge their crimes and ask forgiveness for what they are: "You are all enemies of the people. You are the subjects of the Cultural Revolution. However, the

87. C. Ming, *Nubi nere s'addensano,* 69.
88. Ibid., 70.
89. Ibid., 77.

government is indulgent with you and is offering you the chance to lead a new life. At this moment the people outside are demonstrating their total allegiance to Mao Tse-tung Thought. Since you, monsters and demons, are not allowed to express your allegiance, you will have to demonstrate your support. From now on, when you get up and before you go to bed, you have to admit your crimes and ask for forgiveness before the venerable Chairman Mao. Recognizing and admitting your crimes is the preliminary condition for the reform and to become new people. You should be very grateful to Mao Tse-tung for having been so indulgent with you."[90]

The necessary confessions can be obtained by any means. In some cases, people are led to believe that if they confess their crimes, they will be immediately freed. Driven by the hope of getting out, the victims even confess actions they've never committed. Homosexuality is severely punished: "Our Great Leader, Chairman Mao, teaches us that revolution is not a dinner party!"[91] This phrase is a prelude to greater cruelty, including summary shooting. Worn down by torture, the prisoners pronounce the following words, with tears in their eyes: "I am guilty. I have committed a crime against the party, a crime against the people. I haven't followed the government's instruments to reform myself and thus I have committed a new crime. I ask the government for forgiveness, I ask for another chance."[92] This plea, often pronounced when covered with excrement after days of isolation without food, can be rejected if the officer in service is not convinced of the victim's sincerity.

Prisoners sometimes attempt to kill themselves during the moments of greatest desperation. The party is firmly against this extreme act to put an end to their suffering, since it sees suicide as a "pedagogical failure" to be avoided at any cost. The prisoners who refuse to eat have a rubber tube inserted in their nose with liquid food that causes serious hemorrhages.[93]

The victims must stay alive; only the party can decide their death. When this occurs, the corpses are almost always buried without any mark of recognition. This is not surprising, since family members who visit the tomb of a "counterrevolutionary" are considered to have "impure" feelings and deserve to be punished as well. To avoid being drawn into the concentration camp vortex, relatives are forced to express the greatest disgust for those subjected to "mental reform." Everything follows a preestablished script. Family

---

90. W. Xiaoling, *L'allodola e il drago,* 219.
91. Wu, *Controrivoluzionario,* 321.
92. Ibid., 265.
93. Ibid., 267.

members visiting the reeducation camps dump every responsibility for their condition on their loved ones. After this there is the invitation to repent and diligently study Mao Tse-tung Thought.[94] When the police cannot find sufficient evidence to condemn a "suspect," the children of the victims are forced to denounce their parents for crimes they have never committed.[95]

In the eyes of those outside the "community of absolute revolution," it can seem that the "crime" committed (not showing the necessary enthusiasm for the revolution) has no relation to the punishment inflicted. But we know all too well that a purifier of the world is exactly that and anyone who does not love the revolution—to use the Red Brigades' words—is "a foul being who causes absolute repugnance."

In many cases, the prisoners are forced to live in chains that can weigh from ten to fifteen kilos. Chains around the ankles are very painful and are hammered in, damaging flesh and bone.[96] Even the nighttime yells of an old man in the grip of nightmares are punished with the greatest severity. A high-school teacher is stripped and beaten mercilessly. Corporal punishment causes not only physical stress but also total humiliation: "The camp commander bent over him, tore his trousers off, and ordered him to lie down on his stomach. Roaring like a tiger, he started insulting him and hitting him on his bare behind with all his strength. While he struck him, he ground his teeth. Blow after blow, the prisoner can't stop yelling. His bottom became black and blue and started to bleed. At the end his skin disappeared into a single open wound. 'Mercy,' the prisoner implored. He tried to explain that he had had a nightmare, he certainly hadn't wanted to cause a disturbance. The prison director ignored his words. He continued to hit him, as if trying to kill him, and when he felt that his right hand had no more strength, he continued with his left."[97]

There are no toilet facilities in the reeducation camps. Prisoners found urinating at night outside their cell are shot on the spot.[98] In this atmosphere of terror, haunted by the fear of being killed at any moment, the inmates are continuously interrogated on Mao Tse-tung Thought. They have to demonstrate they know his speeches and some passages have to be learned by heart.

94. Harry Wu's brother, when visiting him during the harshest years of his imprisonment, told him, "You have committed many errors that have wounded not only our family but also the party and the country. Now you must assume responsibility for your behavior. It's all your fault and your family has denounced you. We have disowned you. You have to study Mao Tse-tung diligently, reform, and become a new socialist person." Ibid., 95–96.

95. Ming, *Nubi nere s'addensano,* 92.

96. Ibid., 85–86.

97. Ibid., 94.

98. Ibid., 122.

Even when sleeping they are in danger of death. To ingratiate themselves with the police and in the hope of improving their condition, some prisoners say they have heard the people in their cell express counterrevolutionary thoughts when asleep. These words of a camp officer precede immediate execution: "When you harbor secret counterrevolutionary ideas, they show up in your dreams at night."[99]

Sometimes, "suspect" intellectuals try to protect themselves by showing their appreciation for Mao's works. In the community of absolute revolution, a suspicion is equal to a conviction. There is nothing that you can say or do to save yourself from "mental reform." If no evidence exists, it is constructed. If it can't be constructed, it has to be invented. This conversation between a Chinese intellectual and his interrogator is enlightening; it concluded with immediate deportation to a reeducation camp:

> "Do you read the works chosen by Chairman Mao daily?"
> "Yes, every day, as soon as I have a free moment, I start reading them. I can't go to sleep if I haven't read at least one passage."
> "What? You use Mao's works as a soporific? It's an offense against our Chairman!"[100]

Jung Chang and Jon Halliday, in their powerful biography of Mao, attributed 70 million deaths in peacetime to the Chinese dictator. It is known that the famine of 1959–61, after the failure of Mao's economic policy (the "Great Leap Forward"), caused the death of 37 million Chinese,[101] but the majority were "political" victims, millions of men and women "canceled" from history, whose names have not even been preserved.

The Cambodian Revolution

The gnostic revolutions are particular revolutions. Revolutionary gnosticism is based on an "eschatological" policy that aims at establishing paradise on earth by the physical elimination of those who have been identified with the Devil. The search for "good" and the elimination of "evil" are two inseparable moments of this revolutionary practice. Only the gnostic revolutionaries are driven by the obsession to exterminate their enemies. Neither

---

99. Ibid., 144.
100. Ibid., 151–52.
101. See J. Chang and J. Halliday, *Mao*.

Francisco Villa, Emiliano Zapata,[102] nor Ataturk were among these. The gnostic revolutionaries are the purifiers of the world. When they conquer the coercive apparatus, they do not worry about consolidating their power through a "normalization" based on alliances and compromises with their opponents. Achieving power does not mark the end of their adventure but leads to a "new beginning."

To grasp fully the scope of this political phenomenon, we have to forget the Machiavellian lesson that says ideologies are only a means to embellish the cruel reality of politics, which is the struggle for power. This approach to political phenomena is well covered by literature,[103] but is not relevant to our theme. It does not help us understand. Killing for power is as ancient as humanity. Exterminating millions of individuals to root out "evil" and install paradise on earth is a relatively recent fact, requiring the appropriate interpretative categories. Robespierre, Babeuf, Lenin, Mao, and the Red Brigades think and act according to the same purifying logic. They live to kill. They are not content with power; they want to clean out the "marsh."

The greatest "reclamation" in the history of revolutionary gnosticism took place in Cambodia. Between 1975 and 1978, the Khmer Rouge caused the death of almost 2 million of their fellow citizens. This is an "absolute record"[104] when you think that Cambodia's total population was 7 million at the time. One of the symbols of the fury of the Khmer Rouge is represented by the Tuol Sleng prison camp in the capital, where sixteen thousand people were imprisoned, including women and children, and died amid horrendous torture. The violation of regulations specified whipping with electric cables without being able to cry out.

Sok Thy is fourteen when he is deported with his brother. They haven't committed any crime, but they are Buddhists and this makes them invisible to the Pol Pot regime: "The priests are parasites; they eat rice, but they don't till the soil." After months of starvation and forced labor, the prisoners are exhausted. The hour of execution arrives: "Then the Khmer Rouge tied our hands behind our backs and took plastic bags out of their pockets. My brother died first, his head in the transparent plastic tied around his neck: he rolled on the ground, trying to bite the plastic that stuck to his face and

---

102. Emiliano Zapata was driven by a community ideology and a fierce anticommunism. His dialogue with Soto y Gama is significant in this sense, as he threatens to "shower with bullets" any "representative of the people" who tries to appropriate the fruit of his work for distribution following collectivistic guidelines. See F. McLynn, *Villa e Zapata,* 308.

103. See A. Orsini, "Mutamento sociale e relazioni internazionali," in *Aspetti del mutamento sociale contemporaneo,* ed. A. Agustoni, 113–29.

104. A. Ghirelli, *Tiranni,* 255.

prevented him breathing; he couldn't even cry out....I was so thin I could slip my hands out of the cords, and while the Khmer Rouge were intent on tying bags around the necks of the others, I ran off toward the forest."[105]

For its intransigence, ambition, and radicalism, the Cambodian Revolution went beyond any other revolutionary experiment. In the space of a few months, Pol Pot ordered the elimination of all the political, social, religious, and economic institutions. It was also forbidden to show gratitude as it was considered a bourgeois practice.[106] Saying "thank you" in Cambodia became an offense. Millions of people were required to be "born again," freeing themselves of their past. Currency and private property were abolished in one fell swoop. Princes, intellectuals, technicians, and bonzes (Buddhist monks) were exterminated. The towns, considered the symbol of Western development, underwent "desertification."[107] The central market of Phnom Penh, once the heart of an intense social life with its shops flaunting their neon signs and glittering windows, was razed to the ground. A specific political will rendered the cities uninhabitable.[108] Even the trees were uprooted. No trace remained of the cathedrals and adjacent buildings; the hospitals were destroyed. They were not demolished by enemy bombs but by the pantoclastic fury of the purifiers of the world.

The economist Hou Yuon, one of the founding members of the Khmer Rouge and ideologist of the Cambodian Revolution, had published his theories in a doctoral thesis discussed in Paris fifteen years before the civil war. Steeped in Marxist readings, Yuon's "recipe" is the typical response of a demoted intellectual to the modernization processes: to free Cambodia you have to completely isolate the economy in order to prevent the country from being contaminated by Western civilization, which is corrupt and perverse. It is the myth of the "closed society," proposing a "fusion model" in which individuals are "melted" in the community of equality and absolute happiness.

Before the Khmer Rouge came to power, Cambodia had undergone an intense modernization process. The king, Norodom Sihanouk, was a nationalist leader intent on obtaining his country's independence. On 12 March 1945, Sihanouk signed two ordinances to denounce all treaties and conventions with France and proclaim Cambodia's independence. In his words: "Cambodia must enjoy a freedom fully commensurate with its degree of

---

105. Quoted by F. Debré, *Cambogia,* 18.
106. *Sopravvissuto dalla Cambogia,* 20.
107. J. Lacouture, *Cambogia,* 89.
108. F. Giovannini, *Pol Pot,* 45–46.

evolution and its capacities."[109] In 1955, he announced his abdication in favor of his father. But before doing so, he wanted to ensure the support of the population. He held a referendum in which he asked, "Do the people think the king has been successful in his attempts to gain independence for the country?" In response, 99.8 percent of Cambodians answered yes.

On the back of this success, he founded a political movement (April 1955), the Sangkum Reastr Niyum (People's Socialist Community), that obtained 84 percent of votes, taking all the seats in the National Assembly (September 1955). Sihanouk had given up the throne to become prime minister. With all opposition eliminated from parliament, his control over political life became stronger. Despite the scandals, corruption spread. The middle classes grew rich while the public sector seemed entirely unsuitable for fostering national interests. Public education, in which the compulsory language was French, neglected the history of Asia in favor of that of Western countries. These omissions, combined with inadequate libraries and mediocre teaching staff, prompted Van Molyvann, former minister of education, to declare: "I would rather not be around when the young demand an explanation."

Modernization always provokes rejection. The West, as Toynbee has explained, does not export only the "best" fruits of its civilization. Modernization does not mean only free trade, private ownership, rule of law, and freedom of thought but also exploitation, gambling, pornography, and prostitution. It was Toynbee who coined the "theory of cultural aggression." According to this theory, the "meeting" between two civilizations can produce devastating effects if one of the two has a greater radioactive (or "penetrating") power. By radioactive power he means the capacity to overturn the habits, customs, and traditions of the "assaulted" society. When this occurs, the "inferior" civilization is gradually disorganized until it plunges into a crisis that marks the beginning of its decadence. To keep this from happening, an opposition always forms within the "assaulted" society, divided into the party of the "Herodians" and that of the "zealots." The former are the modernizers. They try to be open to change and plan its development. The latter, instead, are traditionalists and are totally closed to anything that could compromise the spiritual values of the ancestral community. Toynbee has formulated three laws or empirical generalizations. The first says that *the power of penetration of a cultural element is proportional to its degree of futility.* This means that the society with less radioactive power more rapidly receives the superficial cultural elements of the alien culture. Since they are easier for the masses to assimilate,

109. Quoted by Debré, *Cambogia,* 37.

they spread rapidly. The second law asserts that *the dissemination of the alien culture starts to break up the traditional values of the "assaulted" society.* Finally, the third establishes that the *radiation-reception phenomenon creates a "chain reaction."* Since a social system is a set of related parts, changes to one part have repercussions on all the others. These three laws can be summed up as *assault, reception,* and *disintegration:* the society with less radioactive power is first *assaulted,* then *transformed,* and finally *disintegrated*—unless the "zealots" manage to get the better of the "Herodians" and block the change before it is too late. This is exactly what the Khmer Rouge tried to do: to prevent the modernization of Cambodia by isolating it from the rest of the world.

In 1969, Sihanouk opened two state casinos, one in Phnom Penh and the other in Sihanoukville. He wanted this latter to become the Monte Carlo of Asia. To finance the modernization of the country, Sihanouk nationalized gambling and brothels, with their management given to the highest bidder. The institutionalization of gaming provoked a spectacular rush on betting. Not only westerners, Chinese, and Vietnamese filled the casinos. Cambodian students, officials, high-school pupils, professors, soldiers, merchants, and peasants squandered their wages and life savings. They saw the West in the antireligious guise of profit at all costs. Moneylenders and shoe renters (because it was forbidden to enter the casino barefoot) set up shop around the casinos. "The capital's automobiles and apartments changed hands, there were numerous suicides, robberies and thefts multiplied; municipal offices were deserted, schools and universities closed, hospitals were without nurses, the army barracks empty. Nothing existed outside the casino; it was disastrous."[110]

The state got enormously rich while the poor became even poorer. The consequences were soon felt and the masses became restless. The government was considered immoral and acting against the country's interests. Waves of insults greeted the passage of official vehicles. State officials were forbidden to enter the casinos. Attempts were made to placate the crowd, but the country's ruling class was by now viewed with growing mistrust. In a country steeped in superstitious beliefs and magic practices, the people soon became convinced that Sihanouk was no longer in favor with the heavenly forces. Every unpropitious event was interpreted as a premonition. The government prevented the news of a railway accident being published. When it was heard that a bat, a creature considered inauspicious, had been found in the

---

110. Ibid., 64.

house of a royal family member, the alarmed population started to perform exorcisms.

Hatred for Western civilization was the "ideological propellant" of the partisan combatants (the Khmer Rouge) that were to constitute Cambodia's liberation army. With their armed resistance, the Khmer Rouge embraced a radical political ideology based on the idea that contact with Western civilization would have transformed Cambodia into a terrible "marsh." Their leader was Saloth Sar, alias Pol Pot. In all his works there is the obsession to "protect the purity of the Khmer race" from the infiltration of Western customs and habits.[111] When they came to power, on 17 April 1975, the purifiers of the world swept away a millenary society and religion to construct a "new" man and a "perfect" society.

For the Khmer, the revolution could signify only one thing: "To cancel out any trace of the demoniacal presence of the Aggressor, to reject everything that could in some way recall colonial domination—the market, first of all, and then money, profit, science, and so on—to make a clean sweep of a spurious way of life that had polluted the moral 'purity' of the Khmer people and caused its permanent alienation. What was progress for Westernized people could only appear to the Khmer as the devastating rottenness of a demoniacal power, which could only be stopped by the revolutionary call to arms to uproot 'radical evil.' In other words, to the Khmer people—transformed by Western cultural aggression from proud leaders of Cambodia into humble rural proletariat—the society in which they were forced to live appeared like an unnatural world, upside down and radically evil. It thus had to be not just reformed but literally overturned with all means and at any cost. Only in this way could the Macrocosm be reordered and resynchronized with their methodically frustrated needs."[112]

Pol Pot was a firm supporter of the Leninist organization of the political party. He was convinced that only a party based on a rigid hierarchy and a fierce ideological determination would be able to transform the present world. The social composition of the great urban agglomerates encouraged him in his plan to exterminate the "impure" elements. In Cambodia, he observed, there is no problem of a national bourgeoisie. All the bourgeois are French or Chinese. Moreover, there is no opposition between town and country since the towns are foreign creations, populated by foreigners. The urban centers were developed by Vietnamese, Chinese, and Siamese. Their inhabitants are a mixture of these people, and their elimination will not cause

---

111. See M. Callari Galli, *In Cambogia,* 75ff.
112. L. Pellicani, "La rivoluzione cambogiana," in Pellicani, *Rivoluzione e totalitarismo,* 8.

political or psychological reactions. In addition, there is the peasants' hate of citizens from which they are also physically different. They have darker skins than town people.

The only theoretical works left by the leaders of the Cambodian Revolution were by Hou Yuon, cited earlier, and by Khieu Samphan. The former finished his doctoral dissertation in 1955, entitled "The Cambodian Peasants and Their Prospects for Modernization," whereas Samphan's thesis was on "Cambodia's Economy and Industrial Development." Yuon claimed private property was the source of Cambodia's ills, with a country ruled by exploiters and parasites; Samphan thought the answer was a society removed from the influence of the international economy. Complex problems require complex solutions. How do you make the people believe in these ideas? By force. Yuon is advocating the "gnostic scheme": the people can't see and need to be guided.

Every morning, Radio Phnom Penh broadcast the same message: "Cambodia is a vast construction site where the masses can finally find happiness and prosperity." Rejecting the West and its cultural influence was the plan of the "purifiers" of Cambodia.[113] To destroy every aspect of *this world* in order to construct a perfect society is the theme of a speech addressed to the commandant of a village and its inhabitants. This is the manifesto of all gnostic revolutionaries. It contains hatred for present society and pantoclastic fury ("every remnant of the old regime must be destroyed"); the desire to defeat anomie by creating a social fusion model ("we're now a single body"); the desire to found a community in which social control is so suffocating that it cancels out any individuality ("we have to watch each other"); the conviction that "enemies" are everywhere ("the enemies are among us").

In the words of this Khmer Rouge militant: "Until now we've fought to abolish the differences between rich and poor. This objective has almost been achieved, but the last step requires the cooperation of you all. So, friends and comrades, hand over all your goods to the village committee. *We're now a single body....*Every remnant of the old regime must be destroyed and 'new things' must be created for the new regime. We have to help the revolution by watching each other because the enemies are among us."[114]

The ideology of the Khmer Rouge has something we do not find in other similar experiences. The ideal community that Pol Pot had in mind has, at least partly, already existed. In a singular mixture of nationalism and Marxism, the perfect society was that of the glorious Khmer Empire that, between the ninth and fourteenth centuries, included Burma, Thailand, Malaysia,

113. See Y. Oishi, *La mia Cambogia,* 9.
114. *Sopravvissuto dalla Cambogia,* 20. Italics added.

Cambodia, Laos, and part of Vietnam. This helps us understand the political slogan of the Khmer Rouge:

> We work night and day,
> We work until we fall.
> Our reward is imminent.
> Democratic Kampuchea will soon rediscover the glory of Angkor.[115]

To combat individualism, "I" is replaced by "us." It was forbidden to stand with your hands at your sides because it recalled the posture of the soldiers of the previous regime; you couldn't gesticulate when talking; everyone had to have the same haircut. The only permitted way of life was that of the peasants.

Pol Pot, referring to the Marxist doctrine in which the state was the "bourgeoisie's business committee," wanted to dismantle the state totally. Under the Khmer Rouge, there was no more public administration. Letters, post offices, schools, and courts were canceled. International telephone and telegraph connections, mail, and airplanes suffered the same fate. No type of communication was possible with the external world, which was contaminated and contaminating. In January 1976, the Central Committee of the Cambodian Communist Party officially approved the abolition of money. Without money, trade was replaced by barter between the state and the farm cooperatives. Pol Pot justified this measure with the typical arguments of the purifiers of the world: money is the source of privilege and power. You have to get rid of it because it promotes private property and exalts the individual's creativity. Cambodia is a "clean" society; money is corruption.

In his words: "Up to now, the fact that we do not use money has greatly reduced private property and thus has promoted the overall trend toward the collective. If we start using money again, it will bring back sentiments of private property and drive the individual away from the collective. Money is an instrument that creates privilege and power. Those who possess it can use it to corrupt cadres... [and] to undermine our system. If we allow sentiments of private property to develop, little by little people's thoughts will turn only to ways of amassing private property.... If we choose this road, within a year, or in ten or twenty years, what will become of our Cambodian society that up to now has been so clean? Money constitutes a danger, both now and in the future."[116]

---

115. Quoted by C. Ly, *Ritorno in Cambogia,* 119.

116. Quoted by P. Short, *Pol Pot,* 407. Pin Yathay, a survivor of the Khmer Rouge persecution, tells about seeing a Khmer guard throwing in the river thousands of dollars found in the pockets of a victim of the revolutionary terror. P. Yathay, *L'utopie meurtière.*

We learn about the consequences of these measures from Thiounn Mumm, a model student in the most prestigious French universities, and at the time a senior adviser of the Khmer Rouge Ministry of Industry. Returning to Phnom Penh after a trip to Beijing, he is horrified: "I found myself in the Ministry of Industry, working under Vorn Vet. And what did I see? First of all, there was no administration. The cadres sat outside under a tree. When someone arrived, they'd ask him, 'What do you need? You need oil? Go and get it from such-and-such factory.' And they'd give him a voucher. They didn't even keep a copy. Sometimes the man would get to the factory only to be told there was no oil. No one knew and no accounts were kept."[117]

On more than one occasion, Mumm had to keep quiet in the face of Pol Pot's ignorance of economics. The latter once declared to the Central Committee that "if we have a million riels, we use it all for national construction and for defense.... [Other socialist countries] spend half of it on wages and only half on building and defending their country. This puts them half a million riels behind us."[118] It is crass ignorance that drives Pol Pot to laugh at what the other socialist countries have achieved and to boast that what he has done is better. According to this approach, the "new" Cambodians should adopt the ox as their model. The Khmer Rouge were fond of saying, "You see the ox, comrades. Admire him! He eats where we tell him to eat.... When we tell him to pull the plow, he pulls it. He never thinks of his wife or his children."[119]

In Pol Pot's Cambodia, revolutionary education follows the same principles we have encountered in all the communities of absolute revolution. First of all, you have to learn to behave as a revolutionary. All that is considered superfluous is confiscated and destroyed by the Cambodian Communist Party, the Angkar ("organization"), according to the slogan "Luxury poisons the mind." Toothbrushes, clothes, pajamas, cameras, books, radios, mattresses, and armchairs are the expression of a corrupt world that has to be completely buried. Everything is politicized.

Self-criticism sessions are held every evening at a fixed time. The ideological section examines everyone's opinions on the party's role. The "rate" of individualism present in each participant is also measured. To this end, even couples' sentiments and relationships are controlled. Autobiographies are the means for calculating the progress achieved in distancing yourself from and

---

117. Short, *Pol Pot,* 408.
118. Ibid.
119. Ibid., 409. On this point, Short gives the testimony of the young deportee Yi Tan Kim Pho, *Cambodge des Khmers Rouges,* 113.

condemning your previous life. The concept of family has to be destroyed. Eating in your own house is the sign of a bourgeois mentality.[120]

Everyone has the task of controlling other people's thoughts and of denouncing even the most trifling infraction of the revolutionary rule. Those who are sad are condemned because they're regretting the previous regime; those who are joyful are condemned because they're thinking only of personal happiness; those who are indecisive are condemned because they have a "petit bourgeois" inclination; those who ask for help are condemned because they lack a spirit of sacrifice; those who are kind have an ulterior motive; those who establish special relationships with someone are seeking a way to improve their condition to the detriment of others; those who are impatient forget the suffering of the combatants and show they are unsatisfied with the results achieved by the revolution.

It is forbidden to ask questions about the progress in building socialism: the Angkar tells you everything you need to know. It is forbidden to learn the identity of other people, ask questions about their past life, find out where they come from or ask their "real" name, because the Angkar has given a new name to all members of the new society. These bans are institutionalized and are called "law of the secret." They even have to be respected between husband and wife. The Cambodians can pronounce only this phrase: "Everyone participates joyfully in the revolution and in the construction of socialism. The situation is excellent. We have made a great leap forward."[121] The workers are also forbidden to speak to each other. During the workday, the group leader is responsible for relations between members of the same production unit.

The Angkar claims that the people are "bright," but the individual is "bad." You can trust only the representatives of the masses. Permitted conduct is set out in the Ankgar's twelve "commandments":[122]

1. Always defend and serve the people, workers, and peasants; give your unconditional love and devotion to the people.
2. Devote yourself to the people and serve them wholeheartedly everywhere and in all circumstances.
3. Do not touch anything that belongs to the people, not even if very small.

---

120. C. Ly, *Tornata dall'inferno*, 54.

121. O. T. Hoeung, *Ho creduto nei Khmer rossi*, 54. On the annihilation of individual identity in the Khmer regime, see also F. Feher, "Cambogia," 95–107.

122. Hoeung, *Ho creduto nei Khmer rossi*, 55–56.

4. Ask the people for pardon when you commit an error.
5. Behave irreproachably and impeccably in daily life; speak, sleep, walk, eat, stand, sit, and amuse yourself as befits the people.
6. Do not act suspiciously or have an ambivalent attitude to a woman.
7. Do not ever consume anything that has nonrevolutionary characteristics.
8. Do not gamble.
9. Do not touch the goods of the people and of the state.
10. Always act modestly with regard to the people, but be always inflamed with hate for the enemy.
11. Love and constantly practice manual labor.
12. Fight the enemy and obstacles with all your strength, and have the courage to make all the necessary sacrifices for the workers and peasants.

A survivor of Pol Pot's camps, Ong Thong Hoeung, has described how "revolutionary reeducation" courses were carried out. His book—considered a classic on disenchantment with utopia—confirms once again that the mentality of the purifiers of the world is always the same, without distinctions of time or place:

The daily meeting lasts between an hour and a half and two hours. Every three days there is an "in-depth meeting" that lasts far into the night. There are two teams and the chairman of the group directs the session. He has to encourage the others to participate actively while maintaining discipline. . . . There are no dialogues during the criticism/self-criticism. Those who are criticized must not reply, despite the falsity of the accusations. You have to talk in turn. The chairman opens the session and invites N. to speak. N. starts with "My respects to my comrades and to the chairman." Then he recounts what he has done for good or for bad since the last meeting. After that N. asks the others to help him. He solemnly asserts that he's at the disposal of the collectivity. The chairman then intervenes to thank him for having entrusted himself to the collectivity. Then he invites the participants to express their opinion in order to "construct" N. Participation varies from person to person. Every attack is permitted. N. is not disciplined. N. does not work hard enough. N. is not punctual. N. speaks too much or not enough. N. eats too quickly. N. looks sad, he is evidently regretting the old society. N. has a confused mind. During all this, N. has to show interest and accept everything that is said to him. He must never reveal indignation and always demonstrate he is happy to receive "constructive ideas."[123]

Ong Thong Hoeung was a Cambodian who had been studying and living in France since 1965. Steeped in Marxist theories, he greets the victory of Pol Pot with joy. He is convinced that the news reported in the Western press is false and that the photographs of the massacres have been "manipulated" by the bourgeois governments. "I know what the refugees say. That life there is terrible. Some even say that massacres have been carried out. But I refuse to believe that the Khmer could kill other Khmer."[124] Enthusiastic about the revolution, he decides to return home in July 1976. He soon realizes he's been the victim of a tragic illusion. The country is in the hands of a band of fanatics who have plunged the entire population into bereavement and terror. Although he has come back to help the revolution, he is treated as an "impure" element because he has lived in France. Those who had come into contact with Western civilization, he recounts, are treated like "contagious people, contaminated and sullied by the imperialists."[125]

After having felt contempt for the Western world, Hoeung understands the value of freedom, "which we only really appreciate after we've lost it."[126] He is put into a camp and subjected to a severe process of "reeducation" so that he can be cured of his "disease," represented by contact with Western culture. He bitterly regrets his decision to leave France and mourns for the world he disdained. He had believed he was a slave of the capitalist system. He had boasted that he recognized a single authority, that of reason, and now he is as obsequious as a courtier of the ancien régime: "Only yesterday, Phum, the Angkar representative, gestured to me to come over and pick up a stone. I ran to him like a dog called by his master. I respect the Angkar unreservedly. When I'm working and an official approaches, I work even faster so they can see me, I plunge my hands into the excrement."[127] If an "impure element" does not demonstrate the proper enthusiasm for the revolution, he has to be harshly punished; if he works too hard, he's a climber who wants to be noticed. Everyone watches over everyone else: "It all happens as if each of us were at the same time persecuted and persecutor; we are all our own

---

123. Ibid., 56.
124. Ibid., 30.
125. Ibid., 39.
126. Ibid., 59.
127. Ibid., 61.

censors.... We are all at the same time victim and executioner, of ourselves and of the others."[128]

There is a very significant document on the revolutionary experience in Cambodia. It consists of a speech by Khieu Samphan on the road to follow in building communism. The extract given below has a special meaning for us. First of all, it enables us once more to get into the typical mentality of the purifiers of the world; second, it helps us understand the Red Brigades' admiration for Pol Pot.

Samphan points out that the "purification of the mind" (he speaks explicitly of "brainwashing") is more important than removing material obstacles to the revolution. Possessing people's "minds," he explains, is the most important element for the success of the "absolute revolution." He addresses those Cambodian intellectuals who have been in Europe, explaining to them that the "brainwashing" they will undergo is a gesture of love, for which they should be grateful. The thoughts of those who have been in contact with the Western world, he concludes, have to be "disinfected." The length of the citation is justified by its importance. In Samphan's words:

> How do we make a communist revolution? The first thing you have to do is destroy private property. But private property exists on both the material and the mental plane.... To destroy material private property, the appropriate method was the evacuation of towns.... But spiritual private property is more dangerous; it comprises everything that you think is "yours," everything that you think exists in relation to yourself—your parents, your family, your wife. Everything of which you say, "It's mine,"... is spiritual private property. Thinking in terms of "me" and "my" is forbidden. If you say "my wife," that's wrong. You should say "our family." The Cambodian nation is our big family.... That is where we are separated, the men with the men, the women with women, the children with children. You are all under the protection of the Angkar. Each of us—man, woman, and child—is an element of the nation.... We are the child of the Angkar, the man of the Angkar, the woman of the Angkar. Even the knowledge you have in your head, your ideas, are mental private property, too. To become truly revolutionary, you must... wash your mind clean. That knowledge comes from the teaching of colonialists

128. Ibid., 65.

and imperialists...and it must be destroyed. You intellectuals who have come back from abroad bring with you the influence of Europe and what we can call the "sequels of colonialism." So the first thing you must do to make yourself fit to participate in the communist revolution,... [to put yourself on a par with] the ordinary people of Cambodia is to wash your mind....If we can destroy all material and mental private property,...people will be equal. The moment you allow private property, one person will have a little more, another a little less, and they are no longer equal. But if you have nothing—zero for him and zero for you—that is true equality....If you permit even the smallest part of private property, you are no longer as one, and it isn't communism.[129]

For the Cambodian "purifiers," torture is again not a "simple" means to obtain information. It is something more. It is the forceps for extracting "evil" from the body of impure elements. This is very clear in the Khmer Rouge "black book" describing all the "work methods" interrogators have to use. It can be considered the "manual of the perfect inquisitor." You read that the prisoners suspected of having counterrevolutionary thoughts have to write the confession that will condemn them to death. More importance is given to psychological cruelty than to physical violence ("torture is a compliment"). It must be remembered that the purifiers of the world have the power of life and death over their victims. They could kill them with impunity, but this is not the power they want to exercise. Theirs is not "barbarism"; they adopt a specific method. They are carrying out a political and religious ritual that has the final aim of purifying "harmful thoughts." Let us be clear: Pol Pot is not Genghis Khan. In the mental universe of gnostic revolutionaries, the final objective is not physical elimination but the triumph of an idea and the complete submission of your enemies to the "absolute truth" contained in the sacred texts of Marxism-Leninism. It happens in the reeducation camps in China; it happens in Cambodia; it happens in the Red Brigades' "people's prisons," in which the prisoners have to read the classics of Marxism.

It is written in the Khmer Rouge "black book":

Torture has the aim of obtaining a response.
It is not done for amusement.

---

129. Quoted by Short, *Pol Pot,* 418–19.

You have to make prisoners suffer to make them reply faster.

You are asked to break them so as to make them afraid, to terrorize them.

You do not do it to give vent to your anger.

You have to beat them so that they are afraid, but they must never die. Before torturing them, you have to check their health, examine the stick, and not go too fast, because *if they die you lose their statement.*[130]

Interrogation involved the intervention of three groups: "kind," "harsh," and "bitter." The "kind" group tried to obtain a written statement by psychological pressure. Those who did not respond were tortured by the "harsh" group. Any further resistance from the victims (very often because they had not committed the "crimes" for which they were charged) involved passing to the "bitter" group, which had the power to inflict the death penalty. Prisoners were made to kneel with their hands tied behind their back and a scarf over their eyes: "You took an iron bar and hit them on the back of his neck. They fell on their faces. You slaughtered them with a knife."[131]

The "black notebook" continues by codifying the principle of terror. Prisoners have to live in continual fear of being killed. Also in this case the objective to be achieved is complete submission to the party's authority. However, the victims must always be left with the hope of survival, so they are fully aware that their lives depend wholly on the party. This was the Khmer Rouge's "great mission." It is very obvious that terror is the distinctive trait of the culture and mentality of the purifiers of the world.

The purifiers of the world always follow the same reasoning. Cambodians who have had "contacts" with the "previous" world have been contaminated and constitute a constant danger for the revolution. Once victims are suspected of having nourished "impure" thoughts, they have no possibility of escape. Whether they confess or not, their fate is sealed. Pha Than Chan, arrested in 1977, was tortured for years. When the pain became unbearable, he recounts, the victims killed themselves by beating their heads on the ground. Many of them did not manage to die and succeeded only in prolonging their agony.

It would be inconceivable for a purifier of the world not to make use of terror. In the words of a Khmer leader: "You have to leave [prisoners]

---

130. Quoted by R. Panh and C. Chaumeau, *S-21,* 97. Italics added. S-21 was the main "security office" of the Pol Pot regime, set up in a former high school in the Tuol Sleng district in Phnom Penh. Thousands of people died there under torture.

131. Ibid., 129.

in uncertainty, create doubt around them, and above all give them hope of life. You have to make prisoners understand that they are in the hands of the *Santebal* [the Secret Police] Party. In short, make sure that they are uncertain about their future, leave them with the hope of being able to live. They have to be convinced that it is the party's judgment to let them live or die. This is the great mission that the party has assigned to you. You do not have to give prisoners revolutionary respect, because you belong to the *Santebal pâk*."[132]

---

132. Ibid., 101.

Not a Conclusion

Portrait of a Red Brigadist

> If we had come to power in Italy, we would have made even Pol Pot blanch.
>
> —Alberto Franceschini, Red Brigadist

The [Red Brigadist] is a doomed man. He has no personal interests, no business affairs, no emotions, no attachments, no property, no name. Everything in him is wholly absorbed in the single thought and the single passion for revolution.

The [Red Brigadist] knows that in the very depths of his being, not only in words but also in deeds, he has broken all the bonds that tie him to the social order and the civilized world with all its laws, moralities, and customs, and with all its generally accepted conventions. He is their implacable enemy, and if he continues to live with them it is only in order to destroy them more speedily.

The [Red Brigadist] knows only one science: the science of destruction. For this reason, but only for this reason, he will study day and all night the vital science of human beings, their characteristics and circumstances, and all the phenomena of the present social order. The object is perpetually the same: the surest and quickest way of destroying the whole filthy order.

The [Red Brigadist] despises public opinion. He despises and hates the existing social morality in all its manifestations. For him, morality is everything that contributes to the triumph of the revolution. Immoral and criminal is everything that stands in its way.

The [Red Brigadist] is a dedicated man, merciless toward the State and toward the educated classes; and he can expect no mercy from them. Between him and them there exists, declared or concealed, a relentless and irreconcilable war to the death. He must accustom himself to torture.

Tyrannical toward himself, he must be tyrannical toward others. All the gentle and enervating sentiments of kinship, love, friendship, gratitude, and even honor must be suppressed in him and give place to the cold and single-minded passion for revolution. For him, there exists only one pleasure, one consolation, one reward, one satisfaction—the success of the revolution. Night and day he must have but one thought, one aim—merciless destruction. Striving cold-bloodedly and indefatigably toward this end, he must be prepared to destroy himself and to destroy with his own hands everything that stands in the path of the revolution.

The nature of the true [Red Brigadist] excludes all sentimentality, romanticism, infatuation, and exaltation. All private hatred and revenge must also be excluded. Revolutionary passion, practiced at every moment of the day until it becomes a habit, is to be employed with cold calculation. At all times, and in all places, the [Red Brigadist] must obey not his personal impulses, but only those that serve the cause of the revolution....

The [Red Brigadist] enters the world of the State, of the privileged classes, of the so-called civilization, and he lives in this world only for the purpose of bringing about its speedy and total destruction. He is not a [Red Brigadist] if he has any sympathy for this world. He should not hesitate to destroy any position, any place, or any man in this world. He must hate everyone and everything in it with an equal hatred. All the worse for him if he has any relations with parents, friends, or lovers; he is no longer a [Red Brigadist] if he is swayed by these relationships....

This filthy social order can be split up into several categories. The first category comprises those who must be condemned to death without delay. Comrades should compile a list of those to be condemned according to the relative gravity of their crimes; and the executions should be carried out according to the prepared order.

When a list of those who are condemned is made, and the order of execution is prepared, no private sense of outrage should be considered, nor is it necessary to pay attention to the hatred provoked by these people among the comrades or the people. Hatred and the sense of outrage may even be useful insofar as they incite the masses to revolt. It is necessary to be guided only by the relative usefulness of these executions for the sake of revolution. Above all, those who are especially inimical to the revolutionary organization must be destroyed; their violent and sudden deaths will produce the utmost panic in the government, depriving it of its will to action by removing the cleverest and most energetic supporters.

This is the portrait of a Red Brigadist evinced from the documents available. These words are not mine. They were written in 1869 in an anonymous text, *The Revolutionary Catechism,* by a professional revolutionary, probably Sergey Nechaev or maybe even Bakunin.[1] I have simply inserted "Red Brigadist" in place of "revolutionary" in the original document. I hope the reader will permit this liberty.

Having arrived at the end of our story, I want once again to stress my initial thesis: a professional revolutionary is a particular anthropological type who possesses identical features in all places and times.

There is no difference between the Weltanschauung of Robespierre, Babeuf, Buonarrroti, Marx, Lenin, Gramsci, Che Guevara, Stalin, Mao, or Pol Pot and that of Renato Curcio, Mara Cagol, or Mario Moretti. All of them are the "purifiers of the world." They thought they could regenerate humanity through the destruction of *this world,* in the name of a higher knowledge. Although these individuals have not had the same historical weight, they are all the offspring of a shared history: the history of revolutionary gnosticism and the pedagogy of intolerance. To destroy, eliminate, purify, hate, execute, and terrorize. This was the Red Brigades' plan. This is the plan of all the purifiers of the world. The fundamental message is always the same: the world is a putrid and nauseating place. Every single aspect of it must be razed. It is only through the massive use of the pyre, the guillotine, or the gun that humanity can be redeemed and live in the kingdom of absolute happiness.

The Red Brigades' plan is "impressive." However, to destroy the world and totally reconstruct it you need more than a revolutionary theory: ideas are not enough. To have a revolution, you need terror and education. These are the pillars upholding the community of absolute revolution. Terror and the pedagogy of intolerance are the structure of the gnostic revolution. In the communist regimes, terror was not used only in the initial stages of the

---

1. M. Confino, *Il catechismo del rivoluzionario.*

revolution (when there is still political opposition) but also after the purifiers of the world had fully consolidated their power. As Hannah Arendt wrote, terror is the "true essence" of totalitarianism.[2] There is no doubt that the indiscriminate use of violence is a very effective way of obtaining the masses' obedience. But whether it can "reform" the minds not only of the "opponents" but also of the "moderates" is debatable.

To stress the "absolute novelty" of the gnostic revolutionaries' eschatological policy, Luciano Pellicani has distinguished *situational terrorism* from *pedagogical terrorism*. The first has the purpose of consolidating the power of the new dominant elite; the second, instead, goes far beyond this contingent and limited end: it wants to create the "new person" according to the dictates of the Marxist-Leninist doctrine. Pedagogical terror is the "technique" that guarantees the success of the "therapy." Its end is not the restoration of order but the purification of minds. This is because the gnostic activists consider themselves to be the depositaries of an absolute truth. By virtue of a higher knowledge, they are convinced they can foresee the course of human events. The Red Brigadist is a "seer," someone who can see into the future: humanity is inexorably going toward the revolution that—in the Red Brigades' language—will mark "the beginning of the last war: the class war for a communist society."[3] The Red Brigades are respecting the inevitable laws of history, and terror is only their "accelerator." Once power has been achieved, the purifiers of the world want the masses to follow them in their all-destroying adventure. It all starts with an inner transformation (*metanoia*), which—as we learn from the brigadist Fiore's testimony—is a journey "that kills you inside."

The Red Brigades consider themselves "accelerators of History." They want to shorten humanity's labor pains. If *this world* is a horrific place plunged into the "depths of slavery," then you might as well get rid of it. Any attempt to improve the workers' conditions through the tools of "bourgeois democracy" is considered a form of "prolonged artificial life support." In the Red Brigades' mentality, reformers are sadists, people who can't make up their mind to "disconnect the life-support system." This is why Italian reformism has paid such a toll in human lives to the Red Brigades' cause. The idea of killing for love is incomprehensible only to those who cannot penetrate the mental universe of the purifiers of the world. Massimo D'Antona and Marco Biagi were attempting to reform the labor market. They were eliminated for "love."

---

2. H. Arendt, *Le origini del totalitarismo,* 475.

3. *Document of internal reflection,* June 1975, in *Dossier Brigate rosse,* 1:372.

The reforms, when successful, reduce hatred of capitalism and inhibit the revolutionary potential of the working classes. For this reason, anyone seeking to improve the conditions of the proletariat deserves to die. Sergio Lenci, an architect and professor at Sapienza University of Rome, was sentenced to death by the revolutionaries of the Marxist-Leninist group Prima Linea for his architectural projects, which aimed to improve the lives of prisoners. Rome, Friday, 2 May 1980, eight thirty in the morning. Lenci is alone in his private office, talking to his brother on the phone. The building's intercom buzzes, followed by the apartment's doorbell. Lenci opens and is attacked by four militants. He shouts desperately, hoping that his brother, still on the line, will call the police. He is bound, gagged, dragged into the bathroom, and floored by a violent punch to the stomach. The attackers position him with his head next to the toilet. The shot to the nape of his neck is fired by brigadist Ciro Longo, who is supposed to fire a second shot into Lenci's temple but, not daring to turn the head with his hands, fires a second bullet that passes through the victim's hair. While his young attackers flee, convinced that the execution has been carried out, Lenci, miraculously, does not die. He is bleeding from his eyes, nose, and ears. The warm blood that fills his mouth removes the tape that is choking him, and he thus survives until the police arrive. Some years later, Lenci agreed to meet his executioners in the hope of understanding the reasons for the hatred he had been the victim of and that forced him to live with a bullet embedded in his skull. The motivation—revealed, during the trials, by brigadist Michele Viscardi on 3 May 1983 in the prison of Rebibbia—was shocking to Lenci: in the worldview of Prima Linea, all those who sought to improve prison conditions through reforms were guilty of reducing the anger of the prisoners—anger that the Prima Linea needed to keep alive through the oppression and violence of the prison guards.

The Red Brigades' idea of saving the world by destroying it needs further analysis. Some would claim we are talking about psychotic personalities. But the Red Brigades are not "mad." Although some of their documents show a surprising similarity to U.S. psychologist John Weir Perry's accounts of schizophrenics affected by the messianic-hero syndrome,[4] we should not

---

4. J. W. Perry, *La dimensione nascosta della follia*, 119. These are the words of a patient during a psychotic episode: "I know what causes wars—it's commerce; it's a terrible thing, it's the death of humankind . . . those who deal in commerce rarely recognize God—and God does not love them. . . . I want everyone to become alive. . . . I would like all the factories to be destroyed because they are ruining the earth. I love the earth and I want to protect it. . . . I know that Mars is uninhabited because it is a frozen mass. A billion years ago, Mars was like the earth. The earth will become like Mars, but in a few centuries starting from now. The earth is suffocating, so I am going to ask everyone to

make this error. The Red Brigades are aware of how the machine of Italian democracy functions and know how to jam its works. Can we say that we understand the Red Brigades? Judging from the literature available, the Red Brigades phenomenon has not yet been analyzed in depth. There has been extensive coverage only in the media, accompanied by incessant demonization. As Desmoulins said to Robespierre: "Burning is not explaining." For a sociologist, moral condemnation is the antechamber of ignorance.

The Red Brigades belong to a revolutionary tradition that boasts several centuries of history; they did not appear out of the blue. A communist revolution would seem unthinkable today in Italy; but the purifiers of the world do not support the "community of absolute revolution" because of a "vile calculation" of costs and benefits. They are familiar with instrumental logic—it has been said—but this is not what drives them to declare war on the entire world. The Red Brigades have a "mission" to perform. They are prepared to give up their lives "as Christ sacrificed himself to save humanity."[5] These words from an adherent should not surprise us because the Red Brigades, while abiding by a strict atheist logic, have been charged with carrying out the judgment that the Roman Catholic Church and Christianity have pronounced against modern civilization. Capitalism exalts wealth and love of life's comforts; the Church rewards poverty and sacrifice. Capitalism promotes the individual and profit; the Church preaches the communion of goods. "The adversary, in both cases, is presented as the incarnation of the metaphysical Devil, the expression of what is most evil and impure in human nature: egoism, exaggerated individualism, the profit mentality."[6] The Red Brigades are bitter enemies of modernity. They are an antimodern power, exactly like the Catholic Church.

The Red Brigades are thirsty for the "absolute." Their political action originates from a religious need that modern civilization—lay and secularized—has not extinguished. For the victims of modernization, the search for "meaning" is an anguished daily challenge. A man who was very close to Renato Curcio during the early years of his political education in Trento tells us that "he was absorbed in existential problems. For example, I remember that he was fascinated by suicide and read Camus. He often mentioned the

---

abandon the factories, to listen to me. I know this is necessary to save the earth. . . . I am the Savior. I am Nijinsky and not Christ. I love Christ because he was like me. . . . I want to save the entire earth from suffocation. All the scientists must leave their books and come to me and I will help them all because I know many things. I am a man of God. I do not fear death. I will ask people not to fear me. . . . I must not be killed because I love everyone in the same way."

5. Testimony of the Red Brigades terrorist Enzo Fontana to G. Bocca, *Noi terroristi,* 42.

6. D. Settembrini, *Socialismo e rivoluzione dopo Marx,* 109.

fact that he had never had a father and not really a mother; once he said, seriously, 'God is my father.'"[7]

The Red Brigades have great faith in the possibility of humanity's total liberation. It is an impressive undertaking that justifies any means, since—as we have seen—the end "purifies" the means.

Dismantled in the early eighties, the Red Brigades formed again at the start of the new millennium in a very different political and institutional context. They killed Massimo D'Antona and Marco Biagi. Once again wiped out, they reorganized for a third time.

On 12 February 2007, fifteen militants of the New BR are arrested following an antiterrorism raid called Operation Sunset coordinated by the police in Milan, Padua, Turin, and Trieste. The papers talk about plans to attack national names in the media and in cultural and political circles. They were plotting to blow up Silvio Berlusconi with a car bomb. Some of these "true revolutionaries," following a Red Brigades' practice launched in the seventies, declare themselves political prisoners and avail themselves of the right not to speak. They are men ranging in age from twenty-one to fifty-four: Alfredo Mazzamauro, age twenty-one (enrolled in the Faculty of Political Science at Milan University, responsible for signing up young students); Federico Salotto, twenty-two (blue-collar worker); Alessandro Toschi, twenty-four (blue-collar worker); Massimiliano Toschi, twenty-six (blue-collar worker); Amarilli Caprio, twenty-six (trade unionist, Faculty of Political Science at Milan University, responsible for signing up young students); Massimiliano Gaeta, thirty-one (IT manager of the organization); Valentino Rossin, thirty-five (post-office worker, trade unionist, keeper of the group's weapons); Davide Bortolato, thirty-six (identified as leader of the Padua cell); Andrea Scantamburlo, forty-two (trade unionist); Davide Rotondi, forty-five; Alfredo Davanzo, forty-nine (probably the leader of the group, declares himself a political prisoner); Claudio Latino, forty-nine (declares himself a political prisoner); Bruno Ghirardi, fifty (ex–trade unionist); Vincenzo Sisi, fifty-three (previous offender); and Salvatore Scivoli, fifty-four (previous offender).

We can imagine these men as they wander about the cities, on the buses, in the universities, disdainful of everything around them: luxury, wealth, profit, fine bars, glittering shop windows, billboards. They live among us, driven by the desire to destroy *this world* where they can see no place for themselves. They are beside us yet they come from far away. They have a long history behind them. They follow capitalism like a shadow; hiding in the darkness they

---

7. Quoted by A. Silj in *Mai più senza fucile*, 59–60.

Table 4.   Cause of death of far-left militants in Italy, 1969–94

TYPE OF EVENT	NUMBER OF DEATHS	PERCENT
Killed by police or private agents	36	52.94
Accidents when preparing attacks	10	14.71
Suicides in prison or outside	9	13.24
Natural death while in prison or outside	6	8.82
Killed by armed left-wing organizations	4	5.88
Natural death in exile	2	2.94
Killed by others in prison	1	1.47
Total	68	100.00

Source: Progetto memoria.

periodically emerge to bring the "light" to those who do not see it. They hate and want to kill, but they are also prepared to die. They have nothing to lose because they are already "doomed." Rejecting every aspect of *this world,* they have condemned themselves to a nonlife. And they are not frightened. They weren't then, they aren't today.

Table 4 shows the distribution of the far-left militants who died in Italy between 1969 and 1994 divided by type of event in which they died.

In Sesto San Giovanni, on the morning of 15 December 1976, the police are ready to burst into the house of the brigadist Walter Alasia, twenty, former student from a working-class family. Walter was a true revolutionary. Very clever at hiding his hatred for *this world,* those closest to him had no idea of his subversive activity. The police have a search warrant. They have been following him for about a month. They had found a pair of spectacles in a Red Brigades' hideout and managed to trace their owner through the optician who had sold them. They bang on the door, shouting, "Police. Open up!" Alasia's family are all asleep. Walter jumps from his bed and grabs his pistol. He could give himself up. His father opens the front door. A policeman runs through the corridor toward the last room. Suddenly Walter opens the door of his room and shoots at Sergio Bazzega. Then he shifts his aim and shoots the second agent. He finishes his magazine. He is cold, lucid, and determined; he is carrying out a mission. His mother, Ada Tibaldi, recalls: "Walter continues to shoot, lots of shots. I shout at him to stop, for heaven's sake, but he moves his arm and shoots at the other man, but I don't see him fall. Then Walter looks at me without saying a word. *His face is calm, without any sign of agitation.*"[8] He closes the door, reloads his gun, puts on a pair of trousers,

---

8. G. Manzini, *Indagine su un brigatista rosso,* 4. Italics added.

and drops out of the window into the courtyard—it's only a meter down. He starts running and is shot in the legs. He lies on the ground wounded but doesn't surrender. The shoot-out continues. Then at last a shot kills him. The words of Che Guevara, one of the Red Brigades' spiritual fathers, come to mind: "Wherever death may surprise us, let it be welcome, provided that this, our battle cry, may have reached some receptive ear, that another hand may be extended to wield our weapons, and that other men be ready to intone our funeral dirge with the staccato singing of the machine guns and new battle cries of war and victory."[9]

Just like Walter Alasia, the "new" Red Brigades are preparing to attack *this* corrupt *world*. They practice shooting in a house in Mardimago, province of Rovigo.[10] The guns they are using are Kalashnikovs and Uzis, weapons with a devastating effect. Their ideas are published in the underground magazine *Aurora,* in which they stress the importance of uniting armed propaganda with a suitable political scheme. The goal is to insert themselves "into situations like social struggles in the factory, protests against the high-speed railway in the Susa Valley, and violent demonstrations in the suburbs,... to bring the most possible people to the revolutionary cause in preparation for insurrection."[11] They want to "avenge" the bosses' treatment of immigrant workers; they plan punitive expeditions; they are invoking justice; they want to free humanity from unhappiness and pain. For Sergio Segio—twenty-three years spent in prison—"the old and new Red Brigades are the children of the Left. Degenerate certainly. But with a political plan that aims at revolution, at that myth of the Left that, with very few exceptions, has never suggested that nonviolence is one of its ideals."[12]

On 14 February, four people are arrested in Sesto San Giovanni while affixing posters supporting the Red Brigades in prison: "Those who make war are terrorists, not those who fight alongside the people. Comrades, upright or dead, but never kneeling."[13] On 15 February, the "arsenal" of the Political-Military Communist Party is discovered. The media acknowledge that the new Red Brigades "are not only a few obsolete and crazy individuals but extremely dangerous people."[14] In the December 2006 edition of *Aurora,* the government in power, led by Romano Prodi, is chosen as a target. Consistent

---

9. Ernesto Che Guevara, "Creare due, tre, molti Vietnam..." (April 1967) in his *Leggere Che Guevara,* 408.

10. *Corriere della Sera,* 13 February 2007, 5.

11. *Corriere della Sera,* 14 February 2007, 6.

12. Ibid., 8.

13. *Corriere della Sera,* 15 February 2007, 11.

14. *Corriere della Sera,* 16 February 2007, 2.

in their hatred for Western civilization, they applaud the actions of the Iraqi and Afghan guerillas against the Italian army. On 16 February, writing in praise of the Red Brigades appears on the walls of the town hall of Santo Stefano Magra, in the province of La Spezia, in the EUR district in Rome, and in Pordenone.[15]

In August 2008, national news broadcasts talk about the probable reconstitution of the Red Brigades through an alleged "alliance" with Islamic terrorists. On 11 June 2009, after two years of investigations, interceptions, and tailings, six extreme-left militants planning a series of attacks are arrested. Among those investigated is Luigi Fallico, fifty-seven years old, former member of the Combatant Community Unit (UCC). According to investigators, "Fallico was treading in the footsteps of the Red Brigades." In a wiretap, he was heard to say, "The Red Brigades don't retire; the Red Brigades die as Red Brigades."

Revolutionary gnosticism is the response to the *rites of passage* that capitalism continually undergoes. In the perspective of this book, terrorism is the shriek of the "victims" of modernization. It is the outcome of a complex interaction process that culminates in bloodshed.

As Leszek Kolakowski writes: "Revolutionary messianism and the hope for total freedom crop up regularly during periods of crisis, when the system of values breaks down in some crucial points."[16] But anomic disintegration is not enough, in itself, to evoke the forces of the revolution. You need a unilateral and absolute "version of the facts" that encourages and justifies. And you need a revolutionary sect.[17]

Death approaches when the enemy is "a pig who arouses absolute disgust."

---

15. *Corriere della Sera,* 17 February 2007, 6.

16. L. Kolakowski, *Lo spirito rivoluzionario,* 21.

17. As Alan B. Krueger wrote, numerous academic and government studies find that terrorists tend to be drawn from well-educated, middle-class, or high-income families. Among those who have seriously and impartially studied the issue, there is not much question that poverty has little to do with terrorism. In Krueger's words, "For the most part, terrorists are not people who have nothing to live for. On the contrary, they are people who believe in something so strongly that they are willing to die for it." In brief, economic circumstances are not irrelevant, but they are dominated by other forces, such as a commitment to the goals of the terrorist organization. A. B. Krueger, *What Makes a Terrorist,* 3, 48–49.

APPENDIX

Red Brigades and Black Brigades

What do the Red Brigades and the Black Brigades have in common?

From 1975 to 1980 in Italy there are around 8,400 attacks against people and things, most of them carried out over the three years from 1977 to 1979. Of these 8,400 attacks, some 3,000—a little over 35 percent—can be attributed with certainty to the subversive Right.[1]

Fascist revolutionaries have left a long trail of blood behind them. The wait for the end, radical catastrophism, binary-code mentality, apocalyptic vision of historical development, obsession with purification, and identification of evil: these are the typical traits of professional revolutionaries. Whether communists or fascists, they always justify their means through the end.[2]

The neofascist terrorist Pierluigi Concutelli—political and military mind of the Movimento Politico Ordine Nuovo (MPON), multiple murderer, condemned to four life sentences—proposes the same lesson as the brigadist Raffaele Fiore. Before killing, you have to break all the social bonds that prevent the use of revolutionary violence. You have to separate yourself from your family, since these bonds are an obstacle to the professional

---

1. R. Minna, "Il terrorismo di destra," in *Terrorismi in Italia,* ed. D. Della Porta, 63.
2. P. Concutelli, *Io, l'uomo nero,* 56. Concutelli writes, "For the association, the end justifies the means."

revolutionary's salvific mission. Those who embrace "the utopia of the revolution"[3] take a road of no return: "First of all, you had to break contact with all those you had left behind: friends, family, boyfriend or girlfriend. You had to give up the 'middle-class' life and accept that the road you were about to take could lead you either to the cemetery or, at best, to prison for the rest of your days. And you always had to move in a hostile environment. You had to become invisible, never arouse suspicions, and act with extreme caution. It just needed the smallest error, a tiny negligence, and wham: either they arrested you or, worse still, they killed you. And goodbye to your dream of revolution. The most difficult thing for those who make an absolute choice was to overcome taboos. The first is that of emotional ties: they had to be eliminated or removed. Because when you're being hunted, when you live underground, you can't allow them. You can't allow yourself anything."[4]

Concutelli—whose revolutionary vocation sent him to Angola, where he participated in the civil war that broke out in 1975 after the Portuguese left—is an all-around revolutionary just like the Red Brigades. He is part of the same anthropological category as Curcio and Franceschini. Concutelli is a Black Brigadist: "I was prepared and I was a fanatic to the death. I was convinced. I had an unshakeable, blind faith."[5] Ties with *this world* have to be definitively cut to achieve the conditions for conquering "the most important and at the same time the most dramatic taboo: to commit murder, to shed blood. However, a war on the state, a revolution like the one we wanted, couldn't be achieved without blood."[6]

The Obsession with Purity

Like all professional revolutionaries, Concutelli is a pure man. The Red Brigades' contempt for the Communist Party (PCI) is the same as Concutelli's for the Fascist Party (MSI): "I considered the party of Michelini and Almirante a contaminated hothouse where even the most luxuriant plants were destined to become stunted, dry up, and die."[7] The MSI was "the plague itself: a disease to run away from as fast as you could."[8] "I had realized that

---

3. Ibid., 72.
4. Ibid., 77–78.
5. Ibid., 111–12.
6. Ibid., 78.
7. Ibid., 38.
8. Ibid., 133.

the MSI was a party of fascists who weren't fascists at all. It was a masterpiece of political bad faith."[9]

The Black Brigadists feel "chosen." Their mental condition is that of those who live *"in a kind of Indian reserve created for the very few elect. You were quality as opposed to quantity. You were right whereas the others were wrong.* You were the heir to a past, by now remote, that we still considered alive."[10] This obsession with purity condemns the black terrorist to a "life in hell,"[11] to a fanatic and permanent war against the surrounding world: "We are inside a fortress with high wood palisades, the enemies surrounding us with the intent of killing us."[12] "All this continued to make us constantly feel an unjustly persecuted minority. . . . We started to think that someone really wanted our political and physical end. It was this (and not only this) that dragged some of us toward dark shores. It turned us into fugitives and then 'terrorists' and 'murderers.'"[13]

The obsession with purity is exacerbated by the use of violence. Once he has decided to take up the armed struggle, Concutelli launches a "Darwinian selection" among the ranks of his organization. The distinction between pure and impure becomes increasingly suffocating: "I had the honor of choosing the most suitable *camerati:* those were very difficult times and only a few could be capable of measuring up to the task awaiting us. I started to clean up."[14]

The person who is prepared to kill in the name of a revolutionary ideal is pure; those who have already killed are even more so. They are the purest of the pure because they have left their previous humanity to embrace another even more "human" and thus superior. Fascist revolutionaries are "new people" who are directed toward "martyrdom" ("So if you died, you were a 'martyr' of the Idea to be remembered"[15]). They do not have to account for their actions to the ethical categories of *this world,* which is corrupt and putrescent. They have "broken away" from society and now answer only to its "new" revolutionary conscience.

The Black Brigades also kill "for love." The "terrorist despite myself" is also right wing. Just like the Red Brigades, the fascists feel "forced" to violence. The reason is always the same: the world does not understand them,

9. Ibid., 39.
10. Ibid., 41. Italics added.
11. Ibid., 61.
12. Ibid., 70.
13. Ibid., 69.
14. Ibid., 78.
15. Ibid., 73.

it humiliates, rapes, and oppresses them. In the words of the Black Brigadist Stefano Delle Chiaie: "As young people we were violent out of necessity. Our objective political condition meant we had to defend ourselves. We have always replied to violence. And we've always theorized it in our paper *Avanguardia*. Violence is outside my culture, my way of life. I'd always thought my ideas were simple and natural, like anybody else's."[16]

The choice of going underground consigns Concutelli to a "life of hell." Constant nightmares plague him day and night. He feels hunted: "There was an uncomfortable atmosphere. Nothing felt safe, at night I'd wake up with a start, in the middle of a terrible nightmare."[17] In a letter of 4 February 1996, the Black Brigadist Francesca Mambro tells how she had sacrificed everything to the revolutionary cause. She could have run away with the man she loved to start a new life, but the tentacles of the revolutionary sect—tentacles that are mainly psychological—forced her to remain. Referring to her romantic attachment to Valerio Fioravanti, Mambro writes:

> Far away from our race toward death I know that I was happy: we'd been making up a list of dreams to achieve together. Looking at the lake we imagined a village in one of those out-of-the-way countries where we'd be very poor and Valerio and I would've been able to create our "extended family" and, who knows, really give the best of ourselves. We designed utopias: we vied with each other in suggesting the best way to use the money we stole, because in those places we needed only very little to build a school, a hospital. . . . We were naive young people who didn't want to admit the impossibility of turning back, who for a while deluded themselves that they could. . . . I think what was most important for us was the fact of belonging to a group, to our friends. That was the problem. The promises we had made to get those left behind out of trouble. Reason enough not to listen to that voice telling us that our love was the only positive thing worth the sacrifice or our total dedication. And yet, just to mention it would have sounded like an entirely egoistic choice.[18]

Love is considered a bourgeois sentiment. Fascist revolutionaries must not give in to the temptation of life as a couple. They have to criticize everything.

---

16. Quoted by M. Caprara and G. Semprini, *Destra estrema e criminale*, 28.

17. Concutelli, *Io, l'uomo nero*, 79.

18. Letter from Francesca Mambro to P. A. Corsini, 4 February 1996, in P. A. Corsini, *I terroristi della porta accanto*, 184.

It is no surprise to learn that Nechaev is one of the Black Brigades' favorite writers. This is Claudia Serpieri speaking, romantically attached to the fascist multiple murderer Alessandro Alibrandi, a true "missionary" of the revolution, so devoted to the cause that he practiced chastity: "We lived in a microcosm. We never made love. I didn't feel ready. Once, lying beside each other, it was about to happen but I said no and he stopped. He was incredibly shy. But then he left me because he felt his relationship with me was preventing him from doing what he wanted. *He quoted Nechaev: 'The revolutionary must be alone.'* And each goes his own way."[19]

Entering in the revolutionary universe, says Massimo Sparti, key witness against Fioravanti and Mambro for the Bologna massacre, means "losing everything": "I lost family, my shop, my economic security. I didn't just lose 'something.' I lost everything, everything that you can have in life: a wife, children, assets, everything."[20]

Black Brigades and Red Brigades: Their Hatred for "This World"

Whether red or black, revolutionaries relinquish sentiments, emotions, desires, and dreams. Everything has to be sacrificed on the altar of the revolution. Revolutionaries are not allowed to turn back. The Promethean mission of freeing the world from suffering and unhappiness is waiting to be accomplished. Concutelli is a Black Brigadist; he is one of the "elect." He sees, thinks, and acts. All the others are blind, and as such they need his guidance and his sacrifice: "We knew, we thought we were the elite of a minority. A minority of the minority."[21]

Terrorists, red or black, belong to the same anthropological type. They are both professional revolutionaries and purifiers of the world. They live in the "catacombs" and only come to the surface to "clean up."

To grasp the great analogies between the "reds" and "blacks," we have to forget the Marxist approach when defining revolutionary phenomena. According to this tradition, a revolutionary is someone who fights for the abolition of private property and the total nationalization of the means of production. Anything that does not fall within this kind of project, the Marxists say, is "reactionary." Obviously, this way of approaching the problem

---

19. Claudia Serpieri interviewed by Barbara Alberti, 29 July 1985, in ibid., 222. Italics added.

20. Ibid., 234. Massimo Sparti's testimony at the trial of Luigi Ciavardini, Bologna, 15 July 1997.

21. Concutelli, *Io, l'uomo nero*, 77.

meets an ethical-political need that has become a sociological theorem: you can't be revolutionaries without being communists. We are looking at a manifest case of "misappropriation." Concutelli was as much a revolutionary as Curcio or Moretti.

To penetrate the Black Brigades' mental universe, we have to overturn the Marxist approach when defining revolutionary phenomena.

The purifiers of the world do not identify with what they want to create (communism) but with what they want to destroy (capitalism). The dividing line is their pantoclastic fury and their hatred for *this world*. The Red Brigades have also arrived at this conclusion. They all agree that "during those years we never asked ourselves what we had to build, the only thing we knew was that we had to destroy the present."[22]

The professional revolutionaries' different approach to the issue of identification/definition prompts a specific conclusion. All revolutionaries are actually impenitent reactionaries, people angry and resentful about everything that Western modernity represents, whether profit, wealth, competition, opposition, the secularization of the sacred, the rule of law, freedom of expression, or individual rights. The Black Brigades were not born to defend capitalism but to destroy it. This is why Alberto Moravia's arguments to exclude fascists from the ranks of "real" revolutionaries are specious, besides being weak from a historical and sociological angle (it is not true, as Moravia asserts, that fascism and Nazism "did not touch the economic and social frameworks").

Moravia, referring to the death of the violent fascist revolutionary Giancarlo Esposti (30 May 1974), wrote that you can distinguish "true" revolutionaries from "false" ones because of their particular ideology or "vision of the world." According to him, the young communists were altruistic and intent on changing things; the young fascists, instead, were incurably conservative and incapable of changing anything. Moravia replied to Pier Paolo Pasolini, who, commenting on the death of Esposti, had said that the Right and Left had identical values, with these words:[23]

Dear Pier Paolo,
You talked about Esposti, the fascist killed in the shoot-out in Rascino. Esposti, and there can be no doubt about this, was an Italian fascist. Let's investigate further. Was Esposti a conservative or a revolutionary?

---

22. Interview with M. Ferrandi, "Una pistola per riconquistare il paradiso," *Il Manifesto*, 7 March 1984.
23. P. P. Pasolini, "Gli italiani non sono più quelli," 10 June 1974.

The fascists say they are revolutionaries; but are they really?...Perhaps I'm an incorrigible intellectual and attach too much importance to ideas; but I'm certain that Esposti, with his ideas of Nietzsche, of Guenon, and of Evola, with his ideology of the Porsche paid for in installments by his father, with his girlfriend's vision of the world that's both antibourgeois and "profoundly bourgeois," wouldn't have changed the world one iota, even if he really believed he could. And we know all about these ideas, this ideology, this vision of the world. They were those of Nazi Germany, of fascist Italy. They were used for many things, from the concentration camps to the wars against democracies; but they didn't touch the economic and social structures of these two countries that are still those of half a century ago. Changing the world actually means changing part or all of the economic and social structures. So in the end you have to agree that fascism and conservation are synonyms. With this difference, however, that fascism, as we know, claims it is revolutionary and openly praises violence. But revolution and violence are masks that really serve to get possession of power; and having achieved it, without changing anything, fascism empties and becomes petrified in ceremony and in rhetoric. Hyperpublic and hyperrepressive, fascism, with or without Nietzsche, wants the status quo.[24]

What documents have the Red Brigades left about the society they wanted to build? For the very few scholars who have read all their output, there can be only one answer: no document, no idea about "afterward," not even a mention. Hundreds and hundreds of pages to assert a single, entirely negative idea: *this world* is horrible and must be razed to the ground.

After denying that the Red Brigades had a plan for social transformation, we must now ask ourselves who the Black Brigades' enemy was. Was it the Communist Party? The Red Brigades? No, the Black Brigades have the same enemy as the Red Brigades: the SIM, Stato Imperialista delle Multinazionali (Imperialist Multinational State), or capitalism and everything it represents. Concutelli hates the bourgeoisie, the market, competition, contest, egoism, and lack of solidarity. To destroy *this world* he would be willing to fight alongside the Red Brigades. On this point, his words deserve careful reflection: "If, for example, the Red Brigades (also with our 'complicity') had really brought the country to the brink of civil war, then we would have fought on their side. And when the time for the final reckoning arrived, we would

---

24. *L'Espresso,* 23 June 1974.

have been there as well. *Because the enemy was not that different for us fascists and for the Red Brigades. We 'blacks' also wanted to bring down the bourgeois state. We also wanted to destroy the elusive SIM (acronym invented by the Red Brigades), the Imperialist Multinational State: the monster that, according to us, blindly and brutally governed the world, crushing nationalities, values, and ideas under its heel.*"[25] Anticommunism, continues Concutelli, was only a way to cloud the issues. It was capitalism, not communism, that was the true enemy of the fascist revolutionaries. In his words: "I've never killed a communist. After my youthful anger had cooled down, I found anticommunism absurd: a stratagem to keep us occupied and hide what should have been our real targets."[26]

Concutelli feels horror and disdain for the "middle-class mentality" that he wants to abolish in everything around him.[27] The Black Brigadist Stefano Delle Chiaie reproaches him, recalling the early years of his fascist militancy, for having thought the communists were the enemy. He would soon realize that the source of his anger was capitalism and not communism: "When we were young, our enemies were the neighborhood gangs: what rubbish. Power is something else, supranational like the International Monetary Fund, the World Bank, and foreign trade."[28]

The Black Brigadist Valerio Fioravanti wanted to get rid of the middle classes and everything they represented: "Like wanting to kill our fathers, to psychoanalytically kill the social class we came from,... we, who were—and are—bourgeois, fought against the bourgeoisie."[29]

For the Black Brigadists Roberto Fiore and Gabriele Adinolfi, militants in Terza Posizione, an extreme-right group founded in June 1979, the merchant was an example of the type of society to eliminate: "Terza Posizione saw the existential conflict between the figure of the merchant and the archetype of the warrior as the keystone of the revolution. A revolution that, spelled out since the training courses for the younger militants, should first of all be demonstrated in daily life with Sacrifice and with Example. The preparatory courses propagating the ideal of a 'legionary' militia, and the certainty that one day 'a few noble eyes will see the dawn,' made TP a minority that considered itself aristocratic and revolutionary while being clearly of the people."[30]

25. Concutelli, *Io, l'uomo nero*, 80.
26. Ibid., 103.
27. Ibid., 125.
28. Testimony of Stefano Delle Chiaie, quoted in Caprara and Semprini, *Destra estrema e criminale*, 28.
29. Quoted in Corsini, *I terroristi della porta accanto*, 27.
30. G. Adinolfi and R. Fiore, *Noi, Terza posizione*, 27.

Black Brigades take no prisoners: to regenerate humanity you have to destroy capitalism. This world, dominated by the figure of the merchant and thus by profit, must be demolished and rebuilt. Overturn the "overturned world": this was the plan of the Black Brigades who felt violated by *this world* that is corrupt: "Even before they were born, in their education, in health, in freedom, and even in the possibility of survival, they bore the entire weight of a classist society's contradictions. Their revolt was legitimate defense."[31] With these words, Giulio Salierno—ex-militant in the MSI, found guilty of homicide in 1955 and then pardoned in 1968—attempted to sum up the mental universe of the fascist revolutionaries.

The Black Brigades' experience makes Toynbee's concept of the "internal proletariat" even more meaningful. The Black Brigades are mainly children of the bourgeoisie. In many cases they come from well-off families. Giancarlo Esposti, whose father manages the Fiat dealership in Lodi, leaves the MSI to take up the armed struggle. He is accompanied by his friend Antonio Maino, whose father is an engineer. They will both die before their time. The former in a shoot-out with the carabinieri; the latter during a brigadist operation in Palma, Majorca. The Black Brigadist Francesca Mambro is the daughter of a policeman. Alessandro Alibrandi's father is a magistrate. Thanks to his family's support, Valerio Fioravanti can study in the United States. A young actor in advertisements, he then obtains a leading role in the television series *La famiglia Benvenuti,* broadcast in prime time by the RAI in 1968. His father is an RAI news anchor.

At least twenty-five people are killed by militants in the terrorist group founded by Fioravanti, NAR (Armed Revolutionary Nuclei).

It has often been said—because of the Marxist claim, after the Third International, that the fascists had always defended capital and the bourgeoisie[32]— that the subversive universe of the extreme Right was in the pay of the secret services as an anticommunist element. It is a fact that some neofascists worked as "spies";[33] but it is untenable that the more radical components of

---

31. G. Salierno, *Autobiografia di un picchiatore fascista,* 61–62.

32. See Ercoli [P. Togliatti], "A propos du fascisme," 1 August 1928, in R. De Felice, *Il fascismo,* 106–27. Togliatti, after asserting that fascism is a "capitalistic reaction," adds that "fascism is a regime that organizes from top to bottom the country's economic and political life according to the interests of the upper middle classes" (126). No less eloquent was the *Resolution of the Communist International* of 1923, which states that the reformist leaders of the Social Party and workers' associations were mainly responsible for the rise of fascism in Italy, as they had "betrayed" the revolution to defend the interests of capital. Far from improving the workers' conditions—the *Resolution* continues— "the bourgeoisie immediately used fascism in its struggle to crush the proletariat and permanently enslave it" (*Risoluzione dell'Internazionale comunista,* 5 July 1923, in R. De Felice, *Il fascismo,* 65).

33. On this point, see N. Rao, *Il sangue e la celtica.*

Italian neofascism were created to support police investigations and thus to defend the established order.

The Black Brigades brutally killed dozens of policemen and carabinieri, not to mention the magistrates involved in the fight against terrorism. On 10 July 1976, Concutelli takes a machine gun to kill Vittorio Occorsio, deputy public prosecutor in Rome engaged in various Ordine Nuovo and Avanguardia Nazionale cases; on 23 June 1980, Judge Mario Amato, principal investigator of extreme-right terrorism in Rome, is killed by the NAR on viale Jonio while waiting for the bus to take him to the law courts; on 21 October 1981, in Rome, the police captain Francesco Straullu is shot by Alessandro Alibrandi and Francesca Mambro. He was twenty-six. Before acting, the NAR militants fear the reaction of DIGOS (Division for General Investigations and Special Operations) and wonder whether they should carry on with the mission. But it's a risk they have to take because, they conclude, the "guardians" of *this world* deserve only to die. An NAR leaflet from the summer of 1981 states that "the torturers, hit men, and thugs who are to be found in the police stations are and will always be in our sights."[34]

The Black Brigades—with a language and way of thinking almost identical to that of the Red Brigades—proudly claim responsibility for their crimes. For the Black Brigades, killing bourgeois elements is an ethical imperative: "Once again Revolutionary Justice has followed its course and what remains is a warning for the traitors, the slave drivers, and the hacks. Whoever still doubts the revolutionary combatants' determination and capacity should review what has happened this year and they will realize that the time for talking is over and the fighting has begun."[35]

The machine guns used to kill Straullu and his driver, police officer Ciriaco Di Roma, are so powerful that Black Brigadist Alessandro Alibrandi stops Francesca Mambro from approaching the mangled bodies to collect their weapons: "Come away, don't look."

The Black Brigadist Roberto Nistri, militant in the NAR and former member of the Youth Front, on 8 June 1982 kills in cold blood the police officers Franco Sammarco and Giuseppe Carretta near the Flaminio Stadium in Rome. The victims are first disarmed and then forced to lie down on the ground. The policemen are shot in the back of their heads as they plead for mercy. Nistri says that it is his ideological fury that prompts him to shoot. He had learned to distinguish between "assassins"—who shoot out of personal interest—and "revolutionaries"—who kill for the ideal of freeing humanity.

---

34. Quoted in Corsini, *I terroristi della porta accanto,* 217.
35. Ibid., 218–19.

In Nistri's words: "Motivations are what enable those who go to war to perform actions they would normally never dream of. The common ideal was
to change things. You do them only because it is right to do them. If you
only do them out of expediency, then you're another person. Things happen
because you find yourself in a psychological context and condition."[36]

What do the Black Brigades want? Like all the followers of Nechaev, they
want to purify the world; they are not remotely interested in asking themselves about the society they will build after the revolution. They have a single
principle: to destroy the present world through an inordinate use of terrorist
violence. Cold-bloodedly to strike men, women, old people, and children.
Read this document of April 1963, signed by Clemente Graziani, former
member of the Italian Social Republic and founder of Ordine Nuovo:

> To conquer the masses, the revolutionary war doctrine specifies not only the
> use of psychological action but also that of *forms of ruthless and indiscriminate
> terrorism*. It involves conditioning the crowds not only with propaganda
> but also by acting on the innate reaction present both in animals and in the
> psyche of the masses: fear, terror, and the instinct of self-preservation.
>
> Therefore those leading the revolutionary action will take care to
> stress, through abundant case histories, the principle that those who
> betray, oppose, and disagree will be inexorably eliminated. It is neces-
> sary to create in the masses a sense of impotence, of absolute submis-
> sion to the inevitable victory of the revolutionary faction. Large-scale
> terrorism carried out against the forces charged with repressing the
> revolutionary movement always creates discomfort and fatigue, insecu-
> rity [within those forces]. . . . *Indiscriminate terrorism obviously implies the
> possibility of killing or having killed old people, women, and children. These
> types of actions have hitherto been considered universally abhorred and abhor-
> rent crimes and, above all, ineffective and ruinous for the victorious outcome of a
> conflict. But the rules of revolutionary war subvert these moral and humanitar-
> ian principles. These forms of terrorist intimidation are now not only considered
> legitimate but sometimes absolutely necessary to achieve a certain aim.*[37]

The pantoclastic fury typical of professional revolutionaries emerges
even more clearly in a leading article in *Anno Zero,* the magazine of Ordine
Nuovo. This neofascist rant is very similar to what we find in the Red Brigades documents: the world is a nauseating place, irremediably corrupted by

---

36. Quoted by Caprara and Semprini, *Destra estrema e criminale,* 336.
37. C. Graziani, "La guerra rivoluzionaria," 11–13. Italics added.

the values of the middle classes. Exactly what aspects of present society do the Ordine Nuovo revolutionaries want to destroy? They want to destroy it all. They want to make a clean sweep of the bourgeois world; they want to build a new world, although they are unclear about its details because what counts is to annihilate, demolish, purify, execute, and terrorize: these are the pillars of the revolutionary education.

The fascists are certain: the world is about to break up. The end is imminent. A catastrophe is about to strike capitalist civilization. This editorial, dated 20 March 1974, is entitled "Nous sommes si nous marchons":

> Let us welcome the time of action! Let it come. *We're fed up with breathing the putrid air from this rubbish heap* of a democratic and antifascist system. Founded on all the freedoms that don't exist. And on work that, when it exists, is only exploitation and slavery.
>
> We're fed up with being repressed by power, by the democratic dictatorship, with its cops, its magistrates, and its despicable laws. A repression that is becoming increasingly ruthless, as *the bourgeois system feels that its shameful and inevitable end is approaching....*
>
> *We're fed up with living in a world without honor, without principles and higher standards.* And so? And so, let's do it, let's rebel! Let's step up the struggle against this world that no longer has ideals and against the bourgeois society that is its political expression. *There's nothing left to save. We have to destroy everything to rebuild.*[38]

Brescia, 16 February 1974. In front of a Coop supermarket, wrecked by a bomb, a leaflet of the Squadre d'Azione Mussolini announces the imminent end of *this awful world* and predicts the terrible punishments that its "slaves" are about to suffer. A few months later, a bomb hidden in a trash can in Piazza della Loggia kills eight people and wounds ninety-four (28 May 1974). The explosion occurs during a demonstration against neofascist terrorism. No mercy—the fascist revolutionaries announced—not even for women, the elderly, or children. The leaflet ends by extolling the Nazi concentration camps. The fascists also have their own purification doctrine: "Slaves of this rotten system, you have to surrender as the moment of truth is nigh; no one will be saved, all will pay for their sins. We declare war on the communists, the Masons, and the Jews. LONG LIVE DACHAU."[39]

---

38. "Nous sommes si nous marchons," 20 March 1974. Italics added.

39. Squadre d'Azione Mussolini leaflet found in front of the Coop in Brescia blown up with TNT (document reconstructed by the Fascist police). The entire text can be found in M. Franzinelli, *La sottile linea nera*, 263.

While the dead of Piazza della Loggia still lie in the morgue, a document signed "Ordine Nuovo" arrives in the newsroom of the *Giornale di Brescia* (29 May 1974): "Those who do not have the courage to bring arms and death to their own land to defend their own people, their own race, their own heritage, and their own young people, the strength of the future, must and will always be slaves."[40]

Professional revolutionaries are incredibly consistent individuals. They always do what they say. They have had a very strict education—because the revolutionary education is very harsh—aimed at building a "new person." In the name of a boundless love for humanity they are prepared to kill indiscriminately. The professional revolutionary is reborn with a new identity. During an interrogation on 19 February 1981, the Black Brigadist Valerio Fioravanti confirms that *"politics is loving the world and creating a new person. To create a new person you have to destroy the old one, since you can't try to change mentality and morality."*[41]

This is a concept that the magistrates passing judgment on Fioravanti acknowledge. After listening to the accused's statements for many long days, they conclude that Fioravanti, "without any intention of cooperating with the investigators... claims that he is a 'revolutionary' and his group a fighting nucleus carrying out exemplary action as an existential practice, a reason for living, and pure idealism.... Fioravanti's spontaneity has a pedagogical significance because it is aimed at constructing new people who, through dangerous and exemplary action, want to affirm their own nature against a suffocating society."[42]

Julius Evola and the Mental Universe of the Fascist Revolutionaries

The myth of the "new person" is one of the pillars of the revolutionary culture. The Black Brigades mostly obtained it from the philosopher and painter Julius Evola (1898–1974), spiritual father of Italian neofascism.

Although he was pro-German, Evola took part in World War I by serving in the Italian army. After returning to civilian life, he had a profound existential crisis that brought him to the brink of suicide in 1921. He was saved by taking up Buddhism—recounted in his autobiography, *The Path of*

40. A "black" document sent to the newsroom of *Giornale di Brescia,* 29 May 1974.

41. Testimony of Valerio Fioravanti, interrogation of 19 February 1981, quoted by G. Bianconi, *A mano armata,* 47. Italics added.

42. G. Capaldo, L. D'Ambrosio, et al., "L'eversione di destra a Roma dal 1977 al 1983," in *Eversione di destra, terrorismo e stragi,* ed. V. Borraccetti, 236.

Cinnabar[43]—which alleviated his condition as a marginal and alienated man. A prominent representative of Dadaism, he exhibited his paintings in Rome, Paris, and Berlin. Until 1925 he used drugs to achieve an altered state of awareness that led him to interpret Dadaism in a mystic-abstract key. He was not a member of the Fascist Party because he did not consider the fight against the bourgeoisie sufficiently radical.[44] In 1942, he publishes the essay "For a Political and Cultural Alignment of Italy and Germany," in which he expresses his admiration for Nazism, considered superior to Fascism.[45] In 1945, while he is walking in Vienna during a raid, a shell fragment damages his spinal cord. He was to remain paralyzed from the waist down for the rest of his life.

Evola is the spiritual guide of all those who are sickened by bourgeois civilization, but he never identifies with communist ideals. His favorite saying, taken from Ernst Junger, is significant: "Better be a delinquent than a bourgeois."[46] In an interview of January 1970, talking about the possibility of a reaction against the modern world, he states that "it doesn't mean contesting or arguing [against it], but blowing it all up."[47] His remarks are thus directed at the "spiritually disoriented" who are in the painful condition of living in this world without belonging to it. He explains this in his most realistic and pessimistic book, *Ride the Tiger* (1961). It could be defined as a manual of the "perfect alienated man" or that "*particular human type*" who "does not belong inwardly to such a world, nor will he give in to it. He feels himself, in essence, as belonging to a different race from that of the overwhelming majority of his contemporaries."[48]

---

43. J. Evola, *Il cammino del cinabro.*

44. J. Evola, *Gli uomini e le rovine,* 164. Evola writes: "In the past, Fascism adopted an anti-bourgeois stance and, as part of the renewal that it was supposed to usher in, desired the advent of a new man, who was supposed to break with the bourgeois style of thinking, feeling, and behaving. Unfortunately, this was one of the cases where Fascism never got past its own sloganeering; those elements in Fascism that, despite all, remained bourgeois or became bourgeois by contagion constituted one of its weaknesses."

45. See J. Evola, *Fascismo e Terzo Reich* (1964). After comparing the Nazi and Fascist social organization models, Evola writes: "It can be said that, in principle, it was mainly national-socialism that advanced more decisively in the right and traditional direction.... In the case of Germany, one must also think of the influence exerted by the previous structures supported by a similar attitude and a similar tradition, nonexistent in Italy" (81). A more in-depth analysis of Nazi society and its institutions can be found at 195–200, where Evola speaks of the "exceptional performances" of Hitler's state (195).

46. G. de Turris interviewing Julius Evola, published as "Incontro con Julius Evola," November 1970, 812–20.

47. G. de Turris interviewing Julius Evola, published as "La vera contestazione è a Destra: L'uomo di vetta (sette domande a Julius Evola)," 15 January 1970, 16–19.

48. J. Evola, *Cavalcare la tigre,* 19.

Evola's philosophy is a radical attack on the modern world. The plot of the "story" is well known: there is no more light in *this world*. Traditional society is dead, taking with it every transcendent principle. Existence is now without any meaning, any purpose. The bourgeois world—these are Evola's words—is "conformism," "expediency," "baseness," "hypocrisy," "inertia," "nausea," "disgust," and "emptiness." Having cut any ties with transcendence, humanity is condemned to an "absurd" existence in which everything is possible and legitimate: "It is a life without any direction, based on nothing, that uses a system of anesthetics and surrogates as a crutch."[49]

What has caused such a disaster? The human desire for freedom and all that goes with such an endeavor: ethical rationalism, illuminism, liberalism, moral autonomy, individualism, and secularization, up to the emancipation of women, taking in cinema, glossy magazines, television, and beauty contests. Not to mention the "aberration" of jazz. Evola condemns everything that has been contaminated by modernity, meaning that he rejects all aspects of the present. His criticism is a reactionary ax that takes no prisoners. There is no element of the society in which he lives that does not arouse his disgust. We are all "martyrs of modern progress," he says. This is why Tradition is good, modernity bad. The neofascist revolutionary education is entirely built on this contrast. An excellent way of "burning your bridges" in this life would be to isolate yourself completely and avoid any physical or mental contact with inhabitants of the modern world. But this would require material and spiritual resources that few possess. Hence there is the problem of surviving "among the ruins and dissolution." What can one do? Here the philosopher becomes the tutor. He categorically denies that it is possible to come to terms with the bourgeois world (remember, it is a contaminated and contaminating place). He focuses on personal internal conduct: "I want to draw attention to the fact that, before thinking of external actions..., one has to think of training oneself, of acting on oneself, against everything that is nebulous, evasive, or bourgeois."[50]

This is a point that should be clarified: Evola does not advocate political action, because he considers that the evils of the world are by now incurable. The end is nigh; it is better to find refuge, inspired by "strict individual ethics."[51] You have to follow "an extremely strict discipline in life,"[52] which inspires even the rejection of marriage and family, institutions by now

49. Ibid., 43.
50. "A colloquio con Evola" (anonymous interview), January–February 1964, 8–13.
51. Ibid.
52. Ibid.

irredeemably corrupt.[53] Everything should obey a specific slogan: "Make sure that what you cannot change cannot change you."[54] In short, "the essential thing in a man is his 'existential dimension.' And here *the fundamental point is being utterly antibourgeois, intolerant of any bourgeois compromise and conformism,*"[55] because "the differentiated man we are talking about feels completely outside society."[56]

Evola has a lot of respect for those who choose to fight against the bourgeoisie,[57] but his redeeming allegory is addressed to the marginal individual's inner world. Equipped with a "higher spirituality," the man of Tradition is the negation of the modern man. It is difficult to distinguish between people on the basis of their presumed "moral superiority," especially when the criteria are extended to entire human categories. But this does not faze Evola: "Those who share my existential condition, who follow my teachings, are noble spirits; the others are bourgeois and thus corrupt." It is a primitive but effective criterion. The distinction between the pure and impure is a recurrent theme in the revolutionary mentality, as is the obsession with purity, of which the catacombs are the preeminent symbol. It is no coincidence that Evola loves talking about a "front line in the catacombs"[58] to pit against the moral corruption of the "bourgeois forces."

The concept that people should "actively" abstain from any practice that could compromise them with the institutions of *this world* refers to a "theory of passive militancy," aimed at creating an army of "disarmed soldiers." Evola's man is taught to see society as a "hermitage."[59] He feels that he belongs to a different humanity. He sees the desert around him and is isolated even when he interacts with the "others." When the differentiated man wanders

---

53. Evola, *Cavalcare la tigre,* 164. Evola, with an extremely pessimistic view of married life, writes: "In this epoch of dissolution it is hard for the differentiated man to become involved in marriage and family in any way. It is not a matter of ostentatious anticonformism, but a conclusion drawn from a vision consistent with reality, in which the imperative of an inner freedom remains. In a world like the present, the differentiated man must be able to have the self at his disposal, all his life long."

54. "A colloquio con Evola."

55. De Turris, "Incontro con Julius Evola." Italics added.

56. Evola, *Cavalcare la tigre,* 155: "The differentiated man," explains Evola, "cannot feel part of a 'society' that, like the present one, is formless and that, besides having fallen to a level of purely material, economic, and 'physical' values, lives at this level and becomes a mad and absurd race."

57. Evola writes: "A little group seems willing to fight on, even on lost positions. So long as it does not yield, does not compromise itself by giving in to the seductions that would condition any success it might have, its testimony is valid." Ibid., 20.

58. Ibid., 153.

59. Evola writes: "In the current political situation, in a climate of democracy and 'socialism,' the rules of the game are such that the man in question recognizes, as I have said before, that ideas, motives, and goals worthy of the pledge of one's true being do not exist today, nor are there any needs to which one can recognize any moral right or any foundation." Ibid., 151.

around *this world,* it is his "person" that is involved (or his "exteriority"), not his "being" (his "interiority").[60] In short, contact with the bourgeois world, even when freely chosen, must not contaminate the spirit of the elect. This very singular theory of political action refers to the individual and wants to distinguish the "person" who espouses bourgeois politics from his "being," which should instead deeply despise it. It is an authentic form of "associative schizophrenia." Evola calls this "irrevocable interior distance" *apolitìa.* More specifically, *apolitìa* is the condition of those who are spiritually detached from the society in which they live.[61] Isolating yourself, abstaining and purifying yourself, were the ingredients of Evola's "spiritual recipe." He was, *apparently,* the instigator of a passive revolutionary sect. In his works—always excepting the invitation to "blow everything up"—there is no direct incitement to the neofascist fury that was to shake Italy during the "years of lead." But in many cases there is no condemnation of that violence, just as there is—and this is what counts most for an intellectual—no disassociation from the culture that encourages and justifies that type of violence.

Julius Evola: "Let this world blow up!"

Over and above the debate on Evola's moral responsibilities in the genesis of the neofascist strategy of terrorist bombings,[62] we can understand the Black Brigades' mental universe only by studying their "philosophy of marginality."

Evola was loved and respected for having praised alienation, in which the victims of modernization could find a form of psychological compensation for their humiliating condition as permanently defeated people. Living "out of the world" means slowly dying, devoured by envy and resentment. Solitude—and the anxiety that always accompanies it—leads to desperation and can make people accept extreme solutions. In the DRIA model, the pantoclastic adventure starts from a psychological condition of great spiritual unease. Evola was speaking to what he calls "traumatized existences." He rams the lesson home to those young anticommunists who would have destroyed

---

60. Evola is very clear about this distinction. When referring to those who have decided to involve themselves in politics, even though they are men of Tradition, he writes: "We can speak in these cases of a voluntary obligation that concerns the 'person,' not the being, by which—even while one is involved—one remains isolated." Ibid., 152.

61. In Evola's words: "*Apoliteia* is the inner distance unassailable by society and its 'values'; it does not accept being bound by anything spiritual or moral. Once this is firm, the activities that in others would presuppose such bounds can be exercised in a different spirit." Ibid., 152.

62. See G. S. Rossi, *Il razzista totalitario,* 81–89.

this world without using Marxist theories that capitalism is a daily barbarism that has led humanity to an abyss.

Evola uses the term *demonic power of the economy* to indicate all that he despises in the modern world, the center of which is constituted by technology, science, production, productivity, and consumption. "Modern capitalism," he writes in *Men among the Ruins* (1953)—"is subversion."[63] With the typical mentality of the alienated intellectual who blames capitalism for his marginality, Evola wants to restore the philosopher to his original condition, setting the values of the Spirit and Knowledge against those "perverse" and "subversive" values of the market, considered the main source of humanity's degradation: *"What must be questioned is not the value of this or that economic system, but the value of the economy itself."*[64] Nor can one reproach Evola for not having been explicit on this decisive point: "As I have stated previously, I dispute the superiority and the rights of a merely economic class living in a materialistic fashion."[65] The battle thus consists of "defeating the bourgeoisie in general, of taking a resolute stand against the bourgeois type, the bourgeois civilization, and its spirit and its values,"[66] because the bourgeois man is "an inferior type of human."[67] Sweep away the bourgeoisie: this was Evola's rallying cry. "The worst evil for Italy is the bourgeoisie: the bourgeois–priest, the bourgeois–worker, the bourgeois–'noble,' the bourgeois–intellectual. This type is inconsistent, a substance without form, in which there is no 'above' and no 'below.' The watchword or rallying cry should be "Wipe the slate clean!"[68] In his most important work, *Revolt against the Modern World* (1934), Evola, referring to the Hindu doctrine of the four ages, defines the present one as *kali-yuga* ("dark age"). In his words, the triumph of the market economy marks the lowest point ever touched by the human race.[69]

Up to now we have studied the *pars destruens* of Evola's thinking. Let us now ask ourselves what type of society Evola would have wanted to build in place of the present world. Aristocratic principle, hierarchical order, and radical racism were the pillars of his ideal society.

In Evola's traditional society, military virtues predominate over civic ones. It is the bourgeois and not the warrior who has to bow before "the truth

---

63. Evola, *Gli uomini e le rovine,* 112.

64. Ibid., 113. Original italics.

65. Ibid., 115.

66. Ibid., 162.

67. Ibid., 141.

68. Ibid., 164.

69. J. Evola, *Rivolta contro il mondo moderno,* 219 and 406.

professed by those who uphold the *higher right of a warrior view of life.*[70] This does not mean that the military should directly manage public life (the philosophers have the guiding role). It involves—this is the main goal—constructing a state in which everything that is even only "generically bourgeois" is profoundly condemned. The values of productivity and profit will be subject to the love of hierarchy, relationships of obedience and command, courage, heroism, relationships from leader to follower, and feelings of honor and loyalty capable of producing the anonymous sacrifice. These are the typical traits of the closed society, the model of social organization beloved of all professional revolutionaries. They are specifically:[71]

Sacralization of tradition. By sacralizing Tradition, the values, ideals, and beliefs of a society take on a "sacred" and thus unalterable nature. Any deviation from the teaching of the "fathers" is considered an impiety or "sacrilege."

Isolation. To prevent contagion with "other cultures"—bearers of alternative visions of the world—the closed society has to discourage any contact with the external world. Its boundaries must be "hermetic" so that the race of the "pure" does not run the risk of being "infected" by the corruption dominating the world (Evola speaks of "ideological infections"[72]).

Autarky. A closed society has to give up the things of the world and be self-sufficient. It is thus incompatible with the market economy and an enemy of its fundamental institutions. Private property, trade, money, and private initiative compromise its institutional balance, aimed at preventing change. Evola sets the figure of the warrior against that of the merchant. The former is seen as a "guardian," while the latter is a "messenger" who, through "travel" and contact with the outside world, introduces new ideas and new models of behavior.

Hypersocialization. In the closed society, individuals must be stripped of every autonomy of thought and become strictly conformist. They are what the group has established they are. Even the smallest "intuition" is a subversive idea to be forcefully uprooted.

Orthodoxy. Every belief has to conform to the dominant doctrines, dogmas, and institutions. Every "new" idea must be condemned because Tradition is an "enclosed" and "perfect" mental universe and any alteration would mean going toward barbarism.

---

70. Evola, *Gli uomini e le rovine,* 139.

71. L. Pellicani is responsible for the following model, "Genesi della società aperta," in his *Dalla società chiusa alla società aperta,* 98–99.

72. Evola, *Gli uomini e le rovine,* 114.

Holism. The Whole must always be more important than its single parts. The interests of the community are more important than those of individuals. In the closed society, individual rights can never be rigidly fixed because the protection of the individual goes against the holistic principle of the individual in conflict with the community.

Political centralization. Since it has to preserve Tradition and prevent change, the closed society is always autocratic and militarized. Power (political, economic, and religious) has to be concentrated in one unit to stop anything that could alter the balance of the system.

Misoneism. The closed society is against innovations in any sector. Creative people constitute a danger. Their ideas are "unpredictable" and as such risk introducing antitraditional forms of behavior. The creativity of individuals must be "dried up."

These elements—all present in Evola's ideal society—are spiced up by a massive dose of radical racism and fierce antisemitism. Many adjectives have been used to describe this aspect of his philosophy. His racism has been defined as "spiritual" in the attempt to distinguish it (and to "tone it down") from the typically Nazi "biological" one. The documents that Gianni Scipione Rossi has collected speak clearly: Evola's racism was just as radical as that of the Nazis and much more uncompromising than the Fascists'.[73] On several occasions he criticized the "moderation" with which Mussolini's racial laws were applied, at the same time trying to scale down the extent of the Holocaust. These words were addressed to Giorgio Almirante, guilty of having disassociated himself from Fascist racism during a televised party political broadcast. They appear in a letter of 1967 published in *Noi Europa,* organ of Ordine Nuovo:

> You could have first of all pointed out that you were talking about Italian, Fascist racism, which was very milk-and-water with regard to anti-Jewish persecution (up to when Italy defected)...[and that] at first it was a defense against interbreeding and to strengthen the white race's sense of dignity, our nation against the colored peoples....As for the Jews, at the end they were presented as martyrs. But we have to ask ourselves what they would have done if they had had absolute power. As an example, you could have asked your interlocutors if they knew what Purim meant...it's the name of a Jewish national feast day in which they celebrate and continue to celebrate—what?—the

---

73. See Rossi, *Il razzista totalitario,* 61–67.

massacre of almost a hundred thousand of their enemies . . . and if you think of the world's density of population at that time, then a hundred thousand slaughtered is almost equal to the Jews who actually lost their lives in the Nazi concentration camps.[74]

Evola was no less explicit on the fate he had in store for blacks in the United States. He thought a good solution would be to empty one of the minor states "and put in it all the United States' Negroes so that they can enjoy their *Negritude*."[75] This is a very rich sample of his racist expressions. There is also an invitation to the MSI "not to follow the same line as those irresponsible Americans who are moved by the 'poor Negro,' who praise interbreeding, who are not concerned if white girls go to bed and procreate with Negroes."[76]

It is not true that "it is always difficult, debated, and debatable to establish in what sense and to what extent and up to what point an idea can bring about an action," as Piero Di Vona wrote in his *Evola e Guénon*.[77] For many years, Evola welcomed young neofascists who had made a "pilgrimage" to listen to someone they considered their "spiritual guide."[78] He had an enormous influence on their way of thinking. He preached racism, antisemitism, the myth of force, and condemnation for every aspect of *this world*. In January 1970, he urged its physical destruction. A few months later (November 1970), he even sneered at those young fascists he reckoned would only be revolutionaries "in words." There is nothing ambiguous about these statements: "When you are young, it is easy to become passionate about certain ideas (often consigned to the attic when the so-called problems of life appear); it is also easy to be revolutionaries in words, since there is very little possibility of really overturning the present situation."[79] In the most difficult moments of the armed struggle, many in the Black Brigades would have found a "psychological refuge" in these words. Others—the younger ones, the would-be revolutionaries—would find in them a "go-ahead" to

74. J. Evola, "Lettera ad Almirante," 10 March 1967, in Evola, *I testi di Ordine Nuovo,* ed. R. Del Ponte, 127–31.

75. J. Evola, "I tabù dei nostri tempi," 30 January 1969.

76. J. Evola, "Razzismo e altri 'orrori,'" 1959.

77. P. Di Vona, *Evola e Guénon,* 14.

78. On Evola's influence on the young, Giuseppe Parlato has written: "Evola seems to have played a minority and elitist role if you think of the positions and 'spirits' agitating in this political sector, but he did have *a particular capacity to influence, a charisma capable of leaving a clear sign that will not fade easily.*" I quote from the introductory essay by G. Parlato to Evola, *Fascismo e Terzo Reich,* 15 (italics added). The essay is entitled "Fascismo, Nazionalsocialismo, Tradizione."

79. Interview by Gianfranco de Turris, published as "Incontro con Julius Evola."

deploy violence (perhaps even an authentic "encouragement" to "blow everything up").

In times of war, the ambiguity of a "maestro" can be the clearest indication to advance. Evola was a profoundly ambiguous thinker. He exhorted people to withdraw from political life, but always expressed his admiration for those few "elect" who had decided to fight against the bourgeois world.[80] In his main works there is no invitation to carry out violent actions, but equally there is no condemnation of the mentality, symbols, and slogans of these actions. In his thinking, fascist violence is not "wrong," it is "useless" because the world is by now irremediably corrupt.

Let us return to Durkheim's words encountered at the beginning of this book: pedagogical theories have the immediate aim of guiding behavior. They are not action in itself but prepare for it.

Evola might not have led the young neofascists into the hell of terrorism, but he certainly accompanied them to the threshold.

---

80. Evola writes: "If today there are men who are prepared to fight despite everything, even for lost positions, I equally feel respect for them." Anonymous interview published as "A colloquio con Evola."

A NOTE ON METHOD

This book presents the results of a research project that aims to answer three questions:

1. Who are the Red Brigades?
2. Why do they kill?
3. Where do they come from, what is their historic-political tradition?

These three questions correspond to three different stages in my research: descriptive, explicative, and genetic or historic-sociological comparison.

Since I had no specific hypothesis on the reasons for political homicide in extreme-left and neo-Nazi terrorist groups, my first task was to acquire more information on the Red and Black Brigades (fascist groups).

During the first research stage, I studied the characteristics of revolutionary sects (how they recruited, how internal discipline was maintained, how their work was divided up, the incentives to revolutionary violence, the organization chart, etc.) and of the individual members (age, sex, educational level, original social condition, daily life, view of the world, what they think before shooting, how they justify killing people, etc.). These initial explorations are called *descriptive studies* because they aim to give a detailed description of the phenomenon. Descriptive studies pose questions on the *how*, whereas explicative studies ask about the *why*, of social phenomena.

In the second stage I set up a theoretical model to reconstruct the socio-psychological processes leading to violence in extreme-left and neo-Nazi terrorist groups (DRIA model). This is the explicative stage. Since the life of a terrorist group cannot be studied through participant observation, or through the administration of structured questionnaires, the DRIA model was mainly constructed on the basis of the following documents:

1. Testimonies of Red Brigades who had killed
2. Trial affidavits
3. Documents claiming responsibility for aggressions, kidnappings, thefts, assaults, injuries, and homicides

4. Strategic resolutions
5. Documents commemorating Red Brigades members killed by the police
6. Private letters written by Red Brigades members to their families
7. Red Brigades leaflets and writings on the walls in cities or in factories, for which responsibility has been claimed or ascertained

I used the DRIA model to work out a theory, that is, a provisional explanation expressed in a controllable form specifying a particular relationship among several variables. Essentially this theory, the basis for my revolutionary-subversive feedback hypothesis, states that the willingness to give and receive death depends, *in the last analysis,* on how far the gnostic activity has been incorporated into the revolutionary sect.[1] It can be formulated through a bivariate proposal that I express as follows: "The greater the level of integration of the gnostic activity in the revolutionary sect, the higher its propensity to give and receive death." In this explicative stage, Weber's method of *comprehension* and *identification* has played a central role.[2]

I will clarify my point of view through the words of Norbert Elias: "We cannot understand the structure of a society if we cannot manage to see it both through our perspective (speaking about it in the *third* person) and according to its perspective (that is, making its members speak in the *first* person). At the moment it still seems that the only way to achieve a high degree of safety, according to our perspective, is by quantification, enumerating individuals and using statistical measuring tools. But there are also other methods, and they especially are necessary when one tries to determine certain creations for which a scientific approach is possible only by subdividing them conceptually into atoms, single actions, single concepts, variables, or other."[3]

In the third stage I used comparative-historical sociology to investigate the main revolutionary phenomena of modern times in the attempt to find

---

1. The DRIA model and the subversive-revolutionary feedback hypothesis refer above all to the first militants of the Red Brigades. There is, in fact, an important difference between the motivations of militants that form a small group of terrorists such as the Red Brigades in their initial phase, and the motives of those who join when the group has become larger and commands more means and resources. In its initial phase, a terroristic group needs armed individuals who are strongly motivated by ideology. Their members have to accept the idea of kill or be killed. In the second case, ideological motivations can take a back seat to motives of a different nature, for example, economics.

2. As Max Weber teaches, comprehension and identification are not enough in themselves to guarantee the objectivity of sociological research. Researchers must ensure that what they have discovered can be checked and repeated. Hence the importance of documents.

3. N. Elias, *La società di corte,* 59.

the ideological roots of the Red Brigades' plan. I compared the phenomenon with other, similar phenomena. After tracing the sociopsychological profile of the "perfect terrorist," and after reconstructing the determinants of his or her pantoclastic fury, I went back to the past to find their precursors and antecedents, from the revolutionary sects in sixteenth-century Germany to the Pol Pot revolution in Cambodia in 1975. My theory in this third and last part is that the Red Brigades belong to a revolutionary tradition that, in its most complete form, boasts at least two centuries of history. This is the comparative-historical sociology stage.

To understand both red and black terrorists, you have first of all to listen to their activists. The idea behind the entire research project is that the Red Brigades are not "mad." This classification serves only to condemn and hinders comprehension. The Red Brigades are normal people who, through a gradual interaction process (DRIA model), become murderers (revolutionary-subversive feedback theory).

You become a brigadist.

The philosophy behind the research for this work is illustrated in a previous book of mine, *In difesa della sociologia storica* (In Defense of Historical Sociology).

BIBLIOGRAPHY

General

Acquaviva, S. *Guerriglia e guerra rivoluzionaria in Italia: Ideologia, fatti, prospettive.* Rizzoli, Milan, 1979.

Adinolfi, G., and R. Fiore. *Noi, Terza posizione.* Settimo Sigillo, Rome, 2000.

Adornato, F. "Se la violenza sostituisce la politica." *L'Unità,* 26 January 1978.

Aga-Rossi, E., and V. Zaslavsky. *Togliatti e Stalin: Il PCI e la politica estera staliniana negli archivi di Mosca.* Il Mulino, Bologna, 2007.

Agosti, A. *Togliatti: Un uomo di frontiera.* Utet, Turin, 2003.

Agostini, P. *Mara Cagol: Una donna nelle prime Brigate rosse.* Marsilio, Venice, 1980.

Alasia, F., and D. Montaldi. *Milano, Corea: Inchiesta sugli immigrati.* Feltrinelli, Milan, 1975.

Alberoni, F. "Movimenti sociali e società italiana." In *Classi e movimenti in Italia 1970–1985,* edited by C. Carboni. Laterza, Roma-Bari, 1986.

———. *Movimento e istituzione.* Il Mulino, Bologna, 1977.

Almirante, G. "Conferenza stampa." *Il secolo d'Italia,* 1 June 1976.

———. "Intervista a." *Il secolo d'Italia,* 31 January 1975.

Amendola, G. "Dietro il polverone." *Rinascita,* 10 May 1968.

———. "I comunisti e il movimento studentesco." *Rinascita,* 7 June 1968.

———. "Il discorso sulla violenza." *L'Unità,* 11 May 1976.

———. "Il Pci e i giovani." *L'Unità,* 16 May 1972.

———. "Il posto di Togliatti." *Rinascita,* 12 January 1968.

———. "La crisi del Psu: Analisi del significato e della portata di una sconfitta." *Rinascita,* 31 May 1968.

———. *Tra passione e ragione.* Rizzoli, Milan, 1982.

———. "Vigilia elettorale." *Rinascita,* 23 February 1968.

Amerio, P. *Teorie in psicologia sociale.* Il Mulino, Bologna, 1982.

Ammassari, L. *I salari di fatto in Italia.* Giuffré, Milan, 1963.

Ammerman, N. T. *Bible Believers: Fundamentalists in the Modern World.* Rutgers University Press, New Brunswick, 1987.

Ancona, L. *La psicologia sociale in America.* Vita e Pensiero, Milan, 1954.

Applebaum, A. *Gulag: Storia dei campi di concentramento sovietici.* Mondadori, Milan, 2004.

Arendt, H. *Le origini del totalitarismo.* Einaudi, Turin, 2004.

Arfé, G. "Costruire insieme un destino nuovo." *Avanti!* 3 March 1968.

Arvon, H. *Bakunin: La vita, il pensiero, i testi esemplari.* Sansoni, Milan, 1970.

Ascoli, U. *Movimenti migratori in Italia.* Il Mulino, Bologna, 1979.

Aust, S. *Rote Armee Fraktion: Il caso Baader-Meinhoff.* Il Saggiatore, Milan, 2008.

Aylmer, G. E. "England's Spirit Unfoulded; or, An Incouragement to Take the Engagement: A Newly Discovered Pamphlet by Gerrard Winstanley." *Past and Present* 40 (1968).

Babeuf, F.-N. *Il manifesto dei plebei* (1795). In *Il tribuno del popolo,* edited by François-Noël Babeuf. Editori Riuniti, Rome, 1970.

Bailey, K. D. *Methods of Social Research.* The Free Press, New York, 1982.

Bainbridge, W. S. *Satan's Power: Ethnography of a Deviant Psychotherapy Cult.* University of California Press, Berkeley, 1978.

Bakunin, M. A. "I principi della rivoluzione." In *A un vecchio compagno,* edited by A. Herzen. Einaudi, Turin, 1977.

———. *La rivolta.* In *Bakunin: La vita, il pensiero, i testi esemplari,* edited by H. Arvon. Sansoni, Milan, 1970.

———. *La teologia politica di Mazzini e l'internazionale.* In *Scritti editi ed inediti,* by M. A. Bakunin, edited by P. C. Masini. Novecento Grafico, Bergamo, 1960.

———. *Organizzazione anarchica e lotta armata (lettera a uno svedese).* La Rivolta, Ragusa, 1978.

———. *Stato e anarchia.* Feltrinelli, Milan, 1996.

Balch, R. W. "Waiting for the Ships: Disillusionment and the Revitalization of Faith in Bo and Peep's Ufo Cult." In *The Gods Have Landed: New Religions from Other Worlds,* edited by J. R. Lewis. State University of New York Press, Albany, 1995.

Balzerani, B. *Compagna luna.* Feltrinelli, Milan, 1998.

Barbagallo, F. *Lavoro ed esodo nel Sud.* Guida, Naples, 1973.

———. "L'emigrazione." In *Storia dell'Italia repubblicana,* vol. 3/1. Einaudi, Turin, 1996.

Barbagallo, F., and G. Bruno. "Espansione e deriva del Mezzogiorno." In *Storia dell'Italia repubblicana,* vol. 3/2. Einaudi, Turin, 1997.

Barca, F., ed. *Storia del capitalismo italiano.* Donzelli, Rome, 1997.

Barca, L. "Il balletto di Rumor." *Rinascita,* 14 June 1968.

Barkun, M. "Reflections after Waco: Millennialists and the State." In *From the Ashes: Making Sense of Waco,* edited by J. R. Lewis. Lanham, Md., Rowman & Littlefield, 1994.

Basso, L. "Il colpo di Stato di De Gasperi." *Rinascita,* September 1952.

Battafarano, I. M. *Da Müntzer a Gaismair: Teoria della ribellione e progetto comunistico nella guerra dei contadini tedeschi (1524–1526).* Schena Editore, Fasano, 1979.

Bell, D. *The End of Ideology: On the Exhaustion of Political Ideas in the Fifties.* Free Press, New York, 1962.

Bensing. M. *Thomas Müntzer und der Thuringer Aufstand: 1525.* veb Deutscher Verlag der Wissenschaften, Berlin, 1966.

Berger, P. L., and T. Luckmann. *La realtà come costruzione sociale.* Il Mulino, Bologna, 1969.

Bergère, M.-C. *La Cina dal 1949 ai giorni nostri.* Il Mulino, Bologna, 2000.

Berlin, I. *Due concetti di libertà.* Feltrinelli, Milan, 2000.

———. *Karl Marx.* Sansoni, Milan, 2004.

Berlinguer, E. "Alleanze sociali e schieramenti politici." *Rinascita,* 12 October 1973.

———. "Imperialismo e coesistenza alla luce dei fatti cileni." *Rinascita,* 28 September 1973.

———. "Intervista a." *La Repubblica,* 28 July 1981.

———. "Via democratica e violenza reazionaria." *Rinascita,* 5 October 1973.

Bernal, M. "Mao e la rivoluzione cinese." In *Storia del marxismo: Il marxismo nell'età della Terza internazionale.* Vol. 3. Einaudi, Turin, 1980.

Bernstein, E. *Cromwell and Communism.* Frank Cass, London, 1966.

Bettanin, F. *Il lungo terrore: Politica e repressione in Urss 1917–1953.* Editori Riuniti, Rome, 1999.

Bettizza, E. *Il comunismo europeo.* Rizzoli, Milan, 1978.

Biacchessi, D. *Una stella a cinque punte: Le inchieste D'Antona e Biagi e le nuove Br.* Baldini Castoldi Dalai, Milan, 2007.

Bianconi, G. *A mano armata:Vita violenta di Giusva Fioravanti, terrorista neofascista quasi per caso.* Baldini Castoldi Dalai, Milan, 2007.

———. *Mi dichiaro prigioniero politico: Storie delle Brigate rosse.* Einaudi, Turin, 2003.

Biorcio, R. *Sociologia politica: Partiti, movimenti sociali e partecipazione.* Il Mulino, Bologna, 2003.

Blickle, P. *La riforma luterana e la guerra contadina: La rivoluzione del 1525.* Il Mulino, Bologna, 1983.

Bloch, E. *Il principio speranza.* Garzanti, Milan, 2005.

———. *Thomas Müntzer, teologo della rivoluzione.* Edited by S. Zecchi. Feltrinelli, Milan, 1980.

Blumer, H. *Interazionismo simbolico.* Il Mulino, Bologna, 2008.

———. *Symbolic Interactionism: Perspective and Method.* Prentice Hall, Englewood Cliffs, N.J., 1969.

Bobbio, N. *Eguaglianza e libertà.* Einaudi, Turin, 1995.

———. *Il futuro della democrazia.* Einaudi, Turin, 1995.

———. *Né con Marx, né contro Marx.* Editori Riuniti, Rome, 1997.

Bocca, G. *Noi terroristi: Dodici anni di lotta armata ricostruiti e discussi con i protagonisti.* Garzanti, Milan, 1985.

Bonanate, L. *Dimensioni del terrorismo politico.* Angeli, Milan, 1979.

———, ed. *La violenza politica nel mondo contemporaneo.* Angeli, Milan, 1979.

Boock, P.-J. *L'autunno tedesco: Schleyer-Mogadiscio-Stammheim.* DeriveApprodi, Rome, 2003.

Boraso, G. *Mucchio selvaggio: Ascesa, apoteosi, caduta dell'organizzazione Prima Linea.* Castelvecchi, Rome, 2006.

Bordogna, L., and G. C. Provasi. "La conflittualità." In *Relazioni industriali: Manuale per l'analisi dell'esperienza italiana,* edited by G. P. Cella and T. Treu. Il Mulino, Bologna, 1982.

Braghetti, A. L. *Il prigioniero.* Mondadori, Milan, 1998.

Brailsford, H. N. *I livellatori e la Rivoluzione inglese.* Edited by C. Hill. 2 vols. Il Saggiatore, Milan, 1962.

Breschi, D. *Sognando la rivoluzione: La sinistra italiana e le origini del '68.* Mauro Pagliai, Florence, 2008.

Brigate rosse, Le venti tesi finali. Brigadist document of December 1980 (www.brigaterosse.org).

Brinton, C. *Anatomy of Revolution.* Vintage, New York, 1965.

Bromley, D. G., and E. D. Silver. "The Davidian Tradition: From Patronal Clan to Prophetic Movement." In *Armageddon in Waco: Critical Perspectives on the*

Branch Davidian Conflict, edited by S. A. Wright. University of Chicago Press, Chicago, 1995.

Brown, R. *Psicologia sociale dei gruppi.* Il Mulino, Bologna, 1990.

Brunetau, B. *Il secolo dei genocidi.* Il Mulino, Bologna, 2005.

Bufalini, P. "Il Partito e gli studenti." *Rinascita,* 1 March 1968.

Buonarroti, F. *Cospirazione dell'eguaglianza detta di Babeuf.* Einaudi, Turin, 1971.

Burnham, J. *The Machiavellians: Defenders of Freedom.* Gateway, Chicago, 1943.

Callari Galli, M. *In Cambogia: Pedagogia del totalitarismo.* Meltemi, Rome, 1997.

Calvi, G., ed. *Condorcet: I progressi dello spirito umano.* Editori Riuniti, Rome, 1995.

Calvin, J. *Istituzione della religione cristiana.* 1536. Vol. 1. Utet, Turin, 1971.

Camoriano, C. *Nihon Sekigun: L'armata rossa giapponese.* Edizioni Nuova Cultura, Rome, 2006.

Campagna di primavera. Brigadist document of March 1979 (www.brigaterosse.org).

Campi, E. Introduction. In *Scritti politici,* by Thomas Müntzer, edited by E. Campi. Claudiana, Turin, 1972.

——. "Thomas Müntzer: Teologo e rivoluzionario." *Gioventù Evangelica* 20 (1970).

Canfora, L. "Intervista a." *La Stampa,* 10 May 2008.

Canteri, C. *Immigrati a Torino.* Edizioni Avanti, Milan, 1964.

Capaldo, G., L. D'Ambrosio et al. "L'eversione di destra a Roma dal 1977 al 1983: Spunti per una ricostruzione del fenomeno." In *Eversione di destra, terrorismo e stragi: I fatti e l'intervento giudiziario,* edited by V. Borraccetti. Franco Angeli, Milan, 1986.

Capanna, M. *Formidabili quegli anni.* Garzanti, Milan, 2007.

Caprara, M., and G. Semprini. *Destra estrema e criminale.* Newton Compton, Rome, 2007.

Carboni, C., ed. *Classi e movimenti in Italia 1970–1985.* Laterza, Rome and Bari, 1976.

Carr, E. H. *Bakunin: Vita di un rivoluzionario che sognava l'impossibile.* Rizzoli, Milan, 2002.

Casamassima, P. *Il libro nero delle Brigate rosse.* Newton Compton, Rome, 2007.

Cassata, F. *A destra del fascismo: Profilo politico di Julius Evola.* Bollati Boringhieri, Turin, 2003.

Cassirer, E. *Filosofia dell'illuminismo.* La Nuova Italia, Florence, 1985.

——. "Il problema Gian Giacomo Rousseau." In *Tre letture di Rousseau.* Laterza, Rome and Bari, 1994.

Castronovo, V. *L'industria italiana dall'Ottocento a oggi.* Mondadori, Milan, 1990.

Catabiani Umberto, in onore di. Brigadist document, 26 May 1982 (www.brigaterosse. org).

Catanzaro, R., and L. Manconi, eds. *Storie di lotta armata.* Il Mulino, Bologna, 1995.

Chaliand, G., and A. Blin. "Dal 1968 all'islamismo radicale." In *Storia del terrorismo: Dall'antichità ad Al Qaeda,* edited by G. Chaliand and A. Blin. Utet, Turin, 2007.

Chang, J., and J. Halliday. *Mao: La storia sconosciuta.* Longanesi, Milan, 2006.

Chernyshevsky, N. G. *Che fare?* Garzanti, Milan, 2000.

Chiarante, G. "Università '68." *Rinascita,* 9 February 1968.

Chiarini, R., and P. Corsini. *Da Salò a Piazza della Loggia: Blocco d'ordine, neofascismo, radicalismo di destra a Brescia (1945–1974).* Franco Angeli, Milan, 1983.

Chidester, D. *Salvation and Suicide: An Interpretation of Jim Jones, the Peoples Temple, and Jonestown.* Indiana University Press, Bloomington, 1988.

Ciliga, A. *Au pays du grand mensonge.* Gallimard, Paris, 1938.

Cipriani, G. *Brigate rosse: La minaccia del nuovo terrorismo.* Sperling & Kupfer, Milan, 2004.

Clark, R. P. "Patterns in the Lives of ETA Members." *Terrorism: An International Journal* 6 (1983).

Clark, T. J. *Addio a un'idea: Modernismo e arti visive.* Einaudi, Turin, 2005.

Claudio, parla un terrorista a firma di. *Panorama,* 6 June 1978.

Clementi, M. *Storia delle Brigate rosse.* Odradek, Rome, 2007.

Cochin, A. *Lo spirito del giacobinismo: La società di pensiero e la democrazia; Una interpretazione sociologica della Rivoluzione francese.* Bompiani, Milan, 1981.

Codignola, T. "Intervento alla Camera dei Deputati sugli scontri di Valle Giulia." *Avanti!* 2 March 1968.

Codrini, G. *Io, un ex brigatista.* Editrice Fiorentino, Naples, 1981.

Cohn, N. *I fanatici dell'apocalisse.* Edizioni di Comunità, Milan, 1976.

Colarizi, S. *Storia dei partiti nell'Italia repubblicana.* Laterza, Rome and Bari, 1994.

Coleman, J. *Foundations of Social Theory.* Belknap Press of Harvard University Press, Cambridge, Mass., 1990.

Colin, L. *The Structure of the Terror: The example of Javogues and the Loire.* Oxford University Press, London, 1973.

Colletti. L. "Rousseau critico della 'società civile.'" In *Ideologia e società.* Laterza, Rome, 1972.

Collins, Randall. *Violence: A Micro-Sociological Theory.* Princeton University Press, Princeton, N. J., 2008.

Colombo, A., and G. Schiavone, eds. *L'utopia nella storia: La rivoluzione inglese.* Dedalo, Bari, 1992.

Colonna Vilasi, A. *Il terrorismo.* Mursia, Milan, 2009.

Commare, C., and G. Commare, eds. *Presenti e invisibili: Storie e dibattiti degli emigranti di Campobello.* Feltrinelli, Milan, 1978.

Compagna, F. *I terroni in città.* Laterza, Bari, 1959.

———. "L'esodo dal Sud e la ricettività del triangolo industriale." In *Il Nord nella storia d'Italia,* edited by L. Cafagna. Laterza, Bari 1962.

Concutelli, P. *Io, l'uomo nero: Una vita tra politica, violenza e galera.* Marsilio, Venice, 2008.

Condorcet, Nicolas de. *I progressi dello spirito umano.* Edited by G. Calvi. Editori Riuniti, Rome, 1995.

Confino, M. *Il catechismo del rivoluzionario: Bakunin e l'affare Nechaev.* Adelphi, Milan, 1976.

Conquest, R. *Il secolo delle idee assassine.* Mondadori, Milan, 2002.

———. *Stalin: La rivoluzione, il terrore, la guerra.* Mondadori, Milan, 2003.

"Considerazioni sul 18 aprile." *Rinascita,* April–May 1948.

Constant, B. *La libertà degli antichi paragonata a quella dei moderni.* 1819. Einaudi, Turin, 2001.

"Contro il totalitarismo clericale." *Rinascita,* June 1952. The article bears the signature of the PCI Central Committee.

Coppola, A. "L'indimenticabile diciannove maggio." *Rinascita,* 24 May 1968.

Corsi, P. "L'esodo agricolo dagli anni '50 agli anni '70 in Italia e nel Mezzogiorno." *Rassegna Economica* 3 (1977).

Corsini, P. A. *I terroristi della porta accanto.* Newton Compton, Rome, 2007.

Coser, L. *I maestri del pensiero sociologico.* Il Mulino, Bologna, 1989.

Crainz, G. *Il paese mancato: Dal miracolo economico agli anni ottanta.* Donzelli, Rome, 2005.

Cromwell, O. *Discorsi e lettere della rivoluzione.* Doxa, Rome, 1930.

———. *The Writings and Speeches of Oliver Cromwell.* Edited by W. C. Abbott. Harvard University Press, Cambridge, Mass., 1937–47.

Curcio, R. *A viso aperto.* Edited by M. Scialoja. Mondadori, Milan, 1993.

———. In *Nuova resistenza,* January 1971.

———. "Scritto dal carcere di Casale." *Abc* no. 9, 6 March 1975.

Curcio, R., and A. Franceschini. *Gocce di sole nella città degli spettri.* Corrispondenza internazionale, Rome, 1982.

D'Alema, M. "Sedicenti rivoluzionari." *Rinascita,* 10 May 1968.

D'Amato, F. U. "Intervista a." *L'Espresso,* 28 April 1974.

Davies, J. C. "Toward a Theory of Revolution." In *When Men Revolt and Why: A Reader in Political Violence and Revolution,* edited by J. C. Davies. Free Press, New York, 1971.

Dawson, L. L. *Comprehending Cults: The Sociology of New Religious Movements.* Oxford University Press, Oxford, 1998.

Debré, F. *Cambogia: La rivoluzione della foresta.* Città Nuova, Rome, 1978.

De Domenico, S. *Il lavoro nell'Ordine nuovo.* Nuova tipografica, Brescia, 1964.

———. *Introduzione ad Adolf Hitler.* Grafica Federico, Brescia, 1966.

———. *La battaglia è vicina.* Centro studi "Giovane nazione," Brescia, 1962.

De Felice, R. *Il fascismo: Le interpretazioni dei contemporanei e degli storici.* Laterza, Rome and Bari, 2008.

Della Porta, D. *Gli incentivi alla militanza nelle organizzazioni clandestine della sinistra.* Laterza, Rome and Bari, 1986.

———. *Il terrorismo.* Laterza, Rome and Bari, 1985.

———. *Il terrorismo di sinistra.* Il Mulino, Bologna, 1990.

———. *Movimenti collettivi e sistema politico in Italia 1960–1995.* Laterza, Rome and Bari, 1996.

———. *Social Movements and the States: Thoughts on the Policing of Protest.* European University Institute, Florence, 1995.

———. *Terrorismi in Italia: Contributi di G. Caselli.* Il Mulino, Bologna, 1984.

Della Porta, D., and M. Rossi. *Cifre crudeli.* Materiali di Ricerca dell'Istituto Cattaneo, Bologna, 1984.

———. *Cifre crudeli Bilancio dei terrorismi italiani.* Istituto di studi e ricerche Carlo Cattaneo, Bologna, 1984.

Dell'Aringa, C. *Occupazione, salari e prezzi.* Giuffré, Milan, 1969.

Della Volpe, G. *Rousseau e Marx.* Editori Riuniti, Rome, 1997.

De Ruggiero, G. *Storia del liberalismo europeo.* Laterza, Bari, 1945.

Deschamps, D. "Le vrai systeme." In *Illuminismo e utopia: Temi e progetti utopici nella cultura francese (1676–1788),* edited by S. Bartolomei. Il Saggiatore, Milan, 1978.

de Tocqueville, A. *Scritti politici.* Vol. 1, *L'antico regime e la rivoluzione.* Utet, Turin, 1969.

de Turris, G. "Interviewing Julius Evola." Published as "La vera contestazione è a Destra: L'uomo di vetta (sette domande a Julius Evola)," *Il Conciliatore,* no. 1, 15 January 1970.

——. "Interviewing Julius Evola." Published as "Incontro con Julius Evola," *L'Italiano,* no. 11, November 1970.

Diena, L. *Borgata milanese.* Franco Angeli, Milan, 1963.

di Giulio, F. "Lotta sindacale e svolta politica." *Rinascita,* 3 May 1968.

di Loreto, P. *Togliatti e la "doppiezza": Il Pci tra democrazia e insurrezione 1944–49.* Il Mulino, Bologna, 1991.

di Scala, S. M. *Renewing Italian Socialism: Nenni to Craxi.* Oxford University Press, New York, 1988.

"Distensione." *Rinascita,* May 1949.

Di Vona, P. *Evola e Guénon: Tradizione e civiltà.* Società Editrice Napoletana, Naples, 1985.

Djilas, M. *La nuova classe: Una analisi del sistema comunista.* 1957. Il Mulino, Bologna, 1971.

——. *La società imperfetta: Al di là della "nuova classe."* Mondadori, Milan, 1970.

"Documento 'nero' giunto in redazione, Un." *Giornale di Brescia,* 29 May 1974.

Dommanget, M. *Babeuf e la congiura degli uguali.* Samonà e Savelli, Rome, 1970.

Donini, A. "Avanti nella lotta per la pace." *Rinascita,* March 1951.

Dossena, G. "Il polpaccio nel mirino." *L'Espresso,* 3 December 1978.

Dossier "Piano solo." Il generale De Lorenzo, l'arma dei carabinieri, il Sifar. Kaos, Milan, 2005.

Dostoyevsky, F. *I demoni.* Garzanti, Milan, 1973.

Drake, R. *Apostoli e agitatori: La tradizione rivoluzionaria marxista in Italia.* Le Lettere, Florence, 2008.

——. *Il caso Aldo Moro.* Marco Tropea, Milan, 1996.

Durant, W. *Rousseau e la rivoluzione.* Mondadori, Milan, 1970.

Durkheim, E. *Il suicidio.* Utet, Turin, 1969.

——. *L'educazione morale.* Utet, Turin, 2008.

——. *Le forme elementari della vita religiosa.* Comunità, Milan, 1963.

Duverger, M. *Sociologia della politica: Elementi di scienza politica.* Sugarco, Milan, 1973.

Easton, D. *A Systems Analysis of Political Life.* Wiley, New York, 1965.

Eliade, M. *Initiation, rites, sociétés secrètes.* Gallimard, Paris, 1976.

Elias, N. *La società di corte.* Il Mulino, Bologna, 1997.

Engels, F. *Sulle origini del cristianesimo.* Editori Riuniti, Rome, 2000.

Ercoli [P. Togliatti]. "A propos du fascisme." *L'internationale communiste,* 1 August 1928.

Evola, J. "A colloquio con" (anonymous interview). *Ordine Nuovo,* January–February 1964.

——. *Cavalcare la tigre: Orientamenti esistenziali per un'epoca della dissoluzione.* Edizioni Mediterranee, Rome, 2008.

——. *Fascismo e Terzo Reich.* 1964. Edizioni Mediterranee, Rome, 2001.

——. *Gli uomini e le rovine.* Edizioni Mediterranee, Rome, 2002.

——. *Il cammino del cinabro.* All'insegna del pesce d'oro, Milan, 1963.

——. "I tabù dei nostri tempi." *Il Borghese,* 30 January 1969.

——. *I testi di Ordine Nuovo.* Edited by R. Del Ponte. Edizioni di Ar, Padua, 2001.

——. "Lettera ad Almirante." *Noi Europa: Periodico per l'Ordine Nuovo,* 10 March 1967.

——. "Razzismo e altri 'orrori.'" *L'Italiano,* nos. 5–6 (1959).

——. *Rivolta contro il mondo moderno.* Edizioni Mediterranee, Rome, 2007.

Fasanella, G., and A. Franceschini. *Che cosa sono le BR: Le radici, la nascita, la storia, il presente.* Rizzoli, Milan, 2004.

Fazzini, G., ed. *Il libro rosso dei martiri cinesi: Testimonianze e resoconti autobiografici.* San Paolo, Cinisello Balsamo, 2006.

Federico, G., and R. Giannetti. "Le politiche industriali." In *Storia d'Italia,* vol. 15, edited by F. Amatori, D. Bigazzi, R. Giannetti, and L. Segreto. Einaudi, Turin, 1999.

Feher, F. "Cambogia: L'utopia omicida." *Mondoperaio* 3 (1983).

Feltrinelli, G. *Estate 1969: La minaccia incombente di una svolta radicale e autoritaria a destra, di un colpo di Stato all'italiana.* Libreria Feltrinelli, Milan, 1969.

——. "Persiste la minaccia di un colpo di Stato in Italia." *La Sinistra,* no. 3, 1968.

Fenzi, E. *Armi e bagagli: Un diario dalle Brigate rosse.* Costa & Nolan, Genoa and Milan, 1998.

Ferrandi, M. "Una pistola per riconquistare il paradiso." *Il Manifesto,* 7 March 1984.

Ferrara, M. "Responsabilità democratica, irresponsabilità governativa." *L'Unità,* 1 March 1968.

Ferraresi, F. *Minacce alla democrazia: La destra radicale e la strategia della tensione in Italia nel dopoguerra.* Feltrinelli, Milan, 1995.

Ferrero, G. *Le due rivoluzioni francesi.* Sugarco, Milan, 1986.

Fiaschi, G. *Potere, rivoluzione e utopia nell'esperienza di Gerrard Winstanley.* Cedam, Padua, 1982.

Figes, O. *La tragedia di un popolo.* Corbaccio, Milan, 1997.

Filoramo, G. *Il risveglio della gnosi ovvero come si diventa Dio.* Laterza, Rome and Bari, 1990.

——. *L'attesa della fine: Storia della gnosi.* Laterza, Rome and Bari, 1987.

Fisichella, D. *Totalitarismo: Un regime del nostro tempo.* Carocci, Rome, 2002.

Flamigni, S. *La sfinge delle Brigate rosse: Delitti, segreti e bugie del capo terrorista Mario Moretti.* Kaos, Milan, 2004.

——. *La tela del ragno: Il delitto Moro.* Kaos, Milan, 2003.

Fofi, G. *L'immigrazione meridionale a Torino.* Feltrinelli, Milan, 1975.

Franceschini, A. *Mara, Renato e io: Storia dei fondatori delle BR.* Edited by P. V. Buffa and F. Giustolisi. Mondadori, Milan, 1996.

——. *Mara, Renato e io. Storia dei fondatori delle BR.* Mondadori, Milan, 1998.

Franzinelli, M. *La sottile linea nera: Neofascismo e servizi segreti, da Piazza Fontana a Piazza della Loggia.* Rizzoli, Milan, 2008.

Fromm, E. *Fuga dalla libertà.* Mondadori, Milan, 1994.

Furet, F. *Critica della rivoluzione francese.* Laterza, Rome and Bari, 1999.

——. *Le due rivoluzioni: Dalla Francia del 1789 alla Russia del 1917.* Utet, Turin, 2002.

——. *Marx e la rivoluzione francese.* Rizzoli, Milan, 1989.

Furet, F., and D. Richet. *La rivoluzione francese.* 2 vols. Laterza, Rome and Bari, 1998.

Gabriella, G. *La lingua inglese e la rivoluzione puritana: I pamphlets dei livellatori (1640–1660).* Edizioni dell'Orso, Alessandria, 2008.

Galanter, M. *Cults: Faith, Healing and Coercion*. Oxford University Press, Oxford, 1989.

Galeotti, G. *I movimenti migratori interni in Italia: Analisi statistica e programmi di politica*. Cacucci, Bari, 1971.

Galleni. M., ed. *Rapporto sul terrorismo*. Rizzoli, Milan, 1981.

Galli, Giorgio. *Il partito armato: Gli "anni di piombo" in Italia 1968–1986*. Kaos, Milan, 1993.

———. *Piombo rosso: La storia completa della lotta armata in Italia dal 1970 a oggi*. Piemme, Milan, 2007.

Galli, Giuseppe, ed. *Lewin*. Il Mulino, Bologna, 1977.

Gallinari, P. *Un contadino nella metropoli: Ricordi di un militante delle Brigate rosse*. Bompiani, Milan, 2008.

Garavaglia, G. *Storia dell'Inghilterra moderna: Società, economia e istituzioni da Enrico VII alla rivoluzione industriale*. Cisalpino, Bologna, 1998.

Geller, M. *Il mondo dei lager e la letteratura sovietica*. Edizioni Paoline, Rome, 1977.

Germani, G. *Sociologia della modernizzazione*. Laterza, Bari, 1971.

Geschwender, J. A. "Considerazioni sulla teoria dei movimenti sociali e delle rivoluzioni." In *Movimenti di rivolta: Teorie e forme dell'azione collettiva,* edited by A. Melucci. Etas, Milan, 1976.

Ghirelli, A. *Tiranni: Da Hitler a Pol Pot; Gli uomini che hanno insanguinato il Novecento*. Mondadori, Milan, 2002.

Giddens, A. *Capitalismo e teoria sociale*. Saggiatore, Milan, 2002.

Ginsborg, P. *Storia d'Italia dal dopoguerra a oggi: Società e politica 1943–1988*. 2 vols. Einaudi, Turin, 1989.

Giovagnoli, A. *Il caso Moro: Una tragedia repubblicana*. Il Mulino, Bologna, 2005.

Giovannini, F. *Pol Pot: Una tragedia rossa*. Datanews, Rome, 1998.

Gorman, L., and D. Mclean. *Media e società nel mondo contemporaneo: Una introduzione storica*. Il Mulino, Bologna, 2005.

Gramsci, A. "Ai commissari di reparto delle officine *fiat* centro e brevetti." *L'ordine Nuovo,* 13 September 1919.

———. "Chiarezza, democrazia, ordine." *Avanti!* ed. Piedmontese, 17 October 1919.

———. "Cronache dell'Ordine nuovo.'" *L'ordine Nuovo,* 18 October 1919.

———. "Il partito comunista." *L'ordine nuovo,* 4 September 1920.

———. "Il problema della forza." *Avanti!* ed. Piedmontese, 26 March 1920.

———. "Indifferenti." *La Città futura,* no. 1 (published by the Federazione giovanile socialista piemontese), 11 February 1917.

———. "La compagnia di Gesù." ed. Piedmontese, 9 October 1920.

———. "La conquista dello Stato." *L'ordine nuovo,* 12 July 1919.

———. "La forza della rivoluzione." *L'ordine nuovo,* 8 May 1920.

———. "La settimana politica." *L'ordine nuovo,* 4 October 1919.

———. "La sovranità della legge." *Avanti!* ed. Piedmontese, 1 June 1919.

———. "La taglia della storia." *L'ordine nuovo,* 7 June 1919.

———. *Le opere: La prima antologia di tutti gli scritti*. Edited by A. A. Santucci. Editori Riuniti, Rome, 1997.

———. *L'ordine nuovo: 1919–1920*. Edited by V. Gerratana and A. A. Santucci. Einaudi, Turin, 1987.

——. *L'ordine nuovo.* Einaudi, Turin, 1975.

——. "L'organizzazione capitalista." *Avanti!* ed. Piedmontese, 7 September 1920.

——. "Lo sviluppo della rivoluzione." *L'ordine nuovo,* 13 September 1919.

——. "Operai e contadini." *L'ordine nuovo,* 2 August 1919.

——. *Quaderni dal carcere.* Einaudi, Turin, 1975.

——. "Socialisti e anarchici." *L'ordine nuovo,* 20–27 September 1919.

——. "Valori." *Avanti!* ed. Piedmontese, 13 June 1919.

Gramsci, A., and P. Togliatti. "Democrazia operaia." *L'ordine nuovo,* 21 June 1919.

Grandi, A. *L'ultimo brigatista.* Rizzoli, Milan, 2007.

Graziani, A. *Lo sviluppo dell'economia italiana: Dalla ricostruzione alla moneta europea.* Bollati Boringhieri, Turin, 2001.

Graziani, C. "La guerra rivoluzionaria." *Quaderni di Ordine nuovo,* April 1963.

Greer, D. *The Incidence of the Terror during the French Revolution: A Statistical Interpretation.* Harvard University Press, Cambridge, Mass., 1935.

Guagliardo, V. *Di sconfitta in sconfitta: Considerazioni sull'esperienza brigatista alla luce di una critica del rito del capro espiatorio.* Colibrì, Paderno Dugnano (Mi), 2002.

Guevara, E. C. "Al secondo seminario economico sulla solidarietà afroasiatica di Algeri." 24 February 1965. In *Leggere Che Guevara: Scritti su politica e rivoluzione.* Edited by D. Deutschmann. Feltrinelli, Milan, 2008.

——. "Una nuova cultura del lavoro." 21 August 1962. In *Leggere Che Guevara: Scritti su politica e rivoluzione.* Edited by D. Deutschmann. Feltrinelli, Milan, 2008.

Guicciardi, L. *Il tempo del furore: Il fallimento della lotta armata raccontato dai protagonisti.* Rusconi, Milan, 1988.

Guidelli, G. *Operazione Peci: Storia di un sequestro mediatico.* Quattroventi, Urbino, 2005.

Guillemin, H. *Robespierre politico e mistico.* Garzanti, Milan, 1999.

Guitton, J. *Il puro e l'impuro.* Piemme, Casale Monferrato (al), 1993.

Gurr, T. D. *Why Men Rebel.* Princeton University Press, Princeton, N.J., 1970.

Hall, J. R. *Gone from the Promised Land.* Transaction, New Brunswick, N.J., 1987.

Hall, J. R., and P. Schuyler. "The Mystical Apocalypse of the Solar Temple." In *Millennium, Messiahs and Mayhem,* edited by T. Robbins and S. J. Palmer. Routledge, London, 1997.

Hampson, N. *The Life and Opinions of Maximilien Robespierre.* Duckworth, London, 1974.

——. *Storia sociale della rivoluzione francese.* Lucarini, Rome, 1988.

Hasselbach, I. *Diario di un naziskin.* Il Saggiatore, Milan, 1994.

Heller, M., and A. Nekrich. *Storia dell'Urss: Dal 1917 a Eltsin.* Bompiani, Milan, 2001.

Hess, H. *La rivolta ambigua: Storia sociale del terrorismo italiano.* Sansoni, Florence, 1991.

Hill, C., ed. *I livellatori e la Rivoluzione inglese.* 2 vols. Il Saggiatore, Milan, 1962.

——. *Il mondo alla rovescia.* Einaudi, Turin, 1981.

——. *L'Anticristo nel Seicento inglese.* Edited by P. Adamo. Il Saggiatore, Milan, 1990.

Hobsbawm, E. J. *Il secolo breve: 1914–1991.* Rizzoli, Milan, 1997.

Hoeung, O. T. *Ho creduto nei Khmer rossi: Ripensamento di un'illusione.* Guerini e Associati, Milan, 2004.

Hoffer, E. *The True Believer: Thoughts on the Nature of Mass Movements.* New American Library, New York, 1958.

Hunt, L. *La rivoluzione francese: Politica, cultura, classi sociali*. Il Mulino, Bologna, 1989.

Ignazi, P. *Il polo escluso: Profilo storico del Movimento Sociale Italiano*. Il Mulino, Bologna, 1998.

"In memoria di Lumumba." *L'Unità*, 15 February 1961.

Introvigne, M. *Le sette cristiane: Dai testimoni di Geova al reverendo Moon*. Mondadori, Milan, 1990.

———. "Ordeal by Fire: The Tragedy of the Solar Temple." *Religion* 25, 2 (1995).

Izzo, A. *Storia del pensiero sociologico*. Il Mulino, Bologna, 1994.

Juergensmeyer, Mark. *Terror in the Mind of God: The Global Rise of Religious Violence*. University of California Press, 2003.

Kolakowski, L. *Lo spirito rivoluzionario: Cinque saggi per una filosofia della tolleranza*. Sugarco, Milan, 1982.

Kotek, J., and P. Rigoulot. *Il secolo dei campi: Detenzione, concentramento e sterminio; 1900–2000*. Mondadori, Milan, 2001.

Krueger, Alan B. *What Makes a Terrorist: Economics and the Roots of Terrorism*. Princeton University Press, Princeton, N. J., 2007.

La mappa perduta. Sensibili alle foglie, Dogliani (cn), 2007.

La Rocca, T. *Es ist Zeit: Apocalisse e storia; Studio su Thomas Müntzer (1490–1525)*. Cappelli, Bologna, 1988.

Lacouture, J. *Cambogia: I signori del terrore*. Sansoni, Florence, 1978.

Lanaro, S. *Storia dell'Italia repubblicana: Dalla fine della guerra agli anni novanta*. Marsilio, Venice, 1992.

Laski, H. J. *Le origini del liberalismo europeo*. 1947. La Nuova Italia, Florence, 1962.

Lenci, S. *Colpo alla nuca: Memorie di una vittima del terrorismo*. Il Mulino, Bologna, 2009.

Lenin, V. I. *Che fare?* Editori Riuniti, Rome, 1986.

———. "L'estremismo, malattia infantile del comunismo." In *Opere scelte*. Editori Riuniti, Roma 1955.

———. *Opere complete*. Editori Riuniti, Rome, 1957.

———. *Opere scelte*. Editori Riuniti, Rome, 1970.

———. Quoted in Solzhenitsyn, *Arcipelago Gulag*, vol. 1. Mondadori, Milan, 1975.

Levine, J. M., and R. L. Moreland. "Socialization in Small Groups: Temporal Changes in Individual-Group Relations." In *Advances in Experimental Social Psychology*, vol. 15, edited by L. Berkowitz. Academic Press, New York, 1982.

Lewin, K. "The Conflict between Aristotelian and Galileian Modes of Thought in Contemporary Psychology." *Journal of Genetic Psychology* 8 (1933).

———. *Field Theory in Social Science*. Harper & Row, New York, 1951.

———. "Il conflitto fra una concezione aristotelica ed una concezione galileiana nella psicologia contemporanea." In *Teoria dinamica della personalità*. Universitaria, Florence, 1965.

———. *Teoria e sperimentazione in psicologia sociale*. Il Mulino, Bologna, 1972.

Libertini, L. *Capitalismo moderno e movimento operaio*. Samonà e Savelli, Rome, 1965.

Lomartire, C. M. *Insurrezione: 14 luglio 1948; L'attentato a Togliatti e la tentazione rivoluzionaria*. Mondadori, Milan, 2007.

Longo, L. "Ai cittadini italiani." *Rinascita*, April 1951.

———. "Il movimento studentesco nella lotta anticapitalistica." *Rinascita*, 3 May 1968.

——. "Il nostro capo." *Rinascita,* August 1948.

——. "La risposta del popolo." *Rinascita,* July 1948.

——. "Relazione al Comitato centrale del Pci." *L'Unità,* 21 June 1968.

——. "Riflessioni sugli avvenimenti di Francia." *Rinascita,* 14 June 1968.

——. "Risposta alla Dc." *Rinascita,* 9 February 1968.

——. "Tumulti a Battipaglia." *Il Giorno,* 10 April 1969.

Lortz, J., and E. Iserloh. *Storia della riforma.* Il Mulino, Bologna, 1974.

Lumley, R. *Dal '68 agli anni di piombo: Studenti e operai nella crisi italiana.* Giunti, Florence, 1998.

Lutaud, O. *Winstanley: Socialisme et christianisme sous Cromwell.* Didier, Paris, 1976.

Ly, C. *Ritorno in Cambogia: Un cammino di libertà.* Edizioni Paoline, Milan, 2008.

——. *Tornata dall'inferno: La vicenda sconvolgente di una donna sopravvissuta all'orrore dei Khmer rossi.* Edizioni Paoline, Milan, 2006.

Maaga, M. M. *The Most Intimate Other: Hearing the Voices of Jonestown.* Syracuse University Press, Syracuse, N.Y., 1998.

Mably, G. Bonnot de. "Dubbi proposti ai filosofi economisti sull'ordine naturale delle società politiche." In *Scritti politici.* Vol. 2. Utet, Turin, 1965.

Machiavelli, N. *Il principe.* Edited by P. Melograni. Rizzoli, Milan, 1997.

Magnani, M. "La vera occasione mancata degli anni '60." In *Il progresso economico dell'Italia,* edited by P. Ciocca. Il Mulino, Bologna, 1994.

Magrone, N., and G. Pavese. *Ti ricordi di Piazza Fontana? Vent'anni di storia contemporanea nelle pagine di un processo.* 3 vols. Edizioni dall'Interno, Bari, 1987.

Maier, C. H. "Conti e racconti: Interpretazioni della performance dell'economia italiana dal dopoguerra a oggi." In *Storia economica d'Italia,* vol. 1, edited by P. Ciocca and G. Toniolo. Laterza, Rome and Bari, 1999.

Mainardi, M. "Costituzione impossibile." *Riscossa,* 28 June 1962.

——. *L'ultima battaglia per la libertà.* Edizioni Riscossa, Brescia, 1964.

Manconi, L. *Terroristi italiani: Le Brigate rosse e la guerra totale 1970–2008.* Rizzoli, Milan, 2008.

Maniscalco, M. L. *Spirito di setta e società: Significato e dimensioni sociologiche delle forme settarie.* Franco Angeli, Milan, 1992.

Mannheim, K. *Ideologia e utopia.* Il Mulino, Bologna, 1957.

Manuel, F. E. *Requiem per Carlo Marx.* Il Mulino, Bologna, 1998.

Manzini, G. *Indagine su un brigatista rosso: La storia di Walter Alasia.* Einaudi, Turin, 1978.

Mao Tse-tung. *Rivoluzione e costruzione: Scritti e discorsi 1949–1957.* Einaudi, Turin, 1979.

Maréchal, S. "Manifesto degli eguali." In F. Buonarroti, *Cospirazione dell'eguaglianza detta di Babeuf.* Einaudi, Turin, 1971.

Marino, G. C. *Biografia del Sessantotto: Utopie, conquiste, sbandamenti.* Bompiani, Milan, 2008.

Marletti, C. "Immagini pubbliche e ideologia del terrorismo." In *Dimensioni del terrorismo politico,* edited by L. Bonanate. Franco Angeli, Milan, 1979.

Marrow, A. J. *Kurt Lewin tra teoria e pratica.* La Nuova Italia, Florence, 1977.

——. *The Practical Theorist: The Life and Work of Kurt Lewin.* Basic Books, New York, 1969.

Martinelli, F. *Contadini meridionali nella riviera dei fiori.* N.p., n.d.

Martinelli, R., and M. L. Righi, eds. *La politica del partito comunista italiano nel periodo costituente: I verbali della Direzione tra il 5. e il 6. Congresso 1946–1948.* Editori Riuniti, Rome, 1992.

Martinotti, G. "Le caratteristiche dell'apatia politica." *Quaderni di Sociologia* 3–4 (1966).

Marx, K. *Il 18 brumaio di Luigi Napoleone.* 1852. Editori Riuniti, Rome, 1964.

———. Introduction. *Per la critica della filosofia del diritto di Hegel.* 1843. Editori Riuniti, Rome, 1998.

———. *La questione ebraica.* Editori Riuniti, Rome, 1998.

———. "La soppressione della *Neue Rheinische Zeitung.*" In *Il quarantotto,* by K. Marx and F. Engels. La Nuova Italia, Florence, 1970.

Marx, K., and F. Engels. *L'ideologia tedesca.* 1845–46. Editori Riuniti, Rome, 2000.

———. *Opere complete.* Editori Riuniti, Rome, 1977.

Massari, R. *Il terrorismo: Storia, concetti, metodi.* Massari editore, Bolsena, 2002.

Mathieu, V. *La speranza nella rivoluzione: Saggio fenomenologico.* Armando, Rome, 1992.

Mathiez, A., and G. Lefebvre. *La rivoluzione francese.* 2 vols. Einaudi, Turin, 1952.

Matteucci, N. "La strategia del terrorista." *La Nazione,* 23 February 1978.

Mazzocchi, S. *Nell'anno della tigre: Storia di Adriana Faranda.* Baldini Castoldi, Milan, 1994.

McCauley, M. *Stalin e lo stalinismo.* Il Mulino, Bologna, 2004.

McLynn, F. *Villa e Zapata: Una biografia della rivoluzione messicana.* Il Saggiatore, Milan, 2006.

Mead, G. H. *Mente, sé e società.* Editrice Universitaria, Florence, 1965.

———. *Mind, Self and Society.* Open Court, Chicago, 1934.

Melograni, P., ed. *Il principe,* by N. Machiavelli. Rizzoli, Milan, 1997.

Melotti, U. *Rivoluzione e società.* La culturale, Milan, 1965.

Melton, J. G. "Violence and the Cults." *Nebraska Humanist* 8 (1985).

Memorie dalla clandestinità: Un terrorista non pentito si racconta. Cairo, Milan, 2006.

Meneghetti, L. *Aspetti di geografia della popolazione: Italia 1951–67.* Clup, Milan, 1971.

Merton, R. K. *Teoria e struttura sociale.* 3 vols. Il Mulino, Bologna, 2000.

Michelet, J. *Storia della Rivoluzione francese.* Vol. 4. Rizzoli, Milan, 1981.

Michels, R. *La sociologia del partito politico nella democrazia moderna.* Il Mulino, Bologna, 1966.

Miegge, M. *Il sogno del re di babilonia: Profezia storica da Thomas Müntzer a Isaac Newton.* Feltrinelli, Milan, 1995.

Mills, E. W., Jr. "Cult Extremism: The Reduction of Normative Dissonance." In *Violence and Religious Commitment,* edited by K. Levi. Pennsylvania State University Press, University Park, 1982.

Ming, C. *Nubi nere s'addensano: L'autobiografia clandestina di un sopravvissuto alla persecuzione.* Marsilio, Venice, 2006.

Minna, R. "Il terrorismo di destra." In *Terrorismi in Italia: Contributi di G. Caselli,* edited by D. Della Porta. Il Mulino, Bologna, 1984.

Montanelli, I. *Storia d'Italia.* Vol. 11, *1965–1993.* Rizzoli, Milan, 2004.

Monteleone, F. *Storia della radio e della televisione in Italia: Un secolo di suoni e di immagini.* Marsilio, Padua, 1992.

Moravia, A. "Lettera a Pier Paolo Pasolini." *L'Espresso,* 23 June 1974.

Morelly. *Codice della natura.* Edited by E. Piscitelli. Einaudi, Turin, 1975.

Moretti, M. *Brigate rosse. Una storia italiana; Intervista di Carla Mosca e Rossana Rossanda.* Mondadori, Milan, 2007.

Morgenthau, H. J. *Politica tra le nazioni: La lotta per il potere e la pace.* Il Mulino, Bologna, 1997.

Morucci, V. *A guerra finita: Sei racconti.* Il Manifestolibri, Rome, 1994.

——. *La peggio gioventù: Una vita nella lotta armata.* Rizzoli, Milan, 2004.

——. *Ritratto di un terrorista da giovane.* Piemme, Casale Monferrato, 1999.

Mosca, G. "Elementi di scienza politica." In *Scritti politici.* Edited by G. Sola. 2 vols. Utet, Turin, 1982.

Mottura, G., and E. Pugliese. "Mercato del lavoro e caratteristiche della emigrazione italiana nell'ultimo quinquennio." In *Sviluppo economico italiano e forza lavoro,* edited by P. Leon and M. Marocchi. Venice, 1973.

"Mozione finale dell'viii Congresso del Msi." In *L'alternativa in movimento.* Edizioni Nuove Prospettive, Villa S. Lucia, 1984.

Müntzer, T. "Manifesto di Praga." In *Scritti politici.* Edited by E. Campi. Claudiana, Turin, 1972.

Natta, A. "Università da cambiare." *Rinascita,* 15 March 1968.

Negarville, C. "Crociata per la libertà." *Rinascita,* February 1951.

Niebuhr, R. *Uomo morale e società immorale.* 1932. Jaca Book, Milan, 1968.

Nietzsche, F. W. *Genealogia della morale.* Newton Compton, Rome, 1992.

Nomand, M. *Apostles of Revolution.* Collier Books, New York, 1961.

"Nous sommes si nous marchons." *Anno Zero,* 20 March 1974.

Novelli, D., and N. Tranfaglia. *Vite sospese: Le generazioni del terrorismo.* Rizzoli, Milan, 2007.

Occhetto, A. "Cambiare o continuare?" *Rinascita,* 26 April 1968.

——. "Il voto comunista." *Rinascita,* 17 May 1968.

——. "Insurrezione e via democratica." *Rinascita,* 21 June 1968.

——. "Sul movimento studentesco." *Rinascita,* 21 June 1968.

——. "Sulla trasformazione della società." *L'Unità,* 21 November 1976.

——. "Una nuova generazione." *L'Unità,* 17 March 1968.

Ogburn, W. F. *Social Change with Respect to Culture and Original Nature.* 1922. Bell, New York, 1922.

——. *Tecnologia e mutamento sociale.* Edited by G. Iorio. Armando, Rome, 2006.

Oishi, Y. *La mia Cambogia: La drammatica testimonianza di una fotografa reporter nel tormentato paese asiatico dal 1980 ai giorni d'oggi.* Fenice 2000, Milan, 1994.

Orsello, G. P. "I socialisti e l'università." *Avanti!* 1 March 1968.

Orsini, A. *Le origini del capitalismo: Storia e interpretazioni.* Costantino Marco, Lungro di Cosenza, 2008.

——. "Mutamento sociale e relazioni internazionali: Il realismo politico e il problema della guerra." In *Aspetti del mutamento sociale contemporaneo,* edited by A. Agustoni. Aracne, Rome, 2008.

——. "Sociologia politica e scienza politica: I due paradigmi." In *Quaderni di Scienza Politica* 2 and 3 (August–December 2006).

Ortega y Gasset, J. "La ribellione delle masse." In *Scritti politici.* Edited by L. Pellicani. Utet, Turin, 1979.

———. *Una interpretazione della storia universale.* Sugarco, Milan, 1978.

Ossicini, A. *Kurt Lewin e la psicologia moderna.* Armando, Rome, 1972.

Ostrogorski, M. *Democrazia e partiti politici.* Edited by G. Quagliariello. Rusconi, Milan, 1991.

Pace, E. *Le sette.* Il Mulino, Bologna, 1997.

Paci, M. *Mercato del lavoro e classi sociali in Italia: Ricerche sulla composizione del proletariato.* Il Mulino, Bologna, 1975.

Palmer, S. J. "Purity and Danger in the Solar Temple." *Journal of Contemporary Religion* 11, 3 (1996).

Palmer, S. J., and N. Finn. "Coping with Apocalypse in Canada: Experiences of Endtime in 'La Mission de l'Esprit Saint' and the Institute of Applied Metaphysics." *Sociological Analysis* 53, 4 (1992).

Panh, R., and C. Chaumeau. *S-21: La macchina di morte dei Khmer rossi.* O barra o edizioni, Milan, 2004.

Pansa, G. "Annarumma." In *Le bombe di Milano.* Guanda, Parma, 1970.

———. *L'utopia armata: Come è nato il terrorismo in Italia.* Mondadori, Milan, 1992.

Parinetto, L. *La rivolta del diavolo: Müntzer, Lutero e la rivolta dei contadini in Germania e altri saggi.* Rusconi, Santarcangelo di Romagna, 1999.

Parlato, G. "Saggio introduttivo" to J. Evola, *Fascismo e Terzo Reich* (1964). Edizioni Mediterranee, Rome, 2001.

Pasolini, P. P. "Gli italiani non sono più quelli." *Corriere della Sera,* 10 June 1974.

Pasqualini, J. *Prisonnier de Mao.* Gallimard, Paris, 1977.

Pasquino, G. "Sistema politico bloccato e insorgenza del terrorismo: Ipotesi e prime verifiche." In *La prova delle armi.* Il Mulino, Bologna, 1984.

Pavolini, L. "Francia all'opposizione." *Rinascita,* 7 June 1968.

———. "La via di Togliatti." *Rinascita,* 29 March 1968.

Pavone, C. "La continuità dello Stato: Istituzioni e uomini." In *Italia, 1945–1948: Le origini della Repubblica.* Giappichelli, Turin, 1974.

Peci, P. *Io, l'infame.* Edited by Giordano Bruno Guerri. Mondadori, Milan, 1983.

———. "Lettera dal carcere delle Br." *Lotta Continua,* 30 July 1981.

Pelayo, M. G. *Miti e simboli politici.* Borla, Turin, 1970.

Pellicani, L., "Capitalismo, modernizzazione, rivoluzione." In *Sociologia delle rivoluzioni,"* edited by L. Pellicani. Guida, Naples, 1976.

———. *Dalla società chiusa alla società aperta.* Rubbettino, Soveria Mannelli, 2002.

———. *Dinamica delle rivoluzioni: Il ruolo delle guerre di classe nella nascita del mondo moderno.* Sugarco, Milan, 1974.

———. *Il mercato e i socialismi.* Sugarco, Milan, 1979.

———. Introduction. In *L'uomo e la gente,* by J. Ortega y Gasset. Armando, Rome, 2001.

———. *I rivoluzionari di professione.* Franco Angeli, Milan, 2008.

———. *I rivoluzionari di professione.* Vallecchi, Florence, 1975.

———. *La genesi del capitalismo e le origini della modernità.* Costantino Marco, Lungro di Cosenza, 2006. (See also *The Genesis of Capitalism and the Origin of Modernity.* Telos Press, New York, 1994).

——. "La rivoluzione cambogiana." In *Rivoluzione e totalitarismo.* Costantino Marco, Lungro di Cosenza, 2004.

——. *Lenin e Hitler: I due volti del totalitarismo.* Rubbettino, Soveria Mannelli, 2009.

——. *Miseria del marxismo: Da Marx al Gulag.* Sugarco, Milan, 1984.

——. *Revolutionary Apocalypse: Ideological Roots of Terrorism.* Praeger, Westport, Conn., 2003.

——, ed. *Sociologia delle rivoluzioni.* Guida, Naples, 1976.

Pergolizzi, P. *L'appartamento: Br; Dal Pci alla lotta armata.* Aliberti, Reggio Emilia, 2006.

Perry, J. W. *La dimensione nascosta della follia.* Liguori, Naples, 1980.

Petri, R. *Storia economica d'Italia: Dalla Grande guerra al miracolo economico (1918–1963).* Il Mulino, Bologna, 2002.

Petruccioli, C. "Caduto in una battaglia che non ha frontiere." *Rinascita,* 20 October 1967.

——. "Dentro le aule e fuori." *Rinascita,* 16 February 1968.

——. "La spinta dei giovani." *Rinascita,* 31 May 1968.

——. "Studenti: Come andare avanti." *Rinascita,* 12 April 1968.

Petter, G. Introduction to K. Lewin, *Teoria dinamica della personalità,* edited by G. Petter. Universitaria, Florence, 1965.

Pipes, R. *Il regime bolscevico: Dal terrore rosso alla morte di Lenin.* Mondadori, Milan, 2000.

Pisano, I. *Io terrorista: Parlano i protagonisti.* Marco Tropea Editore, Milan, 2004.

Pisetta, E. "Per una storia del terrorismo nero." *Il Mulino* 289 (1983).

Pizzorno, A. *Le radici della politica assoluta.* Feltrinelli, Milan, 1993.

——. "Mutamenti nelle istituzioni rappresentative e sviluppo dei partiti politici." In *Storia d'Europa: L'età contemporanea.* Vol. 5. Einaudi, Turin, 1996.

Plato. *La Repubblica.* In *Opere.* Vol. 2. Laterza, Rome and Bari, 1974.

Platone, F. "Stato di polizia." *Rinascita,* June 1948.

——. "Trent'anni." *Rinascita,* January 1951.

Poggio, P. P. "Il difficile rapporto tra intellettuali e popolo nel lungo Novecento." *Agalma: Rivista di studi culturali e di estetica* 15 (March 2008).

Polanyi, K. *La grande trasformazione: Le origini economiche e politiche della nostra epoca.* Einaudi, Turin, 2000.

Polo, G. *I tamburi di Mirafiori: Testimonianze operaie attorno all'autunno caldo alla FIAT.* CRIC, Turin, 1989.

Popper, K. *La società aperta e i suoi nemici.* 2 vols. Armando, Rome, 1996.

Pons, S. *L'egemonia impossibile: L'Urss, il Pci e le origini della guerra fredda (1943–1948).* Carocci, Rome, 1999.

Pozzi, E. *Il carisma malato: Il People's temple e il suicidio collettivo di Jonestown.* Liguori, Naples, 1992.

Progetto memoria: La mappa perduta. Sensibili alle foglie, Dogliani, 2007.

Prosperi, A., and P. Viola. *Storia moderna e contemporanea: Dalla Rivoluzione inglese alla Rivoluzione francese.* 4 vols. Einaudi, Turin, 2000.

Rao, N. *Il sangue e la celtica: Dalle vendette antipartigiane alla strategia della tensione; Storia armata del neofascismo.* Sperling & Kupfer, Milan, 2008.

Reck-Malleczewen, F. P. *Il re degli anabattisti: Storia di una rivoluzione moderna.* Rusconi, Milan, 1971.

Regalia, I., M. Regini, and E. Reyneri. "Conflitti di lavoro e relazioni industriali in Italia." In *Conflitti in Europa: Lotte di classe, sindacati e Stato dopo il '68,* edited by C. Crouch and A. Pizzorno. Etas, Milan, 1977.

Reineri, E. "Il 'maggio strisciante': L'inizio della mobilitazione operaia." In *Lotte operaie e sindacato in Italia.* Il Mulino, Bologna, 1978.

Reiterman, T. *Raven: The Untold Story of Rev. Jim Jones and His People.* With J. Jacobs. Dutton, New York, 1982.

Ries, J., ed. *I riti di iniziazione.* Jaca Book, Milan, 1989.

Ro, M. "La brutale irruzione poliziesca nell'ateneo romano." *L'Unità,* 1 March 1968.

Robbins, T., and D. Anthony. "Sects and Violence: Factors Enhancing the Volatility of Marginal Religious Movements." In *Armageddon in Waco: Critical Perspectives on the Branch Davidian Conflict,* edited by S. A. Wright. University of Chicago Press, Chicago, 1995.

Roberts, J. A. G. *Storia della Cina.* Il Mulino, Bologna, 2007.

Robespierre, M. *La rivoluzione giacobina.* Editori Riuniti, Rome, 1967.

Rodari, A. "La rivolta degli studenti." *L'Unità,* 3 March 1968.

Rokeach. M. *The Open and Closed Mind: Investigations into the Nature of Belief Systems and Personality Systems.* Basic Books, New York, 1960.

——. "Political and Religious Dogmatism: An Alternative to the Authoritarian Personality." *Psychological Monographs* 70 (1956).

Rossanda, R. "Il discorso sulla Dc." *Il Manifesto,* 28 March 1978.

Rossi, G. S. *Il razzista totalitario: Evola e la leggenda dell'antisemitismo spirituale.* Rubbettino, Soveria Mannelli, 2007.

Rossi, J. *Le manuel du goulag.* Le Cherche-Midi, Paris, 1996.

Rousseau, J.-J. *Il contratto sociale.* In *Scritti politici.* Utet, Turin, 1970.

——. *Origine della disuguaglianza.* Edited by G. Preti. Feltrinelli, Milan, 1997.

——. "Progetto di Costituzione per la Corsica." In *Scritti politici.* Utet, Turin, 1970.

——. "Rousseau giudice di Jean-Jacques." In *Opere.* Sansoni, Florence, 1988.

Ruggiero, L., ed. *Dossier Brigate rosse 1969–1975: La lotta armata nei documenti e nei comunicati delle prime Br.* Kaos, Milan, n.d.

——. *Dossier Brigate rosse 1976–1978: Le Br sanguinarie di Moretti; Documenti, comunicati e censure.* Kaos, Milan, 2007.

Rummel, R. J. *Stati assassini: La violenza omicida dei governi.* Rubbettino, Soveria Mannelli, 2005.

Runciman, W. G. *Relative Deprivation and Social Justice.* University of California Press, Berkeley, 1966.

Rutigliano, E. *Teorie sociologiche classiche.* Bollati Boringhieri, Turin, 2002.

Sabine, G. H. *Storia delle dottrine politiche.* Edizioni di Comunità, Milan, 1953.

Šafarevič, I. *Il socialismo come fenomeno storico mondiale.* Effedieffe, Milan, 1999.

Saint-Just, L. A. de. *Terrore e libertà.* Editori Riuniti, Rome, 1966.

Salierno, G. *Autobiografia di un picchiatore fascista.* 1976. Edizioni minimum fax, Rome, 2008.

Salvadori, M. L. *Storia dell'età contemporanea: Dalla restaurazione all'eurocomunismo.* Loescher, Turin, 1977.

Salvati, M. "Effetti reali o nominali della svalutazione? Commento all'articolo di Andreatta e D'Adda." *Politica economica* 2 (1985).

Sartori, G. *Democrazia: Cosa è?* Rizzoli, Milan, 1997.

Schiavone, G. *Winstanley: Il profeta della rivoluzione inglese.* Dedalo, Bari, 1990.

Schmalenbach, H. *La categoria sociologica del Bund: Comunità, società e sodalità.* 1922. Edited by A. Vitiello. Ipermedium libri, S. Maria C.V. (Ce), 2006.

Schumpeter, J. A. *Capitalismo, socialismo, democrazia.* Comunità, Milan, 1964.

———. *Teoria dello sviluppo economico.* Sansoni, Florence, 1971.

Scoppola, P. *La Repubblica dei partiti: Evoluzione crisi di un sistema politico 1945–1996.* Il Mulino, Bologna, 1997.

Segio, S. *Una vita in prima linea.* Rizzoli, Milan, 2006.

Sémelin, J. *Purificare e distruggere: Usi politici dei massacri e dei genocidi.* Einaudi, Turin, 2007.

Senzani, G. *L'esclusione anticipata: Rapporto da 118 case di rieducazione per minorenni.* Jaca Book, Milan, 1973.

Service, R. *L'uomo, il leader, il mito.* Mondadori, Milan, 2001.

Servier, J. *Le terrorisme.* Puf, Paris, 1979.

Settembrini, D. *Il labirinto rivoluzionario: L'idea anarchica; L'impatto con la realtà 1917–1978.* 2 vols. Rizzoli, Milan, 1979.

———. "Il Pci e la violenza rivoluzionaria." In *Socialismo, marxismo e mercato: Per un bilancio dell'idea socialista.* Marco, Lungro di Cosenza.

———. *Socialismo e rivoluzione dopo Marx.* Guida, Naples, 1974.

Shalamov, V. *Racconti di Kolyma.* Einaudi, Turin, 1999.

Short, P. *Mao: L'uomo, il rivoluzionario, il tiranno.* Rizzoli, Milan, 2006.

———. *Pol Pot: Anatomia di uno sterminio.* Rizzoli, Milan, 2005.

Silj, A. *Mai più senza fucile.* Vallecchi, Florence, 1977.

Simmel, G. *La differenziazione sociale.* Edited by B. Accarino. Laterza, Rome and Bari, 1982.

———. *Sociologia.* Comunità, Milan, 1998.

Sinclair, A. *Storia del terrorismo.* Newton Compton, Rome, 2003.

Smelser, N. J. *Il comportamento collettivo.* Vallecchi, Florence, 1968.

———. *Manuale di sociologia.* Il Mulino, Bologna, 1984.

Soboul, A. *La rivoluzione francese.* Newton Compton, Rome, 1988.

Sola, G. *I paradigmi della scienza politica.* Il Mulino, Bologna, 2005.

Solzhenitsyn, A. *Arcipelago Gulag.* Mondadori, Milan, 1975.

Sopravvissuto dalla Cambogia: Il protagonista, Someth May, narra l'infernale vita nella Cambogia di Pol Pot e nei campi di lavoro dei Khmer rossi. De Agostini, Novara, 1989.

Sossi, M. *Nella prigione delle Br.* Editoriale Nuova, Milan, 1975.

Speltini, G., and A. Palmonari. *I gruppi sociali.* Il Mulino, Bologna, 2007.

Spriano, P. "L'Italia disse no." *L'Unità,* 13 July 1968.

Stajano, C. *Il sovversivo: L'Italia nichilista; Storie di una società ferita.* Einaudi, Turin, 1992.

Stark, R., and W. S. Bainbridge. *The Future of Religion: Secularization, Revival and Cult Formation.* University of California Press, Berkeley, 1985.

———. "Scientology: To Be Perfectly Clear." *Sociological Analysis* 41, 2 (1980).

Stark, W. *The Sociology of Religion: A Study of Christendom.* Routledge and Kegan Paul, London 1967.

Steinhoff, P., "Death by Defeatism and Other Fables: The Social Dynamics of the Rengo Sekigun Purge." In *Japanese Social Organization,* edited by Takie Sugiyama Lebra. University of Hawaii Press, Honolulu, 1992.

Stern, Jessica. *Terror in the Name of God: Why Religious Militants Kill.* Harper Collins, New York, 2003.

Sternberger, D. *Le tre radici della politica.* Il Mulino, Bologna, 2001.

Stoppino, M. *Potere e teoria politica.* Giuffrè, Milan, 2001.

Stouffer, S. A. *The American Soldier.* Princeton University Press, Princeton, N. J., 1949.

Strada, V. *Etica del terrore: Da Fëdor Dostoevskij a Thomas Mann.* Liberal edizioni, Rome, 2008.

"Sugli scontri di Valle Giulia." *L'Unità,* 1 March 1968.

"Sugli scontri di Valle Giulia: Resoconto della Segreteria nazionale del Psi." *Avanti!* 6 March 1968.

"Sugli scontri in Parlamento." *L'Unità,* 30 April 1966.

"Sulla nostra politica." *Rinascita,* September–October 1948.

"Sulla protesta studentesca." *L'Unità,* 8 March 1968.

"Sull'arresto di Jordi Sole-Tura." *L'Unità,* 12 March 1968.

"Sulle violenze della polizia contro gli studenti." *L'Unità,* 2 March 1968.

Sullivan, L. E. "'No Longer the Messiah': U.S. Federal Law Enforcement Views of Religion in Connection with the 1993 Siege Mount Carmel near Waco, Texas." *Numen* 43, 2 (1996).

"Sul terrorismo irlandese." *L'Unità,* 1 February 1972.

Suyin, H. *Mao Tsetung: Una vita per la rivoluzione.* Bompiani, Milan, 1972.

Szamuely, T. *The Russian Tradition.* Fontana, London, 1988.

Tabor, J., and E. Gallagher. *Why Waco?* University of California Press, Berkeley, 1995.

Tagliente, G., and S. Mensurati. *Il FUAN: Trent'anni di presenza politica all'Università.* Edizioni Atheneum, Rome, 1982.

Taine, H. *Le origini della Francia contemporanea.* Treves, Milan, 1930.

Talmon, J. *The Origins of Totalitarian Democracy.* Mercury Books, London, 1961.

Tarrow, S. *Democrazia e disordine: Movimenti di protesta e politica in Italia 1965–1975.* Laterza, Rome and Bari, 1990.

Teodori, M. *Storia delle nuove sinistre in Europa (1956–1976).* Il Mulino, Bologna, 1976.

Tessandori, V. *Br. imputazione: Banda armata.* Baldini Castoldi Dalai, Milan, 2004.

Tetlock, P. E. "Cognitive Style and Political Belief Systems in the British House of Commons." *Journal of Personality and Social Psychology* 31 (1975).

Thiers, A. *Storia della rivoluzione francese.* Dall'Oglio, Milan, 1965.

Togliatti, P. "Governo anticomunista." *Rinascita,* March 1950.

———. "Intervento al Comitato Centrale del pci." *L'Unità,* 12 June 1958.

———. "Le decisioni del xx congresso e il Partito socialista italiano." *Rinascita,* October 1958.

———. "Piano del lavoro." *Rinascita,* February 1950.

———. *Opere.* Editori Riuniti, Rome, 1967.

———. "Tentazioni e minacce." *Rinascita,* June 1949.

Tönnies, F. *Comunità e società.* Edizioni di Comunità, Milan, 1963.

Topitsch, E. *Per una critica del marxismo.* Bulzoni, Rome, 1977.

Toynbee, A. J. *A Study of History.* Vol. 5. Oxford University Press, London 1962.

Trentin, B. *Autunno caldo: Il secondo biennio rosso 1968–1969.* Editori Riuniti, Rome, 1999.

——. *Da sfruttati a produttori: Lotte operaie e sviluppo capitalistico dal miracolo economico alla crisi.* De Donato, Bari, 1977.

Trockij, L. *Giacobinismo e socialdemocrazia.* In *Che fare?* by V. I. Lenin. Einaudi, Torino, 1971.

Troeltsch, E. *Le dottrine sociali delle chiese e dei gruppi cristiani.* 2 vols. La Nuova Italia, Florence, 1941.

Trotsky, L. *La rivoluzione tradita.* A. C. Editoriale, Milan, 2000.

——. *Storia della rivoluzione russa.* Sugarco, Milan, 1967.

Vacca, G. "Il problema storico del terrorismo in Italia." Preface to *L'appartamento: Br; dal Pci alla lotta armata,* by P. Pergolizzi. Aliberti, Reggio Emilia, 2006.

——. *Saggio su Togliatti.* De Donato, Bari, 1974.

Valentinov, N. *I miei colloqui con Lenin.* Il Saggiatore, Milan, 1968.

Veblen, T. *La teoria della classe agiata.* Einaudi, Turin, 1999.

Venturi, F. *Il populismo russo: Herzen, Bakunin, Chernyshevskij.* Vol. 1. Einaudi, Turin, 1977.

Visalberghi, A. "Cosa fare per l'università." *Avanti!* 5 March 1968.

Voegelin, E. *Il mito del mondo nuovo: Saggi sui movimenti rivoluzionari del nostro tempo.* Rusconi, Milan, 1970.

Voltaire. *Saggio sui costumi e lo spirito delle nazioni.* Vol 4. De Agostini, Novara, 1967.

Vovelle, M. *La mentalità rivoluzionaria.* Laterza, Rome and Bari, 1999.

Walzer, M. *La rivoluzione dei santi: Il puritanesimo alle origini del radicalismo politico.* Claudiana, Torino 1996.

Weber, M. *Economia e società.* 4 vols. Edizioni di Comunità, Milan, 1999.

——. *La politica come professione.* Edizioni di Comunità, Turin, 2001.

——. *L'etica protestante e lo spirito del capitalismo.* Rizzoli, Milan, 2002.

Webster, C., ed. *The Intellectual Revolution of the Seventeenth Century.* Routledge & Kegan Paul, London, 1974.

Werth, N. "Violenze, repressioni, terrori nell'Unione Sovietica." In *Il libro nero del comunismo: Crimini, terrore, repressione.* Mondadori, Milan, 2000.

Wheen, F. *Marx: Vita pubblica e privata.* Mondadori, Milan, 2000.

Wilson, B. *Religious Sects: A Sociological Study.* Weidenfeld & Nicolson, London, 1970.

Winstanley, G. *The Works: With an Appendix of Documents Relating to the Digger Movement.* Edited by George H. Sabine. Russell & Russell, New York, 1965.

Wright, S. A. "Another View of the Mt. Carmel Standoff." In *Armageddon in Waco: Critical Perspectives on the Branch Davidian Conflict,* edited by Wright. University of Chicago Press, Chicago, 1995.

Wu, H. *Controrivoluzionario: I miei anni nei gulag cinesi.* San Paolo, Cinisello Balsamo, 2008.

Xiaoling, W. *L'allodola e il drago: Sopravvissuta nei gulag della Cina.* Piemme, Casale Monferrato, 1993.

Yathay, P. *L'utopie meurtrière: Un rescape du genocide cambodgien temoigne.* Robert Laffont, Paris, 1980.

Yi, Tan Kim Pho. *Cambodge des Khmers Rouges: Chronique de la vie quotidienne.* Editions L'Harmattan, Paris, 1990.

Yinger, J. M., ed. *The Scientific Study of Religion.* Macmillan, New York, 1970.

Zamagni, V. *Storia economica dell'Italia.* Il Mulino, Bologna, 2007.

———. "Un'analisi critica del 'miracolo economico' italiano: Nuovi mercati e tecnologia americana." In *L'Italia e la politica di potenza in Europa 1950–1960,* edited by A. Di Nolfo, T. H. Rainero, and B. Vigezzi. Edizioni Marzorati, Milan, 1992.

Zaslavsky, V. *Pulizia di classe: Il massacro di Katyn.* Il Mulino, Bologna, 2006.

Zavoli, S. *La notte della Repubblica.* Mondadori, Milan, 1995.

Brigadist Documents

Unless indicated otherwise, these brigadist documents appear in *Dossier Brigate rosse 1969–1975: La lotta armata nei documenti e nei comunicati delle Br (1969–1978).* 2 vols. Edited by L. Ruggiero. Kaos, Milan, n.d.

Autointervista. Opuscolo Br, September 1971.

Brigata rossa Pirelli. Comunicato no. 6. Volantino brigatista, 5 February 1971.

Cagol, M. *Lettera ai genitori* (Letter to her parents), 18 September 1974.

———. *Lettera alla madre* (Letter to her mother), 1969.

"Classe contro classe: guerra di classe." Enclosure with *Brigate rosse: Giornale comunista rivoluzionario proletario,* Milan, 1971.

"Comunicato congiunto Br-Nap." *Controinformazione,* no. 7–8, June 1976.

Comunicato di esproprio a Lonigo. Comunicato brigatista, 14 July 1975.

Comunicato no. 1—Campagna D'Urso (see www.brigaterosse.org).

Comunicato no. 2—Campagna D'Urso. Documento brigatista of 15 December 1980 (www.brigaterosse.org).

Comunicato no. 4—Campagna D'Urso. Documento brigatista of 23 December 1980 (www.brigaterosse.org).

Comunicato no. 5—Campagna D'Urso. Documento brigatista, 28 December 1980 (www.brigaterosse.org).

Comunicato no. 10—Campagna D'Urso. Documento brigatista, 14 January 1981 (www.brigaterosse.org).

Comunicato per la liberazione di Curcio. Documento brigatista in *Corriere della Sera,* 21 February 1975.

Comunicato per la morte di Mara Cagol. Documento brigatista, 5 June 1975 in *Corriere della Sera,* 7 June 1975.

Contro il neogollismo portare l'attacco al cuore dello Stato. Documento brigatista, April 1974.

Curcio, R. "L'ultrarevisionismo." *Controinformazione,* no. 7–8, 1976.

Diario di lotta: Tribunali speciali di Bologna, Torino, Milano. Documento brigatista of September 1977.

"Documento di riflessione interna." *Brigate rosse,* no. 1, June 1975.

Emancipazione della donna? Volantino brigatista, March 1970.

Fogli di lotta di Sinistra proletaria, July–October 1970.

Forza di massa. Volantino brigatista, 18 December 1972.

"Giornale 'Brigate rosse' no. 2. Br di Roma." *Brigate rosse* no. 2, May 1971.

Il voto non paga, prendiamo il fucile! Documento brigatista, April 1972.

Interrogatorio del detenuto Mario Sossi arrestato da un nucleo armato delle Brigate rosse condotto in un carcere del popolo. Partial document published in the weekly *Panorama,* 10 July 1975.

La campagna di primavera. Documento brigatista, March 1979 (www.brigaterosse. org).

Lettera aperta al processo di Bologna. Documento brigatista in *Controinformazione* no. 9–10, November 1977.

"Lettera di Roberto Peci dal carcere delle Br." *Lotta Continua,* 30 July 1981.

Lotta sociale e organizzazione nella metropoli. Documento brigatista, autumn 1969.

Norme di sicurezza e stile di lavoro. Documento interno brigatista, date believed to be 1974.

Opuscolo Brigate rosse no. 4. Attaccare, colpire, liquidare e disperdere la Democrazia cristiana, asse portante della ristrutturazione dello Stato e della controrivoluzione imperialista. Risoluzione della direzione strategica delle Brigate rosse. November 1977.

Processo di Milano. Comunicato Br no. 1. Documento brigatista, 15 June 1977.

Processo di Milano. Comunicato Br no. 2. Documento brigatista, 20 June 1977.

Processo di Torino. Documento brigatista, 3 May 1977.

Risoluzione della direzione strategica. Documento brigatista, April 1975.

Rivendicazione assalto sede Associazione piccola industria di Torino, 4 January 1976. Documento della formazione rivoluzionaria Prima Linea (Document on the formation of the revolutionary organization Prima Linea).

Rivendicazione assassinio di Padova. Brigadist leaflet reproduced in *Paese Sera,* 19 June 1974.

Rivendicazione attentati a Brescia. Brigadist leaflet in *Controinformazione* no. 7–8, June 1976.

Rivendicazione attentati a Roma. Communiqué disseminated in Rome by the Red Brigades, 27 April 1978.

Rivendicazione attentato all'ispettorato carceri. Communiqué published in *Controinformazione* no. 7–8, June 1976.

Rivendicazione attentato Borello. In *Controinformazione,* no. 7–8, June 1976.

Rivendicazione attentato Cacciafesta. Documento brigatista, 21 June 1977.

Rivendicazione attentato Traversi. Documento brigatista, 13 February 1977.

Rivendicazione delitto Casalegno. Comunicato brigatista, 16 November 1977.

Rivendicazione delitto Coco. Documento brigatista, 8 June 1976.

Rivendicazione del sequestro Labate. Documento brigatista, 12 February 1973.

Rivendicazione del sequestro Macchiarini. Documento brigatista, 3 March 1972.

Rivendicazione ferimento consulente Ministero del Lavoro—Gino Giugni. Documento delle Brigate rosse—Partito Comunista Combattente, 3 May 1983 (www. brigaterosse.org).

Rivendicazione ferimento Rossi. Purported Brigadist leaflet, published in *Il Messaggero,* 4 June 1977.

Rivendicazione incendio auto. Volantino brigatista, 15 January 1972.

Rivendicazione irruzione nella sede di "Iniziativa democratica." *Corriere della Sera,* 16 May 1975.

Rivendicazione omicidio Biagi. Documento brigatista, March 2002 (www.brigaterosse. org).

Rivendicazione omicidio docente di Economia politica—Ezio Tarantelli. Documento brigatista, 27 March 1985 (www.brigaterosse.org).

Rivendicazione omicidio ex sindaco di Firenze—Lando Conti. Documento delle Brigate rosse Partito Comunista Combattente (br-pcc) of 10 February 1986 (www. brigaterosse.org).

Rivendicazione omicidio Generale USA—Ray Leamon Hunt. Documento brigatista, 15 February 1982 (www.brigaterosse.org).

Rivendicazione omicidio Marco Biagi. Documento brigatista of 19 March 2002 (www. brigaterosse.org).

Rivendicazione omicidio operaio comunista Italsider di Genova—Guido Rossa, 24 January 1979 (www.brigaterosse.org).

Rivendicazione sequestro Amerio—Comunicato no. 1. Documento brigatista, 10 December 1973.

Rivendicazione sequestro Sossi—Comunicato no. 1. Documento brigatista in *Il Messaggero,* 20 April 1974.

Rivendicazione sequestro Sossi—Comunicato no. 8. Documento brigatista, 23 May 1974, in *Il Giornale d'Italia,* 24–25 May 1974.

Rivendicazione sequestro Taliercio. Documento brigatista, 11 June 1981.

Scelte di campo. Comunicato brigatista, 30 March 1972.

Schiacciamo i fascisti a Mirafiori e Rivalta! Cacciamoli dalle nostre fabbriche e dai nostri quartieri. Volantino brigatista, 26 November 1972.

Sequestro Moro. Comunicato Br no. 1. Documento brigatista, 18 March 1978.

Sequestro Moro. Comunicato Br no. 2. Documento brigatista, 25 March 1978.

Sequestro Moro. Comunicato Br no. 3. Documento brigatista, 29 March 1978.

Sequestro Moro. Comunicato Br no. 4. Documento brigatista, 4 April 1978.

Sequestro Moro. Comunicato Br no. 5. Documento brigatista, 10 April 1978.

Sequestro Moro. Comunicato Br no. 6. Documento brigatista, 15 April 1978.

Sequestro Moro. Comunicato Br no. 7. Documento brigatista, 20 April 1978.

Sequestro Moro. Comunicato Br no. 8. Documento brigatista, 24 April 1978.

Sequestro Moro. Comunicato Br no. 9. Documento brigatista, 5 May 1978.

Sequestro Peci. Comunicato no. 5. In *Lotta Continua,* 30 July 1981.

Un destino perfido. Documento brigatista, November 1971.

Volantino di commemorazione dei quattro militanti uccisi in Via Fracchia a Genova. Documento brigatista of 29 March 1980 (www.brigaterosse.org).

INDEX OF NAMES

Acquaviva, Sabino, 7n44, 104
Adinolfi, Gabriele, 270
Adornato, Ferdinando, 148
Alasia, Walter, 260–61
Alberoni, Francesco, 76, 107
Alibrandi, Alessandro, 267, 271, 272
Allende, Salvador, 147
Almirante, Giorgio, 101, 102, 282
Amato, Mario, 272
Amendola, Giorgio, 134, 138, 141, 142–44, 148
Amerio, Ettore, 8n47
Annarumma, Antonio, 139–40
Annenkov, Pavel, 195
Arancio, Silvia, 3
Arendt, Hannah, 214, 256
Arfé, Gaetano, 145
Aristotle, 26, 69, 166
Augustine, Saint, 26–27

Babeuf, François-Noël, 170, 184–87
Baglioni, Enrico, 31, 61
Bailey, Kenneth D., 67n84
Bakunin, Mikhail, 195, 196, 198–200, 224, 255
Balzerani, Barbara, 8
Barca, F., 94n9
Barère, Bertrand, 183
Basso, Lelio, 133–34
Battafarano, Italo Michele, 160
Bensing, Manfred, 159
Berardi, Francesco, 74
Berger, P. L., 87
Bergère, Marie-Claire, 226
Berlinguer, Enrico, 129, 147, 149, 150
Berlusconi, Silvio, 259
Bernal, Martin, 230
Bettanin, F., 218n34
Biagi, Marco, 16, 66, 256, 259
Biancone, Maria Grazia, 74
Bianconi, G., 86

Bloch, Ernst, 159
Blumer, Herbert, 71
Bonanate, Luigi, 37
Bonch-Bruyevich, Vladimir, 203–4
Bonisoli, Franco, 61
Borelli, Giulia, 2n9
Borello, Giuseppe, 43n57
Bortolato, Davide, 259
Braghetti, Anna Laura, 72, 75
    on brigadist ideology, 28, 62
    on daily life in Red Brigades, 49n6
    on motivation, 4, 20, 41, 79
Breschi, Danilo, 120n138
Bridge, William, 168
Brinton, Crane, 122
Brunelli, Giorgio, 55n26
Bufalini, P., 138
Buonarroti, Filippo, 186–87
Buonavita, Alfredo, 28, 32
Burroughs, Jeremiah, 168
Burton, Henry, 168

Cagol, Margherita (Mara), 12–13, 15–16, 21
Calvin, John, 166
Campi, Emidio, 156, 159
Canfora, Luciano, 122–23
Caprio, Amarilli, 259
Carretta, Giuseppe, 272
Carrier, Jean-Baptiste, 175
Casalegno, Andrea, 123
Casalegno, Carlo, 59n50
Casimirri, Alessio, 14
Cassirer, Ernst, 171
Catabiani, Umberto, 11n10
Chang, Jung, 237
Chaumeau, C., 251
Chernyshevsky, Nikolay, 196, 200–202
Chiarante, G., 137
Chieco, Mario, 55n26
Clark, R. P., 88
"Claudio," 48, 60, 79

Cochin, Augustin, 181–82
Coco, Francesco, 42n56, 59n48, 65
Cocozzello, Antonio, 64
Codignola, Tristano, 144–45
Codrini, Gianluca, 4, 34, 73, 77–78
Cohn, Norman, 20
Colletti, Lucio, 171–72
Collins, Randall, 68n90
Concutelli, Pierluigi, 263–70, 272
Condorcet, Marquis de, 172–73
Conti, Lando, 59n51
Corsini, P. A., 272
Costa, Maurizio, 61
Croce, Fulvio, 84
Cromwell, Oliver, 166–67
Curcio, Renato, 11–13, 15, 43, 104–5, 127
     Chiavari address, 119–20
     life story of, 109–11, 118–19, 258–59

D'Alema, Massimo, 141
D'Amato, Federico Umberto, 123
D'Antona, Massimo, 256, 259
Davanzo, Alfredo, 259
Davies, James C., 114
De Andrade, Marcelo, 120
De Domenico, Salvatore, 101
De Gasperi, Alcide, 132–34, 135
Dejana, Antioco, 65
Della Porta, Donatella, 37
Della Volpe, Galvano, 172
Delle Chiaie, Stefano, 266, 270
De Marsanich, Augusto, 101
De Ruggiero, Guido, 172
De Sario, Giacomo, 102n68
Deschamps, Léger-Marie, dom, 171
Desmoulins, Camille, 177–79, 258
de Tocqueville, Alexis, 117
Di Rocco, Ennio, 74
Di Roma, Ciriaco, 272
Di Vona, Piero, 283
Djilas, Milovan, 75–76, 196, 214, 218
Dommanget, Maurice, 184
Dostoyevsky, Fyodor, 203–4
Durkheim, Émile, 2, 76, 111, 284
D'Urso, Giovanni, 2n4
Duverger, Maurice, 116

Easton, David, 117
Eliade, Mircea, 87
Elias, Norbert, 286
Engels, Friedrich, 7–8, 159, 190–91, 195
Ercoli, 271n32. See also Togliatti, Palmiro
Esposti, Giancarlo, 268–69, 271
Evola, Julius, 101, 275–84

Fallico, Luigi, 262
Faranda, Adriana, 17, 50n8, 57–58, 72, 105
Feltrinelli, Giangiacomo, 119
Fenzi, Enrico, 4, 12, 17–18, 54, 61, 123–24
Ferrandi, Mario, 4–5, 61, 76–77, 268
Ferrero, Guglielmo, 182
Filoramo, G., 3n15, 4n16
Fioravanti, Valerio, 266–67, 270, 271, 275
Fiore, Raffaele, 10n3, 256
     on daily life in Red Brigades, 48, 50–51
     on initiation rites, 88
     on killing, 59–60, 66
     life story of, 21–23
     on sociopolitical shifts in Italy, 95–96
Fiore, Roberto, 270
Fioroni, Vincenza, 12
Fontana, Enzo, 4
Fouquier-Tinville, Antoine Quentin, 174, 197
Franceschini, Alberto, 13, 106, 127
     on brigadist ideology, 28
     on founding of Red Brigades, 15n26,
        119–21
     on Italian Communist Party, 152, 153
Furet, François, 180

Gaeta, Massimiliano, 259
Galileo, 69
Gallinari, Prospero, 35, 62, 84, 105
     on founding of Red Brigades, 121
     on Italian Communist Party, 151–53
     life story of, 79n123, 108–9
Galmozzi, Enrico, 16, 61, 62n68
Germani, Gino, 112–13
Ghirardi, Bruno, 259
Ginsborg, Paul, 97
Giralucci, Graziano, 25n70, 104n84
Graglia, Barbara, 4n19
Gramsci, Antonio, 125–29, 149–50
Graziani, Clemente, 273
Greer, Donald, 178
Guagliardo, Vincenzo, 21, 41, 51, 54, 62, 68,
        75
Guevara, Ernesto Che, 76, 81–82, 148, 151,
        261
     on "perfect society," 7n41
     response to death of, 136
Guitton, Jean, 40, 41, 72
Gurr, Ted R., 113–14

Halliday, Jon, 237
Hampson, N., 179n88
Harrison, Thomas, 167
Hasselbach, Ingo, 71–72
Herzen, Alexander, 196–98

Hitler, Adolf, 101
Hobsbawm, Eric J., 3n10, 212
Hoeung, Ong Thong, 246, 247–49
Hoffer, E., 107
Hunt, Lynn, 183
Hunt, Ray Leamon, 66
Hus, Jan, 157

Ingrao, Pietro, 151
Ishutin, Nikolai, 202

John of Leiden (Jan Beukelszoon),
    162–65
Juergensmeyer, Mark, 32n12
Junger, Ernst, 276

Kang Sheng, 228
Karakozov, Dmitri, 206
Karlstadt, Andreas, 157
Kazuko, Koojima, 88, 89
Kolakowski, Leszek, 262
Kostylev, Mikhail, 131
Kotek, Joël, 231
Krueger, Alan B., 262n17
Künzli, Arnold, 191–92

Labate, Bruno, 2n5, 10, 58n33
Lapponi, Paolo, 28
La Rocca, Tommaso, 156
Latino, Claudio, 259
Lenci, Sergio, 257
Lenin, Vladimir, 2n7, 208–13, 215, 222
    brigadist ideology and, 122
    Chernyshevsky and, 200
    dacha of, 219
    establishment of concentration camps by,
        225
    on hate, 5
    Nechaev and, 203
Levine, J. M., 87
Lewin, Kurt, 69–70, 72
Lintrami, Arialdo, 22
Longo, Luigi, 132, 133, 137, 141, 146–47
Longo, P., 103
Luckmann, T., 87
Lumumba, Patrice, 135–36
Luther, Martin, 156–58

Mably, Gabriel Bonnot de, 170–71
Macchiarini, Idalgo, 45, 59n38
Machiavelli, Niccolò, 26, 166, 183
Maino, Antonio, 271
Malevich, Kasimir, 223
Mambro, Francesca, 266–67, 271, 272

Mannheim, Karl, 28
Mantovani, Cesare, 101–2
Manuel, Frank E., 194
Mao Tse-tung, 226–37
Maréchal, Sylvain, 185
Marletti, Carlo, 37–38
Marshall, Stephen, 168
Martinelli, Franco, 99
Marx, Karl, 78, 122, 187–96, 198–99
Masakuni, Yoshino, 89
Masi, Pino, 45
Massa, Maria Giovanna, 74
Massari, Roberto, 212
Mathieu, Vittorio, 53, 165
Mathiez, Albert, 179, 181
Matteucci, N., 4
Matthys, Jan, 162–63
Mazzamauro, Alfredo, 259
Mazzola, Giuseppe, 25n70, 104n84
Mead, George Herbert, 71
Meinhof, Ulrike, 40, 41n45
Melotti, Umberto, 104n84
Michelet, Jules, 175
Michels, Robert, 219, 222
Mieko, Toyama, 88–89
Minervino, Roberto, 7
Ming, Chen, 233–34, 236–37
Mitsuo, Ozaki, 88
Moravia, Alberto, 268–69
Moreland, R. L., 87
Morelly, 170
Moretti, Mario, 15, 35, 54, 62, 86, 105–6
Morgenthau, Hans J., 27
Mori, Tsuneo, 88
Moro, Aldo, 8n48, 58, 59n52, 129–30,
    134–35
Morucci, Valerio, 18, 31–32, 44, 85, 86
    on daily life in Red Brigades, 48, 49–50,
        89, 91
    on founding of Red Brigades, 121
    on hate, 24
    on Italian Communist Party, 153–54
    on killing, 28, 59, 65–66
    on Leninism, 53, 91–92
    life story of, 40, 118
    on politics of Red Brigades, 8, 9
Mosca, G., 26n72
Mumm, Thiounn, 245
Munari, Antonio, 24
Müntzer, Thomas, 155–61
Mussolini, Benito, 101

Nagata, Hiroko, 88
Nechaev, Sergei, 32, 202–3, 255, 267

Nietzsche, Friedrich, 107
Nie Yuanzi, 227
Nistri, Roberto, 272–73
Nitta, 19–20, 23, 27, 59, 83
  on politics, 3, 7n40, 30–31

Occhetto, Achille, 139, 140, 141–42, 143, 146, 149
Occorsio, Vittorio, 272
Ogburn, William F., 112
Orsello, Gian Piero, 144
Ortega y Gasset, José, 68
Ostrogorski, Moisei, 224–25

Pace, E., 6n36
Pagliarini, Mauro, 55n26
Pallotto, Marino, 74
Palmieri, Sergio, 65
Panh, R., 251
Parlanti, Luciano, 100
Parlato, Giuseppe, 283
Pasolini, Pier Paolo, 268
Pasqualini, Jean, 231–32, 233
Pasquino, Gianfranco, 37
Pavolini, L., 143
Peci, Patrizio, 54, 56, 86, 89–91
  brother Roberto and, 46
  on killing, 24, 62, 64–65, 83–84
  on motivation, 10, 11, 21, 106, 191
  on Red Brigades vs. fascists, 33
  on trade unions, 43
  on underground life, 51, 73
Peci, Roberto, 46–47, 74
Pedenovi, Enrico, 16n36
Pellicani, Luciano, 32n11, 93, 104n84, 242, 256, 281
Perry, John Weir, 257
Petri, R., 96
Petruccioli, C., 136, 138n227, 143
Pfeiffer, Heinrich, 158–59
"Piero," 28
Plato, 188
Polanyi, Karl, 94
Pol Pot, 239, 242, 244–45
Pons, S., 131
Prosperi, A., 167
Pyatakov, Yuri, 222–23

Rigoulot, Pierre, 231
Robespierre, Maximilien, 170, 174–75, 177–78, 180–81, 183–84, 226
Rokeach, Milton, 32
Roppoli, Maria Rosaria, 21, 86
Rossa, Guido, 55, 85

Rossanda, Rossana, 129, 130
Rossi, Emilio, 38
Rossi, Gianni Scipione, 282
Rossi, Jacques, 226
Rossi, Paolo, 136
Rossin, Valentino, 259
Rosso, Roberto, 20, 30, 67n85
Rotaris, Maurizio, 118
Rotondi, Davide, 259
Rousseau, Jean-Jacques, 170–73
Rummel, Rudolph J., 213–14
Rüsher, Hubert, 163
Russo, Silveria, 61, 62

Šafarevič, Igor, 159
Saint-Just, Louis-Antoine de, 175
Salierno, Guido, 271
Salotto, Federico, 259
Salvati, Michele, 100n48
Sammarco, Franco, 272
Samphan, Khieu, 243, 249–50
Saponara, Giovanni, 65
Sartori, Giovanni, 172
Savasta, Antonio, 8n48
Scantamburlo, Andrea, 259
Schleyer, Hanns-Martin, 53n16
Schmalenbach, Herman, 39
Schumpeter, Joseph A., 93
Scivoli, Salvatore, 259
Segio, Sergio, 11, 20, 151, 261
Senzani, Giovanni, 124
Serpieri, Claudia, 267
Settembrini, D., 258
Shalamov, V., 226
Sidorov, Vasily Klementovich, 214–17
Sihanouk, Norodom, 239–41
Simmel, Georg, 71
Sinclair, Andrew, 183–84
Sisi, Vincenzo, 259
Smelser, Neil J., 115
Soboul, Albert, 179–81
Sok Thy, 238
Soldati, Giorgio, 74
Sole-Tura, Jordi, 139
Solzhenitsyn, Aleksandr, 225
Sossi, Mario, 23n63, 63–64
Spadolini, Giovanni, 59n51
Sparti, Massimo, 267
Spriano, Paolo, 137
Stalin, Joseph, 132, 212, 214, 218, 219, 230
Steinhoff, Patricia, 89
Stern, Jessica, 32n12
Sternberger, Dolf, 26–27
Strada, Vittorio, 203

Straullu, Francesco, 272
Suyin, Han, 229

Taliercio, Giuseppe, 2n6
Talmon, J., 6–7
Tarantelli, Ezio, 55, 83
Tessandori, Vincenzo, 110n110
Tetlock, P. E., 33n16
Tkachev, Pyotr Nikitich, 206–7
Togliatti, Palmiro, 129, 131–34, 137, 144
    on fascism, 271n32
    on violence, 139, 153, 154
Tönnies, Ferdinand, 39
Toschi, Alessandro, 259
Toschi, Massimiliano, 259
Toynbee, Arnold J., 78–79, 113, 240, 271
Traversi, Valerio, 43n60
Trentin, B., 96
Trimarchi, Pietro, 139
Troeltsch, Ernst, 6
Trotsky, Leon, 116, 219, 220

Vacca, G., 151
Vai, Angela, 14, 65, 84
Valentinov, Nikolai, 209, 210

Viola, P., 167
Visalberghi, Aldo, 145
Viscardi, Michele, 257
Voegelin, Eric, 52
Voltaire (François-Marie Arouet), 173

Waccher, William, 74
Walzer, Michael, 166
Weber, Max, 5, 25, 67n84, 94, 146, 286n1
Weitling, Wilhelm, 194–95
Winstanley, Gerrard, 168–69
Wu, Harry, 232, 236n94

Xiaoling, Wang, 234–35

Yathay, Pin, 244n116
Yoshitaka, Kato, 88
Yuon, Hou, 239, 243

Zaichnevsky, Pyotr, 204–6
Zamagni, Vera, 100
Zambianchi, Paolo, 18, 85
Zapata, Emiliano, 238
Zaslavsky, Victor, 220
Zavoli, S., 5